MOON

Death Valley National Park

JENNA BLOUGH

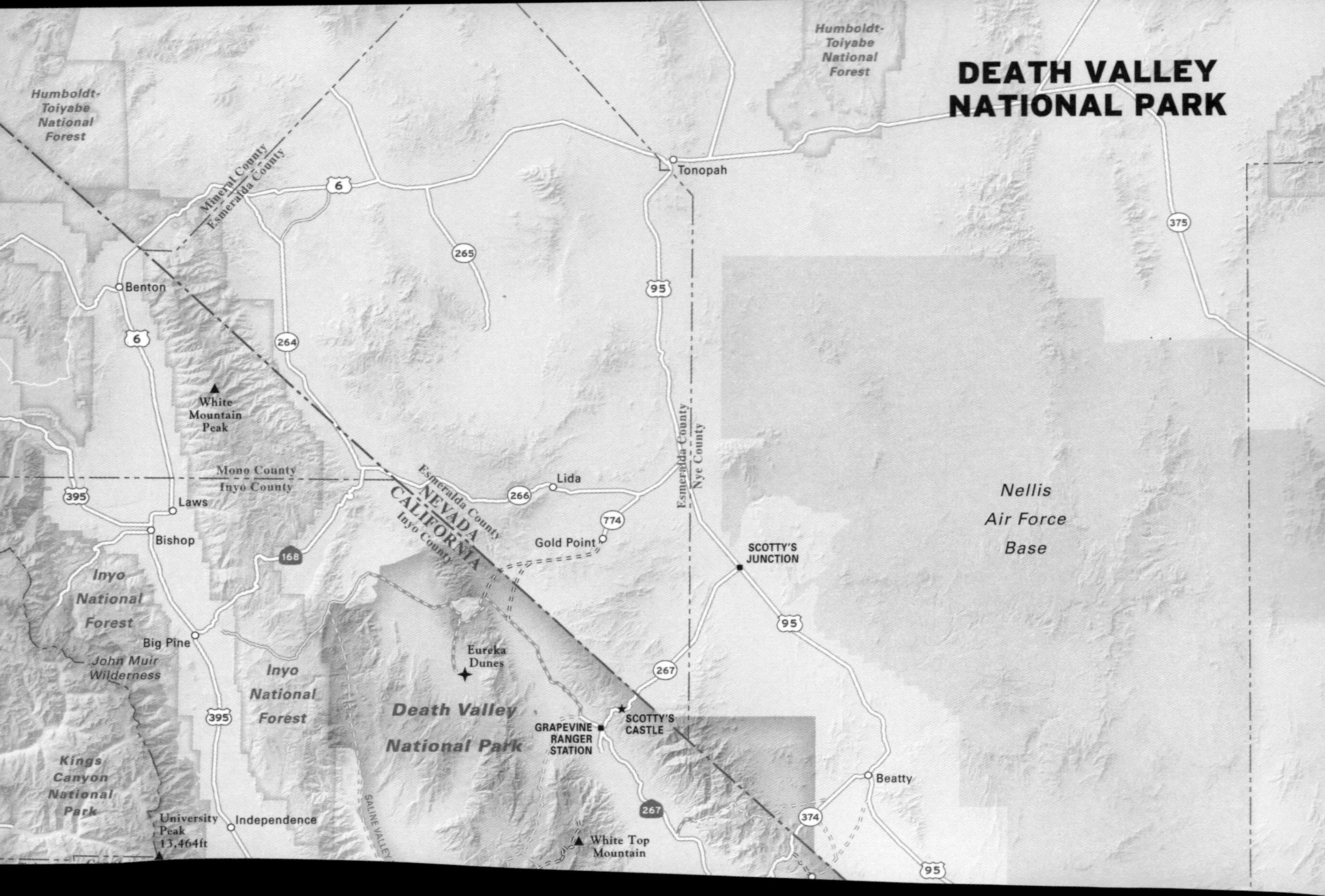

DEATH VALLEY
NATIONAL PARK
Humboldt-Toiyabe National Forest
Humboldt-Toiyabe National Forest
Tonopah
Mineral County
Esmeralda County
Benton
6
6
265
264
95
375
White Mountain Peak
Mono County
Inyo County
Esmeralda County
Nye County
Esmeralda County
NEVADA
CALIFORNIA
Inyo County
Lida
266
774
Gold Point
Nellis
Air Force
Base
SCOTTY'S JUNCTION
395
Laws
Bishop
168
Inyo National Forest
Big Pine
John Muir Wilderness
Eureka Dunes
Inyo National Forest
Death Valley
National Park
95
267
SCOTTY'S CASTLE
GRAPEVINE RANGER STATION
395
Kings Canyon National Park
University Peak 13,464ft
Independence
SALINE VALLEY
267
White Top Mountain
Beatty
374
95

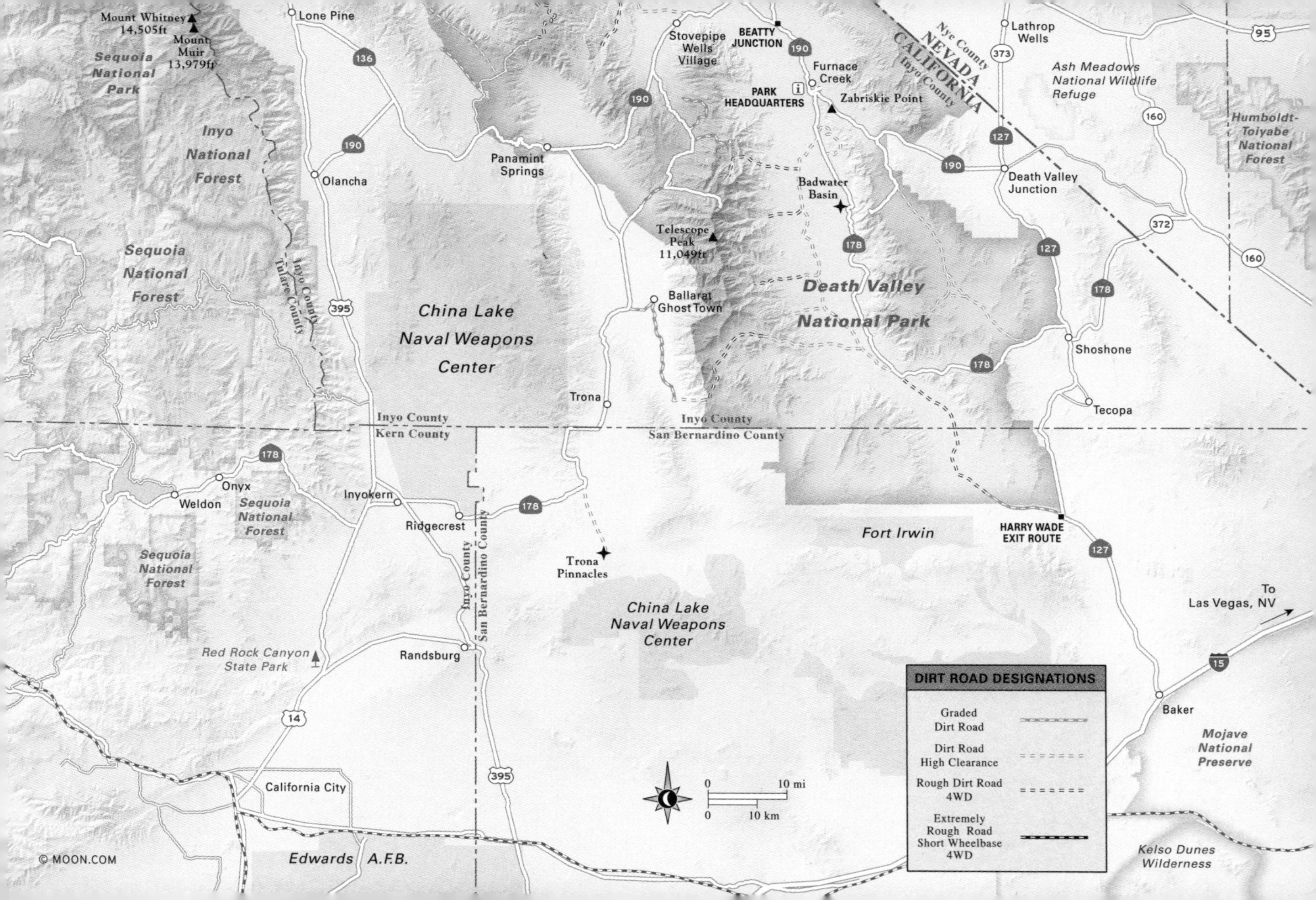

Mount Whitney 14,505ft
Mount Muir 13,979ft
Sequoia National Park
Inyo National Forest
Sequoia National Forest
Inyo County
Tulare County
Lone Pine
136
190
Olancha
395
Panamint Springs
China Lake Naval Weapons Center
Stovepipe Wells Village
BEATTY JUNCTION
PARK HEADQUARTERS
Furnace Creek
Zabriskie Point
Nye County
NEVADA
CALIFORNIA
Inyo County
Lathrop Wells
373
95
Ash Meadows National Wildlife Refuge
Humboldt-Toiyabe National Forest
160
127
Death Valley Junction
372
Badwater Basin
Telescope Peak 11,049ft
178
Death Valley National Park
Ballarat Ghost Town
Shoshone
Tecopa
Trona
Inyo County
Kern County
San Bernardino County
Onyx
Weldon
Inyokern
Ridgecrest
Trona Pinnacles
Fort Irwin
HARRY WADE EXIT ROUTE
To Las Vegas, NV
15
Baker
Mojave National Preserve
Red Rock Canyon State Park
Randsburg
14
California City
Edwards A.F.B.
0 10 mi
0 10 km
DIRT ROAD DESIGNATIONS
Graded Dirt Road
Dirt Road High Clearance
Rough Dirt Road 4WD
Extremely Rough Road Short Wheelbase 4WD
Kelso Dunes Wilderness
© MOON.COM

Contents

spring wildflowers

WELCOME TO

Death Valley National Park

Death Valley may be as close as you'll ever get to visiting another planet. Its sculpted sand dunes, crusted salt flats, towering rocks, and polished marble canyons will make you consider your place in the universe.

Declared a national monument in 1933, then signed into national park status in 1994, Death Valley is the largest national park in the lower 48 states. Located within the northern Mojave Desert, the park boasts extremes of temperatures and elevation. One early travel advertisement promised "all the advantages of hell without the inconveniences." From the oppressive salt flats of Badwater Basin 282 feet (86 m) below sea level to the snow line at Telescope Peak 11,049 feet (3,368 m) above, a complex and varied geology spans eras of seas and volcanoes, tectonic forces and fault lines.

Death Valley holds spectacular sights for all to see, but its secrets are not so easily given up. Dotting the landscape are hidden springs, mining camps, ghost towns, and the sacred spots of Indigenous people who call the valley home. Get out of the car to walk the twisting canyons, search for waterfalls or petroglyphs, and listen to the wild landscape. Decaying or preserved, battered by wind or watered by secret oases, these places stand as a testament to the frenzy of human hopes and the fury of imagination.

This was and still is a place for dreamers—pyramid schemes and tall tales abound. Thousands came here to seek their fortunes. Some remain etched into popular history, while others have faded into local lore.

Come to Death Valley to be awed and humbled, dazzled, and pushed out of your comfort zone. You'll wonder whether the searing heat and whipping cold are creating a mirage—or lifting the scales from your eyes.

Zabriskie Point

6 TOP
EXPERIENCES

1 Hiking the park's trails, old mining roads, and canyons from **Mosaic Canyon** (page 104) to **Telescope Peak** (page 169).

2 Roaming the pristine sandscapes at **Ibex Dunes** (page 73), **Mesquite Flat Sand Dunes** (page 92), and **Eureka Dunes** (page 122).

3 Seeing countless glowing stars from this **International Dark Sky Park** (page 33).

4 Off-roading on **Titus Canyon Road,** one of the best four-wheel drives (page 97).

5 Finding paradise in the desert at **Saratoga Spring** (page 74) and **Surprise Canyon** (page 166).

6 Walking on the otherworldly **Badwater Basin** salt flats (page 46).

Planning Your Trip

WHERE TO GO

Furnace Creek and the Amargosa Range

Iconic views, short hikes, and easy access make Furnace Creek and the Amargosa Range an excellent introduction to Death Valley. The village of **Furnace Creek** serves as the park headquarters, with a plethora of services—**lodging, campgrounds, restaurants,** and even gas. The most popular sights are in this region, including **Badwater Basin, Artist's Drive, Devil's Golf Course,** and **Natural Bridge.**

The Amargosa Range provides opportunities for in-depth **hiking, biking,** and **rock climbing.** Dig into Death Valley's mining past by traveling the **West Side Road** to the rugged canyons of the Panamint Range, the orchards of **Hungry Bill's Ranch,** or the bubbling oases of **Hanaupah Canyon.** An easy two-hour drive to the park's lightly visited **Southeastern Corner** yields scenic springs, ghost mines, and pristine dunes.

Stovepipe Wells and the Nevada Triangle

Stovepipe Wells and the Nevada Triangle are home to steep alluvial fans that lead to the wind-sculpted and colorful canyons of the Cottonwood and Grapevine Mountains, including **Marble Canyon.** The tiny visitor hub of **Stovepipe Wells** occupies a central location on Highway 190, with the scenic **Mesquite Flat Sand Dunes** within sight.

The Nevada Triangle serves as a jumping-off point to the spectacular—and popular—**Titus**

salt flats of Badwater Basin

Canyon drive, as well as the haunting ghost town of **Rhyolite.** Nearby **Beatty, Nevada,** offers services in this tiny corner of the park.

Scotty's Castle and the Eureka Valley

The Eureka Valley is the most **lightly visited** park region. There are **no services,** so a trip here means roughing it, but you'll be rewarded with solitude and natural wonders. The exception is popular **Scotty's Castle,** a 1920s mansion tucked in the folds of the Grapevine Mountains. Scotty's Castle was one of the most popular destinations in the park until severe flash floods in October 2015 damaged the historical buildings, infrastructure, and grounds of the popular destination. Scotty's Castle is set to reopen in late 2025.

The **Eureka Dunes** are the main draw in the Eureka Valley, towering more than 680 feet (207 m) above the valley floor. In the secluded Racetrack Valley, hardy souls make the long, difficult drive to **The Racetrack,** a dry lake bed scattered with the mysterious trails of rocks that skate across its surface.

Panamint Springs and the Saline Valley

Panamint Springs and the Saline Valley are filled with creeks and springs, historical mining roads, and camps. Old cabins and ghost towns,

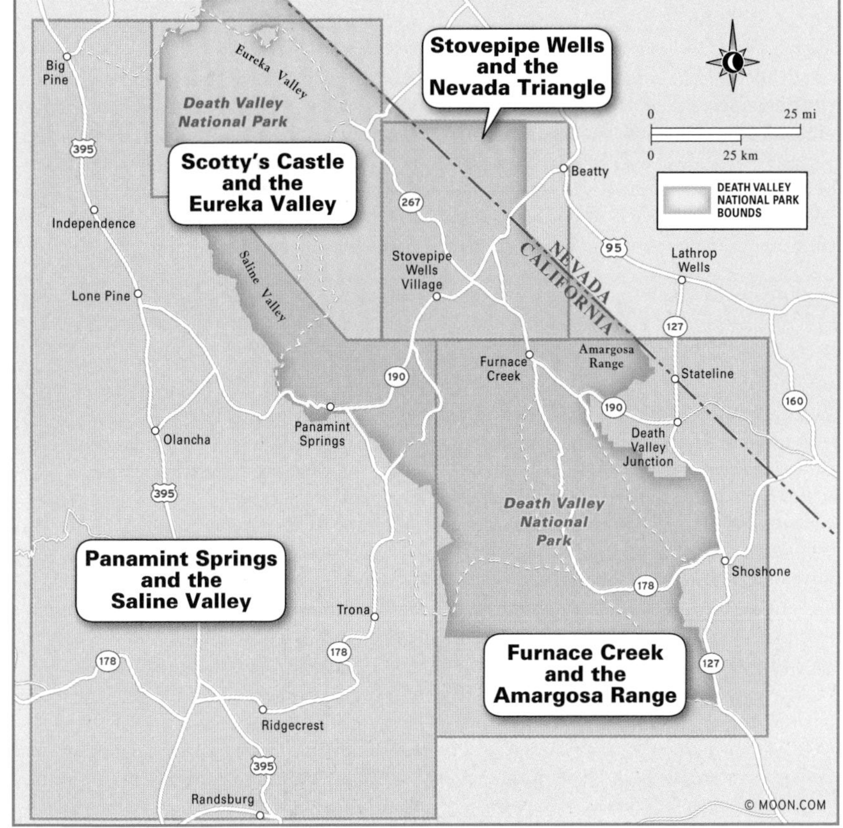

like **Skidoo** and **Panamint City,** are scattered through the wrinkled folds of the western Panamint Mountains, which are home to **Telescope Peak,** the highest peak in Death Valley. The village of **Panamint Springs** is the region's hub, with **lodging,** a **restaurant,** and a few services.

The Saline Valley brings it back to the basics with sheer quiet remoteness. The long, washboard **Saline Valley Road** offers rough access to the **Lee Flat Joshua Tree Forest,** rarely visited **Saline Valley Dunes, hot springs,** and the remains of the Salt Tramway.

WHEN TO GO

Death Valley's steep mountains and low valleys mean that temperatures fluctuate wildly depending on where you are at what time of year. High elevations are cooler and low elevations are hotter.

High Season (mid-Oct.-mid-May)

The most popular time to visit Death Valley is **spring** (March, April, and May), for its **wildflowers** and mild temperatures at all elevations. **Fall** is also lovely and moderate; however, a few businesses, especially those beyond the boundaries, may be closed.

Winter is a great time to visit—there are few crowds and the temperatures are pleasant at lower elevations, such as Furnace Creek. Winter brings snow to higher elevations, such as Wildrose and Telescope Peaks in the Panamint Mountains. **Roads may close;** check road conditions and carry chains.

Off-Season (mid-May-mid-Oct.)

Death Valley may be a year-round destination, but **summer** is the off-season due to extreme heat. **Services are limited,** and it can be brutally hot everywhere, particularly in the valleys. **Hiking is strongly discouraged** at low elevations in summer. Still, many visitors come to the park in summer despite the heat.

BEFORE YOU GO

Services

There are **limited services** within Death Valley. Stock up on water, food, and any necessary supplies before entering the park. Gas, ice, and limited food and supplies are available at **Furnace Creek, Stovepipe Wells,** and **Panamint Springs.**

There is **no cell phone reception** in Death Valley National Park, with the exception of Furnace Creek and Stovepipe Wells. Depending on your provider, you may also luck into a tiny window of cell service at unpredictable moments. Do not rely on your cell phone for communication.

Cell service is unpredictable to nonexistent in many areas around the park. On the western side of the park, there is cell service in the town of Lone Pine and along US 395. On the eastern side of the park, there is cell service in the town of Beatty and along US 95. Many individual businesses provide wireless internet for guests.

Park Fees and Passes

The park entrance fee is **$30 per vehicle,** good for seven days; an **annual pass** is available for $55. **Furnace Creek,** accessed via **Highway 190,** serves as the main park entrance station. Fees can also be paid at the Furnace Creek Visitor Center, the Stovepipe Wells Ranger Station, and at self-pay kiosks within the park.

US citizens or permanent residents ages 62 and older can purchase an **America the Beautiful Senior Pass** (lifetime $80, annual $20) at any

If You Have...

- **Two Hours:** Drive Badwater Basin Road south from Furnace Creek to see iconic Death Valley sights: Badwater Basin, the Devil's Golf Course, the Artist's Drive, and Zabriskie Point.
- **One Day:** Hike Mosaic Canyon near Stovepipe Wells and take the scenic drive on the one-way dirt road through Titus Canyon.
- **Two Days:** Add a hike like Desolation Canyon or Sidewinder Canyon in the Furnace Creek region, then visit the Mesquite Flat Sand Dunes near Stovepipe Wells.
- **Three Days:** Make the adventurous trek out to The Racetrack with a high-clearance vehicle; consider camping in the Racetrack Valley.
- **Four Days:** Attempt the rugged Saline Valley Road and backcountry camp in the Saline Valley. Alternatively, add a trip to the remote Eureka Dunes.
- **One Week:** Base yourself in the Panamint Springs region and explore the Emigrant and Wildrose Canyons, hike Wildrose Peak and Telescope Peak, and backpack to Surprise Canyon and Panamint City.

Above: Artist's Drive

In-Park Lodging

	LOCATION	PRICE	SEASON	AMENITIES
Sunset Campground	Furnace Creek elev. 190 feet (58 m)	$14 or $7 with senior or access pass	Oct. 15.-Apr. 15	tent and RV sites, shower and pool access at the Ranch for small fee
Texas Springs Campground	Furnace Creek elev. 190 feet (58 m)	$16	Oct. 15-Apr. 15	tent and RV sites, shower and pool access at the Ranch for small fee
Fiddlers' Campground	Furnace Creek elev. 190 feet (58 m)	$34	year-round; reservations	tent and RV sites, shower and pool access at the Ranch
Furnace Creek Campground	Furnace Creek elev. 190 feet (58 m)	$22, hookups $36 or $18 with senior or access pass plus $14 utility fee	year-round; reservations Oct. 15-Apr. 15	tent and RV sites, shower and pool access at the Ranch for small fee
The Ranch at Death Valley	Furnace Creek	$199-400	year-round	motel rooms, cottages, restaurants, pool
The Inn at Death Valley	Furnace Creek	$400-699	year-round	hotel rooms, casitas, restaurants, pool
Stovepipe Wells Campground	Stovepipe Wells elev. 10 feet (3 m)	$14 or $7 with senior or access pass	Oct. 15.-Apr. 15	tent and RV sites, shower and pool access for small fee
Stovepipe Wells RV Park	Stovepipe Wells elev. 10 feet (3 m)	$40	year-round; reservations	RV sites, shower and pool access
Stovepipe Wells Hotel	Stovepipe Wells	$144-226	year-round	motel rooms, restaurant, pool

visitor center or ranger station in Death Valley or online at www.nps.gov. The pass is part of the National Parks and Federal Recreational Lands Pass Series and can be used to cover entrance fees at 2,000 locations, including national parks and national wildlife refuges. It also provides discounts on some facility amenities, useful at campgrounds. If you already have a Golden Age or Golden Access Pass, both are good for entry into the park.

	LOCATION	PRICE	SEASON	AMENITIES
Mesquite Spring Campground	Northern Death Valley elev. 1,800 feet (549 m)	$14	year-round	tent sites
Eureka Dunes Dry Camp	Eureka Valley elev. 2,880 feet (878 m)	free	year-round, weather permitting	primitive sites
Homestake Dry Camp	Racetrack Valley elev. 3,785 feet (1,154 m)	free	year-round, weather permitting	primitive sites
Panamint Springs Resort Campground	Panamint Springs elev. 1,926 feet (587 m)	$15-85	year-round; reservations	tent sites, RV sites, tent cabins, restaurant, showers
Panamint Springs Resort	Panamint Springs	$226-326	year-round	motel rooms, cottage, cabins, restaurant
Emigrant Campground	Emigrant Canyon elev. 2,100 feet (640 m)	free	year-round	tent sites
Wildrose Campground	Wildrose Canyon elev. 4,100 feet (1,250 m)	free	year-round	tent sites
Thorndike Campground	Wildrose Canyon elev. 7,400 feet (2,256 m)	free	mid-Apr.- Nov.	tent sites
Mahogany Flat Campground	Wildrose Canyon elev. 8,200 feet (2,499 m)	free	mid-Apr.- Nov.	tent sites
Saline Valley Campground	Saline Valley elev. 1,375 feet (419 m)	free	year-round, weather permitting	primitive sites

Reservations

Spring, fall, and **holiday weekends** can be competitive times for lodging. Make reservations a few weeks to several months in advance if you want to stay inside the park. If all park lodging is booked, your next option is in one of the gateway towns such as Lone Pine, California, or Beatty, Nevada.

Furnace Creek Campground (Furnace Creek; 877/444-6777; www.recreation.gov; year-round) is the only park campground that accepts reservations (Oct. 15-Apr. 15). All other park campgrounds are first-come, first-served. Privately owned campgrounds within the park that also take reservations include **Panamint**

Springs Resort Campground (Panamint Springs; 775/482-7680; www.panamintsprings.com; year-round), the Ranch at Death Valley's **Fiddlers' Campground** (Furnace Creek; 760/786-2345 or 800/236-7916; www.oasisatdeathvalley.com; year-round), and **Stovepipe Wells RV Park** (Stovepipe Wells; 760/786-7090; www.deathvalleyhotels.com; year-round).

IN THE PARK

Visitor Center

The **Furnace Creek Visitor Center** (Furnace Creek Ranch, Hwy. 190; 760/786-3200; www.nps.gov/deva; 8am-5pm daily) serves as the main park hub year-round.

Where to Stay

There are only four accommodation options within the park. If you're not staying at one of these, you're camping.

- **Ranch at Death Valley** (Furnace Creek; 800/236-7916; www.oasisatdeathvalley.com; year-round)
- **Inn at Death Valley** (Furnace Creek; 800/236-7916; www.oasisatdeathvalley.com; year-round)
- **Stovepipe Wells Hotel** (Stovepipe Wells; 760/786-7090; www.deathvalleyhotels.com; year-round)
- **Panamint Springs Resort** (Panamint Springs; 775/482-7680; www.panamintsprings.com; year-round)

There are **15 campgrounds** in the park; with the exception of Furnace Creek Campground, Fiddlers' Campground, Panamint Springs Resort Campground, and Stovepipe Wells RV Park, all are **first-come, first-served.** Finding an open site may be a problem on spring weekends. Texas Spring Campground, in Furnace Creek, routinely fills. High-elevation campgrounds can fill during weekends in summer.

Campgrounds are open seasonally (either fall-spring or spring-fall), depending on their elevation. There are also primitive campgrounds and many opportunities for backcountry camping.

Getting Around

Most visitors fly into Los Angeles or Las Vegas and rent a car to drive to Death Valley. There are no park shuttles or public transportation available within the park—**you will need your own vehicle.** For back-road excursions, **4WD rentals** are available through **Farabee's** (Furnace Creek; 760/786-9872; https://farabeejeeps.com; Sept.-May); advance reservations are recommended during high season.

Gas is available within the park, but it's best to fill up at one of the gateway or service towns instead, as distances are great and gas prices are expensive. If entering from the south, fill up at **Ridgecrest** or **Trona;** from the west, stop in **Olancha** or **Lone Pine;** if entering from Nevada, **Beatty** has gas; on the southeastern route into the park, gas is available in **Shoshone.**

BEST OF Death Valley

Day 1

Fly into **Las Vegas, Nevada,** and rent a car for the road trip to Death Valley. From Las Vegas, travelers will access the eastern side of the park, a drive of about 2.5-3 hours (150 mi/242 km) to the park hub of Furnace Creek.

Day 2

Set yourself up in the village of **Furnace Creek,** the main park hub, to enjoy Death Valley's most iconic sights. The casual Ranch at Death Valley and the upscale Inn at Death Valley are your only accommodation options. Texas Springs is the most scenic campground, but it can get crowded; make sure you've lined up your space early.

Just south of Furnace Creek, **Badwater Road** offers a scenic driving tour. Fill up with breakfast at **1849 Restaurant** in Furnace Creek before heading out. Your first stop is **Golden Canyon,** where you can beat the heat (and the crowds) with a lovely morning hike.

Continuing south along Badwater Road, take a quick side trip to enjoy the relaxing and scenic drive along **Artist's Drive** and through the colorful, jumbled rock formations.

Just over 6 miles (9.7 km) south of the Artist's Drive exit along Badwater Road, the **Devil's Golf Course** surprises with its bizarre salt formations, but you can only see these if you stop and get up close.

Two miles (3.2 km) south is the turnoff to an easy stroll through impressively large **Natural Bridge.** Continue 4 miles (6.4 km) south on the park road to admire **Badwater Basin**'s surreal salt flats, the lowest point in North America at 282 feet (86 m) below sea level.

From Badwater, turn around and retrace your route north to the junction with Highway 190 and turn right (east). Follow Highway 190 to its junction with Dante's View Road to end at **Dante's View** after 22 miles (35 km) for sweeping views of the valley below. Retrace your steps and make a detour through **Twenty Mule Team Canyon,** 17.7 miles (28.5 km) north of the viewpoint. Finish your scenic driving tour at **Zabriskie Point** for more spectacular views of the valley below and up-close views of the eroded badlands below the point.

Furnace Creek

Leave yourself enough time to enjoy the warm spring-fed pool at the Ranch at Death Valley before heading to dinner. Reserve a table at the **Inn at Death Valley** for a sunset meal at one of the outdoor tables or in the historical dining room. The inn also has a cocktail lounge where you can enjoy the same view.

Day 3

Today, explore the Stovepipe Wells and Nevada Triangle region. The short hike through **Mosaic Canyon** is a great introduction to the canyons—wander through polished marble, colorful mosaic stone, and satisfying narrows. Just across Highway 190, the sculpted sand dunes of **Mesquite Flat** are visible from Stovepipe Wells but are definitely worth a closer view.

From Stovepipe Wells, head east for 26 miles (42 km) along Daylight Pass Road to **Beatty, Nevada,** the jumping-off point for your next adventure. Beatty is a good place to fill up on gas and food. Try **Happy Burro Chili & Beer,** a charming saloon-style bar and restaurant with an outdoor patio.

The ghost town of **Rhyolite** is just 4 miles (6.4 km) west of Beatty. Wander the impressive ruins of this once-rich gold-mining town, then stop at the **Goldwell Open Air Museum** next door to peruse the hauntingly beautiful outdoor art exhibits set incongruously against the desert backdrop.

The crowning point of your day will be driving the **Titus Canyon Road**—the most popular backcountry route in Death Valley. The one-way access point begins 2.1 miles (3.4 km) south of Rhyolite, just off Daylight Pass Road. The washboard road winds 27 miles (43 km) past rugged rock formations, sweeping canyon views, petroglyphs, and even a ghost town to eventually end at Scotty's Castle Road, 20 miles (32 km) north of Stovepipe Wells.

End your day with a celebratory drink at the **Badwater Saloon** back in Stovepipe Wells Village. Enjoy a dip in the pool or a casual dinner before retiring to one of the basic motel rooms.

Bank ruins tower over the ghost town of Rhyolite.

Day 4

You'll need an early start to explore Eureka Valley. Pack your car with all the food and water you'll need for a full day, and bring your camping gear.

Continue north to the **Eureka Dunes,** a drive of nearly 50 miles (81 km) from Mesquite Spring Campground. It's a two-hour haul to the northernmost destination in the park, but it's well worth it to enjoy the isolated and pristine setting. The Eureka Dunes are the tallest dunes in Death Valley, rising from the Eureka Valley floor and framed by the Last Chance Range.

The Best of Death Valley in One Day

If you only have one day to spend, this driving tour of the park will help you experience some of the most iconic sights, stretch your legs, and even enjoy a back-road adventure. Fill your gas tank before entering the park, and be sure to have plenty of food and water on hand, as services are limited.

- Start the day at **Furnace Creek,** a tourism outpost since 1933. Orient yourself at the **Furnace Creek Visitor Center** (page 39), where you can pick up a park map and pay the entrance fee. Furnace Creek is also home to a few restaurants and a general store; this is a good place to fill up on breakfast or lunch before hitting the road.
- Drive south along Badwater Basin Road to **Badwater Basin** (page 46), a Death Valley classic. The lowest point in North America, these vast salt flats lie 282 feet (86 m) below sea level and encapsulate the mesmerizing yet unforgiving landscape of Death Valley. Walk out onto the salt flats to look for delicate salt crystal formations.
- Head north, back to Highway 190, and continue past Furnace Creek to the **Mesquite Flat Sand Dunes** (page 92), near Stovepipe Wells. These sculpted, windswept dunes sit perched on a slope of the valley floor and are the most popular dunes in the park.
- Take a minor detour west along Highway 190 to the trailhead for **Mosaic Canyon** (page 104). Hike through narrows of sculpted, polished marble and colorful mosaic stone on this short, popular hike near Stovepipe Wells.
- Two miles (3.2 km) east of Rhyolite, **Titus Canyon Road** (page 97) begins. The 27-mile (43-km) one-way dirt road is one of the most popular backcountry routes in the park. It sweeps past rugged rock formations and a ghost town before the grand finale, the canyon narrows. The narrows tower overhead, barely allowing a car to squeeze through before they open wide to reveal the salty and barren Death Valley floor.

When you've had your fill, head back down to Scotty's Castle Road (a 1-hour drive) and camp at **Mesquite Spring.** The sites at this quiet, pretty campground are dotted with its namesake trees and sheltered along a wash. If you're not camping, Stovepipe Wells has the closest accommodations, but this will add an extra hour of driving.

Day 5

Today's destination is the Racetrack Valley. (If you've camped at Mesquite Spring, you're well positioned for this trip.) The long, high-clearance, gravel Racetrack Valley Road begins just beyond **Ubehebe Crater.** Make a quick pit stop at this colorful volcanic overlook before heading south toward the Racetrack Valley. The destination for most people is the Racetrack, 26 miles (42 km) in.

At 19.4 miles (31.2 km), the colorful **Teakettle Junction** signpost comes into view. Take a left turn at Teakettle Junction for a quick detour to the picturesque and weathered cabin of the **Lost Burro Mine** (at 3.2 mi/5.1 km, you will reach a four-way junction; park and walk along the right spur, which ends at the Lost Burro Mine in 1.1 mi/1.8 km).

Head back to Racetrack Valley Road and turn left to continue to **The Racetrack.** This dry lake bed, or playa, is famous for its moving rocks, which glide across the surface and leave mysterious trails. Soak in the surreal sight, then tackle the ambitious hike to **Ubehebe Peak.** The trail starts at **The Grandstand** parking area, then switchbacks up the side of the mountain with increasingly spectacular views of the Racetrack and the surrounding valley. Leave enough time for the hike back down and the long drive back out.

Teakettle Junction

Spend another night camping at Mesquite Spring, or drive the 66 miles (106 km, 1.5 hours) south to the **Panamint Springs Resort** on Highway 190. Tuck into a rustic cabin, motel room, or campsite and enjoy a relaxing dinner on the stone patio. Swap stories of your day's adventure with the other visitors at this friendly outpost on the western side of the park.

Day 6

Fill up on breakfast at Panamint Springs before heading out for a full day of exploring and hiking in the **Emigrant and Wildrose Canyons** on the western side of the Panamint Range. The first stop is the historic **Wildrose Charcoal Kilns.** Once used to make charcoal for the mining efforts in the area, they now stand as works of hand-engineered beauty.

The **Wildrose Peak** trail starts from the charcoal kilns parking area. This colorful forested trail leads through juniper trees to a big payoff at Wildrose Peak with its panoramic views.

Wind down with two final stops on your way back to Panamint Springs Resort. Located off Aguereberry Road, **Aguereberry Camp** provides a great perspective of a small mining camp and life in the desert. Enjoy the spectacular views from **Aguereberry Point** across Death Valley below.

You've definitely earned your relaxing dinner at Panamint Springs Resort after this day. If you're camping, **Wildrose Campground** is a great choice, tucked away in Wildrose Canyon.

Day 7

From Panamint Springs, it's about 50 miles (81 km) west to **Lone Pine,** an outpost of civilization on US 395 and your western exit from Death Valley. Spend a few hours exploring the town before driving south to **Los Angeles** (200 mi/320 km, 3 hours) or returning to **Las Vegas** (300 mi/485 km, 5 hours) for your flight home.

Mining Camps and Ghost Towns

From small Western towns that refused to die to forgotten mining camps, these destinations tell Death Valley's history, geology, and human experience.

- **Ashford Mine Camp** (page 59): Gold mining caught on in Ashford Canyon in 1907, and the Ashford Mine was worked until the 1940s. The well-preserved Ashford Mine Camp is home to abandoned cabins and the remnants of camp life.
- **Ballarat** (page 151): A caretaker is the sole year-round resident, running the general store and keeping Ballarat from ghost-town status. The town had its heyday between 1897 and 1905; original adobe structures and wood cabins remain.
- **Cerro Gordo** (page 202): High in the Inyo Mountains, the well-preserved wood and corrugated metal remains stand as a monument to Cerro Gordo's history as a thriving silver producer supplying Los Angeles, 275 miles (445 km) away, with a financial lifeline. Mines were in operation 1865-1938.
- **Gold Point** (page 136): Gold Point was a mining camp in the 1860s. The abandoned property was bought and rehabilitated in the early 1980s, resulting in a Wild West gem.
- **Inyo Mine Camp** (page 42): Inyo Mine is a bona fide ghost town, with a boardinghouse, cookhouse, several cabins, and mine works.
- **Lost Burro Mine** (page 124): Hidden in a corner of the Racetrack Valley, the Lost Burro Mine's camp and hand-painted sign are especially picturesque.
- **Panamint City** (page 167): The silver-boom ghost town of Panamint City is scenic and well preserved, with cabins, a mill, and artifacts for days.
- **Rhyolite** (page 94): At its peak, Rhyolite was home to 3,500-5,000 people; by 1920, only 14 remained. Today you can walk the main road past crumbling two-story bank ruins, a red-light district, a cemetery, and mine remains.
- **Saratoga Mines** (page 74): A peaceful walk along the Ibex Hills follows a former mining road that served several groups of talc mines in the hillsides.

Above: the Lost Burro Mine

Best Hikes

While there are few maintained trails in the park, old mining roads, narrow canyons, and natural features offer spectacular hiking opportunities.

Gower Gulch and Golden Canyon

Hike through glowing **Golden Canyon** (page 53) and past historical borax mining ruins to the spectacular views from **Zabriskie Point,** the stunning halfway point on this **7.8-mile (12.6-km) round-trip** trek. Shorter destinations include the equally striking **Red Cathedral.**

Hungry Bill's Ranch

Historic **Hungry Bill's Ranch** (page 57) was tied to one of the biggest silver rushes in the area. The **3.3-mile (5.3-km) round-trip** hike is via **Johnson Canyon,** one of the most-watered canyons in Death Valley. Gorgeous canyon views and hand-built rock walls make this well worth the effort it takes to drive the rough, four-wheel-drive-only road to get here.

Ashford Canyon

Colorful **Ashford Canyon** (page 59) leads to the tucked-away and well-preserved **Ashford Mine Camp**. Gold mining caught on in the area in 1907; the Ashford Mine was worked until the 1940s, when it was finally abandoned, leaving behind cabins, underground rooms, and the trappings of camp life. The steep **4.2-mile (6.8-km) round-trip** hike follows the canyon and pieces of the old mining road.

Sidewinder Canyon

Half the fun of **Sidewinder Canyon** (page 63) is the fun of discovery. Hikes range **2-4 miles (3.2-6.4 km)** or more to explore three different slot canyons and the twisting arches, hollows, natural bridges, and sculpted narrows that make up this sinewy maze at the base of Smith Mountain. The trailhead is south of Badwater Basin off Badwater Road.

Mosaic Canyon

Mosaic Canyon (page 104) is a popular hiking destination. This **2.8-mile (4.5-km) round-trip** trek through the canyons of the **Cottonwood**

Mountains wanders through polished marble and colorful mosaic stone. The trailhead is just outside Stovepipe Wells.

Ubehebe Peak

Unlike other Death Valley hikes, there is an actual trail to **Ubehebe Peak** (page 129); miners built it as a mule trail to haul out copper ore. A difficult **6-mile (9.7-km) round-trip** climb rewards with sweeping views of **The Racetrack** and the **Saline Valley.**

Telescope Peak

At 11,049 feet (3,368 m), **Telescope Peak** (page 169) is the highest point in Death Valley. Covered in snow most of the year, this **14-mile (22.5-km) round-trip** hike is strenuous but worth it. Plan your attempt in **May or June** for premium views.

Wildrose Peak

The steep hike to 9,064-foot (2,763-m) **Wildrose Peak** (page 171) leads through conifer forests, offering some welcome shade for hiking. The limber and bristlecone pine-studded trail stretches **9 miles (14.5 km) round-trip** but pays off with impressive views of Death Valley Canyon and Trail Canyon.

Surprise Canyon to Panamint City

The silver-boom ghost town of **Panamint City** (page 167) can only be reached via a long, strenuous hike through the scenic and well-watered **Surprise Canyon** (page 166). This **11-mile (17.7-km) round-trip** hike is best done as a backpacking trip: plan one day to hike in, a day to explore, and a day to hike out.

Mosaic Canyon's polished narrows

Best Four-Wheel Drives

Hundreds of miles of unmaintained four-wheel-drive (4WD) roads in the park provide access to remote destinations. **Farabee's Jeep Rentals** in Furnace Creek rents 4WD vehicles and has up-to-date backcountry road information. Check the visitor centers and ranger stations to confirm current road conditions, which can change from one day to the next.

- **Cottonwood Canyon Road** (page 98): This 19-mile (31-km) primitive road travels deep into the Cottonwood Mountains. The road starts off through semi-deep sand, eventually becoming more solid (washboard and gravel) and then much rougher as it enters the Cottonwood Canyon wash.
- **Echo Canyon to Inyo Mine Camp** (page 50): The 19-mile (31-km) round-trip drive is popular for its scenic, winding canyon and ghost camp ruins. Access starts from Highway 190, east of Badwater Road, and requires a high-clearance vehicle for the 3 miles (4.8 km) to the canyon mouth and 4WD beyond to the mining camp.
- **Racetrack Valley Road** (page 128): High-clearance vehicles can make the long, white-knuckle drive 26 rocky miles (42 km) into the Racetrack Valley, but 4WD may be necessary at times.
- **Saline Valley Road** (page 159): This rough yet graded dirt road travels 78 lonely miles (126 km) from Highway 190 to Big Pine-Death Valley Road. Although a high-clearance vehicle is suitable during good weather, 4WD may be necessary at times to access the remote Saline Valley.
- **Warm Spring Canyon to Butte Valley** (page 50): The lower canyon is easily accessible, following a good graded road the first 11 miles (17.7 km) to Warm Springs Camp. The upper canyon is harder to navigate and requires 4WD for the additional 11 miles (17.7 km) into Butte Valley.
- **Titus Canyon Road** (page 97): Beginning near Beatty, Nevada, the one-way Titus Canyon Road switchbacks 27 miles (43 km) along colorful, high-pitched slopes to end on the salty Death Valley floor. High clearance is suitable during good weather, but 4WD may be necessary at times.
- **Phinney Canyon Road and Strozzi Ranch Road** (page 98): A high-clearance then 4WD road cuts into the Grapevine Mountains and Nevada Triangle from the Nevada side. In 19 miles (31 km), it crosses a high desert plain then climbs through pinyon-pine forest to end at the historic Strozzi Ranch.

Hidden Springs and Desert Oases

The most surprising feature in Death Valley may be the presence of wetlands. These rare environments support distinct fish populations and provide life-giving watering holes for plants, animals, and humans.

Salt Creek

Salt Creek supports its own species of **pupfish** in the delicate riparian environment. A short walk along the wooden **wheelchair-accessible trail** (page 94) and the incongruous sight of a rushing creek in the tortured expanse of the valley floor give this place a lot of bang for the easy effort to get here.

Johnson Canyon

The energetic creek here has literally shaped **Johnson Canyon** (page 58), carving out the sheer walls that tower above. Stroll along the creek's edge or hike the steep ridge of the canyon to look down on this powerful thicket.

Hanaupah Canyon

A short hike leads to a charming creek and the historical site of **Shorty Borden**'s camp (page 56), a friendly prospector who made a name in Death Valley history. The creek is fed by snow from the Panamint Mountains, and the hike is scenically framed by views of Telescope Peak.

Warm Springs Camp

Nestled within **Warm Spring Canyon,** a luxurious spring was the site of the **Warm Springs Camp** (page 48), a mining camp established in the 1930s by Louise Grantham. Wandering amid the abandoned buildings, you'll come across the last thing you might expect—a swimming pool (now drained), which was fed from the spring's source behind the camp.

Ash Meadows National Wildlife Refuge

This magical swatch of open desert in the **Amargosa Valley** (page 77) contains crystal-blue pools of warm water, its own fish population, and the **Devil's Hole,** a deep window into an ancient aquifer system.

Amargosa River

The elusive **Amargosa River** surfaces in only two places during its 185-mile (300-km) length. It makes one of its rare appearances at the **China Ranch Date Farm** (page 82), near **Tecopa,** creating valuable habitat for migratory birds and other animals.

Saratoga Spring

These **springs** (page 74), hidden away in the **park's southeast corner,** quietly mirror the desert sky. Surrounded by reeds and desert grasses, they provided water for mining camps in the area and formed the backbone of a short-lived but enterprising water-bottling plant.

Cottonwood Canyon

The luxuriant springs of **Cottonwood Canyon** (page 98) are the crowning set of wonders along an action-packed 4WD trail. The first spring begins just beyond the end of the road as an energetic desert stream. Two more springs beyond give rise to the canyon's signature cottonwood trees and a shady oasis, a miracle of desert life that's surprising in this rugged canyon.

McElvoy Canyon

The spur road to **McElvoy Canyon** (page 164) is a faint track off the dusty Saline Valley Road that has you trudging over a hot alluvial fan until you hit the clear, luscious creek. Following it to the canyon mouth will take you to a grotto waterfall, cool with hanging ferns. A second waterfall lies beyond if you're up for a short rock climb.

wetland at Salt Creek

Best Spots for Stargazing

Death Valley has some of the most stellar stargazing in America. With the park's remote location and special lighting to reduce sky glow and glare, it earned an **International Dark Sky Park** certification. The closest urban center is Las Vegas, 110 miles (177 km) to the east as the crow flies; the tiny towns to the west are blocked by the sheer wall of the Panamint Range. The dazzling skies can be observed year-round; however, the park service offers **night sky events** on some weekends (Thurs.-Sun.) December-March.

TIPS

Pick a large, **open area** with **higher elevation;** lower elevations may mean that surrounding mountains block some of the sky. No fancy equipment is needed, but **binoculars** can give you a closer look. Use the red-light function on your headlamp to help your eyes adjust, and stay outside for at least 30 minutes. To do more than gaze in awe, check out a **night sky almanac** or one of the stargazing apps. Some apps rely on your phone's camera and do not require Wi-Fi, cellular service, or GPS, which is helpful in notoriously off-grid Death Valley.

BEST SPOTS

- Located in the northernmost section of the park, the **Eureka Dunes** (page 122) offer remoteness, elevation, and a striking backdrop. The pale dunes rise nearly 700 feet (213 m) and contrast with the dark, limestone cliff face of the Last Chance Mountains. There is a tiny campground so you can set up and soak it in.
- **Mesquite Spring Campground** (page 135) is dotted with its namesake mesquite, a low shrub that leaves the night sky wide open for craning your neck upwards. The congestion is far less here than campgrounds in Furnace Creek, meaning there is little to stand between you and the universe.
- Set up in the sea of sand that is the **Mesquite Flat Sand Dunes** (page 92) to take in the sea of stars overhead. This popular destination transforms into a quiet harbor at night with the clean lines of the dunes making for unobstructed views.
- The historical buildings and mule cart at the **Harmony Borax Works** (page 42) add a picturesque foreground while the salt flats beyond give way to big skies. The site is also easy to reach, located close to the Furnace Creek Visitor Center.
- The great wide open of **Emigrant Campground** (page 174) means that you can admire the celestial interplay over distant mountain ranges. The tent-only rule means that the only hum will be your communion with the starry universe.
- The expansive dazzle of the salt flats and sky counterbalance each other at **Badwater Basin** (page 46). At 282 feet (86 m) below sea level, some of the Milky Way may be blocked by mountain ranges, but the uniqueness of the experience plus the otherworldly foreground make it a special nighttime place.

Above: stars in Death Valley National Park

Furnace Creek and the Amargosa Range

The Amargosa Range rides the eastern boundary of Death Valley National Park, from the California-Nevada border south to the Amargosa River in the southeastern corner of the park.

The Grapevine, Funeral, and Black Mountains roll down into alluvial fans as the valley trends north in a wash of salt-crusted desert floor the length of the park. At its most extreme, the valley sinks below sea level, generating hot winds that lick at the mountain slopes. Shimmering heat and the unrelenting blue sky inspire wonder at the resourcefulness of the Indigenous people who called this area home. How did pioneers cross this expanse with their lives intact?

The park hub of Furnace Creek provides a good introduction for first-time visitors and gives easy access to many of the park's highlights:

Highlights

Look for ★ to find recommended sights, activities, dining, and lodging.

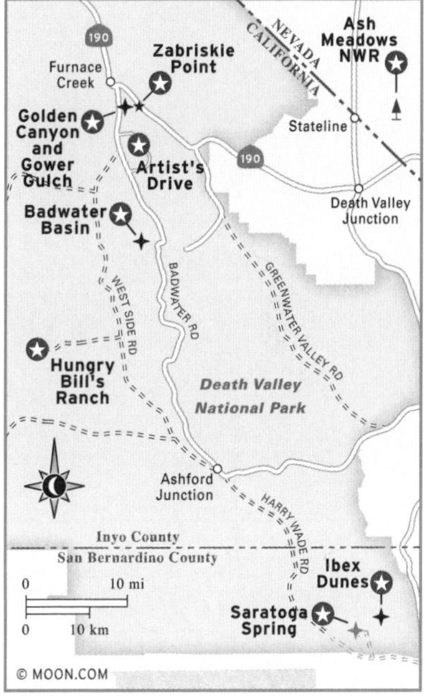

★ **Zabriskie Point:** A popular stop for photographers and visitors, this iconic Death Valley vantage point overlooks eroded badlands. The colors kindle at sunrise and sunset, revealing the magnificent desolation of the valley (page 44).

★ **Badwater Basin:** The lowest point in North America at 282 feet (86 m) below sea level, these vast salt flats encapsulate the mesmerizing yet unforgiving landscape of Death Valley (page 46).

★ **Artist's Drive:** Named for its shifting palette of colors, this gentle drive rises along an alluvial fan fed by the Black Mountains, proffering a chaotic jumble of hues from oxidized metals (page 48).

★ **Golden Canyon and Gower Gulch via Zabriskie Point:** The eroded hills of the badlands, glowing Golden Canyon, and historical borax mining ruins are the highlights of this rewarding hike (page 53).

★ **Hungry Bill's Ranch:** If you have a high-clearance 4WD vehicle, it's worth braving every boulder and washout in Johnson Canyon to access the hike to this ranch in the remote and wild Panamint Mountains (page 57).

★ **Ibex Dunes:** Admire these pristine sand scapes from a distance against the sharp backdrop of the Saddle Peak Hills or hike 1 mile (1.6 km) to their steep slopes (page 73).

★ **Saratoga Spring:** These beautiful ponds, tucked away in the often overlooked southeastern section of the park, are a rare sight in Death Valley (page 74).

★ **Ash Meadows National Wildlife Refuge:** Fossil water, melted from the last ice age, supplies the largest remaining oasis in the Mojave Desert, home to nearly 30 endemic plant and animal species (page 77).

Furnace Creek and the Amargosa Range

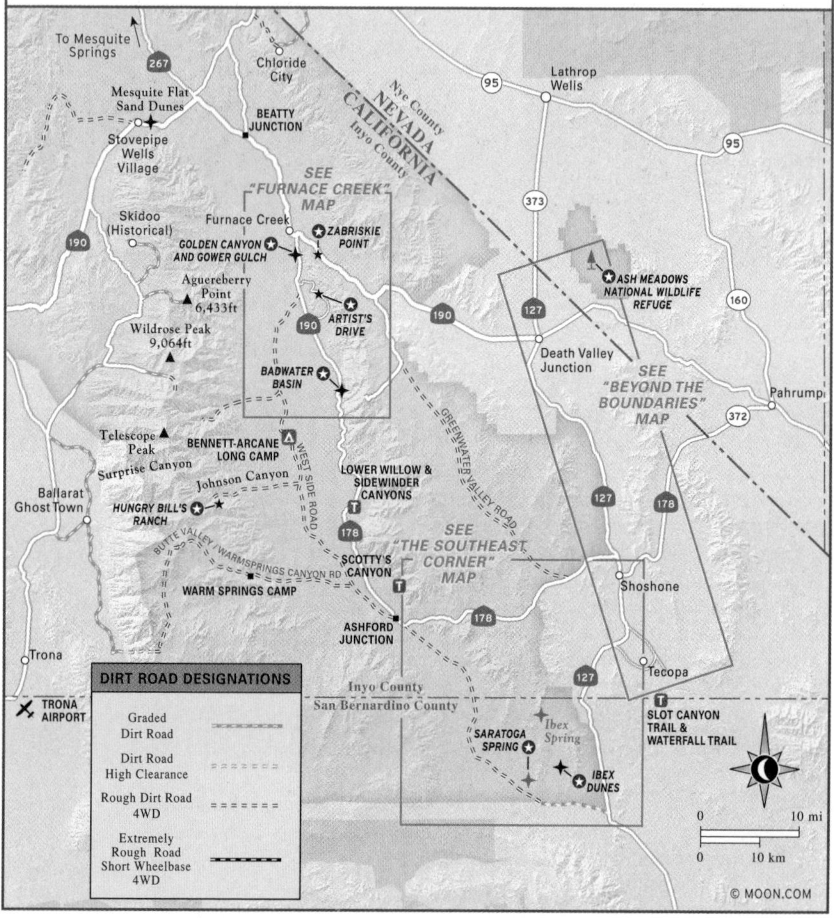

Zabriskie Point, Badwater Basin, and Artist's Drive. Wander among alien salt formations, red canyons, pioneer camps, or muted mineral tones with the mountains as canvas.

Like the chaotic geography that makes Death Valley famous, this area bucks easy categorization. Heading away from the magnetic pull of the valley's center reveals pristine sand dunes, bubbling oases, and forgotten mines.

PLANNING YOUR TIME

Furnace Creek is the park hub, an outpost of comfort and civilization with a visitor center, accommodations, campgrounds, restaurants, and even gas. This is the only area of the park where you will regularly encounter crowds, but even here, solitude is easy to achieve.

The two main, paved roads in the park—**Highway 190** and **Badwater Basin**

Previous: Badwater Basin; signpost in the village of Shoshone; Harmony Borax Works.

Furnace Creek

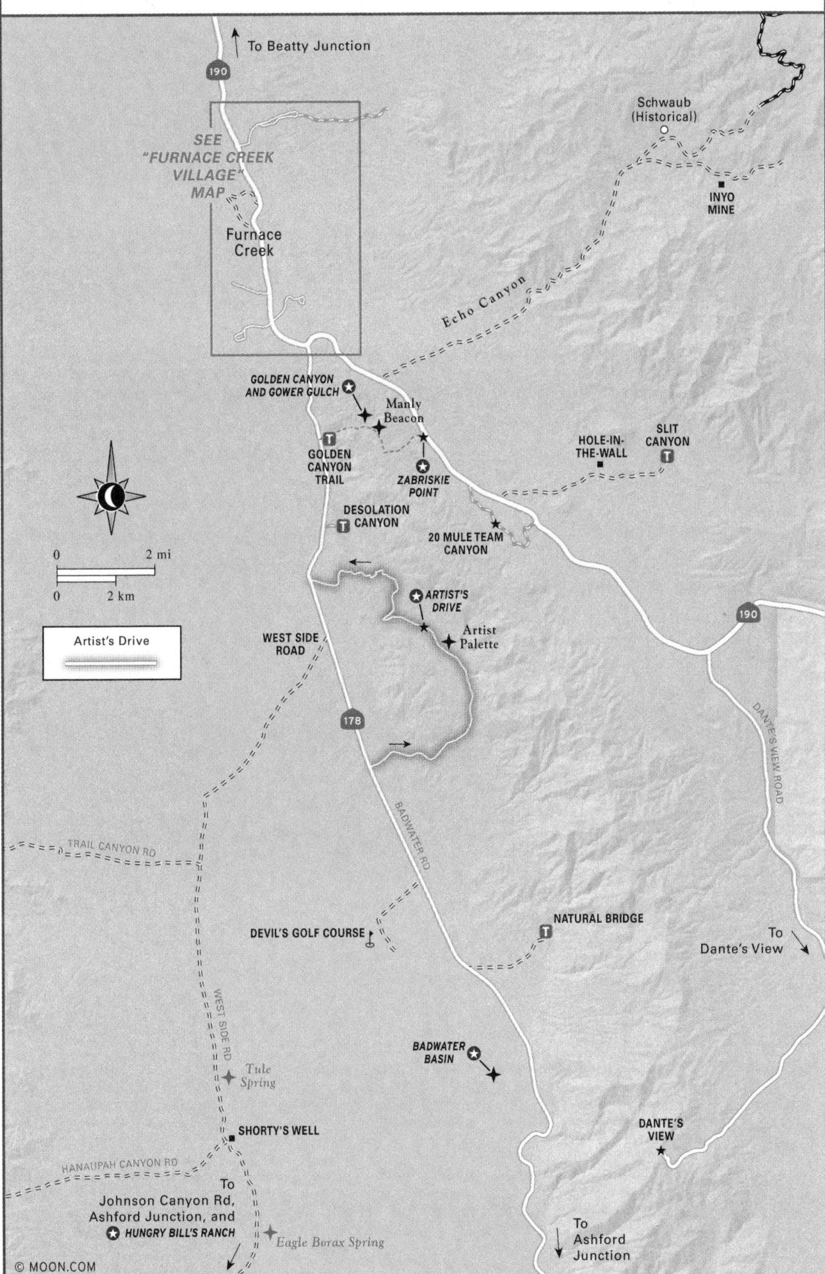

Where Can I Find . . . ?

The Oasis at Death Valley, a tourist facility located in the village of Furnace Creek, provides several basic visitor services. For more information, call 760/786-2345.

- **ATMs:** Located at the Ranch at Death Valley.
- **Cell phone reception:** The village of Furnace Creek, including the Ranch at Death Valley and the Inn at Death Valley, has the only cell reception in the park. Wi-Fi is available to all registered hotel guests.
- **Gas and auto repair:** The gas station at the Ranch performs basic auto repairs. For major repairs or towing, services will come from Beatty or Pahrump, Nevada.
- **Gift shops:** The Ranch General Store (760/786-2345; 7am-9pm daily) and Oasis Shoppe (760/786-2345; 9am-5pm daily).
- **Camping equipment:** Desert Outfitters (760/786-2345; 9am-5pm daily).
- **Laundromat:** Ranch at Death Valley (24 hours daily; change available from the Ranch General Store).
- **Post office:** Ranch at Death Valley (8am-1pm and 1:30pm-4pm Mon.-Fri.).
- **Showers:** Ranch at Death Valley (day pass $10).
- **Supplies:** Ranch at Death Valley General Store (760/786-2345; 7am-9pm daily) sells basic groceries, beer, wine, apparel, and gifts.

Road—intersect at Furnace Creek. A drive here is a pretty straightforward experience if you plan to stay on paved roads and see the popular destinations within an easy day trip from Furnace Creek. Most visitors concentrate their time on the sights along **Badwater Road,** touring the highlights in an afternoon; adding a hike can turn the trip into a full day.

Set aside **two days** to travel the length of the road, visit all the sights, and complete several hikes. Exploring some of the more rugged hikes and drives accessed from the graded, dirt West Side Road can add an additional day or two. To visit the southeastern section of the park with its cluster of natural and historical sites, allow an extra day.

When to Go

The village of Furnace Creek lies 190 feet (58 m) below sea level, making it an inferno in summer with temperatures soaring to well over 100°F (38°C) and dropping by as much as 40 degrees at night. The heat and wind of the valley floor are omnipresent. Certain times of the day and year are lovely, but prepare for extreme fluctuations in temperature and oppressive heat from **mid-May to the beginning of October.** Most services remain open in summer, but some business hours may fluctuate in the off-season. It's a good idea to call ahead if you're traveling in the summer. Hiking is strongly discouraged at lower elevations during summer.

Spring is the peak season to visit—daytime temperatures are pleasantly warm and nighttime temperatures are moderate. Seasonal businesses are open, and there may even be wildflowers during wetter years. **Fall** has equally lovely temperatures and is generally less crowded. **Winter** can be a great time to visit the lower elevations around Furnace Creek. There are fewer crowds, and skies are often clear. However, some park roads may be closed due to snow.

Driving Distances

From Furnace Creek to:	Distance	Duration
Stovepipe Wells	25 mi/40 km	30 min
Scotty's Castle	54 mi/87 km	1 hr 10 min
Panamint Springs	55 mi/89 km	1 hr
The Racetrack	83 mi/134 km	3-4 hrs
Eureka Dunes	97 mi/156 km	3 hrs
Southeast Corner	80 mi/129 km	2 hrs
Death Valley Junction	30 mi/48 km	30 min
Shoshone	56 mi/90 km	1 hr
Tecopa	68 mi/109 km	1 hr 10 min
Olancha	102 mi/164 km	2 hrs
Baker	112 mi/180 km	2 hrs

Exploring the Park

The Amargosa Range owes its creation to the Northern Death Valley Fault Zone, but despite its tumultuous formation, this is the most visited and accessible area of the park. The Grapevine, Funeral, and Black Mountains roll down into alluvial fans, and the popular Badwater Basin Road will take you past the famous sights: the haunting and eroded Zabriskie Point badlands, stifling and strange Badwater Basin, and the colorful mineral palette of Artist's Drive.

The village of Furnace Creek offers lodging, dining, gas, souvenirs, supplies, a post office, restrooms, a visitor center, the Borax Museum, and a golf course. Visitors casually gather around outdoor seating, an outdoor fireplace, and the saloon patio with a backdrop of palm trees fed by Furnace Creek's natural oasis.

VISITOR CENTER

Hwy. 190; 760/786-3200; www.nps.gov/deva; 8am-5pm daily

The Furnace Creek Visitor Center is located within the Western-themed village of Furnace Creek and provides information on park sights, activities, and programs, as well as camping and hiking. Interpretive displays offer an overview of the park's natural and cultural history. Park passes, permits, and information are available here. Park passes are also available from a cash or card kiosk outside the visitor center as well as at strategic locations in the park. The **Death Valley Natural History Association** (http://dvnha.org) maintains an outlet filled with books on the natural and cultural history of the park. Take a few minutes to stroll through the visitor center's museum exhibits, which take a fresh and engaging approach to presenting background on the area's cultural and natural history and phenomena. Restrooms are available outside the visitor center, and water is available to refill reusable water bottles.

PARK ENTRANCES

Highway 190 leads to the park hub at Furnace Creek; it is the most popular and efficient way to access the park's most-visited sights. The road is fully paved, and if you are visiting for the first time, the visitor center can be a source of helpful information.

Highway 190 can be accessed from the **east** via **Death Valley Junction** and Highway 127, a distance of approximately 30 miles (48 km, 30 minutes). Furnace Creek can also be accessed from the **west** via Highway 190, which connects with US 395 at the town of **Olancha** (100 mi/161 km, 1.75 hours).

Aside from Furnace Creek, there are no other entrance stations; however, there is an automated **kiosk** on Highway 190 across from Dante's View Road. The kiosk accepts cash and major credit cards. Visitor guides with basic park maps and information are available for free.

There are several routes from Las Vegas to the park hub at Furnace Creek whether you are looking for the shortest, easiest, or most scenic drive. Count on covering between 120 and 172 miles (193-275 km) with commute times ranging 2-3.5 hours.

To take the **shortest route** (120 mi/193 km, 2 hours), from I-15 South, exit on Nevada Highway 160 West. Drive 60 miles (97 km) to Pahrump, Nevada. Turn left on Bell Vista Road and drive 30 miles (48 km) to Death Valley Junction, California. Turn right on Highway 127 then left on Highway 190 after approximately 300 feet (91 km). Drive 30 miles (48 km) to the Furnace Creek Visitor Center.

For the **most straightforward route,** (145 mi/233 km, 2.5 hours) from I-15, exit on US 95 North. Drive 90 miles (145 km) to Lathrop Wells, Nevada. Turn left on Nevada Highway 373, which becomes California Highway 127. Drive 25 miles (40 km) to Death Valley Junction. Turn right on Highway 190 and continue for 30 miles (48 km) to the Furnace Creek Visitor Center.

To follow what the National Park Service (NPS) has dubbed the **ghost town route** (160 mi/260 km, 3 hours), from I-15, exit on US 95 North. Drive 120 miles (193 km) to Beatty, Nevada. Turn left on Highway 374. The access road for Rhyolite ghost town is 4 miles (6.4 km) south of town (1.5 mi/2.4 km to town site from Hwy. 374). Continue on Highway 374 for 19 miles (31 km) to Hells Gate. Turn left on the signed Beatty Cutoff Road. Drive 10 miles (16.1 km). Turn left on Highway 190 and continue 11 miles (17.7 km) to the Furnace Creek Visitor Center.

The **most scenic route** (172 mi/275 km, 3.5 hours) approaches from the south through the tiny town of Tecopa and traverses Badwater Road, giving access to Death Valley's famed salt flats. From I-15 South, exit on Highway 160 West. Drive 45 miles (72 km). Turn left on Tecopa Road (Old Spanish Trail) and drive 41 miles (66 km). Turn right on Highway 127 for 10 miles (16.1 km). Turn left on Highway 178 West (Badwater Rd.) for 75 miles (121 km). Turn left on Highway 190 and drive 1 mile (1.6 km) to the Furnace Creek Visitor Center.

GAS AND SERVICES

While Furnace Creek is conveniently located and a good place to explore this popular region of the park, food, supplies, and accommodations can be pricey. Plan ahead to stock up on gas and other supplies at larger towns outside the park.

Gas and limited supplies are available in **Shoshone,** 57 miles (92 km) southeast of Furnace Creek at the junction of Highways 190 and 178. Outside the park boundaries, gas and limited supplies are available 56 miles (90 km) farther south in the town of **Baker,** at the junction of I-15 and Highway 127.

Furnace Creek and the Amargosa Range in One Day

- Begin your day at the **Furnace Creek Visitor Center.** Pick up a hiking map and check out the exhibits.
- Head south on Badwater Road to explore Death Valley's highlights: **Artist's Drive, Devil's Golf Course,** and the salt flats of **Badwater Basin.**
- Fit in a hike to colorful **Desolation Canyon** or make the extra drive to explore the twisting slots of **Sidewinder Canyon,** 17 miles (27 km) south of Badwater Basin.
- Pack a picnic or return to **Furnace Creek** for lunch.
- The afternoon is all about the views. Travel Highway 190 east of Furnace Creek to look across the striking badlands from famous **Zabriskie Point.** Drive or walk the 2.7-mile (4.3-km) loop through the strangely eroded hills of **Twenty Mule Team Canyon,** and end on a high note at the **Dante's View** overlook, which offers sweeping west-facing views.
- **Furnace Creek** will be your hub for dinner.

Sights

FURNACE CREEK VILLAGE

With its Wild West theme and visitor-friendly amenities, the village of Furnace Creek could fool you into thinking it has never been anything more than that. In reality, the site of the Ranch at Death Valley has some serious park cred when it comes to history.

Located at the mouth of Furnace Creek, the site was a working ranch from the 1870s on, growing alfalfa, dates, produce, and later livestock for distribution to nearby mining camps. More importantly, it provided relief from the relentless sun and loneliness of travelers and prospectors making their way against the merciless salt and sky, seeking riches but more often just scraping a living. Even after Furnace Creek became a homestead and ranch, it remained a meeting point for three different Native American groups: the Shoshone from the north, the Southern Paiute from east of the valley, and the Kawaiisu from southern Death and Panamint Valleys. Currently, the Timbisha Shoshone Band of California has a community here.

The Pacific Coast Borax Company took a big role in steering the historical course of the ranch when it took over sometime after 1889. The ranch served as terminus for the famous 20-mule-team runs, distributing borax from major mines in the region. In the 1920s the company added tourism to its repertoire in Death Valley. It commissioned the building of the elegant Furnace Creek Inn, which opened to visitors in 1927. Furnace Creek Ranch opened as a tourist destination in 1933.

Today the village of Furnace Creek is the site of the re-branded Oasis at Death Valley (formerly Furnace Creek Resort), comprising the inn and the ranch, located 1 mile (1.6 km) apart. **The Ranch at Death Valley** is home to a cabin and motel complex as well as restaurants, a general store, a high-end gift shop, outfitters, a saloon, a post office, a golf course, the **Borax Museum,** horse stables, a **gas station,** park headquarters, and a **visitor center.** The **Inn at Death Valley** is terraced into a hillside near the ranch, with its own restaurant and hotel amenities. **Jeep rentals** are available next to the Ranch.

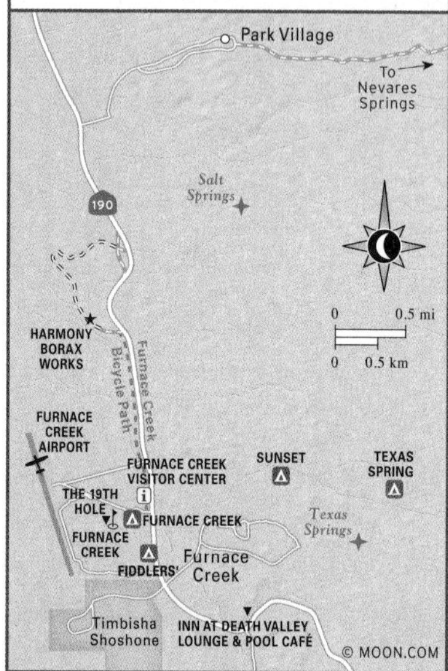

Borax Museum

760/786-2345; 9am-9pm daily; donation

The Borax Museum, located at Furnace Creek between the restaurants and golf course, is housed in the oldest building in Death Valley. Built in 1883, it was once the assay office for the Monte Blanco Mine in what is now the Twenty Mule Team Canyon. It was moved to Furnace Creek, where it packs in exhibits on Native Americans in Death Valley as well as mining history and the history of borax, the "white gold" of the valley. The outdoor exhibits include a 60-ton oil-burning locomotive that hauled borate, which gives some idea of the brute force it took to tackle mining in the harsh environment.

Harmony Borax Works

Access via Hwy. 190, 1 mile (1.6 km) north of Furnace Creek

Just 1 mile (1.6 km) north of Furnace Creek, a short paved path leads to the site of the Harmony Borax Works. A 20-mule-team wagon, the remains of a borax refinery, and interpretive signs tell the textbook history of the site as a base of operations for borax mining and processing from 1883 to 1888. The deeper history may well be in the harsh, exposed salt flats that extend in a white glare north and west. It was here that mostly Chinese laborers lived in tent communities, harvesting borate, which they raked into mounded "haystacks" for processing. Mercifully, the temperatures were too hot in Furnace Creek for the operations to continue in summer.

It is possible to see the faint eroded remains of some of the **borax haystacks** on a 1.5-mile (2.4-km) walk across the salt pan. From the parking area, drive the graded road as it begins to veer right into Mustard Canyon. Park here and walk 1.5 miles (2.4 km) westward across exposed open desert, passing strange salt formations and eventually hitting the rows of haystacks, which run north and south. The salt flats form a shallow seasonal lake, making this walk impossible at times. Even when it is passable, mud can make the passage difficult, and footprints can remain for years. Do not walk through the haystacks; instead, enjoy them from a safe distance. Do not attempt this in summer due to the extreme heat or after a rain.

INYO MINE CAMP

Access via Hwy. 190 starting 2 miles (3.2 km) east of Badwater Rd.

A rocky four-wheel drive takes you through the rugged gorge of Echo Canyon to the remains of a gold-mining camp deep in the Funeral Mountains. In 1905 gold-bearing quartz veins were discovered in Echo Canyon. From 1905-1907, high-grade ore and the profitable mines kept the humble mining camp busy until funds and investors dwindled. The mine was abandoned in 1912 then revitalized in 1935-1936 and again in 1939-1941. Scattered across the remote hills are a boardinghouse, a cookhouse, cabins, and the mine works, providing plenty

1: a locomotive at the Borax Museum **2:** Inyo Mine **3:** Zabriskie Point **4:** the Borax Museum

1
DVRR
DVRR
2
2
3
4
THE
Borax Museum
NO
Smoking

to explore. The 19-mile (31-km) round-trip drive is scenic, and the canyon with its narrows and stone arch (Eye of the Needle, at 4.8 mi/7.7 km) makes it a worthy trip. The route begins 2 miles (3.2 km) east of Badwater Road. For the first few miles, the road may be passable with a high-clearance vehicle. Once the road enters the canyon mouth, it requires four-wheel drive due to slanted bedrock and deep gravel. Allow 2-3 hours to complete the drive and explore the camp.

★ ZABRISKIE POINT

Off Hwy. 190, 7 miles (11.3 km) south of Furnace Creek

Iconic Zabriskie Point overlooks otherworldly and eroded badlands from a vantage point just off Highway 190, 7 miles (11.3 km) south of Furnace Creek. It's a popular stop for photographers and other visitors; the colors kindle at sunrise and sunset, capturing the magnificent desolation of the valley.

Manly Beacon, a rock outcropping to the north, commemorates William L. Manly, who, along with John Rogers, guided a group of 49ers, migrant pioneers headed to the California goldfields, out of danger during an 1849 crossing of Death Valley. The site was once ancient Lake Manly, and the hills began eroding into the shape seen today by the formation of the Black Mountains to the west. The darker ridgelines are formed by lava.

This is a beautiful and haunting place to soak it all in, as well as an excellent hiking destination (or starting point) for hikes through **Golden Canyon** and **Gower Gulch** to experience the splendid desolation on a closer scale.

TWENTY MULE TEAM CANYON

Access via Hwy. 190, 5.7 miles (9.2 km) from Furance Creek

A short, graded dirt road leads about 3 miles (4.8 km) through a mudstone canyon past badlands and the site of historical mining prospects at Twenty Mule Team Canyon. The road is not accessible to vehicles over 25 feet (7.6 m) long, and the route is prone to washouts, so check to make sure it's open before you make the trip.

At 1.8 miles (2.9 km), **Twenty Mule Team Canyon Road** veers to the left, toward the **Monte Blanco assay office,** a large wooden house built in 1883 to serve miners. (The building was moved and now houses the Borax Museum at the Ranch at Death Valley.) The area was never extensively mined, but old adits (tunnels) are visible.

Although the name of the canyon evokes the big wagon teams from tales of the Wild West, the Monte Blanco mining district was never fully developed and might not have seen the big wagon teams. Instead, look toward the gold-and-white hills to understand what all the fuss was about. The white striations are borate ore. Although not as romantic as gold, borax was Death Valley's bread and butter.

Directions

From Furnace Creek, drive south to the intersection of Highway 190 and Badwater Basin Road. Continue east on Highway 190 for 4.7 miles (7.6 km). Look for a small signed intersection on the right indicating the one-way drive through Twenty Mule Team Canyon. The drive through the canyon is 2.7 miles (4.3 km); the total drive from Furnace Creek is about 16 miles (26 km).

DANTE'S VIEW

As the name suggests, Dante's View provides spectacular panoramic views of Death Valley. The Panamint Mountains rise dramatically from the stiflingly low Badwater Basin salt flats at 282 feet (86 m) below sea level to Telescope Peak, snowcapped much of the year and the highest point in the park at 11,049 feet (3,368 m). On a clear day you can see Mount Whitney, the highest point in the contiguous 48 states, in the same view. The Owlshead Mountains to the south, the Funeral Mountains to the north, and the Greenwater Mountains to the east make this a good place to get your bearings and be dazzled at the same time. Visit at sunrise to see the whole valley suffused with morning light. Some people bring telescopes out at night for unparalleled **stargazing.**

A Galaxy Not So Far Away: *Star Wars* in Death Valley

"What a desolate place this is."—C-3PO

Artist's Drive

Death Valley is often described as "otherworldly," and that alien look earned it a role as the sparsely inhabited planet Tatooine in the original *Star Wars* trilogy. The mythical planet was characterized by scorching sun, lack of surface water, and abandoned mining equipment. Sound familiar?

Crucial scenes for *Star Wars: Episode IV - A New Hope* and *Star Wars: Episode VI - Return of the Jedi* were shot in Death Valley, including the scene where Obi-Wan Kenobi meets Luke Skywalker, R2-D2, and C-3PO for the first time.

Despite Tatooine's fictional location on the outer rim of the galaxy, film locations are an easy drive on pavement from **Furnace Creek** and include many of the park's highlights:

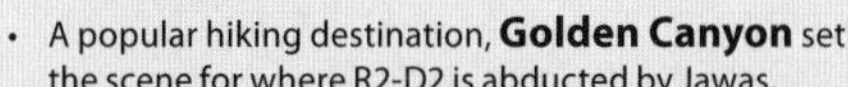

- A popular hiking destination, **Golden Canyon** set the scene for where R2-D2 is abducted by Jawas.
- **Mesquite Flat Sand Dunes,** the largest dune field in the park, was the vast backdrop for the scene where R2-D2 and C-3PO part ways after crashing their escape pod on Tatooine.
- The dark, sculpted entrance to **Desolation Canyon** marks the spot where Tusken Raiders mount banthas before Luke Skywalker is attacked.
- The 9-mile (14.5-km) scenic loop of **Artist's Drive** takes you through striking volcanic rock as well as the place where a miniature Sandcrawler was filmed so that R2-D2 could be carried to it by Jawas. Stop at **Artist's Palette** for colorful views and more *Star Wars* scenery.
- Jabba the Hutt's palace was accessible by a single dirt road that stretched through a canyon. Visit **Twenty Mule Team Canyon** to see where R2-D2 and C-3PO made the journey.
- At 5,475 feet (1,669 m), **Dante's View** offers sweeping views across Death Valley and was used as an establishing shot of Mos Eisley, Tatooine's large spaceport. As described by Obi-Wan Kenobi to Luke Skywalker, "Mos Eisley Spaceport. You will never find a more wretched hive of scum and villainy."

Have fun visiting all the locations. May the force be with you!

Directions

From Furnace Creek, drive south to the intersection of Highway 190 and Badwater Basin Road. Follow Highway 190 east for 10.7 miles (17.2 km), then turn right onto Furnace Creek Wash Road. At 7.5 miles (12.1 km), continue onto Dante's View Road. Drive 5.5 miles (8.9 km) to the parking area and overlook. The total drive from Furnace Creek is about 24 miles (39 km) and takes approximately 30 minutes.

ARTIST'S PALETTE

Badwater Rd., 5 miles (8 km) south of Furnace Creek, 9 miles (14.5 km) one-way

A popular stop along Artist's Drive is the Artist's Palette, a scenic viewpoint 4.5 miles (7.2 km) into the 9-mile (14.5-km) paved drive. Compound-rich volcanic deposits have tinged the hills at the foot of the Black Mountains, giving rise to a rainbow effect across the eroded landscape. It is most concentrated at the Artist's Palette, where a jumble of green, rose, yellow, purple, and red create a dramatic backdrop. Artist's Palette is less than one hour round-trip from Furnace Creek and has a parking area and scenic viewpoint.

DEVIL'S GOLF COURSE

Badwater Rd., 11 miles (17.7 km) south of Furnace Creek

You'll want to put your camera on the macro setting to capture the controlled chaos of the Devil's Golf Course. Located on the northern end of the eerie, stark salt flats of Badwater Basin, Devil's Golf Course is filled with spiky salt crystals that you have to see close up to appreciate. Groundwater seeps up to the surface, prompting the jagged pinnacles.

It's extremely difficult to walk out here. Take the graded dirt road to a small parking lot, where you can see the formations at closer range. If you step out into them, place your feet carefully between the pinnacles. A few awkward steps into the frenetic landscape will reveal tiny salt crystals sprouting wildly in the barbed ground.

TOP EXPERIENCE

★ BADWATER BASIN

Badwater Rd., 16 miles (26 km) south of Furnace Creek

Badwater Basin is a Death Valley classic. If you're going to visit one place in Death Valley, this is it. The lowest point in North America, at 282 feet (86 m) below sea level, these vast salt flats encapsulate the mesmerizing yet unforgiving landscape of Death Valley. Walk out onto the salt flats to feel the sea of air and look for delicate salt-crystal formations. The blinding glare, emanating heat, and scale of humans next to the surrounding Black Mountains puts our existence into perspective and gives us a sense of the earth's extremes.

WEST SIDE ROAD

Badwater Rd., 6 miles (9.7 km) south of Furnace Creek, 37 miles (60 km) one-way

Unlike the valley floor from Badwater Basin Road, the West Side Road parallels a wide swath of vegetation supported by the four main springs: **Tule Spring, Shorty's Well, Eagle Borax Spring,** and Bennett's Well, at the **Bennett-Arcane Long Camp.** The mesquite trees and other tenacious vegetation have adapted to the saline environment and offset the white austerity of the salt playa and mountain backdrop.

Directions

The West Side Road starts on Badwater Road, opposite the Artist's Drive loop, and continues south for 37 miles (60 km), ending just before the ruins of Ashford Mill. The road has a few rough patches, and a **high-clearance vehicle** is generally recommended. At times the road may be passable in a passenger car, but conditions change, especially after rain, when the water creates mud and washouts. The road may close during summer due to extreme heat. Check at the visitor center or online for road conditions.

To reach the northern entrance from Furnace Creek, drive 6 miles (9.7 km) south on Badwater Road and turn right at the signed junction.

Eagle Borax Works

12.6 miles (20.3 km) from the northern entrance

The Eagle Borax Spring is the site of the Eagle Borax Works, and its historical remains are worth a quick stop. The area includes the **Bennett-Arcane Long Camp** (15.6 mi/25 km), where a famous group of 49ers, migrant pioneers headed to the California goldfields in 1849, set up a desperate camp after nearly dying on an ill-fated shortcut through Death Valley. Members of the party who went to seek supplies on foot eventually returned to rescue them. Upon leaving, one of the members of the party was said to have turned for a last look at their narrow escape and said, "Goodbye, death valley," even though only one of the party actually died. Understandably, the name stuck.

1: Devil's Golf Course 2: Badwater Basin salt flats

1
2 
BADWATER BASIN
282 FEET/85.5 METERS
BELOW SEA LEVEL

Warm Springs Camp

44 miles (71 km) from the northern entrance

From the 1880s, miners used the region around Warm Springs as a camp. In the early 1930s, Louise Grantham established Warm Springs Camp to serve her mines. Grantham was one of the most famous and financially successful women miners in Death Valley. She moved here from Ohio at age 25 and began staking claims in Warm Spring Canyon in the early 1900s. Her camp was a step above many of the rough subsistence camps elsewhere and included her private residence, a mess hall, a shop, a dormitory, and several houses. There were also showers and flush toilets. A swimming pool was added later, fed with the water that tumbles from the spring in the cliffs behind the camp.

Driving up to the site today, it looks like it could still be inhabited. Bright yellow buildings poke out behind tamarisks and the overgrowth from the spring. This is a fun place to explore; the spring, the camp, and the mine works are easily visible in the surrounding hills. Between the camp and the road, **Gold Hill Mill** is a historic gold-processing plant, with a stone arrastre (used for grinding gold-bearing rocks into dust) and myriad wheels and pulleys. In the hills on the north side of the road, the **Pink Elephant Mine** inspires the imagination with its psychedelic moniker and the aerial tramway visible from the camp.

Warm Springs Camp is easily accessible via Warm Spring Canyon Road, a well-maintained graded road suitable for any **high-clearance vehicle** (and possibly passenger vehicles, depending on road conditions). From West Side Road, 2.9 miles (4.7 km) from its southern end or 33 miles (53 km) from its northern end, a sign marks Warm Spring Canyon Road. Along the 11 miles (17.7 km) to Warm Springs Camp, the road passes many mining claims; those on the north side are older and more historical.

Scenic Drives

Many visitors treat a visit to Death Valley as a car-only tour, an approach that makes sense during summer due to the extreme heat. But during spring, fall, and winter, you can experience the nuance of the desert and enjoy your own little piece of it by hiking some of the canyons or taking one of the many lightly traveled roads.

Dirt roads vary in their accessibility. Some roads require only high clearance and may be passable with a passenger car, while others require a serious four-wheel-drive (4WD) vehicle. Several of the dirt roads in this area, including the **West Side Road** and the **Greenwater Valley Road,** are graded and may be passable with a passenger car in good weather and road conditions. A 4WD vehicle opens up your possibilities for canyon or other more remote exploration.

★ ARTIST'S DRIVE

Distance: *9 mile (14.5 km) loop*
Duration: *Less than 1 hour*
Start: *Badwater Rd., 5 miles (8 km) south of Furnace Creek*
Road surface: *Paved*
Vehicle: *Passenger*

Named for the shifting palette of colors, gentle Artist's Drive rises along an alluvial fan fed by the Black Mountains. The road loops through rainbow-tinged, eroded hills, juxtaposed with the rugged Black Mountains and giving views of the salt flats below. The colors, caused by the oxidizing of different metals on the volcanic rock, proffer a chaotic jumble of hues, including green, rose, yellow, purple, and red. The highlight of the Artist's Drive is **Artist's Palette,** a section of hills named for its concentrated rainbow of color, 4.5 miles (7.2 km) into the drive. The paved 9-mile (14.5-km) **scenic loop** is a one-way road starting on Badwater Road, 5 miles (8 km) south of Furnace Creek. There are plenty of places to pull over for the many pictures you will want to take.

As with many good things in Death Valley, they get even better once you step out of your car. It's possible to explore a **short, colorful canyon** 3.5 miles (5.6 km) in, at the second dip in the road. There is a small turnout at the top of the rise on the right side where you can park. Hike up the wash at the bottom of the dip about 50 yards (46 m), where a pink fall marks the entrance to the canyon. Look for mud drippings and slickensides (rocks polished smooth by movement along a fault) and enjoy the scramble over several boulder jams. If you haven't given up before this, the last stretch of the canyon is a vertical narrows that ends at a 20-foot (6.1-m) fall.

WEST SIDE ROAD

Distance: *37 miles (60 km) one-way*
Duration: *1 hour*
Start: *6 miles (9.7 km) south of the Hwy. 190-Badwater Rd. junction; may be closed in summer due to extreme heat*
End: *3.8 miles (6.1 km) north of Ashford Junction*
Road surface: *Dirt*
Vehicle: *High-clearance recommended*

This graded dirt road runs along the west side of Badwater Basin, skirting the foot of the Panamint Range and offering a unique perspective of the Death Valley floor different from the more heavily traveled Badwater Road to the east. West Side Road crosses the **Devil's Golf Course** to head south, skirting the shimmering oven of the Badwater salt pan. It is generally used as an access road to the rugged and scenic canyons on the eastern side of the Panamint Mountains. Rugged roads that demand high-clearance and 4WD vehicles cross the alluvial fans to a series of deep and scenic canyons with hidden streams, mining ruins, and beautiful canyon walls. Experience the orchards of **Hungry Bill's Ranch** or the bubbling oases of **Hanaupah Canyon.** There are plenty of backcountry campsites and hikes where you can enjoy the intense quiet of the desert and the translucent glow of the night sky from the salt-crusted valley floor.

High clearance is recommended due to washboards and pockets of soft dirt. After rain the road may be closed due to washouts or flooding. There are two access points: From the junction of Highway 190 and Badwater Road, the northern access is 6 miles (9.7 km)

Artist's Palette

south; the southern access is 39.2 miles (63 km) farther south.

FOUR-WHEEL DRIVES

Echo Canyon to Inyo Mine Camp

Distance: *19 miles (31 km) round-trip*
Duration: *2-3 hours*
Start: *Hwy. 190, 2 miles (3.2 km) east of Badwater Rd.*
End: *Hwy. 190, 2 miles (3.2 km) east of Badwater Rd.*
Road surface: *Gravel*
Vehicle: *High-clearance 4WD required*

The Echo Canyon drive is popular for its scenic and winding canyon, stone arch, and ghost camp ruins. Echo Canyon starts from Highway 190, at an inconspicuously signed junction 2 miles (3.2 km) east of Badwater Road. For the first couple of miles, as the road crawls toward the canyon mouth, it may be passable with a high-clearance vehicle. Once the road approaches the mouth of the canyon, things change—from here to the mining camp, a high-clearance 4WD vehicle is required due to deep gravel and a rocky wash.

After entering the canyon mouth, the road winds through canyon narrows, reaching the **Eye of the Needle,** a sharp stone arch that juts into the canyon, at 4.8 miles (7.7 km). The canyon broadens into a valley that may be filled with flowers in springtime. Just below the mining camp (about 0.5 mi/0.8 km), a signed junction marks a small triangular intersection. Continue right toward the Inyo Mine Camp. The road leads to a small parking area below the mine. There are enough buildings here to elevate the site beyond the level of camp to a bona fide ghost town with a boardinghouse, cookhouse, several cabins, and, of course, the mine works. It is possible to visit the camp in 2-3 hours from Furnace Creek, including the drive and time to explore the camp.

Warm Spring Canyon to Butte Valley

Distance: *44.6 miles (72 km) round-trip*
Duration: *3-4 hours*
Start: *Warm Springs Canyon Rd.*
End: *Warm Springs Canyon Rd.*
Road surface: *Dirt*
Vehicle: *High-clearance 4WD required*

This scenic drive leads through Warm Spring Canyon to Butte Valley. The drive begins on Warm Spring Canyon Road, accessed from the West Side Road 2.9 miles (4.7 km) from its southern end or 33 miles (53 km) from its northern entrance. A good graded road leads 11 miles (17.7 km) to Warm Springs Camp. While lower Warm Spring Canyon is easily accessible, the upper canyon is harder to navigate once you're there, requiring a 4WD vehicle to access remote springs, secluded cabins, and the lovely geology of Butte Valley.

From Warm Springs Camp, the road spurs to the northwest at 4.4 miles (7.1 km) (15.4 mi/24.8 km into the drive) to **Arrastre Spring** and the **Gold Hill** area; little remains from its brief time as a gold-mining location. Arrastre Spring was named for the stone arrastres (now obscured by willows) used to grind gold. It is most famous as the spot where some historians think the infamous Bennett-Arcane party spoke the words "Goodbye, death valley" as they escaped their near-death ordeal.

The road continues as Butte Valley Road. The road condition worsens, but the scenery improves as the road drops into Butte Valley at 17.8 miles (28.6 km). The impressive **Striped Butte,** an unmistakable geologic feature for which this area was named, is straight ahead. Access to Striped Butte is via a northwest road into **Redlands Canyon** at 20.3 miles (32.7 km). Continuing on Butte Valley Road will take you to **Anvil Spring Junction** at 22.3 miles (35.9 km) (look for an unsigned but obvious junction). From here, a right turn leads to Anvil Spring and the well-known **Geologist's Cabin.** A left turn leads to **Willow Spring.** Straight on, the road continues to **Russel's Camp,** Mengel Pass, and Goler Wash. Historical interest groups, the public, and the National Park Service maintain **cabins** in the area. If you are visiting the cabins, be aware of the threat of hantavirus, which exists in old buildings.

To complete the drive, turn around in Butte Valley and head back out the way you came in. From Anvil Spring Junction, it is a 22.3-mile (35.9-km) drive to return to the West Side Road. Allow at least three hours for the drive back. (It is sometimes possible to continue an additional 11 miles/17.7 kilometers via Mengel Pass into Goler Wash and the western side of the Panamint Mountains, but this is one of the worst and most dangerous drives in the park. The road is often impassable and should not be attempted if you are not an experienced 4WD driver.)

Harry Wade Road

Distance: *31 miles (50 km) one-way*
Duration: *1 hour*
Start: *Ashford Junction*
End: *Hwy. 127*
Road surface: *Dirt, sand*
Vehicle: *High-clearance required*

This lightly traveled road in the southeastern corner of Death Valley connects Badwater Road to the north with Saratoga Spring Road to the south in a shortcut (the type that is shorter in miles but longer in time and scenery) worth the trek for its sweeping solitude, dark and eroded rocks of the Owlshead Mountains, and glimpses of far-off talc mines in the Ibex Hills. Pavement to pavement, the drive is 31 miles (50 km). It begins at Ashford Junction (where Highway 178/Jubilee Pass Road turns north to become Badwater Road). It ends at the Harry Wade Monument on Highway 127, 26 miles (42 km) south of Shoshone or 29 miles (47 km) north of Baker. The Harry Wade Route or Harry Wade Exit Route was once thought to have been the escape route for the Harry Wade family, seekers of the western goldfields, who sought a shortcut through Death Valley to the Sierra Nevada range and got bogged down in Death Valley's treacherous landscape. Now, they are thought to have made their way out via Wingate Wash, a southwest pass beginning a few miles north of Jubilee Pass.

From Jubilee Pass, the sometimes-graded dirt road sweeps through open desert. At 19 miles (31 km), Owl Hole Spring Road juts off to the west (right). Over the next few miles look for distant talc mines (Moorehouse and Monarch Mines) on your left. At 25 miles (40 km), the signed Saratoga Spring Road on the left (north) leads to Saratoga Spring in 4 miles (6.4 km). The Ibex Dunes are visible from this junction, and the shortest hiking access is from the Saratoga Spring Road. Continuing straight takes you to the pavement of Highway 127.

Road conditions can be a breeze and suitable for any high-clearance vehicle if the road is dry and maintained, with only a few brief sandy stretches where the road crosses the Amargosa River bed (often dry and underground at this point). However, the road is prone to washouts, washboards, mud, and closures. When the Amargosa River is flooded, the road is impassable with any vehicle.

Recreation

HIKING

Golden Canyon to Red Cathedral

Distance: *3 miles (4.8 km) round-trip*
Duration: *1-2 hours*
Elevation gain: *530 feet (162 m)*
Effort: *Easy*
Access: *Passenger vehicles*
Trailhead: *Badwater Basin Road at the Golden Canyon turnoff, 2 miles (3.2 km) south of the Badwater Road junction. Take the signed, graded dirt road on the east (left) side of the road to the parking area. Follow the marked trail sign to Golden Canyon (see map page 53).*

This canyon has gentle grades that lead to sheer red stone walls with majestic creases, earning its name. The mouth of the canyon

Furnace Creek and Southeast Corner Hikes

Natural Bridge

Trail	Effort	Distance	Duration
Natural Bridge	Easy	0.7-1.4 mi/1.1-2.3 km rt	30-45 min
Hanaupah Canyon	Easy	2 mi/3.2 km rt	1 hr
Sidewinder Canyon	Easy	2-4 mi/3.2-6.4 km rt	2-3 hrs
Golden Canyon to Red Cathedral	Easy	3 mi/4.8 km rt	1-2 hrs
Saratoga Spring	Moderate	2.2 mi/3.5 km rt	1.5-2.5 hrs
Desolation Canyon	Moderate	3.6 mi/5.8 km rt	1.5-2 hrs
Lower Willow Canyon	Moderate	4.5 mi/7.2 km rt	2-3 hrs
Ibex Spring	Moderate	5 mi/8 km rt	2.5-3 hrs
Scotty's Canyon	Moderate	6 mi/9.7 km rt	3-4 hrs
★ **Golden Canyon and Gower Gulch via Zabriskie Point**	Moderate	7.8 mi/12.6 km rt	4-5 hrs
★ **Hungry Bill's Ranch**	Difficult	3.3 mi/5.3 km rt	2-3 hrs
Ashford Canyon	Difficult	4.2 mi/6.8 km rt	3-4 hrs

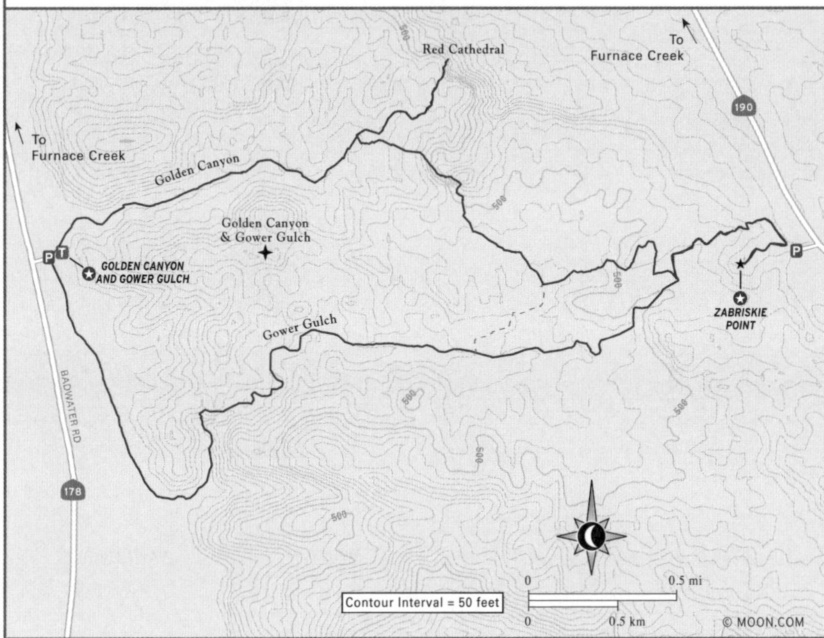

begins along a gravel wash through short narrows with sedimentary and volcanic rocks on the passage walls. The hike can be crowded, but it clears up a bit the farther into the canyon you go. Numbered markers along the way indicate interpretive sights, and a pamphlet is available at the visitor center or at the trailhead. When the canyon opens up, it is to a gold corridor of badlands, both bright and desolate. The trail ends at a fork about 1 mile (1.6 km) in; to reach the **Red Cathedral,** continue hiking another 0.5 mi (0.8 km).

★ Golden Canyon and Gower Gulch via Zabriskie Point

Distance: *2.7-7.8 miles (4.3-12.6 km) round-trip*
Duration: *1.5-4.5 hours*
Elevation gain: *875 feet (267 m)*
Effort: *Moderate*
Access: *Passenger vehicles*
Trailhead: *For Golden Canyon (to Red Cathedral, Zabriskie Point, and Gower Gulch Loop), access the trailhead from Badwater Basin Road at the Golden Canyon turnoff, 2 miles (3.2 km) south of the Badwater Road junction. Take the signed, graded dirt road on the east (left) side of the road to the parking area. Follow the marked trail sign to Golden Canyon (see map page 53). To complete the 4.3-mile badlands loop, access from Zabriskie Point.*

This hike is a Death Valley classic that leads through eroded badlands, old mining claims, shifting canyon scenery, and the spectacular views from Zabriskie Point, which offers views of Manly Beacon, a lava cap in stark contrast to the eroded landscape.

The full loop begins at the Golden Canyon parking area, continues to Red Cathedral, winds through badlands to iconic Zabriskie Point, and returns to the Golden Canyon parking area off Badwater Road via Gower Gulch. It can also be broken into shorter hikes: Golden Canyon to Red Cathedral (3 mi/4.8 km out and back), Gower Gulch loop (4.3-mi/6.9-km loop; 5.3 mi/8.5 km with spur

Desolation Canyon

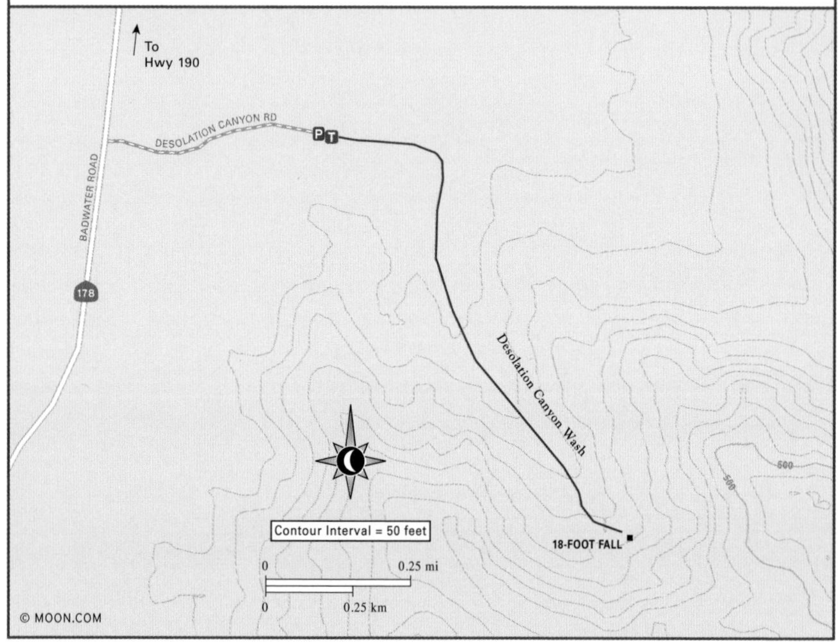

to Red Cathedral), and the Badlands loop (2.7-mi/4.3-km loop starting from Zabriskie Point). The trailhead from Golden Canyon is very popular and can be crowded along the first mile.

For Golden Canyon to Red Cathedral (3 mi/4.8 km out and back), Gower Gulch Loop (4.3-5.3 mi/6.9-8.5 km), or the full loop (7.8 mi/12.6 km), begin the hike on the interpretive trail in Golden Canyon. Pamphlets, available at the trailhead, draw your attention to the canyon's geologic features. There is also a hike description and downloadable GPX track available on the NPS website: www.nps.gov/deva/planyourvisit/golden-canyon.htm. Carry a map and hike description with you on the hike.

The Golden Canyon Trail leads up a gravel wash for about 1 mile (1.6 km) toward the huge **Red Cathedral** formation. Look for the signed junction for Red Cathedral or Zabriskie Point. The trail to Zabriskie Point continues up Golden Canyon for another 1.9 miles (3.1 km). For Zabriskie Point, head east. (Reaching Zabriskie Point might be a proud moment—or you might wonder why you didn't just drive here, as visitors roll up to the famous vista for some photo ops.)

To return from Zabriskie Point via Gower Gulch, retrace your steps (approximately 0.5 mi/0.8 km from the trailhead) to a signed intersection to Golden Canyon or Gower Gulch. Head left into Gower Gulch and follow the wash for 3 miles (4.8 km) back to the parking area. As the canyon walls narrow, look for colorful mineral deposits. You'll also pass some old **borax mines;** signs warn to stay away for fear of being crushed or poisoned. Once you emerge from the gulch, you're on the home stretch back to the Golden Canyon trailhead. Another 0.8 mile (1.3 km) west across exposed desert will bring you back to the trailhead.

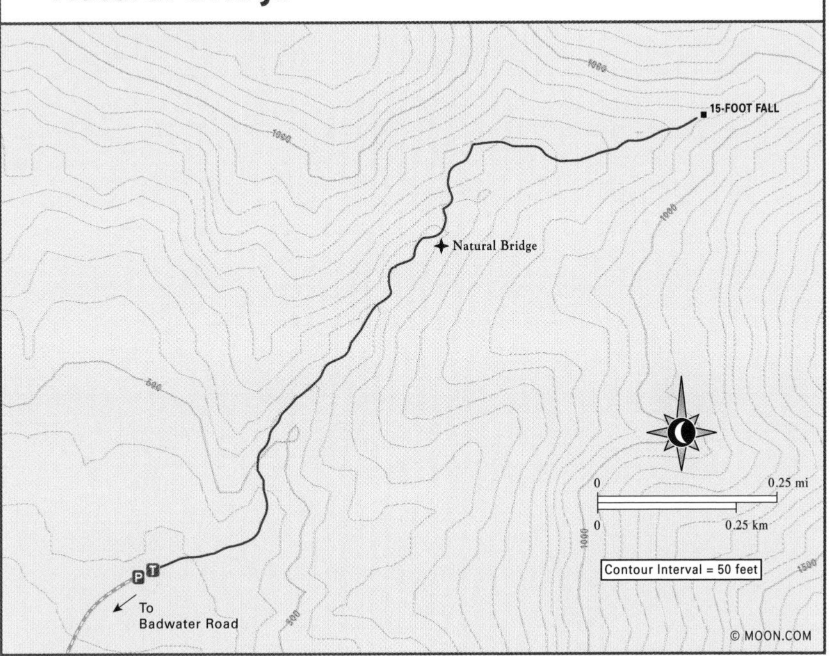

Desolation Canyon

Distance: *3.6 miles (5.8 km) round-trip*
Duration: *1.5-2 hours*
Elevation gain: *755 feet (230 m)*
Effort: *Moderate*
Access: *Passenger vehicles*
Trailhead: *Desolation Canyon Road is an unmarked 0.5-mile (0.8-km) graded road off Badwater Road, 3.7 miles (6 km) south of Highway 190 (south of Golden Canyon and before Artist's Drive). The road leads to a small parking lot and the start of the trail (see map page 54).*

This is a colorful and less-crowded out-and-back alternative to Golden Canyon. Desolation Canyon shares the sedimentary rocks of the Artist's Palette and the volcanic minerals that gave this area its splashes of muted color. It is also clearly a child of the Black Mountains, with its eroded badlands, also found in Golden Canyon and Gower Gulch slightly north. The result is a pleasant walk through a colorful canyon gorge and mud hills. Note that these hills are very fragile; stay in the canyon wash and do not walk on the hills.

From the parking area, head east toward the wide canyon and Black Mountains (avoid the smaller canyon to the south) to enter **Desolation Canyon** wash. The trail follows the mostly hard-packed wash through narrows and badlands. The trail continues over two rough-hewn **falls** that you will need to scramble over; the first is 8 feet (2.4 m) and 1 mile in and the second is 6 feet (1.8 m) and 1.8 miles (2.9 km) in. They are easy to navigate and will not stop most hikers. The trail **forks** at 1.2 and 1.5 miles (1.9 and 2.4 km); stay right to remain in the main canyon, gradually winding up to a ridgeline where you have sweeping views of Death Valley below.

Natural Bridge

Distance: *0.7-1.4 miles (1.1-2.3 km) round-trip*
Duration: *30-45 minutes*

Hanaupah Canyon

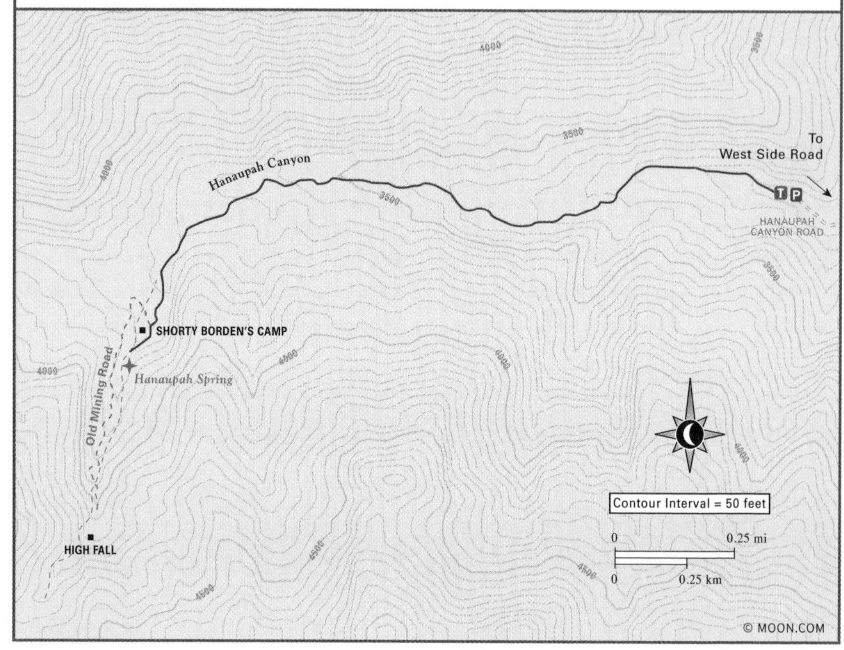

Elevation gain: *180-470 feet (55-143 m)*
Effort: *Easy*
Access: *Passenger vehicles*
Trailhead: *Badwater Road, 13.1 miles (21.1 km) south of Highway 190. Take the signed and graded dirt road east for 1.8 miles (2.9 km) to a small parking lot (see map page 55).*

Natural Bridge is one of the few natural bridges in the park, and it's definitely the biggest. This easy hike is popular, so be prepared to share it. Just 0.7 mile (1.1 km) in from the trailhead, Natural Bridge spans a red-wall canyon that contrasts with the bright sky above. Look back toward Badwater Basin to see Telescope Peak in the distance.

Most people turn around at the bridge, but the canyon continues another 0.7 mile (1.1 km). Shortly past the arch, check out the polished conglomerate **falls** on the right and look for mud formations that resemble candle drippings high up on the canyon walls. There are two places where you will have to scramble up a few small rock falls, but nothing that is a hike-stopper. The trail effectively ends at a vertical **15-foot (4.6 m) fall** another 0.7 mile (1.1 km) in. Turn around and retrace your steps to the trailhead.

Hanaupah Canyon

Distance: *2 miles (3.2 km) round-trip*
Duration: *1 hour*
Elevation gain: *640 feet (195 m)*
Effort: *Easy*
Access: *High-clearance/4WD*
Trailhead: *From Badwater Basin Road, drive south 10.7 miles (17.2 km) on the West Side Road to the signed Hanaupah Canyon Road and turn west. The rough road ends in about 8 miles (12.9 km), just short of Hanaupah Spring. A clearly marked trail with a trail marker begins at the end of the road (see map page 56).*

This short, pleasant hike through lower Hanaupah Canyon leads to Shorty Borden's camp and a pretty bubbling creek. From the end of **Hanaupah Canyon Road,** the trailhead is signed with a marker. Head west into the scenic canyon, which starts with deep red walls and eventually opens up. The trail is well defined and easy to follow along a rocky wash for the first mile (1.6 km), but avoid hiking directly in the rocky wash, if you can. You will come to **Shorty Borden's camp and mine** in about 1 mile (1.6 km). There's not a whole lot left of the camp, which once had a cabin and a shower house. A picturesque wood-framed mine tunnel that doubled as a workroom sits perched up a steep side trail on the south side of the canyon.

Just past the camp, the stream surfaces, fed by **Hanaupah Spring** as well as rain and snow from the Panamint Mountains. In some years it's an energetic creek with plenty of water; at other times it's a small and charming stream. Here the canyon widens and splits. Stay to the left and enjoy the creek. At this point, I would call it time well spent and return the way you came.

However, this trail does continue, and if you're really lucky, you'll see the creek at full volume. Vegetation is very thick, but it's easy to bypass this section by using the **old mining road** on the north side of the camp at 1 mile (1.6 km). The road swings around a hill and then drops back down to the creek. When it does go creek-side again, it's difficult to follow, and you may end up fighting your way through more vegetation. The trail is unmarked and difficult to follow for the rest of the hike. If the creek is running full force, you will have nice views of the narrows at points. If not, it's vegetation city with the occasional teasing sound of running water. The trail finally comes out with a view of a high fall at about 1.5 miles (2.4 km). In some years, water will be streaming out of a hole in the cliff; you may also just be looking at an impressive rock wall with watermarks. Don't say I didn't warn you.

★ Hungry Bill's Ranch

Distance: *3.3 miles (5.3 km) round-trip*
Duration: *2-3 hours*
Elevation gain: *1,514 feet (461 m)*
Effort: *Difficult*
Access: *High-clearance/4WD*
Trailhead: *From Badwater Basin Road, take West Side Road south for 21.7 miles (34.9 km). Turn west onto the marked Johnson Canyon Road and drive 10 rough miles (16.1 km) west to the road's end at Wilson Spring. The well-worn trail starts from the end of the road and heads into the canyon (see map page 58).*

This is a hike that just keeps giving. One of the most well-watered canyons in Death Valley, gorgeous canyon views, mysteriously constructed stone walls, a historic ranch tied to one of the biggest silver rushes in the area, and the site of a Native American village make this well worth the effort.

Getting here is half the fun, with the proper vehicle. **High clearance** is definitely necessary, and **4WD** is required starting at mile 5 of Johnson Canyon Road, which is rough, with rocky washouts that will rattle you across the alluvial fan as you climb toward the canyon mouth. Just past the midway point, around the 5-mile (8-km) mark, look for a picturesque rock wall and rusted car with a lovely desert patina. From here the road drops into a wash and becomes extremely rough with large rocks and limited turnarounds. The trail begins at the end of the road, just before Wilson Spring, which you can spot from its small cluster of willow trees. Park and leave the road clear.

In 1873 a frenzied silver strike occurred just over the Panamint Mountains from Johnson Canyon. To capitalize on the rush, William Johnson, for whom the canyon is named, built a ranch over the mountain pass to feed unruly groups of fortune seekers on their way to Panamint City. The Shoshone people were already living seasonally in the canyon, but Johnson set up camp anyway, creating terraced, irrigated gardens for beans, squash, melons, and corn along with fruit and nut orchards. When a flood nearly wiped out Panamint City, the rush was over and Johnson moved on, leaving trees that hadn't even had a chance to bear fruit. Hungry Bill, a Shoshone man known for his insatiable appetite, took over the ranch with his family and cultivated

Hungry Bill's Ranch

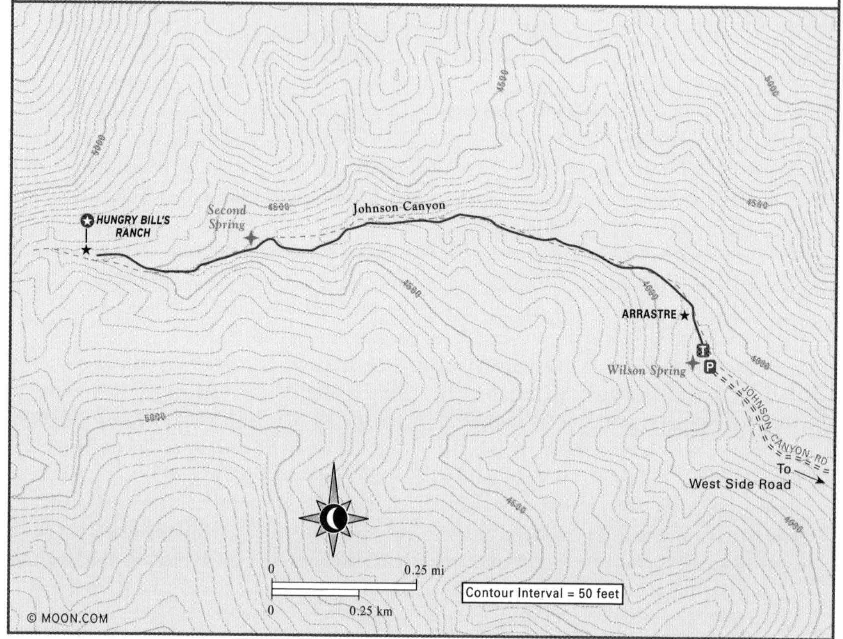

vegetables and apple, pear, fig, and walnut trees. The site was an ancestral Shoshone village, so it makes sense that he would establish his ranch here.

The hike to Hungry Bill's Ranch doesn't look long on a map, but the intense elevation gain necessary to bypass the springs and creeks throughout the hike makes it fairly strenuous. **Wilson Spring** lies just beyond the road's end, marked by telltale willows. The other springs at 1.2 and 2.1 miles (1.9 and 3.4 km) (past Hungry Bill's Ranch) are unnamed. Note that almost all the elevation gain on the hike to Hungry Bill's occurs over approximately 1.7 miles (2.7 km).

The trail starts out well-defined at the end of the Johnson Canyon Road and leads up **Johnson Canyon,** following the stream formed by the intermittent springs; the stream disappears underground at points. Look for an old stone **arrastre** on the left side of the trail in about 0.1 mile (0.16 km). To the untrained eye, this may look like a stone fire pit, but it was actually a simple mill used to pulverize precious ores (like gold) in order to extract the metals. There are two more arrastres on the same side of the creek in another 0.5 mile (0.8 km) and 1 mile (1.6 km), but they are not as well preserved and are harder to spot.

About 0.3 mile (0.5 km) into the hike, the canyon walls begin to narrow and rise dramatically as the first surface water starts to appear. A **bubbling creek** with small pools causes the canyon wash to become too choked with vegetation to continue as a main route. Stay on the south side of the creek and follow the trail as it climbs steeply to bypass the creek from the top of the canyon walls. Pay attention to follow the trail and find the path of least resistance. The elevation gain is especially tough over the next mile (1.6 km), but it offers beautiful views of the canyon walls. Look down to see **stone walls,** which are part of the charm and historical significance of the

Shorty Borden

Shorty Borden went far in Death Valley history on the strength of his personality, earning his reputation by being friendly and hospitable. A US Cavalry soldier during World War I, Borden came to Death Valley in the 1920s to prospect. He thought he had found rich silver-lead outcroppings in **Hanaupah Canyon** and set about developing it, singlehandedly digging out the present 9-mile (14.5-km) road from the valley floor to his camp with only a pick, a crowbar, a shovel, a little dynamite, and a burro (which might also tell you a little about the road). Apparently this wasn't enough, so he also dug out the well off **West Side Road** that is now named after him. Shorty did all of this at the age of 66. After the park began attracting visitors in the 1930s, he got by again on his natural friendliness, sharing his meager diet of coffee and beans in exchange for better provisions with any unsuspecting visitor who, against all odds, stumbled on his place.

canyon. No one knows who made the walls or exactly what they were for, but they're beautifully constructed and it's intriguing to see them snake along the steep canyon sides.

At 1.2 miles (1.9 km), the canyon makes a sharp turn around the **second spring;** cross the creek twice in succession. **Hungry Bill's Ranch** will be evident by its green cleared fields and stone walls. The area farther upcanyon with a larger field was thought to be the site of Johnson's ranch. For most people this is an excellent place to end the hike and retrace your steps.

For a **backcountry campsite,** look at the midway point along Johnson Canyon Road, near the rusted car; it's sheltered and obvious that others have used it. In spring, wildflowers will make this little corner extra special. There are other good spots for backcountry camping near the road's end and Wilson Spring. Though this is a popular spot, there's a good chance you will have the place to yourself.

Ashford Canyon

Distance: *4.2 miles (6.8 km) round-trip*

Duration: *3-4 hours*

Elevation gain: *More than 1,000 feet (305 m)*

Effort: *Difficult*

Access: *High-clearance possible/4WD preferable due to steep, rough, rocky road*

Trailhead: *Access the trail via an unmarked dirt road across from Ashford Mill. The 2.8-mile (4.5-km) road requires a high-clearance vehicle (4WD preferable) and has a few rough patches. The trailhead begins at the end of a small parking area (see map page 60). Trailhead parking is the same for Ashford Canyon and Scotty's Canyon.*

As with many hikes in Death Valley, the biggest battle is getting to the trailhead, but the results are rewarding. This is a beautiful, colorful canyon hike with a well-preserved and well-hidden mining camp at the end. The hike follows relics of the old mining road up to Ashford Mine Camp, steadily gaining elevation.

The trail starts at a wilderness marker at the end of a small parking area and follows the first canyon's wash for about 0.3 mile (0.5 km) until an **old mining road** becomes visible on the left (north); look for a flat place running along the hill. If you pass the mining road, don't worry. This first canyon is lovely, ending at a **high fall** with rock-climbing possibilities. Just backtrack and look again for the old mining road. Once you've found it, you'll see pieces of the old pavement poking through. Follow the old mining road for about 0.3 mile (0.5 km) until it drops back into the main canyon again.

As you hike, look for intersecting side canyons. The **first side canyon** intersects at about 1.2 miles (1.9 km). After the **second side canyon,** at 1.6 miles (2.6 km), look for signs of the old road on your left heading up into the hills to the **Ashford Mine Camp.** The road appears at about 1.8 miles (2.9 km). From here it's only another 0.3 mile (0.5 km) to the camp. Follow the old road as it leads up

Ashford Canyon

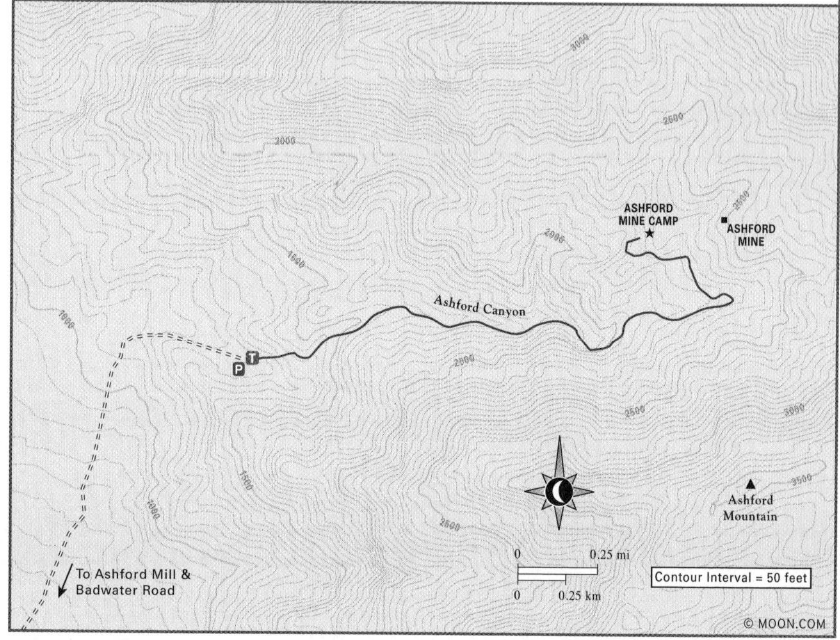

and over the canyon wall, and you will soon be looking down at the camp.

The Ashford Mine Camp is a strangely moving sight, perched in its forgotten ring of hills, exposed to the wind and relentless sun. Continue to follow the old road to explore the old cabins and dugouts, partially furnished, telling of life in a lonely mining camp.

Scotty's Canyon

Distance: *6 miles (9.7 km) round-trip*
Duration: *3-4 hours*
Elevation gain: *1,014 feet (309 m)*
Effort: *Moderate*
Access: *High-clearance possible/4WD preferable due to steep, rough, rocky road*
Trailhead: *Access the trail via an unmarked dirt road across from Ashford Mill. The 2.8-mile (4.5-km) road requires a high-clearance vehicle (4WD preferable but not necessary) and has a few rough patches. The trailhead begins at the end of a small parking area. Trailhead parking is the same for Ashford Canyon and Scotty's Canyon.*

Starting in the same tiny parking lot as Ashford Canyon, Scotty's Canyon is similarly rewarding, meandering past the surprising rock piles of the Amargosa Chaos and the sculpted conglomerate beds of lower Scotty's Canyon to end at a hidden grotto and tiny stream where the infamous Death Valley Scotty, of Scotty's Castle fame, once lived in a camp he called Camp Hold Out.

Walter Edward Scott, or Death Valley Scotty, may be most well known for his friendship with the benefactors he inspired (some say swindled) to build Scotty's Castle, the Spanish colonial-style mansion in the Grapevine Mountains. But his schemes and ties to Death Valley history run deep. Beginning in 1902, Scotty conned would-be

1: hikers heading into Desolation Canyon
2: Ashford Mine Camp

1

2

investors with tales of a rich gold mine in Death Valley. He was able to string them along and secure bankrolling for himself through his entertaining personality and flashy wealth (always temporary) and by producing high-grade ore from other mines from time to time. He kept these same investors away with wild tales of Death Valley's hellish landscape, temperatures, and supposed outlaw ambushes, even staging some of these attacks himself. The ruse lasted for a good 10 years, during which time he made a media name for himself and secured a place in Death Valley history. During this period, his Death Valley headquarters was Camp Hold Out in what today is named Scotty's Canyon. He eventually fell into disgrace, pressed by investors and the law, and confessed that his mine was a hoax. Luckily, in the meantime he had befriended benefactors Albert and Bessie Johnson, a friendship that proved lifelong, with Scotty's Castle as monument to this colorful piece of Death Valley history.

Scotty's Canyon is one canyon to the north of Ashford Canyon. The trail shares the same tiny parking area, but it starts on the opposite side. From the top of the rise where the road ends, follow a very faint Jeep trail to your left that swings down to the wash in 0.3 mile (0.5 km). Continue across the wash toward the brown hills at the foot of the black rock formation. The brown and red jumble you see is part of an unusual rock formation called the Amargosa Chaos, outcroppings of quartz monzonite and granite that are unique to this region of Death Valley.

The trail proper begins at about 0.7 mile (1.1 km) on the other side of the wash. It switchbacks up the brown hills before it cuts down through a colorful pink passage that spills into the wash of Scotty's Canyon, within view of the canyon mouth. Get the trail in your sights before beginning across the wash. It's easier to see from a slight distance and may save you from an exposed desert odyssey as you scramble through rocky washouts (ahem, not that I am speaking from experience) to try to make it to Scotty's Canyon wash.

The canyon segment of the hike begins as a wide wash. The canyon walls taper down past the mouth. The hike gains steady elevation, passing sculpted conglomerate formations that look like polished concrete and enough eclectic rock formations to keep you entertained. You will know you are approaching the grotto and Camp Hold Out when you see a tiny trickle of water in the sand and a cluster of mesquite trees. The grotto itself is a contrast of green vegetation and blistered rock. Listen for the incongruous sound of dripping water. Camp Hold Out was the low overhang on the south side of the canyon.

Lower Willow Canyon

Distance: *4.5 miles (7.2 km) round-trip*
Duration: *2-3 hours*
Elevation gain: *740 feet (226 m)*
Effort: *Moderate*
Access: *All vehicles*
Trailhead: *Short dirt road and large parking area near old gravel pit 31.4 miles (50.5 km) south of Furnace Creek (on left). Coming from the south, the dirt road and parking area is 11.5 miles (18.5 km) north of the Ashford Mill ruins (on right). Trailhead parking is the same for Willow Canyon and Sidewinder Canyon hikes.*

Willow Canyon is named for the bountiful willow trees in upper Willow Canyon, located in the remote Gold Valley (4WD access only from Greenwater Valley Road). The upper canyon is well watered with springs that drain down through the Black Mountains to the dramatic lower canyon. Here the last of Willow Creek slides down a slanted, rocky chasm in a 50-foot (15-m) fall. There is usually water here except for the driest years. The upper and lower canyons are divided by impassable cliffs, and it is not possible to hike through. But the lower canyon is easy to visit and hike.

The hike begins on the left (north) side of the parking area. A faint but well-traveled trail follows a fairly tame alluvial fan toward the canyon mouth. The canyon begins as a wild, rocky wash, lined with fanglomerate formed when all types of rock fragments washed

Sidewinder Canyon

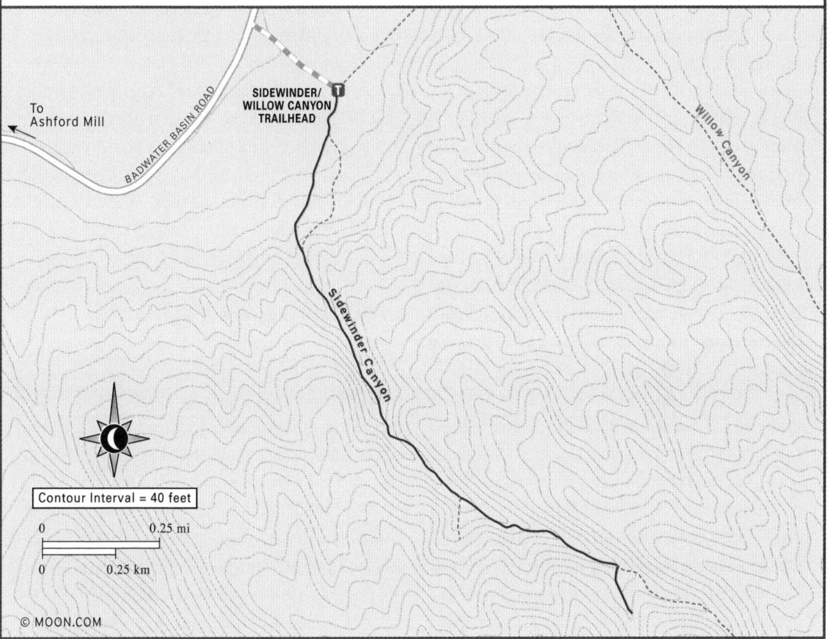

down the canyon to form choppy cliffs. The wash gets rockier as you approach the canyon mouth (about 0.5 mi/0.8 km in). The dark canyon walls are rough-hewn diorite. They gradually narrow and become more imposing until the canyon narrows at about 1.5 miles (2.4 km). The hike ends at the fall in a dark and towering enclave. Evidence of bighorn sheep is everywhere; otherwise you might feel like this is a place not fit for habitation. If you are lucky, you may see one.

Sidewinder Canyon

Distance: *2-4 miles (3.2-6.4 km)*
Duration: *2-3 hours*
Elevation gain: *600-800 feet (183-244 m)*
Effort: *Easy*
Access: *All vehicles*
Trailhead: *Short dirt road and large parking area near old gravel pit 31.4 miles (50.5 km) south of Furnace Creek (on left). Coming from the south, the dirt road and parking area is 11.5 miles (18.5 km) north of the Ashford Mill ruins (on right). Trailhead parking is the same for Willow Canyon and Sidewinder Canyon hikes* *(see map page 63).*

The unassuming hills at the base of Smith Mountain do not hold any particular draw from the road, but delving in quickly brings you to a sinewy maze of slot canyons, some of the deepest in Death Valley, with hidden natural bridges and sculpted alcoves. This hike is not a straightforward out and back with one defining destination. A series of slot canyons intersect the main canyon and give you the fun of discovery in the twisting arches and hollows that leave only a glimpse of sky at times as some passages narrow to less than arm's length.

The hike begins on the right (south) side of the parking area. A faint but well-traveled trail heads toward the dark opening of Sidewinder Canyon, which begins as a low gravel trench. There are three main slots (some hiking literature counts six, although some of these dead-end quickly). The first slot canyon is 1 mile (1.6 km) in from the trailhead on your right. Over the next 0.5 mile (0.8 km) you will come across two more. This is a fun hike for making your own discoveries, literally around each new turn.

BIKING

There are a few easy routes within riding distance of Furnace Creek. E-bikes and road bike rentals are available at Desert Outfitters in Furnace Creek (9am-5pm daily).

More difficult rides include the hilly paved loop of **Artist's Drive** (9 mi/14.5 km one-way) and the exposed gravel loop of the **West Side Road** (up to 40 mi/64 km), running along the valley floor.

Furnace Creek Bicycle Path

Access via Furnace Creek Visitor Center

Starting from the Furnace Creek Visitor Center, the easy Furnace Creek Bicycle Path (3.5 mi/5.6 km round-trip) goes along a flat, paved bicycle route for 1 mile (1.6 km) to the historical site of the Harmony Borax Works. It continues along open desert, past white-crusted borax mining fields, and then takes a short and scenic 1 mile (1.6-km) detour through Mustard Canyon's gravel road, before heading back to the visitor center in 1.5 miles (2.4 km).

Twenty Mule Team Canyon

Access via Hwy. 190, 5 miles (8 km) south of Furnace Creek

The short, graded road through Twenty Mule Team Canyon takes you 2.7 miles (4.3 km) on a one-way loop through a mudstone canyon past badlands and the site of historical mining prospects. The loop begins about 5 miles (8 km) south of Furnace Creek on Highway 190 and exits back onto Highway 190 about 8 miles (12.9 km) south of Furnace Creek. Complete the loop in about 5.5 miles (8.9 km).

Greenwater Valley Road

Access via Dante's View Road, 7.5 miles (12.1 km) south of Hwy. 190

A lightly traveled road (34.2 mi/55 km one-way) that traverses a large swath of Death Valley, Greenwater Valley Road is a quiet route across a wide and gentle valley. The road is well graded, and on a bicycle you will notice it runs slightly uphill.

The road begins 7.5 miles (12.1 km) south of Highway 190 from a junction with Dante's View Road. It runs straight for 34.2 miles (55 km) southeast to end at the cheerful town of **Shoshone.** (On some maps and at road entrances, Greenwater Valley Road is marked as Furnace Creek Wash Road.) A few people

bikers on the Furnace Creek Bicycle Path

use the road as a quiet backcountry entrance to the park. Still fewer people use Greenwater Valley Road to connect to a network of 4WD-only roads leading to remote backcountry mining sites and springs.

Beyond this, it is a pleasant ride and overall experience, although with few specific sights to recommend it. However, this is an area of great archaeological significance for the numerous Native American sites that date back thousands of years. Somewhere out there are pictographs, petroglyphs, stone circles, rock walls, and more.

CLIMBING

There is no shortage of rocks in Death Valley, but for some reason it is not as common to see rock climbers as it is in, say, Joshua Tree National Park. Don't let this stop you if rock climbing is your thing. There are hundreds of canyons with dry falls as well as excellent bouldering sites. The Furnace Creek area has a few, although there are more challenging rock climbing opportunities in other areas of the park.

Although it's a remote location, one potential bouldering site is far out on **Warm Spring Canyon Road.** As the road nears the pass into Butte Valley, large granitic boulders dot a field.

Slit Canyon

Access via the end of Hole-in-the-Wall Road

Hike from the end of **Hole-in-the-Wall Road** for 1.2 miles (1.9 km) northeast across the alluvial fan to where a long, low, yellow-and-tan mudstone hill meets the Funeral Mountains. Slit Canyon has three polished gray dolomite falls within the first 2 miles (3.2 km) of the canyon, not to mention the tall recessed cavern for which the canyon is named.

Ashford Canyon

Access via Badwater Basin Rd.

Ashford Canyon, on the western side of the **Black Mountains,** offers a canyon with a steep-walled narrows and four falls. Ashford Canyon can be reached via an unmarked turnoff across from the Ashford Mill on the southern end of Badwater Basin Road. A rough dirt road takes you to a small parking area that ends at the wilderness area.

GOLF

Furnace Creek Golf Course

Hwy. 190; 760/786-3373; www.oasisatdeathvalley.com; 6am-4pm daily, call for seasonal hours; greens fees $30-74

If vacation means golf to you, you're in luck. The Furnace Creek Golf Course claims to be the lowest-elevation golf course in the world. At 214 feet (65 m) below sea level, it's hard to dispute. This 18-hole golf course doesn't let you forget that it's on an oasis; it's lined with palm and tamarisk trees and dotted with water. Temperatures soar in summer, but the resort takes a tongue-in-cheek approach, hosting the Heatstroke tournament every June.

Food

The village of Furnace Creek is home to the Ranch at Death Valley and the Inn at Death Valley restaurants. Food can be pricey, so stock up on supplies outside the park.

The only other location that offers food on the eastern side of the park is the village of **Stovepipe Wells,** 25 miles (40 km) northwest. Food is available outside the park at the Longstreet Inn and Casino, 30 miles (48 km) east in the Amargosa Valley. There are no other stops for food and water. If you're planning a long day of sightseeing far from the park hub, plan to take a cooler packed with picnic supplies, ice, and drinks.

Around dinnertime the **Ranch at Death Valley** (Hwy. 190; 760/786-2345; www.

oasisatdeathvalley.com; year-round) buzzes with visitors in its mission-style town square, sharing a glass of wine, debriefing on the day's sights, or waiting for a table. The restaurants are fairly casual and are open year-round, but hours may be shorter in summer (mid-May-mid-Oct.). Hours listed are for high-season (mid-Oct.-mid-May). It is best to check with the main office at the Ranch when you arrive for the most up-to-date hours.

General Store

Ranch at Death Valley; 7am-9pm daily

If your travel supplies run low, the Ranch General Store is well stocked with prepared picnic items to take on day adventures and camping staples like eggs, milk, bacon, produce, and canned goods. The store also offers snacks, ice cream, beer, wine, and cold beverages. Prices reflect the fact that you're in the middle of nowhere, but the store is good for a treat or supplemental items.

Last Kind Words Saloon

Ranch at Death Valley; 760/786-3335; noon-3pm lunch, 3pm-5pm bar bites, 5pm-9pm dinner; $41-75

The Last Kind Words Saloon is the heart of the Ranch at Death Valley for midday refueling or post-adventure steaks and fireside cocktails. The high-ceilinged tavern is decked out with Wild West photos and relics, taxidermied animals, and Native American rugs, all capped by a stamped copper ceiling. A giant mission-style fireplace on the exterior is enticing for alfresco drinks or dining. Head indoors for casual eats at the café tables, booths, or long bar. The attention to design detail may upstage the food, which is decent if pricey even by tourist standards. Lunch keeps it simple with sandwiches, salads, and pizza. The dinner menu features steaks rounded out by pasta, fish, and appetizers. Dinner reservations are highly recommended and can be made up to three months in advance.

1849 Restaurant

Ranch at Death Valley; 760/786-2345; 6am-10am breakfast $21 adults, $10.50 children 5-12, under 5 free, 11am-2pm lunch $23 adults, $11.50 children 5-12, under 5 free, 4pm-9pm dinner $34 adults, $17 children 5-12, under 5 free

The Ranch 1849 Restaurant is a family-friendly buffet-style restaurant serving breakfast, lunch, and dinner, centrally located at the Ranch between the saloon and general store. Breakfast includes breakfast entrées and meats, along with a selection of baked goods and fruit. Lunch and dinner feature a salad bar, a rotating selection of entrées, and desserts.

Ice Cream Parlor

Ranch at Death Valley; 760/786-2345; 11am-7pm daily for coffee and ice cream, noon-6pm daily for grill items

The Ice Cream Parlor, the newest addition to the Ranch town square, features a retro interior with a classic soda fountain counter and stained-glass accents. Shakes, sundaes, housemade sodas, and floats are the reason you're here, with burgers, hot dogs, fries, and a coffee menu rounding out the offerings.

The 19th Hole

Hwy. 190; 760/786-2345; 11am-7pm daily Oct.-May, closed June-Sept.

Located just off the golf course, The 19th Hole is a seasonal, open-air venue known for its burgers. It is open for lunch and early dinner, and with a full bar and cold beer for golf course takeout.

INN AT DEATH VALLEY

Inn at Death Valley Dining Room

760/786-3385; 7am-10am breakfast $14-19, 5pm-9pm dinner $28-71

The real star of the show at the Inn at Death Valley Dining Room may be the view. At sunset, the west-facing bank of windows frames the sun's fiery drop behind the rugged Panamint Mountains. Gilbert Stanley Underwood, the same architect who designed the iconic Ahwahnee Hotel in Yosemite, laid the plans for the Furnace Creek Inn in the 1920s, and the dining room is reflective of classic lodges of the time, with its beamed ceiling, exposed brick and adobe fireplace, and upscale rustic look. Weather permitting, an outdoor terrace offers the same service, menu, and striking views. An eclectic and seasonally changing menu hits continental, Southwestern, and classic dishes that include steak, fish, and pasta. The dining room is open for breakfast and dinner. Reservations are required.

The inn caters to lodge guests and those staying at the Ranch; a light dress code (no tank tops or T-shirts) is expected.

Inn at Death Valley Lounge

760/786-3385; 4pm-9pm daily

Stop in at the elegant lounge for a cocktail or appetizer before dinner. The limited lounge menu features a charcuterie board and shrimp cocktail as well as upscale bar food—think tuna poke nachos and beef sliders with house-made accompaniments.

Inn at Death Valley Pool Café

760/786-3385; 11am-5pm daily, hours vary based on season, weather, and staffing

A casual café at pool level ensures you don't have to give up your poolside spot. A limited menu offers sandwiches, snacks, signature cocktails, beer, wine, and other cold beverages.

Accommodations

HOTELS

Ranch at Death Valley

Hwy. 190; 760/786-2345, reservations 800/236-7916; www.oasisatdeathvalley.com; year-round; $199-400

The Ranch at Death Valley was originally built to be the less-formal lodging counterpart to the Inn at Death Valley, and that tradition continues even as the property underwent a major renovation. From a midday stroll around the date palm-studded grounds, it's evident that some guests never leave the comfortable vicinity of the spring-fed pool and air-conditioned rooms. There's something wildly luxurious about lounging in the perfect temperature water under the blazing sun with sharp desert mountains in the background. Communal fire pits, horseshoe pits, a kids' playground, and tennis, volleyball, and basketball courts add to the vacation experience.

Casual and family-friendly accommodations are set in a sprawling complex of cottages, two-story standard rooms, and deluxe motel-style rooms adjacent to the Spanish colonial revival-style town square. All rooms feature French doors with small patios or balconies affording views of the surrounding desert and mountains.

Restaurants and other amenities are just a few steps away.

Inn at Death Valley

Hwy. 190; 760/786-2345, reservations 800/236-7916; www.oasisatdeathvalley.com; year-round; $400-699

Death Valley is known for its contrasts, and the Inn at Death Valley provides the ultimate contrast to the austerity of the valley floor with its well-watered grounds and luxury accommodations.

The Pacific Coast Borax Company opened the inn in 1927. Driving in on Highway 190, you'll see the red tile roofs, palm trees, and classic stucco sculpted into the hillside and set against a backdrop of the Funeral Mountains. Albert C. Martin, a prominent Los Angeles architect, designed the mission-style hotel; its archways and tower are inspired by the Spanish missions on the California coast. Daniel Hull, the original landscape architect, created verdant grounds that complement the stark and rocky hillside.

The inn offers a variety of rooms, as well as

THE RANCH AT DEATH VALLEY
1
2 
3 
4

22 two-room casitas added in 2018. **Standard rooms** include either a king bed or a double with a twin and have a private bath. Rooms may be located in the main building or on the terrace above the pool and feature views of the gardens, desert, or mountains.

The resort boasts a spring-fed swimming pool with cabanas and a poolside bar, a wellness center with treatment rooms, and an on-site restaurant and lounge all set amid lush oasis gardens. Prices have come a long way from the original $10 per night, which included meals.

CAMPING

There are **four campgrounds** clustered around Furnace Creek, all with their pros and cons. Furnace Creek and Sunset Campgrounds both sit at 196 feet (60 m) below sea level, making them oppressively hot in summer, and Texas Spring, at sea level, is not much higher or cooler. Site passes for Sunset and Texas Spring are sold at automated kiosks that take major credit cards and cash. Passes are for general overnight admission but do not specify sites.

Summer at Furnace Creek can create its own kind of ghost town due to the excessive heat at lower elevations. If you are planning to camp in Death Valley in summer, you would be wise to camp at higher elevations in other sections of the park.

Tip: All campgrounds can get very windy at night regardless of the time of year or the temperature. If you are tent camping, make sure you have your tent properly staked, and make sure everything that could be blown away is secured (camp chairs love to catch air when you're not watching). If you're relying on RV electrical hookups, don't be surprised by electricity surges.

Fiddlers' Campground

760/786-2345 or 800/236-7916; www.oasisatdeathvalley.com; year-round; $34

Located at the Ranch at Death Valley, the privately run Fiddlers' Campground offers RV sites (no hookups, back-in only). One tent is allowed per site. While not the place for those seeking desert solitude, it does include amenities such as wireless internet and access to the Ranch at Death Valley's pool, showers, and sports facilities. Communal picnic tables and fire pits are available within the campground but not at individual sites. Sites can be reserved year-round through Oasis at Death Valley.

Furnace Creek

877/444-6777; www.recreation.gov; year-round; $22, $36 with hookups

Furnace Creek Campground is a year-round RV and tent campground with 136 sites. It's the only public campground in Death Valley that takes **reservations** (Oct. 15-Apr. 15), so for busy weekends in spring or on holidays, or for travelers who like to have a set itinerary, this is a good option. From mid-April to mid-October, sites are first-come, first-served; reservations are not accepted. The campground is right next to the Ranch, so while it's easy to walk to dining and amenities, it also means this is not the serene desert escape you might be looking for. The surrounding valley and hills provide a beautiful setting, but the campground itself can be crowded and disorderly. There are some walk-in tent sites, which afford slightly more serenity. **Day passes** ($10) are available for the Ranch pool and showers. Pro tip: These pool and shower passes are available to anyone, not just campground guests. This might be a selling point if you're staying for several days or are visiting in the hotter parts of the year.

Sunset

First-come, first-served; Oct. 15.-April 15; $14

Sunset Campground is across the road from Furnace Creek Campground and conveniently located near the services at the Ranch at Death Valley. With 270 sites, it caters mainly to RVs and is peaceful but spare, meaning it is basically a very scenically located parking lot.

1: entrance to the Ranch at Death Valley **2:** the historic Inn at Death Valley **3:** Last Kind Words Saloon **4:** pool at the Inn at Death Valley

Amenities include water, flush toilets, and a dump station. It's useful as an overflow if Furnace Creek Campground is full or to avoid some of the congestion there.

Texas Springs

First-come, first-served; Oct. 15.-April 15; $16

Texas Springs shares an entrance with Sunset Campground, but it is a little more scenic, tucked farther into the hills with tamarisks offering shade at a few of the sites. This also means that it is the most popular campground in the area, and its 92 tent and RV sites fill up quickly. Amenities include water, picnic tables, fire pits, flush toilets, and a dump station.

Backcountry Camping

The Furnace Creek region has the most restrictions on where backcountry camping is allowed. Camping is not allowed on the valley floor from Ashford Mill in the south to 2 miles (3.2 km) north of Stovepipe Wells. Camping is also not allowed directly off the West Side Road, but it is permitted along some of the Panamint Mountain canyon roads that are accessed by **West Side Road.** To camp off the canyon roads, such as in **Johnson** and **Hanaupah Canyons,** you must drive at least 2 miles (3.2 km) in along any of the canyon roads from the West Side Road. (Pay attention to any posted signs, as the 2-mile (3.2-km) mark is a general rule of thumb, and some canyon roads may require you to go farther from West Side Road.) A backcountry camping permit is required for roadside camping in **Echo Canyon** and may be obtained from the Furnace Creek Visitor Center.

Backcountry sites are unmarked and have no amenities; look for spots that are flat, have easy turnouts, or look like they have been camped in before. The roads in this area become increasingly rough farther toward the canyon; if you're driving a basic, high-clearance vehicle, such as a city SUV, you might not want to venture much past the 2-mile (3.2-km) mark. If you do snag one of these canyon spots, they can be austere and quiet, with views of Badwater Basin glowing in the distance; however, they can be very windy, especially at night.

Furnace Creek Campground

The Southeast Corner

The lightly visited Southeast Corner of Death Valley makes an excellent **weekend trip.** Sand dunes, mining camps, and lovely springs show off the diversity of Death Valley without the need to brave more formidable expanses. Stay in nearby **Shoshone** or **Tecopa** or camp in the backcountry.

The Southeast Corner is in the southern end of the Black Mountains and remains somewhat disconnected from the Furnace Creek region, since no major park road allows access. There are two main areas of exploration: Saratoga Spring/Ibex Dunes and Ibex Spring.

Getting There

The backcountry **Harry Wade Exit Route,** or **Harry Wade Road,** cuts through the region, joining Badwater Road with the Saratoga Spring/Ibex Dunes area. From its unsigned intersection at Jubilee Pass, it is possible to drive the Harry Wade Road 25.6 miles (41.2 km) south to the signed junction with Saratoga Spring Road. This junction gives access to Saratoga Spring and Ibex Dunes. Beyond the Saratoga Spring Road intersection, the Harry Wade Road connects to paved Highway 127 near the Dumont Dunes Off-Highway Vehicle (OHV) area in 5.8 miles (9.3 km). The Harry Wade Road is an infrequently traveled dirt road that is usually passable with a high-clearance vehicle. At times, a 4WD vehicle may be necessary, especially in spring when the Amargosa River may cover portions of the road.

IBEX SPRING

Access via Ibex Spring Rd. off of Hwy. 127

What the Ibex Spring mining camp lacks in rip-roaring history—there were no saloon shoot-outs or land swindles—it makes up for in buildings that are still around for us to check out. In the 1940s, when the camp was built, wild speculation had largely been replaced by a more prosaic approach—mine steadily for what's there instead of the fabled ores that brought prospectors out in droves in the gold rush of 1849. Mining companies in this area went for talc instead of gold (even though "talc fever" doesn't really have the same ring).

The Saratoga Hills, Ibex Dunes, and Black Mountains serve as a backdrop as you make your way across barren desert on the old Ibex Spring Road toward the Ibex Spring mining camp.

Directions

From Furnace Creek, head east on Highway 190 to the intersection with Highway 127 at Death Valley Junction. From Death Valley Junction, head south 27 miles (43 km) to the town of Shoshone. From Shoshone, drive south on Highway 127 for 16.3 miles (26.2 km) to an unmarked dirt road on the right (west). This is the **Ibex Spring Road.**

The road has deep washouts along with surviving bits of pavement, making for a schizophrenic road condition. It's a decent dirt road, suitable for **high-clearance** vehicles; however, some washouts at the start may make a **4WD** vehicle desirable. When the road forks at 2.1 miles (3.4 km), follow the right fork toward the low Ibex Hills in the distance. At 3.2 miles (5.1 km) from the highway, there is a major washout, and a 4WD vehicle is necessary to navigate this. Without a 4WD vehicle, this is a good place to park and walk the rest of the way to the site. With the right vehicle, it is possible to drive all the way to the camp.

Hiking

Ibex Spring

Distance: *5 miles (8 km) round-trip to Ibex Spring mining camp; 6.2 miles (10 km) with a side trip to Monarch-Pleasanton Mine*

Duration: *2.5-3 hours*

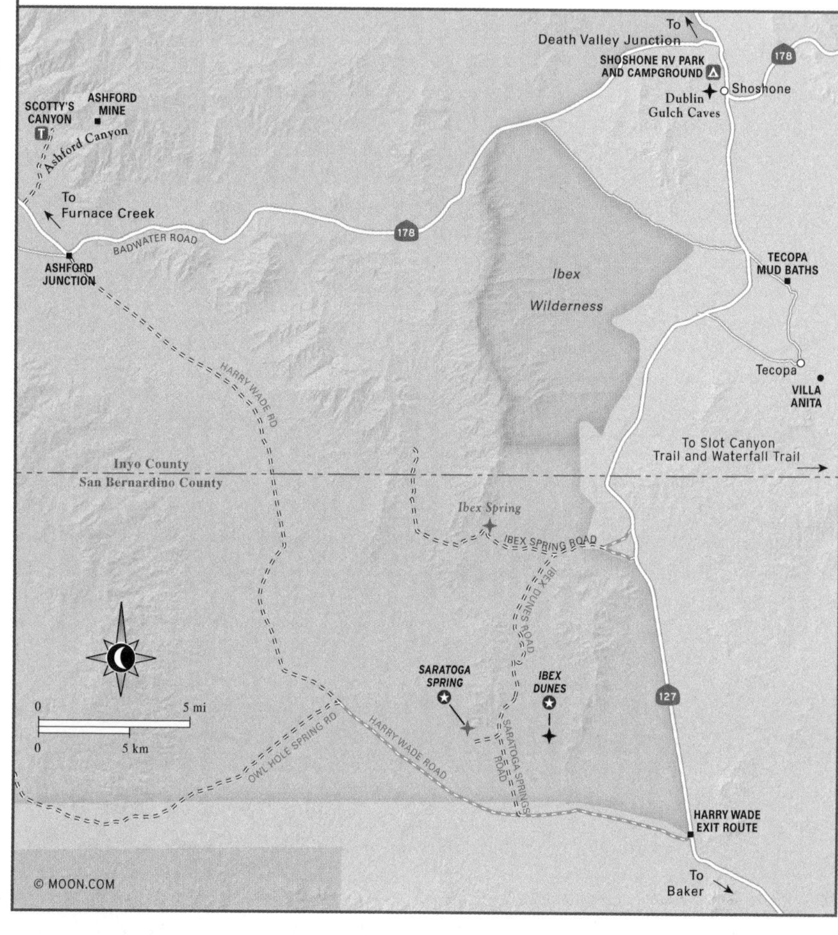

The Southeast Corner

Elevation gain: *400 feet (122 m)*
Effort: *Moderate*
Access: *High-clearance vehicle and a short hike, or a 4WD road*
Trailhead: *Ibex Spring Road washout, 3.2 miles (5.1 km) from Highway 127*

This pleasant walk along the old road gets more interesting as the Ibex Spring mining camp comes into sight. From the washout, follow the well-defined mining road across open desert toward the mining camp, faintly visible tucked against the Saddle Peak Hills. You will reach the site in 2.5 miles (4 km).

Ibex Spring mining camp was built on a natural oasis. Cottonwood and tamarisk trees shade a lonely **cabin,** and palm trees flash unexpectedly in the sunlight. This area was previously mined for gold during the Bullfrog era, in the early 1900s; look carefully for the foundations of two stone houses and an unmarked grave from this era. Most of the newer buildings were cabins used to house miners during a talc mining boom in

Ibex Spring

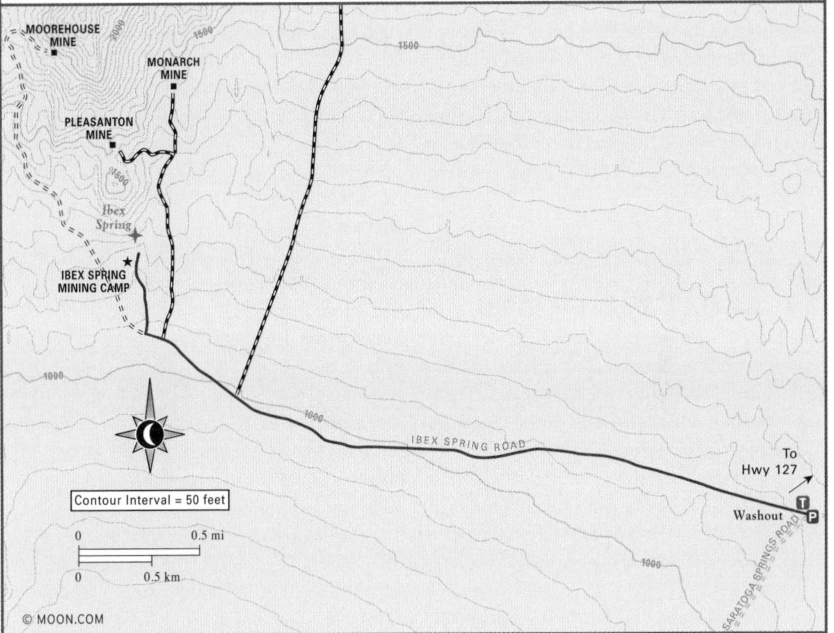

the 1930s and 1940s; remnants from this era include a **springhouse** full of water, the chaotic crisscrossing of pipes on the ground, and the concrete-floor shower house.

The **Monarch-Pleasanton Mine** is within view of the Ibex Spring mining camp—its white talc tailings are a dead giveaway. The **Moorehouse Mine** is another mile (1.6 km) up the road beyond the Ibex Spring mining camp. The road is rougher past the camp, and even if you've driven this far, you may opt to walk. Plan on 30 minutes-1.5 hours to explore these mining sites.

TOP EXPERIENCE

★ IBEX DUNES

Access via Saratoga Spring Rd. off of Hwy. 127

The Ibex Dunes are marked by seclusion and pristine sandscapes set against the austere cragginess of the Saddle Peak Hills. Although easily accessible, they are very lightly visited due to their remote location. Combine a trip to the Ibex Dunes with a trip to Saratoga Spring, with its lovely ponds and well-preserved mine ruins, for an enjoyable day trip. Admiring the dunes from a distance is rewarding, but there's something about the sight of all that smooth sand that inspires us to climb them.

The closest access is about 1.5 miles (2.4 km) past the turnoff to Saratoga Spring, where there is a tiny pullout along the road on the right. A cross-country walk to the base of the dunes is about **1.2 miles** (1.9 km) **one-way.** The dunes are steep and slippery, making them difficult but fun to climb. From the top you can catch a glimpse of an old talc mine in the Saddle Peak Hills.

Directions

From Shoshone, drive 26.2 miles (42.2 km) south on Highway 127 to an unassuming dirt road on the right, marked with a historical marker for the Harry Wade Exit Route. Harry

Wade requires a **high-clearance vehicle** and can be sandy or rough in places, but a city SUV should be fine for the section to the spring and dunes. In 5.8 miles (9.3 km), turn right onto Saratoga Spring Road and continue another 2.7 miles (4.3 km) to a junction. A left (west) turn leads to Saratoga Spring; turn north (straight right) toward the Ibex Dunes. Stop within 1-1.5 miles (1.6-2.4 km), within sight of the dunes.

TOP EXPERIENCE

★ SARATOGA SPRING

Access via Hwy. 127

Any spring in Death Valley is cause for excitement. While most springs are marked only by a small overgrowth of vegetation, Saratoga Spring is a marvelous sight, with a cluster of shining ponds and swishing cane. If you travel to this tucked-away corner in the extreme southeastern end of Death Valley, you have a good chance of having this rare spring to yourself.

From the parking area, a well-marked **trail** (a former mining road) leads past the ponds while providing beautiful views. Tread lightly and be careful not to trample on any of the vegetation around the ponds. Reflecting the desert sky, they are the last thing you might expect to see in the Black Mountains and on this austere valley floor. The trail will quickly take you past the Saratoga Spring in about 0.5 mile (0.8 km). Even this area saw some enterprise; one entrepreneurial man bottled the water, starting the Saratoga Water Company as well as a small resort for a time.

Directions

From Furnace Creek, follow Highway 190 east for 30 miles (48 km) to its junction with Highway 127 at Death Valley Junction. Take Highway 127 south for 27 miles (43 km) to the town of Shoshone. Continue south on Highway 127 for another 26.2 miles (42.2 km). Turn right (west) on an unassuming dirt road marked with a historical marker for the Harry Wade Exit Route. The road requires a **high-clearance vehicle** and can be sandy or rough in places. In 5.8 miles (9.3 km), turn right onto Saratoga Spring Road and continue north for 2.7 miles (4.3 km) to a junction. The left (west) fork ends at a small parking area for Saratoga Spring.

Hiking

Saratoga Spring

Distance: *2.2 miles (3.5 km) round-trip to the first group of mines (south group); 3.4 miles (5.5 km) round-trip to the second group of mines*

Duration: *1.5-2.5 hours*

Elevation gain: *270 feet (82 m)*

Effort: *Moderate*

Access: *High-clearance vehicle*

Trailhead: *The trailhead begins at the parking area for Saratoga Spring. It is clearly marked with a sign forbidding vehicles. It is actually the continuance of the mining road, which now serves as the trail.*

The shining ponds of Saratoga Spring, peaceful walks along the Ibex Hills, and historical talc mines make this a lovely place to explore. A trail follows what used to be the mining road that served several groups of talc mines. Beginning at Saratoga Spring, the trail winds along the base of the hills where you will see the **Saratoga Mines** nestled, a cluster of talc mining sites with well-preserved and picturesque ruins.

Historically, there was a lot of wishful thinking in this area. The first wave of mining exploration began in 1902 when hundreds of people and agencies made a frenzied dash to mine nitrates. Saratoga Spring was pretty inaccessible, however, and niter, used primarily in agriculture, was already cheap. The scheme would never pay off.

A second wave in 1907 had people clinging to tales of gold. The theory was that gold would have washed down to the valley floor through erosion (disregarding the fact that gold traveling downhill breaks up and disperses). Ordinary talc, easily accessible in the

1: Ibex Dunes **2:** the shining ponds of Saratoga Spring, a rarity in Death Valley

1
2

Ibex Hills, was eventually settled on, and several mines sprang up in the area.

From the trailhead, look for the faint mining road on the east side of the spring and follow it north past Saratoga Spring. The road passes two **stone buildings,** remains from an earlier mining era (probably gold mining). In 0.9 mile (1.4 km) is a faint junction, with a road leading east to the **first group** of mines, picturesque ruins with a tin shack and wooden chute visible from the main trail.

The junction to the **second group** of mines awaits 0.3 mile (0.5 km) farther along the main trail. Reaching the ruins takes another 0.5 mile (0.8 km). They include a well-preserved headframe, beautifully weathered and standing tall against the backdrop of the hills.

The main road continues north with a spur (in 0.5 mi/0.8 km) to the Whitecap (1 mi/1.6 km) and Superior (2.2 mi/3.5 km) Mines. The Pongo Mine requires an additional hike of 0.5 mile (0.8 km) along the main road, then 2.1 miles (3.4 km) east to the mine site; however, with the exception of the Whitecap Mine, the ruins beyond the second group are minimal.

For an easy and rewarding **half-day hike,** visit Saratoga Spring and then hike to the second mine group (3.4 mi/5.5 km round-trip). A visit to the Pongo Mine extends this to about 9 miles (14.5 km) round-trip—a short full-day hike.

Beyond the Boundaries

If you plan to enter the park from the east via Highway 190, **Death Valley Junction,** the **Amargosa Valley, Shoshone,** and **Tecopa** are gateways into the park. These towns stretch north to south along Highway 127, which intersects Highway 190 at Death Valley Junction. From Death Valley Junction, Highway 190 heads west for approximately 30 miles (48 km) to Furnace Creek.

Visitors using the travel hub of **Las Vegas** will follow US 95 north to Amargosa Valley before dropping south across the state line via Highway 373/127 to Death Valley Junction. From **Los Angeles,** I-15 connects with Highway 127 at its southern terminus.

DEATH VALLEY JUNCTION

Entering the park from the east via **Highway 190** takes you through Death Valley Junction, the small historic outpost at the crossroads of Highway 127 and Highway 190. Lodging is available, but there is **no gas, food, or supplies.** The closest gas station is in the Amargosa Valley, 8 miles (12.9 km) north of Death Valley Junction just across the Nevada state line. The next closest gas and supplies are in Furnace Creek, 31 miles (50 km) west, or Pahrump, Nevada, 30 miles (48 km) east. The 30-mile (48-km) drive west from Death Valley Junction to Furnace Creek takes about half an hour.

Sights

The **Death Valley Junction Historic District** includes the tiny town, hotel, and surrounding property, and it is on the National Register of Historic Places. It's well worth a stop, if not a stay. The hotel staff allows curious visitors to wander through the lobby and some of the open hotel rooms, where you will see the hotel's famous murals, all hand-painted by Marta Becket. The place retains its air of colorful history but has declined over the years.

Amargosa Opera House and Hotel

Hwy. 127, Death Valley Junction; 760/852-4441; www.amargosa-opera-house.com; 8am-8pm daily

The Amargosa Opera House and Hotel is a place with a past. This functioning hotel rises like a mirage along the alkali desert floor. Originally constructed by the Pacific Coast Borax Company, the Amargosa Hotel

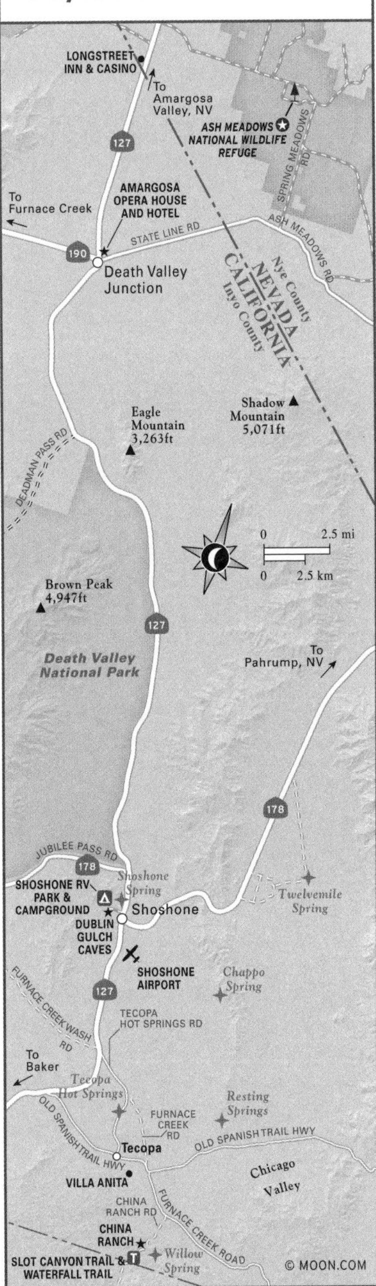

was called Corkhill Hall and had a dormitory for miners, a 23-room hotel, a store, and a dining room. The hotel and the rest of the town fell into decline in the mid-20th century, crumbling and all but forgotten in the desert sun for many years. In the late 1960s Marta Becket, traveling through from New York with her husband, had a flat tire in this desolate place. She ended up staying, painting murals and breathing life into the old hotel, or maybe kicking up the dust of a life that had never quite expired. The hotel has a reputation for being haunted and has been featured on ghost-hunter TV shows like the Travel Channel's *Ghost Adventures.* Marta Becket passed away in 2017, leaving behind the strange hotel still draped with her murals and a tradition of music and dance performance in the desert.

Getting There

From Furnace Creek, take Highway 190 east for approximately 30 miles (48 km) to Death Valley Junction. Plan on **30 minutes** for the drive.

AMARGOSA VALLEY

The Amargosa Valley stretches north of Death Valley Junction along **Highway 127** and crosses the state line into Nevada. The Ash Meadows National Wildlife Refuge offers a lovely side trip, while the Longstreet Inn and Casino provides basic **supplies,** accommodations, Wi-Fi, and **gas.**

★ Ash Meadows National Wildlife Refuge

610 Springs Meadows Rd., Amargosa Valley, NV; 775/372-5435; www.fws.gov; sunrise-sunset daily; free

Fossil water, melted and remaining from the last ice age, supplies this largest remaining oasis in the Mojave Desert, home to nearly 30 endemic plant and animal species. The springs of the Ash Meadows National Wildlife Refuge are clear and warm, reflecting blue against rocky hills and an austere desert backdrop.

However, if things had gone according to plan, you might have been shopping at a select retail space instead of admiring native plants. It's hard to believe, but this was almost a large-scale housing development in the 1980s, complete with shops, 34,000 homes, hotels, airports, and all the comforts of planned living. It was saved from that fate by efforts from The Nature Conservancy and the US Fish and Wildlife Service, which ultimately purchased the land.

A visit to the beautiful, serene oasis is an enjoyable hour or two. There are easy interpretive trails, accessible to wheelchairs, and a **visitor center** (9am-4pm daily) with exhibits and a bookstore. In addition to clear waters and native flora and fauna, the refuge is known for **Devil's Hole,** managed by Death Valley National Park. Devil's Hole is a geothermal pool surfacing in a limestone cave that goes more than 500 feet (152 m) deep. Its claims to fame are the rare Devil's Hole pupfish and the fact that the bottom has never been found. A visit to the site will confirm that it is, indeed, a very deep hole.

Food and Accommodations

Longstreet Inn and Casino

4400 Hwy. 373, Amargosa Valley, NV; 775/372-1777; www.longstreetcasino.com; from $135

The Longstreet Inn and Casino is outside California, just far enough into Nevada to make the casino legal. Most people don't come here for the slots, but it is the only option in town if you want a hotel room, a restaurant, and a bar rolled into one. Located just 8 miles (12.9 km) north of Highway 190, the main eastern route into the park, it's a good lodging alternative to the pricier options in Death Valley.

The rooms are basic budget rooms, but after a day of exploring in the desert, the Longstreet has what you need: Wi-Fi, a laundry room, a convenience store, a bar, and a restaurant. There is also a 51-space **RV resort.** An outdoor pool is open in summer. The **café** (8am-8pm Sun.-Thurs., 8am-9pm Fri.-Sat.; $9-19) serves basic American food for breakfast, lunch, and dinner. Depending on the time of day, expect friendly bartenders, fried food, and old-timers singing karaoke.

Information and Services

The convenience store at the Longstreet Inn and Casino offers basic **groceries, supplies,** and **gas.** There is also an ATM, Wi-Fi, and cell phone reception inside the hotel. The next closest gas station is in Furnace Creek, 31 miles (50 km) west, or Pahrump, Nevada, 30 miles (48 km) east. The closest official park information is inside the park at Furnace Creek, but both the Longstreet and Amargosa hotel staff are friendly and may be able to answer questions about the area.

Getting There

From Death Valley Junction, head north on Highway 127 for 7.5 miles (12.1 km), continuing as it crosses the Nevada state line and turns into Highway 373. The Longstreet Inn and Casino will be on the left just across the state line and marks the beginning of the Amargosa Valley.

To reach the Ash Meadows National Wildlife Refuge, continue north on Highway 373 and turn right (east) onto Spring Meadows Road; drive 5 miles (8 km) to the refuge entrance. Plan **one hour** for the drive from Furnace Creek.

PAHRUMP, NEVADA

Pahrump has hotels, RV parks, restaurants, gas, and places to buy a new tire, replace camping equipment, fill prescriptions, or restock groceries and travel supplies. All **services,** including a Walmart and other big-box stores, are located along Highway 160, which slices through the center of town. There is also cell phone reception in Pahrump.

Food and Accommodations

Pahrump Nugget Hotel and Casino

681 S. Hwy. 160; 866/751-6500; www.goldencasinogroup.com; from $99

For a lodging option that meets all your travel needs and then some, the Nugget offers 69 remodeled guest rooms as well as on-site restaurants that range from casual cafés and snack bars to a fine-dining steakhouse. The property also offers a bowling alley, casino, and several bars with gaming.

Getting There

Pahrump, Nevada, is 74 miles (119 km) southeast of Beatty via US 95 and 28 miles (45 km) northeast of Shoshone at the junction of Highways 160 and 372.

SHOSHONE

Shoshone functions as the **southern gateway** to Death Valley. The town sits at the junction of **Highway 127** (from Baker to the south) and **Highway 178** (from Pahrump, Nevada, to the east). Shoshone (www.shoshonevillage.com) is a charming bubble of a town, stuck in a pleasant time warp. It has history as a railroad stop on the Tidewater and Tonopah Railroad but today is known primarily as a hospitable gateway. The fact that it rests on a hot springs oasis lends a lush and relaxed air to this tiny town, which also conveniently has a post office, **a gas station, a café, a saloon,** and **a convenience store.** It's the last stop before Death Valley and a great place to use as a base camp when exploring the southeastern section of the park.

Sights

Dublin Gulch Caves

Access off of Hwy. 127

The Dublin Gulch Caves were hand-dug into the soft hills on the edge of town and used as residences by miners. Wooden doors lead into shadowy rooms that originally held stoves, beds, and all the comforts of home. Most of them are locked, but you can still peer through open windows to see fireplaces and bedsprings in some. They were in use until the 1970s, and the word is that as one occupant died or otherwise moved on, neighbors quickly jumped on the vacancy, upgrading to the more desirable caves. What makes one cave more desirable over another is something to think about as you wander among the hills. Look for roof stovepipes, outhouses, and a can graveyard. This area is for day use only, so camping is not allowed. The caves are on the south end of town. Park in the dirt parking area and walk past the **Shoshone Cemetery,** where some of the cave residents are buried, along with members of the town's founding family. Dublin Gulch Caves are located in the Village Center, walkable from any point in the village.

Shoshone Museum and Visitor Center

118 Hwy. 127; 760/852-4224; www.shoshonevillage.com; 9am-3pm daily; donation

The Shoshone Museum and Visitor Center is housed in an old gas station and features exhibits and a well-stocked bookstore on the area's geology and cultural and natural history. The excavated remains of a prehistoric mammoth are a surprise amid the other exhibits.

Food

Crowbar Café and Saloon

Shoshone Village, Hwy. 178; 760/852-4123; 8am-9:30pm daily; breakfast $11-14, lunch $13-20, dinner $13-46

Dig the clean shirt out of your bag and head over to the Crowbar Café and Saloon for breakfast, lunch, dinner, or drinks. The Crowbar leans a little more heavily toward travelers than locals, but don't hold that against them; there are just more of us. It has been around since the 1930s, and the stripped-down Western atmosphere and well-executed comfort food, from veggie burgers to prime rib, hits the spot in a land of few options. The saloon offers a full bar as well as a few local brews. The Crowbar doesn't take reservations, and it can get busy for dinner, depending on the season. One caveat: The Crowbar has been known to close early and without notice. The next closest dining option is in Pahrump or, depending on the day, there are limited options in Tecopa.

Accommodations

Staying at the Shoshone Inn or Shoshone RV Park and Campground will give you access to a hot springs pool at just the right temperature year-round. Both, along with several vacation rentals, are reservable online (www.shoshonevillage.com).

1
2
SHOSHONE INN
3
SHOSHONE
MUSEUM
GIFT SHOP
VISITOR CENTER
4
The Famous
CROWBAR
Cafe
Saloon

★ Shoshone Inn

Shoshone Village, Hwy. 178; 760/852-4335; www.shoshonevillage.com; front desk 8am-10pm daily, check-in 2pm-10pm daily; $160-185

The Shoshone Inn greets its visitors with turtle murals and relics from the town's mining days on the site of the old-style motor court motel. Inside, the motel's 17 rooms and one suite exceed expectations for their bright, clean style and fresh renovations. Ask for a key to the inn's private hot springs pool, complete with an artificial waterfall. This is a bright and charming spot, and a great place to set up a base camp for exploring areas in and around the southeastern edge of the park or as a last stop to wash off the dust at the end of your desert vacation. Note the inn's 2pm-10pm check-in time. The office is locked and there is no way to check in after 10pm. The next closest lodging after 10pm is in Pahrump.

Shoshone RV Park and Campground

Shoshone Village, Hwy. 178; 760/852-4335; www.shoshonevillage.com; front desk 8am-10pm daily, check-in 1pm-9pm daily; $35 tent, $50 RV

This is no wild-and-scenic backcountry camping adventure, but instead has some comfy amenities. The Shoshone RV Park and Campground has 25 full hookup sites, tent camping, very clean flush restrooms and showers, a library, a community room, and a fire pit set around a grassy lawn with palm trees. It's right off the main road, but there is little traffic on this north end of town, so it's relatively peaceful. The best part of the campground is use of the natural warm spring-fed pool. It's big enough to swim laps, and the pool water is at a perfect temperature—it can feel refreshing on a blazing sunny day and warm at cooler times of the year or in the evening. Despite its loveliness and the fact that it's shared with the Shoshone Inn, it's easy to have the pool to yourself.

The place caters mainly to RVs, but the tent sites have grassy spaces and privacy walls that keep out the wind. It's a short walk to the café and saloon in town. If you've been roughing it for a few days, this is a good place to take advantage of the showers or to set up a base camp to explore the southeastern part of the park.

Shoshone Vacation Rentals

Shoshone Village, Hwy. 178; 760/852-4335; www.shoshonevillage.com; front desk 8am-10pm daily, check-in noon-10pm daily; $210

The Shoshone RV Park and Campground also offers two vacation rentals located on the grounds. The Black Rock Cabin accommodates up to six with a full kitchen and dining area. Dutch's Retreat sleeps up to four with a full kitchen and dining and living area. Reserving these bungalows also gives you access to the campground's spring-fed swimming pool.

Information and Services

Shoshone has very basic supplies, dining, lodging, tent and RV camping, gas, and propane. There is no cell phone reception in town, but a few places offer Wi-Fi. The **Shoshone Museum and Visitor Center** (Shoshone Village, Hwy. 178; 760/852-4224; www.shoshonevillage.com; 9am-3pm daily) provides free Wi-Fi on-site as well as information about Death Valley. The Shoshone Inn and the Shoshone RV Park and Campground provide free Wi-Fi to guests.

The **Charles Brown General Store** (Shoshone Village, Hwy. 178; 760/852-4224; 7am-8:30pm daily, gas available 24 hours daily) is the last stop for gas and basic supplies before entering Death Valley. The store offers an RV propane station, convenience-store groceries, hot coffee, ice, beer and wine, and gift items such as Native American jewelry. For some reason, buying lottery tickets is also a popular pastime here, and visitors from all over the world on their way into Death Valley line up to contribute to the California economy.

If your **gas** tank isn't full, this is a good

1: pools and streams at Ash Meadows National Wildlife Refuge **2:** Shoshone Inn **3:** Shoshone Museum and Visitor Center **4:** Crowbar Café and Saloon

place to refuel. Shoshone is relatively isolated, and gas prices reflect this, but prices are still much better than the expensive fuel you will find in the park.

Getting There

The drive west from Shoshone to Furnace Creek takes about **one hour.** Take Highway 127 north to Death Valley Junction, and then continue 30 miles (48 km) west via Highway 190 to Furnace Creek. It is also possible to take scenic Highway 178, also known as Badwater Basin Road, to Furnace Creek; expect this drive to take about 1.75 hours without stops.

TECOPA

Once the largest Native American settlement in the area, Tecopa would have likely faded into the history of mining camps and rail stops of the Mojave if it weren't for the natural **hot springs** that bubble to the surface. Visitors to Death Valley usually blow right past the Tecopa turnoff from **Highway 127,** instead stopping in Shoshone 12 miles (19.3 km) north. Those who do make the detour come through for a **motel,** a soak, or to explore the Amargosa River Natural Area and China Ranch. Named after Chief Tecopa, a Paiute chief known for his peacemaking, the region also saw brief mining efforts and had a moment as a stop on the Tonopah and Tidewater Railroad. Today it is home to Vegas expats who fled the bright lights, beer makers, hot springs seekers, weekenders, lifers, and the occasional Death Valley visitor who detours off the main road to stop over in this funky outpost.

Two motels, a private campground, a county campground with developed hot springs, a restaurant, a bakery, and two breweries round out the few services. Most services are seasonal (Oct.-Apr.). Summer is too hot. There is **no gas.** There is **no cell reception** and **limited Wi-Fi.** Bring your own drinking water.

Sights

China Ranch Date Farm

China Ranch Rd.; 760/852-4415; www.chinaranch.com; 9am-5pm daily; free

The painted roadside signs for date shakes may lure you in even if you don't know anything about the China Ranch Date Farm. Follow the signs from Highway 127 just outside Tecopa to the ranch. China Ranch Road is a 1.5-lane dirt road that winds through mud hills deep into a scenic canyon to end at the ranch and the Amargosa River Natural Area, a lush riparian environment along the banks of the Amargosa River.

China Ranch is a working family farm with a gift shop, picnic area, and access to hiking trails in the Amargosa River Natural Area. It has an interesting history that you can learn about at the tiny **museum** housed in an outbuilding on the property. The ranch is open to visitors, and you can stroll through the date trees and picnic at several charming spots with a view of date palms set against the rocky canyon hills. The short interpretive **Creek Trail,** accessed behind the gift shop, follows China Ranch Creek through labeled native vegetation. There are picnic tables along this walk. Bring your own lunch or make an impromptu picnic with salsas, pickles, date nut bread, and other treats from the gift shop.

Hot Springs

Natural hot springs in the area have given rise to a small, low-key desert community enjoying the sun and solitude. You might wonder how anyone ever ended up here in the first place, but it seems clear that once here, many people have no intention of leaving anytime soon. RVs dot the landscape, and the several sun-beaten resorts in the area cater to this lifestyle. Visitors to the area can choose from several developed hot springs to bathe in. Tubs at all resorts are concrete and fed with piped-in natural hot spring water. There are several hot spring resorts, with motel cabins, RV spaces, and tent camping. Resorts may close in summer; check before visiting. Bring your own drinking water.

Tecopa Palms Therapeutic Hot Springs RV Park & Resort

155 Tecopa Hot Springs Rd.; 760/852-4347; www.tecopapalmstherapeutichotspringsresort.com; $20 per day

Day-use is possible at Tecopa Palms, a small resort that caters mainly to RV camping. It offers private, reservable indoor tubs for daily soaking in hot mineral water.

Delight's Hot Springs

368 Hot Springs Rd.; 760/852-4343; www.delightshotspringsresort.com; 8am-midnight daily; $25-35 per day

Delight's Hot Springs is unique in town for having a large, warm, spring-fed outdoor swimming pool. There are also four smaller, hotter soaking tubs in the central outdoor area, varying in temperature. Four private indoor soaking tubs are available with changing areas and shower. The pools are available to adults age 21 and over.

Tecopa Hot Springs Campground and Pools

400 Tecopa Hot Springs Rd.; 760/852-4377; www.tecopahotspringscampground.com; 6am-11pm daily; $10-25 per day

Tecopa Hot Springs Campground and Pools offers separate communal clothing-prohibited (by county health ordinance) tubs for men and women as well as a private, reservable tub.

Tecopa Mud Baths

Tecopa Hot Springs Rd.

There is also a natural hot spring approximately 1 mile (1.6 km) from the town of Tecopa Hot Springs. The springs are undeveloped with a silty base, giving the site its name. Water levels and temperatures can vary by season and year. The site is considered clothing optional by many people who frequent it. From the center of town next to the Tecopa Hot Springs Campground and Pools, head northwest toward Highway 127. Parking for the spring, known as the Tecopa Mud Baths, is on the right in a small turnout. The pond is located in open desert a short walk (200 yd/183 m) from the road.

Hiking

For most of its 185-mile (300-km) journey through the desert, the Amargosa River disappears underground, but here it swishes along on the surface. If you take one of several trails in the area, you may even have to do some rock-hopping. These hikes are accessed from **Amargosa River Natural Area,** adjoining the China Ranch Date Farm.

natural hot springs in the open desert near Tecopa

The natural area has several different well-marked trails for any ability. Trails lead to the river as well as a slot canyon, through badlands, and past historical remains, including an old saloon and a stop on the Tonopah and Tidewater Railroad. History, water, desert, and natural contrasts abound, but you're never uncomfortably far from freshly baked goodies and a place to rest in the shade.

Keep in mind, this is still desert hiking, and it requires all the same precautions. Carry plenty of water, know your route, use sunscreen and sunglasses, wear proper shoes and clothing, and use common sense. Ask in the gift shop for more information about the trails listed here or other hikes in the area.

Note: These two hikes can be combined for an extra 0.2 mile (0.3 km) and half an hour.

Slot Canyon Trail

Distance: *4 miles (6.4 km) round-trip*
Duration: *1.5 hours*
Elevation gain: *350 feet (107 m)*
Effort: *Easy*
Trailhead: *Behind the gift shop heading south into the canyon*
Directions: *Access the hike from the China Ranch Date Farm, approximately 5 miles (8 km) from Tecopa.*

If your favorite type of hike is the "everything" hike, the Slot Canyon Trail is an excellent way to spend an hour or two. The highlights include an **old stone saloon building** and **assay office,** delicate mud hills, a Tonopah and Tidewater Railroad stop, the Amargosa River, and a lovely slot canyon.

Start the hike behind the China Ranch gift shop and head downcanyon. The beginning of the trail is clear, but there are no name markers. The trail **forks** after about 0.25 mile (0.4 km). Take the right fork and you will eventually pass the picturesque saloon remains. The trail winds through mud hills and then comes out onto a mesa overlooking the remains of **Acme Siding,** an ore-loading site and stop on the Tonopah and Tidewater Railroad from 1905 until 1938. Take the trail off the mesa to the right and continue toward the river. The **slot canyon** will be visible in the distance. Once you cross the river (yes, there's water!), continue up the wash and into the slot canyon, with its sandy floor and beautifully eroded igneous rhyolite rock. The canyon is eventually blocked by two vertical dry falls.

Waterfall Trail

Distance: *4 miles (6.4 km) round-trip*
Duration: *1.5 hours*
Elevation gain: *350 feet (107 m)*
Effort: *Easy*
Trailhead: *Behind the gift shop, heading south into the canyon*
Directions: *Access the hike from the China Ranch Date Farm, approximately 5 miles (8 km) from Tecopa.*

We're not talking Yosemite here, but after an exposed hike along the remains of the Tonopah and Tidewater Railroad rail bed, this tiny pocket of falling water is a sight to behold.

This hike follows the same trail directions as the Slot Canyon Trail, starting behind the China Ranch gift shop and heading downcanyon toward the mesa overlook. The trail switchbacks down the left side to the ore-loading site and Tonopah and Tidewater Railroad bed. Follow the rail bed, avoiding washouts, until you get to a **trail** heading left. Take this trail and you'll soon see a **waterfall** sign as the trail continues to a pool on Willow Creek, shortly before it reaches the Amargosa River.

To combine this hike with the **Slot Canyon Trail,** retrace your steps to the Tonopah and Tidewater Railroad bed and follow the tracks. When you get to a fork with a cairn, turn right and follow the trail to the Amargosa River. Cross the river and head up the wash into the slot canyon, which will be visible from the river.

Food and Accommodations

Renaissance would be too strong a word, but let's just say that when I first visited Tecopa in 2014 the most exciting thing going to the uninitiated eye (in addition to the hot springs) was the free Wi-Fi at the community center. Now the tiny town boasts a legit good restaurant, two small breweries, and a bakery.

These are in addition to the hot springs, decent camping, and (still very basic) lodging. With prices in the park being what they are (expensive), Tecopa may even be an option for setting up a base camp to explore Death Valley if no-frills, offbeat outpost is your vibe. This is a seasonal town (Oct.-Apr.) with many businesses closed in summer. Check before you go.

Tecopa Brewing Company

760/852-4343; https://delightshotspringsresort.com; 3pm-9pm Thurs., noon-9pm Fri.-Sun., noon-8pm Mon.

Founded by Westley McNeal, Tecopa Brewing Company is a small, family-run business that makes small batches of their own beer (which they can run out of). The brewery also offers a decent California craft beer selection, pulled pork, brisket, and sides. Located at Delight's, inside it's an unassuming space that feels like a living room; sometimes they have the game on. Outside tables are on the patio.

★ Steaks and Beer

860 Tecopa Hot Springs Rd.; 702/334-3431; 5pm-8pm Fri.-Tues.; $20-55

Chef and owner Eric Scott of Steaks and Beer skipped out on Las Vegas to preside over Tecopa's worst-kept secret. The restaurant has expanded slightly from its hole-in-the-wall location in "downtown" Tecopa to its current location at the Tecopa Hot Springs Resort. Scott nails every course in the kitchen, from salads to sides, but the farm-raised steaks are why you come here. Stick with the program, and you will not be disappointed (hint: Steaks and Beer). There are no vegan options, although it is possible to eat vegetarian. The menu is also not particularly child-friendly unless your children crave an expertly cooked ribeye or filet mignon. To accompany, Steaks and Beer serves generous offerings of beer and wine. Table service is casual, and Scott also comes out from behind the grill to keep things moving along. This place is tiny and popular; reservations are highly recommended.

Death Valley Brewing

102 Old Spanish Trail Hwy.; 760/298-7014; www.deathvalleybrewing.com; 1pm-8pm Fri.-Mon.

The motto of Death Valley Brewing is "beer the way the miners used to drink it." This guiding principle of proprietor and brewer Jon Zellhoefer results in potent small batches of unfiltered and unpasteurized brews. If these were the beers of the Wild West, it gives you some insight into all the barroom brawls. Beware the crystal skull mugs, which hold two of these homebrews.

Kit Fox Café

59 Tecopa Hot Springs Rd.; 970/388-4805; hours vary

Kit Fox Café is the newest addition to Tecopa's food and drink scene. The café filled a much-needed gap in the area with espresso, coffee, and tea. The small shop also serves smoothies, bakery items, and a limited breakfast and sandwich menu on house-made bread. There is a wood-fired pizza oven that staff fires up sometimes.

Tecopa Palms Therapeutic Hot Springs RV Park & Resort

155 Tecopa Hot Springs Rd.; 760/852-4347; www.tecopapalmstherapeutichotspringsresort.com; $105-168 RVs and cabins, $55 personal RV, $45 tent

Tecopa Palms has parked RVs and cabins on-site that are available for overnight stays. It also has personal RV parking with 30- and 50-amp hookups and a few tent sites. Access to private indoor hot soaking tubs is included with your stay. Additional amenities include laundry facilities and free Wi-Fi.

Delight's Hot Springs Resort

368 Hot Springs Rd.; 760/852-4343; www.delightshotspringsresort.com; $75-220 rooms, $40 RV site with hookup

Delight's Hot Springs Resort offers cottages and motel rooms with kitchenettes and RV spots with hookups. There are no showers or bathtubs inside the accommodations; guests use showers by the private mineral baths. Accommodations are very basic, but the grounds have nice desert views and some character. No children are permitted.

Tecopa Hot Springs Campground and Pools

Tecopa Hot Springs Rd.; 760/852-4377; www.tecopahotspringscampground.com; $21-25

Tecopa Hot Springs Campground and Pools has over 100 sites for tent and RV camping, some with electrical hookups. Campground fees include the hot pools and shower facilities. Sites are spare with no picnic tables. Fire pits are available at some sites, and firewood can sometimes be purchased at check-in, depending on availability. The campground has plenty of space—reservations are not necessary.

Tecopa Hot Springs Resort

860 Tecopa Hot Springs Rd.; 760/852-4420; www.tecopahotsprings.org; motel rooms $132-142, cabins $115-130, RV sites $35-45

The cluster of RVs and cement-block buildings at Tecopa Hot Springs Resort might not immediately suggest it, but this is a resort open for business, falling on the far rustic end of the "resort" spectrum. Its cinder-block motel rooms and rail-tie cabins are strewn back from the Tecopa Hot Springs Road, dotted with palm trees and framed by low hills. Some have kitchenettes. An RV-only campground has full hookups and concrete pads. There is no Wi-Fi on the property. The natural mineral hot springs, in semiprivate soaking tubs available for resort guests, are the real draw, of course.

★ Villa Anita

10 Sunset Rd.; 760/852-4595; https://villaanitadv.com; $242-375

Founded by artist Carlo Roncancio in 2010, Villa Anita is equal parts art installation, boutique hotel, and experiential desert living destination. The unique property is run by Roncancio and partner and artist Jack Holloman, who provide the hospitality and keep the artistic vision flowing. Villa Anita spans 10 acres (4 ha) and incorporates the original 1951 house as well as trailers and other units into a dwelling sculpture interconnected by pathways, gardens, and lounging spaces. You can book suites like the one-bedroom Bottle Cottage, giving a nod to houses from Death Valley mining towns built with the plentiful resource, or the charming retro Bird's Nest, giving new life to a 1970s trailer. Accommodations typically have a bedroom, a living space, a bathroom with shower, and an outdoor space. Breakfast and dinner are served family style for an additional fee. This place is not for everyone but recommended if you like Noah Purifoy, junk dada, assemblage art, and off-beat getaways.

Information and Services

Free Wi-Fi is available from the parking lot of the **Tecopa Community Center** (400 Tecopa Hot Springs Rd.; 760/852-4262). It's worth taking advantage of, since there is little to no cell service available for miles around, even in the town of Shoshone. There are no other services in Tecopa.

Getting There

Tecopa is about 70 miles (113 km) southeast of Furnace Creek and is accessed via **Tecopa Hot Springs Road,** between Baker and Shoshone. From Tecopa, drive 4 miles (6.4 km) west along Old Spanish Trail Highway to Highway 127. Take Highway 127 north for 35 miles (56 km), then turn left (west) on Highway 190 and continue 30 miles (48 km) to Furnace Creek. Plan about **75 minutes** for the drive from Furnace Creek.

Stovepipe Wells and the Nevada Triangle

For such a small slice of Death Valley, the Nevada Triangle holds many attractions.

On a map, the region opens, fanlike, toward northern Death Valley, between the Grapevine and Cottonwood Mountains. Squeezing through the Grapevine Mountains is Titus Canyon Road, which winds more than 27 spectacular backcountry miles (43 km) down to the valley floor, dense with salt and sand and with little human population. Here, boulder-filled alluvial fans lead to steep mountains and the area's signature wind-sculpted canyons.

Stovepipe Wells, a touring outpost built in 1926, still sits on the toll road (now Highway 190) that officially kicked off tourism in Death Valley. The road was originally built to join Stovepipe Wells with Lone

Highlights

Look for ★ to find recommended sights, activities, dining, and lodging.

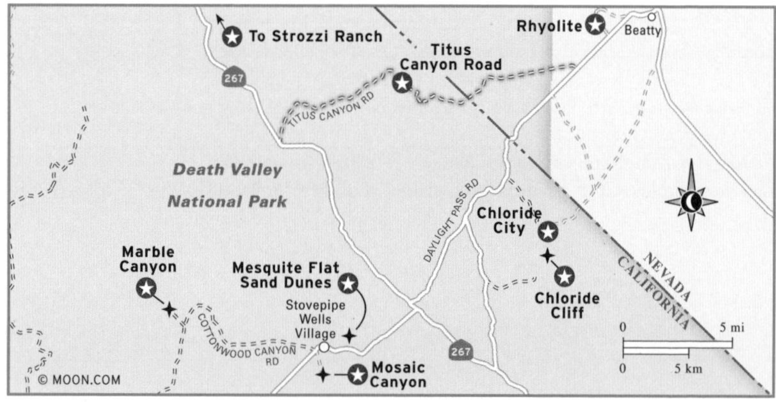

★ **Mesquite Flat Sand Dunes:** These iconic sand dunes are the most popular in the park (page 92).

★ **Rhyolite:** The ghost town of Rhyolite was so rich in its heyday that it was home to an opera house and a stock exchange. Today, the dirt road leads past crumbling banks once bursting with gold (page 94).

★ **Strozzi Ranch:** A high-clearance then 4WD road ends at the beautifully weathered remains of this historic ranch, set amid high-elevation pinyon-pine forest (page 97).

★ **Titus Canyon Road:** This one-way, 27-mile (43-km) road winds past rugged rock formations, sweeping canyon views, petroglyphs, and even a ghost town, all eventually leading to the salty and barren Death Valley floor (page 97).

★ **Chloride City and Chloride Cliff:** This forgotten silver- and lead-mining district is one of the oldest historical sites in Death Valley. Remains include an old mill, the marked grave of James McKay, and dugout houses scattered around a short loop trail (page 100).

★ **Mosaic Canyon:** Wander through polished marble, colorful mosaic stone, and satisfying narrows on this short and sweet hike (page 104).

★ **Marble Canyon:** A rough but scenic drive into the Cottonwood Mountains pays off in a hike through sculpted narrows and petroglyphs (page 105).

Stovepipe Wells and the Nevada Triangle in One Day

- Start your day with a short hike through polished **Mosaic Canyon.**
- After your hike, head toward the Nevada side of the park via Highway 190 and the Beatty Cutoff Road. Make a stop at the historic **Keane Wonder Mine** to take in the remains of one of the most successful gold-mining operations in Death Valley.
- Have lunch at the **Happy Burro Chili & Beer** in **Beatty, Nevada.**
- Reenter the park via the spectacular, one-way **Titus Canyon Road,** which winds down through carved hills to spill out onto the Death Valley floor. If there's time, detour through the ghost town of **Rhyolite** on your way to the entrance for Titus Canyon. Along Titus Canyon Road, stretch your legs at one of several viewpoints or along the 1-mile (1.6 km) stroll around the remains of **Leadfield** ghost town. After you reach the valley floor, take in golden hour at the **Mesquite Flat Sand Dunes.**
- **Stovepipe Wells** has a restaurant and saloon to end your day.

Pine in the Sierra Nevada and now serves as the park hub for this region, with a campground, a hotel, a restaurant, and a gas station.

Black dust clouds have been known to sweep down into Stovepipe Wells seemingly from nowhere. Camping at Stovepipe Wells one spring evening at dinnertime, we noticed a big dark cloud hovering over the Cottonwood Mountains. We had just enough time to look up and wonder if it could possibly be rain on this clear sunny day when the dust storm hit. A downburst of cold air pummeled the campground as we all held on. It swept out as quickly as it came, leaving the campground strewn with equipment—unstaked tents had taken off like kites. Shell shock gave way to awe as a double rainbow appeared, and we realized we had experienced the sheer intensity of the desert.

PLANNING YOUR TIME

The Nevada Triangle sits on the northeastern edge of Death Valley. Navigating this region can be a little tricky and involves some forethought. Some sights, like the ghost town of Chloride City, the beautifully weathered remains of the Strozzi Ranch, or the spectacular one-way Titus Canyon Road, can only be accessed from outside the park on the Nevada side. **Beatty, Nevada,** offers the closest access to these sights.

Titus Canyon Road was closed in 2024 due to flood damage. Check the National Park Service's Alerts page (www.nps.gov/deva/planyourvisit/conditions.htm) for current road conditions.

Stovepipe Wells is the park hub for this region and is a good place to set up base camp. The village is at 10 feet (3 m) above sea level. It is hot much of the year and windswept the rest. Using Stovepipe Wells as a base, it's possible to see the highlights and get in one good meaty canyon hike, such as Marble Canyon, in **three days.**

Spend one day near Stovepipe Wells Village, which offers proximity to the Mesquite Flat Sand Dunes and several canyon hikes. Visiting Rhyolite or Chloride City, then driving the Titus Canyon Road, will fill a second day. A third day could be spent exploring the Red Wall and Fall Canyons along Highway 190, north of Titus Canyon Road.

Previous: a hiker on the Mesquite Flat Sand Dunes; tent camping at Stovepipe Wells Campground; Happy Burro Chili & Beer.

Stovepipe Wells and the Nevada Triangle

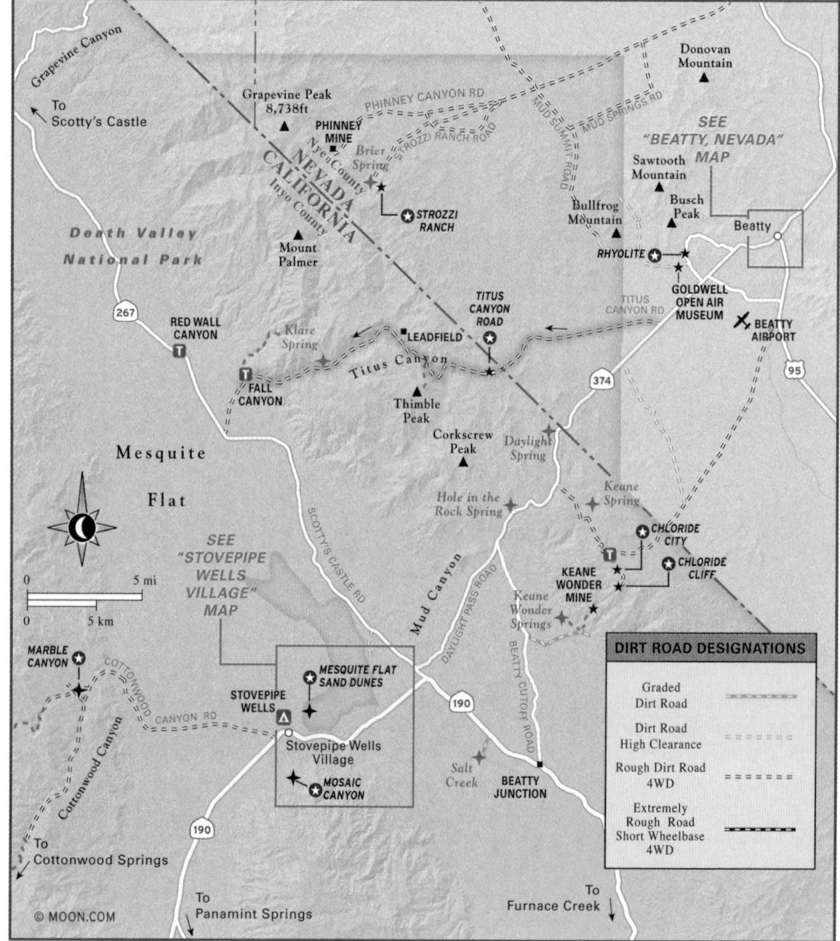

Exploring the Park

Stovepipe Wells is along Highway 190, the main route through the park, about 25 miles (40 km) northwest of Furnace Creek. A stay here offers convenient access to the Nevada Triangle, as well as parts of Scotty's Castle, Furnace Creek, and even some western locations around Panamint Springs.

RANGER STATION

Although this is the second major park hub in Death Valley, after Furnace Creek, Stovepipe Wells does not have a visitor center. You can pay entrance fees and get general information and backcountry information at the **Stovepipe Wells Ranger Station**

Driving Distances

From Stovepipe Wells to:	Distance	Duration
Furnace Creek	25 mi/40 km	30 min
Panamint Springs	30 mi/48 km	30 min
Beatty, NV	34 mi/55 km	45 min
Scotty's Castle	44 mi/71 km	1 hr
The Racetrack	83 mi/134 km	3-4 hrs
Eureka Dunes	98 mi/158 km	3 hrs

(760/786-2342; 10am-5pm daily, open variably). Books and maps are available at the Furnace Creek Visitor Center and the general store in Furnace Creek. After business hours, entrance fees can be paid using an automated kiosk outside the ranger station that takes cash and plastic.

PARK ENTRANCES

The village of Stovepipe Wells has been a waypoint since the toll road through Death Valley was finished in 1926. Today, **Highway 190** follows much of the original road. From its western terminus in the Owens Valley, at the junction with US 395, Highway 190 runs east for 45 miles (72 km), passing through Panamint Springs and swooping over to Stovepipe Wells, an easy 30 miles (48 km) away.

The small gateway town of **Beatty, Nevada,** is just beyond the eastern park boundary on **US 95,** about 120 miles (193 km) northwest of Las Vegas. If you're coming through Las Vegas, it can serve as a good base camp or as a jumping-off point for exploring the park. Beatty is close to the ghost towns of Rhyolite and Chloride City and the scenic Titus Canyon Road. Access to Stovepipe Wells from Beatty is via **Highway 374** (Daylight Pass Rd.), only 34 miles (55 km) and less than an hour's drive, a snap in Death Valley time.

Gas and Services

Stovepipe Wells has a full-service hotel, a campground, a restaurant, a saloon, and gas. The gift shop and convenience store are primarily invested in T-shirts and novelty items; neither offers a supply of books or information. Your best bet for these is to drive to **Furnace Creek,** 30 minutes southeast.

Beatty, Nevada, just 9 miles (14.5 km) outside the park boundary, is a tiny but full-service town with hotels, restaurants, gas, and basic groceries. Its rough-hewn main street of saloons, motels, and casinos may better satisfy a craving for a Wild West experience than Stovepipe Wells. Beatty is a 45-minute drive from Stovepipe Wells.

Sights

STOVEPIPE WELLS

Hwy. 190; www.deathvalleyhotels.com; year-round

Stovepipe Wells was named for a rusty pipe sticking out of shifting sands that helped travelers, pioneers, and prospectors find the murky well just below the surface. Some enterprising businessperson opened the first services by building a dugout of mud and beer bottles. It was effectively a cellar just below the surface, but it served to keep travelers cool in the blazing desert sun. Beer, supplied from Tonopah, Nevada, was kept cool in tubs covered with sacks soaked in water. This first incarnation of Stovepipe Wells evolved into a tent outpost and way station as the mining towns of Rhyolite and Skidoo began cranking out their ores in the early 1900s. When the mines closed and the towns faded, so did Stovepipe Wells, returning once again to a humble well amid arid desert.

Windswept, exposed, and sandy, Stovepipe Wells has a certain beauty in its austerity, but it can also feel more like an outpost against the elements than a resort. The toll road was abolished in 1933 when Death Valley became a national monument, but the present Highway 190 follows most of its old route. Stovepipe Wells itself has been remodeled extensively over the years, but it still offers hospitality in this often inhospitable environment.

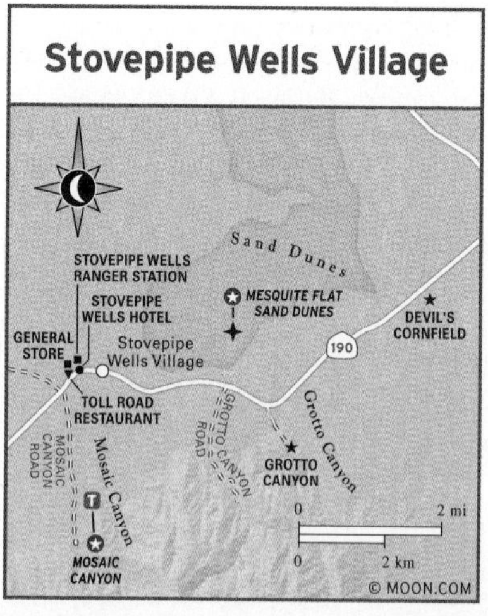

TOP EXPERIENCE

★ Mesquite Flat Sand Dunes

2 miles (3.2 km) east of Stovepipe Wells; year-round; free

The Mesquite Flat Sand Dunes are iconic to Death Valley and a popular sight in the park. In order to form, dunes require wind, sand, and a place for the sand to collect. These three things exist in spades in this austere section of the park, just east of the village of Stovepipe Wells. The sculpted dunes are visible from Stovepipe Wells and beyond, rising out of the desert floor to catch the light of the sky in smooth, unbroken crests and lines. Such is the power of the dunes that they seem to draw people from miles around, and you'll find that lots of other people are here to enjoy these vast expanses. The simplicity of the dunes provides a rich experience where you can hike, run in the sand, admire the ripples of the wind, or look for tiny animal tracks.

Directions

From Stovepipe Wells, drive 2 miles (3.2 km) east on Highway 190 and look for a signed parking area. From here it's less than 0.5 mile (0.8 km) to the base of the dunes. A quieter approach is via the Historic Stovepipe Wells Road, 3 miles (4.8 km) north of Highway 190 off Scotty's Castle Road. A walk to the base of the dunes from here is about 1 mile (1.6 km). There are several dune fields in the park, but Mesquite Flat is the easiest to visit—although it's still a long walk across the sand.

1: Mesquite Flat Sand Dunes **2:** Devil's Cornfield **3:** Rhyolite **4:** Titus Canyon

1
2
3
4

DEVIL'S CORNFIELD

6 miles (9.7 km) east of Stovepipe Wells; year-round; free

What would a field of plants growing in an eternal fiery inferno look like? Very possibly like the Devil's Cornfield, just east of Stovepipe Wells. Mounded clumps of these bursting plants stretch in neat rows along the sandy desert floor. The plants are actually the not-so-humble arrowweed plant (the "corn" part of the Devil's Cornfield), in the sunflower family. The salt-tolerant plant has adapted to harsh life in Death Valley and the Sonoran Desert, growing in clumps in order to take root against the shifting sands and incessant desert winds. Native Americans used the plants medicinally, as well as for housing thatch and arrow shafts. The plants themselves make sense, but the effect of the carefully plotted rows of wild plants against the backdrop of the Funeral Mountains is surreal. In the spring the haystacks can blossom, leaving them with blue tops.

Directions

From Stovepipe Wells, drive east on Highway 190 for approximately 6 miles (9.7 km). An interpretive sign and a few flat, paved parking spaces next to the road mark the Devil's Cornfield; however, the area extends on either side of the road for a good part of the drive. Park and wander among the plants, which get bigger a little farther from the road.

SALT CREEK

11 miles (17.7 km) east of Stovepipe Wells; year-round; free

Salt Creek feels strangely like East Coast beaches known for salty air, heat, humidity, dunes, and sand grasses—the air smells salty and even feels slightly humid. A wheelchair-accessible boardwalk follows the miraculous Salt Creek, winding 0.5 mile (0.8 km) toward pale, eroded mud hills through an expanse of pickleweed, a salt-resistant desert plant. This place is as desert as it gets, yet here is Salt Creek, valiantly flowing along, supporting a tiny riparian environment, including the endemic **Salt Creek pupfish.** The park is quite proud of this little pupfish, and if you visit Salt Creek, you will understand why. Salt Creek may be a miracle by desert standards, but it's a trickle by forest standards.

Salt Creek is a fragile ecosystem, and your visit can have a swift and negative impact. Respect the desert and other visitors by remaining on the boardwalk. The area was severely impacted by floods in summer 2022, which changed the course of the creek and destroyed the boardwalk. Restoration is in progress.

Directions

Salt Creek is about 11 miles (17.7 km) east of Stovepipe Wells. Take Highway 190 east for approximately 7 miles (11.3 km) to the intersection with Scotty's Castle Road. Turn south. After another 4 miles (6.4 km), turn right onto the signed, graded dirt road for Salt Creek and drive to the parking area at the end.

KLARE SPRING

Titus Canyon Rd.; year-round; free

The **petroglyphs** at Klare Spring are among the few petroglyph locations in the park that are publicized. Sadly, this means they've been defaced; people have unfathomably added their own writing on top of these ancient works. Still, the large panel of ancient drawings chipped into rock is a fine one and worth the stop.

Look for Klare Spring on the right, 18.1 miles (29 km) from the start of the Titus Canyon Road (reopening 2025) and less than 3 miles (4.8 km) past Leadfield.

★ RHYOLITE

Hwy. 374; year-round; free

Shorty Harris and E. L. Cross sparked the birth of Rhyolite in 1904. While prospecting in the area, they found gold in the Bullfrog Hills, named for their green-spotted rocks. Thousands of people began streaming into the area. The first post office opened in 1905; at its peak in 1907-1908, Rhyolite was probably home to between 3,500 and 5,000 people. The town boasted an ice cream parlor, a school, an ice plant, banks, and a train station. As quickly as Rhyolite sprang up, it started to deflate when the financial panic of 1907 kicked off a rush in the opposite direction. By 1911, the mine had closed, and by 1920, the last holdouts had dwindled to 14 lonely souls.

Today, the main road through the **ghost town** leads past crumbling banks once bursting with gold. Some ruins are two stories tall, towering like era monuments. The beautiful mission-style **train station** remains intact and looks like it could open tomorrow. Side roads lead to the red-light district, **cemetery,** and mine ruins.

Rhyolite might be most famous for its **bottle house,** built by enterprising miner Tom Kelly out of a plentiful material on hand—beer and liquor bottles. It took over 50,000 bottles to make this structure, which was restored by Paramount Pictures in 1925, as Rhyolite began to be used as a filming location.

Directions

Rhyolite is approximately 4 miles (6.4 km) west of Beatty, Nevada, off Highway 374. Take Highway 374 west from Beatty and turn right into the well-marked entrance.

From Stovepipe Wells, Rhyolite is about 30 miles (48 km) northeast. Head east on Highway 190 to Daylight Pass Road. A well-marked entrance on the left indicates the 2-mile (3.2-km) road to Rhyolite. Plan to spend an hour or two strolling among the crumbling buildings and art.

Goldwell Open Air Museum

1 Golden St.; 702/870-9946; www.goldwellmuseum.org; year-round; free

The Goldwell Open Air Museum is a sculpture installation and art park just south of Rhyolite, located off of Rhyolite Road. Belgian artists began the museum in the 1980s using the surreal location to showcase larger-than-life sculptures.

The Last Supper, Lady Desert: The Venus of Nevada, and *Tribute to Shorty Harris* are all impossibly big and very haunting. ***The Last Supper,*** the most prominent piece, features ghostly life-size hollow figures huddled on a wooden platform in an eerie plaster sculpture rendition of Leonardo Da Vinci's famous fresco. ***The Venus of Nevada*** represents a 3-D woman made of 2-D computer pixels; it stands larger than life, pink and yellow cinder blocks incongruous against the desert browns and golds. Taken together, the collection is disjointed and surreal against the desert landscape.

A tiny **visitor center** (10am-4pm Wed.-Sat.) sits centrally located among the sculptures, with T-shirts and museum gifts for sale; there are no services.

KEANE WONDER MINE

Beatty Cutoff Rd.; www.nps.gov; year-round; free

Keane Wonder Mine was one of the most successful gold mines in Death Valley. With its well-preserved aerial tramway, the site has long attracted visitors to its rugged location in the Funeral Mountains. It is one of the best historical examples of a gold-mining operation in the park. Gold was discovered here in 1904, and serious mining efforts began in 1907 when the 20-stamp mill and tramway were installed. By 1912, the mines had mostly played out and operations ended. They were picked up again in 1913, 1915, 1935, and 1940, but each time production was less than 10 percent of the earlier period. The mine's glory days were over. The aerial tramway makes this site truly unique. The 1-mile-long (1.6-km) feat of engineering was designed to haul ore from 1,500 feet (457 m) up the steep Funeral Mountains and across a 500-foot-deep (152-m) canyon to an extensive milling complex below.

Directions

From Stovepipe Wells, take Highway 190 13.7 miles (22 km) east to the signed Beatty Cutoff Road. Turn left and travel 5.7 miles (9.2 km) north to the signed road for Keane Wonder Mine. Drive 2.8 miles (4.5 km) to a parking area. From here stroll around the site where

1

2

the camp and mill were located. For views of the lower tram terminal and first few tram towers, take the short trail at the end of the road. To reach the upper tramway terminal and Keane Wonder Mine, follow the old mining road for 1.4 miles (2.3 km) and a 1,500-foot (457-m) ascent.

★ STROZZI RANCH

Access via the 4WD Phinney Canyon Rd. off US 95; year-round; free

The historical site of this ranch from the 1930s is a lightly visited time capsule set in a forested canyon unusual for Death Valley. Because it is accessed by a 4WD road from outside the park, it receives few visitors. Strozzi Ranch was created by Beatty cattle and goat rancher Caesar Strozzi in 1931 as a summer headquarters. The remains today include two structures, a "Cousin Jack" dugout, and chicken coops. The National Park Service (NPS) has completed some restoration, and the ranch is a beautifully weathered piece of history, salted with artifacts. Look for the uniquely fenced corral 0.2 mile (0.3 km) before the ranch.

Directions

Access to this site is via high-clearance then 4WD road. Begin at the town center of Beatty, the intersection of Daylight Pass Road (Hwy. 374) and US 95. Head north on US 95 for 11.8 miles (19 km). The primitive road to Strozzi Ranch begins on the left behind a barbed-wire gate and Keep Gate Closed sign. There are several of these gates within a few miles of each other. Look for the gate between highway mile markers 71 and 72. As another check, to the east of the highway you will see a dirt road heading northeast across the base of Oasis Mountain. Phinney Canyon/Strozzi Ranch Road begins as an easily passable dirt track, requiring only high clearance as you travel across the desert plains of Sarcobatus Flat. At 12.2 miles (19.6 km), you will reach an obvious fork in the road, the Strozzi-Phinney Junction. Beyond this junction 4WD is best due to high, rocky crowns. The south fork leads to Strozzi Ranch in 7 miles (11.3 km).

Scenic Drives

This region as a whole is well worth exploring. Mining wasn't as prevalent here as it was in other areas of Death Valley, and the main features are the deep, scenic canyons in the Cottonwood and Grapevine Mountains. The region is a strange mix of the very inaccessible and the easily accessible. The Cottonwood Mountains are so remote that there is not a single road that traverses the entire range. The only road that even attempts it is the **Cottonwood Canyon Road,** which runs for 19 miles (31 km) from its starting point at Highway 190 outside Stovepipe Wells. It ends beyond the canyon mouth at Cottonwood Springs.

The Grapevine Mountains are relatively accessible compared to the other mountain ranges in the region. The paved **Scotty's Castle Road** runs north-south along the base of the Grapevine Mountains, giving access to scenic canyons such as Fall Canyon and Red Wall Canyon. The Titus Canyon Road ends at an intersection with Scotty's Castle Road. The final section is two-way for 2.7 miles (4.3 km) to give access to Fall Canyon.

TOP EXPERIENCE

★ TITUS CANYON ROAD

Distance: *27 miles (43 km) one-way*
Duration: *3 hours*
Start: *Hwy. 374, 6 mi (9.7 km) south of Beatty, NV*
End: *Scotty's Castle Road*

1: *Ghost Rider* by Albert Szukalski at the Goldwell Open Air Museum **2:** Strozzi Ranch

Road surface: *Dirt*
Vehicle: *High-clearance recommended*

If you're looking to make a dramatic entrance into Death Valley, drive Titus Canyon Road. The 27-mile (43-km) one-way dirt road sweeps through rugged rock formations, hangs over canyon views, skirts past petroglyphs, and even rolls through a ghost town, eventually passing through what is arguably the grand finale: the canyon narrows. The narrows tower overhead, barely letting cars squeeze through before they open wide to reveal the barren Death Valley floor.

Titus Canyon Road has some of the most interesting geology in the park. Aside from taking in the spectacular views that dominate the entire drive, there are some key spots to stop.

The ruins of **Leadfield** lie scattered on the left side of Titus Canyon Road, 15.7 miles (25.3 km) from the start of the drive. A 1-mile (1.6-km) **hiking trail** passes through the remains of the town, including several large structures, a dugout, and the remains of the old post office.

Look for **Klare Spring** on the right, 18.1 miles (29.1 km) from the start of the Titus Canyon Road and less than 3 miles (4.8 km) past Leadfield. There are **petroglyphs** on a large rock at the site.

The one-way Titus Canyon Road starts from Highway 374 (Daylight Pass Rd.), 6 miles (9.7 km) south of Beatty, Nevada. Plan to spend three hours driving Titus Canyon Road to its terminus at Scotty's Castle Road. It's a slow drive on a one-lane dirt road that can be rutted or rocky, and it hugs the canyon wall at points. The NPS officially recommends a two-wheel-drive high-clearance vehicle (an urban SUV is usually fine) but cautions that a 4WD vehicle may be needed in inclement weather.

If you choose to drive this road in the evening, give yourself enough time to reach the valley floor before dark. The NPS does not recommend this drive in summer; the area is lightly patrolled, and any breakdown can be dangerous due to the heat.

Titus Canyon Road was closed in 2024 due to flood damage. Check the National Park Service's Alerts page (www.nps.gov/deva/planyourvisit/conditions.htm) for current road conditions.

FOUR-WHEEL DRIVES

Cottonwood Canyon Road

Distance: *19 miles (31 km) one-way*
Duration: *2-3 hours*
Start: *Stovepipe Wells*
End: *Cottonwood Canyon*
Road surface: *Sand and gravel*
Vehicle: *4WD*

Cottonwood Canyon Road is a primitive 19-mile (31-km) road that goes deep into the Cottonwood Mountains. Rough and scenic, it runs through two sets of narrows and past fossils and side canyons to end at lush hidden springs and a series of oases. A hiking trail continues beyond the end of the road to explore **Lower, Middle,** and **Cottonwood Springs.**

To drive Cottonwood Canyon Road, start from Stovepipe Wells to the left of the campground entrance. You'll know you're in the right place when you see a small airstrip. The road starts off with a bang, spitting through semi-deep sand. The ground eventually becomes more solid, and the road is washboard with some gravel near the end of this stretch. At the 8.6-mile (13.8-km) mark, the road enters the Cottonwood Canyon wash and becomes much rougher. At 10.8 miles (17.4 km), the road splits; look for the very faint sign and follow the road to the left toward Cottonwood Canyon.

Because of its scenery and supply of water, a rarity in Death Valley, this is a popular driving, camping, and hiking destination.

Phinney Canyon Road and Strozzi Ranch Road

Distance: *19 miles (31 km) from Beatty to Strozzi Ranch, 20.8 miles (33.5 km) from Beatty to Phinney Canyon*
Duration: *2-3 hours*
Start: *Beatty, NV*
End: *Phinney Canyon and Strozzi Ranch*
Road surface: *Dirt and gravel*

Vehicle: *High-clearance 4WD recommended*

Phinney Canyon and Strozzi Ranch Roads are two of only a handful of roads that cut into the Grapevine Mountains from the Nevada Triangle. The road spins across the high desert plain of Sarcobatus Flat and forks. The south fork climbs into the Grapevine Mountains to end at the beautifully patinaed remains of the historic Strozzi Ranch. The north fork climbs through pinyon pine-forested canyon to end about 1 mile (1.6 km) before a 7,500-foot (2,286-m) crest in the Grapevine Mountains.

Strozzi Ranch and Phinney Canyon share the same starting point. Begin at the town center of Beatty, the intersection of Daylight Pass Road (Hwy. 374) and US 95. Head north on US 95 for 11.8 miles (19 km). The primitive road begins on the left behind a barbed-wire gate and Keep Gate Closed sign between highway mile markers 71 and 72. There are several of these gates within a few miles of each other north of town. To the east of the highway you will see another dirt road heading northeast across the base of Oasis Mountain as well as the raised, graded dirt of the Bullfrog Goldfield Railroad.

Phinney Canyon/Strozzi Ranch Road begins as an easily passable dirt track, requiring only high clearance as you travel across the strangely named Sarcobatus Flat (the name refers to a species of flowering plant, commonly greasewood or saltbush), drawing closer to the Grapevine Mountains in the distance. Ranching roads and old mining roads intersect at points; continue straight at all intersections. You may see wild burros ranging across the public land.

At 12.2 miles (19.6 km), you will reach an obvious fork in the road, the Strozzi-Phinney Junction. Beyond this junction 4WD is best.

South Fork

The south fork continues for another 7 miles (11.3 km), dropping into the Strozzi wash before climbing into the Grapevine Mountains. Desert turns to mountain: The air becomes crisper, the road becomes rockier, and vegetation turns from sagebrush and Joshua tree to pinyon and pine. The road ends at the Strozzi Ranch, elevation 6,220 feet (1,896 m). Constructed in 1931 by Caesar Strozzi for his summer cattle and goat ranch (his winter ranch was in Beatty), the site has picturesque remains, including two buildings, a dugout, and chicken coops. There is also a well-maintained picnic area, surprising for a spot so remote.

Cottonwood Canyon

Stovepipe Wells Hikes

Trail	Effort	Distance	Duration
★ **Chloride City and Chloride Cliff**	Easy	1.5-4.5 mi/2.4-7.2 km rt	1.5-3 hrs
★ **Mosaic Canyon**	Easy	2.8 mi/4.5 km rt	1 hr
★ **Marble Canyon**	Moderate	3.2 mi/5.1 km rt	2-4 hrs
Fall Canyon	Moderate	6.8 mi/10.9 km rt	3 hrs
Red Wall Canyon	Moderate	6.4-9.2 mi/10.3-14.8 km rt	3-6 hrs

North Fork

The right (north) fork of the junction continues for 8.6 miles (13.8 km) into Phinney Canyon. The first 5 miles (8 km) follow an alluvial fan, eventually dropping into the wash of Phinney Canyon. The last 3-plus (4.8 km) miles are steep and rocky with a deteriorated road. The road ends at 20.8 miles (33.5 km), just beyond a nice campsite. This is a good parking spot and place to turn around. At 20.5 miles (33 km), you can find the small remains of the 1930s Phinney Mine up a small side canyon. Another mile (1.6 km) on foot along the main road takes you to a rocky pass overlooking the wild and sweeping slopes of Moonlight Canyon, deep in the Grapevine Mountains.

Recreation

HIKING

★ Chloride City and Chloride Cliff

Distance: *1.5-4.5 miles (2.4-7.2 km) round-trip*
Duration: *1.5-3 hours*
Elevation gain: *230-920 feet (70-280 m)*
Effort: *Easy*
Access: *High-clearance or passenger vehicle; 4WD not required*
Trailhead: *From Beatty, drive south on Highway 374 for 8.9 miles (14.3 km). Just outside the park boundary, take Chloride Cliff Road southeast. Drive 6.8 miles (10.9 km) to a T junction. Turn right and drive an additional 2 miles (3.2 km) to a fork in the road. If you are not driving a 4WD vehicle, park at the bottom of the hill and walk 1 mile (1.6 km) to the top of the hill, where you will see the scattered remains of Chloride City (see map page 101).*

Chloride Cliff, high up in the Funeral Mountains, offers one of the oldest historical sites in Death Valley, along with sweeping views of the valley below.

Chloride Cliff's history is too slow and uneven to call it a boom. In 1871, silver-lead ore was discovered in Chloride Cliff. August Franklin, a civil engineer sent to survey the California-Nevada boundary, staked the first claims and began running a small mining operation. The quality of the ore was good, but the closest town was 180 miles (290 km) southeast across salt flats, through desolate mountain passes, and without roads or

Chloride City and Chloride Cliff

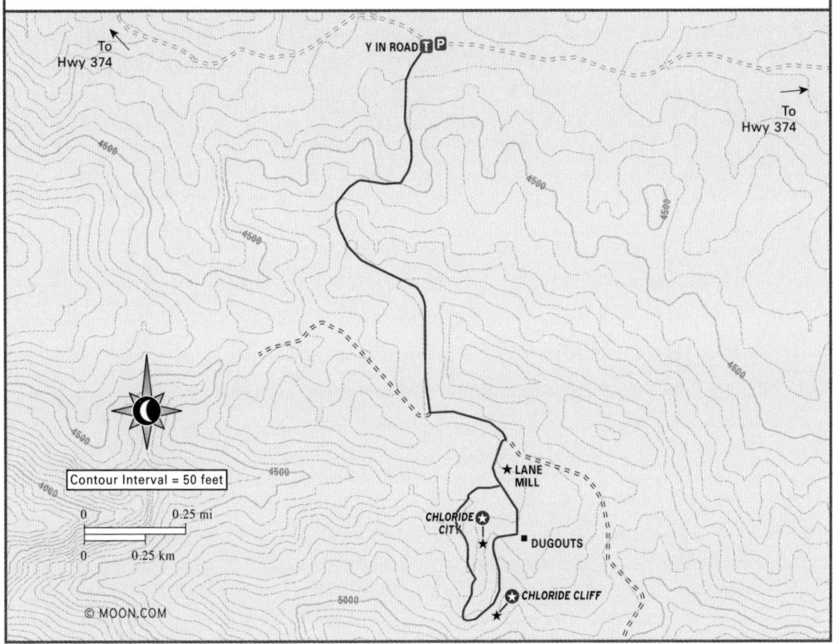

settlements. The mining efforts folded after two years.

Franklin died in 1904, just missing the next boom in 1905, which spanned the areas below the cliffs and the Bullfrog District around Rhyolite. Chloride City boomed on and off until 1912, and was then intermittently resuscitated by different owners and lessees until the early 1940s. Each time the remoteness was too formidable, even in a region accustomed to being remote.

Today, the town of Chloride City is strewn across a bowl in the steep hills of the Funeral Mountains, rusting quietly in windswept desolation. Even though services can now be found less than an hour away, the site still has the power to evoke the isolation that must have been pervasive here.

After parking, head to the left up the hill for 1 mile (1.6 km). The top of the hill provides a panoramic view of **Chloride City.** It's an exciting prospect to stand on the edge of the town and see the ruins. An **old road** rings the site and forms the basis for the hike. A **1.5-mile (2.4-km) loop** through Chloride City will take you past the 1916 Lane Mill, several dugouts, and the original mines and mill. Start at the **water tower** and walk clockwise from north to south past the flattened buildings of Chloride City. Follow the loop to **Lane Mill** (0.4 mi/0.6 km) and the miners' hillside **dugout dwellings** (0.8 mi/1.3 km), and pick up a trail (2 mi/3.2 km out and back) to see the immense views of Death Valley from **Chloride Cliff** (on the southern end).

Chloride City is only about 20 miles (32 km, less than an hour's drive) from the ghost town of **Rhyolite.** Combine a trip to these two sites to get a sense of this region, which has been connected by mining efforts for more than 100 years. From either Beatty or Stovepipe Wells, allow at least four hours to get to the site and explore.

Fall Canyon

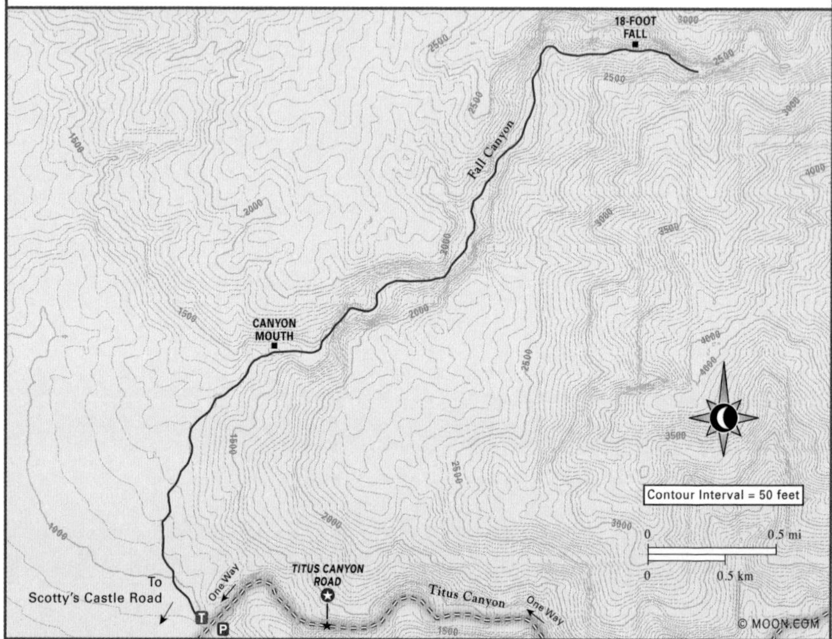

Fall Canyon

Distance: *6.8 miles (10.9 km) round-trip to 18-foot (5.5 m) fall*

Duration: *3 hours*

Elevation gain: *1,330 feet (405 m)*

Effort: *Moderate*

Access: *Passenger vehicle from graded dirt road*

Trailhead: *From Stovepipe Wells, drive east on Highway 190 for 7 miles (11.3 km). Turn left onto Scotty's Castle Road and drive 14.9 miles (24 km) north to Titus Canyon Road (reopening in 2025). Turn right onto Titus Canyon Road and drive 2.7 miles (4.3 km) to where the two-way section ends. Park in the small parking area near the restrooms (see map page 102).*

Fall Canyon is presumably named for the sleek 18-foot (5.5-m) fall that interrupts the first narrows, but it could just as likely have been named for its colors. Yellow, tan, brown, and red hues shift along the towering canyon walls, lovely in the late afternoon. Fall Canyon is a great balance of easy access, spectacular canyon, and moderate hiking. It is the first canyon north of Titus Canyon.

The well-beaten trail starts on the north side of the parking area. This exposed trail follows the foot of the mountains, drops into a wash, then swings toward the canyon mouth. This is the type of hike you will do with your neck craned up to look at the soaring canyon walls. The angle of the canyon walls along with the very slight, almost imperceptible elevation gain creates its own world of strange angles, and you may not realize that you are slowly gaining elevation. At 0.9 mile (1.4 km) the hike enters **Fall Canyon,** and for the next 2.5 miles (4 km) you will be rewarded with sweeping cliffs and narrows that are finally broken by an **18-foot (5.5-m) fall.** This is a great stopping point; however, as at many of the canyons in this area, the best part lies just beyond.

A rock-climbing maneuver on the south (right) side of the fall will put you in the final

Red Wall Canyon

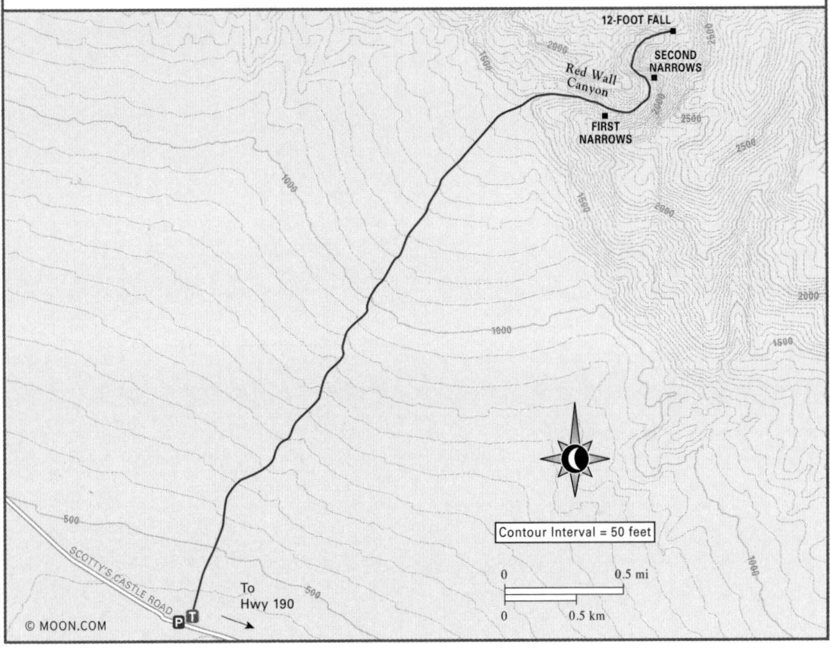

stretch of the **first narrows.** This last 0.3-mile (0.5-km) stretch is winding, polished, deep, and the slimmest of the narrows, a spectacular end to the hike.

Red Wall Canyon

Distance: *6.4 miles (10.3 km) round-trip to first narrows; 9.2 miles (14.8 km) round-trip to second narrows*

Duration: *3-6 hours*

Elevation gain: *1,520-2,420 feet (463-738 m)*

Effort: *Moderate*

Access: *Passenger vehicle from paved road*

Trailhead: *Park at mile 19 on Scotty's Castle Road north of where Titus Canyon Road crosses the main highway (see map page 103).*

Red Wall Canyon lives up to its name, boasting lofty red walls and red-walled narrows made of limestone and dolomite stained by oxides. Red Wall Canyon is in the Grapevine Mountains near the spectacular Titus Canyon Road. This whole area is graced with soaring canyon walls and scenically shifting landscapes.

Start hiking northeast across the alluvial fan toward the mouth of Red Wall Canyon. There will be several red rock formations in your line of sight, but keep your eyes on the apex of the fan where there is a red and brown gap. This gap is the mouth of Red Wall Canyon. Don't be thrown off by the red rock formations to the left (north).

Crossing the alluvial fan is tough and seemingly endless. Alluvial fans are made when water deposits sediment at the base of a mountain. By nature they are rocky and rise in elevation. If you're wondering why this part of the hike seems so hard, it's because you're slowly gaining elevation, although it's hard to tell without any perspective. You're walking on a tilted world. This section of the hike is also fully exposed, adding to the treadmill feeling. Sweet relief and payoff will be yours once you enter **Red Wall Canyon** at 2.3 miles

Mosaic Canyon

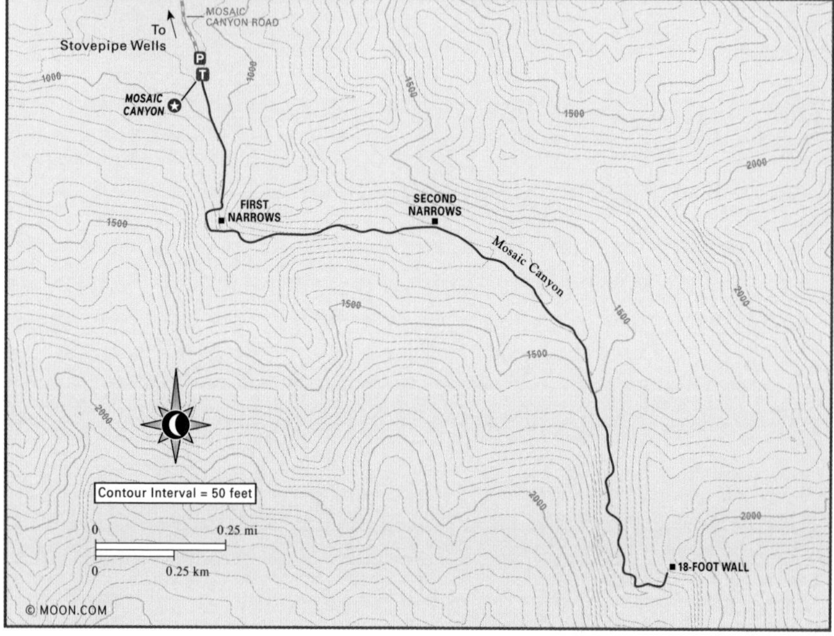

(3.7 km). There's a good chance you'll have the canyon to yourself.

The **narrows** start 0.5 mile (0.8 km) in, winding beneath rich red cliffs. For all the work you've put in to get here, the fun soon comes to an end at less than 0.5 mile (0.8 km) farther, when the canyon hits a **25-foot (7.6-m) blockage.** If you're a rock climber or an advanced hiker not afraid to attempt some rock-climbing moves, your fun may just be getting started. Climbing shoes are helpful here, as well as some experience.

Of course, the best narrows in the canyon are just beyond this snag. The **first narrows** continue with tortured and folded dolomite for your geological hiking adventure. In another 0.4 mile (0.6 km) you will reach the **second narrows,** which last for just under 1 mile (1.6 km), broken once by a **12-foot (3.7-m) fall;** again, a minimal amount of rock climbing comes in handy. Even if you're not rock climbing, the canyon holds a lot of beauty and solitude. Pick the route that suits you, and turn around when you need to.

TOP EXPERIENCE

★ Mosaic Canyon

Distance: *2.8 miles (4.5 km) round-trip (through second narrows)*
Duration: *1 hour*
Elevation gain: *730 feet (223 m)*
Effort: *Easy*
Access: *Passenger vehicles*
Trailhead: *Mosaic Canyon Road, on the western edge of Stovepipe Wells Village (on the same side of the road as Stovepipe Wells Hotel). Turn left (south) onto Mosaic Canyon Road and drive 2.4 miles (3.9 km) along a graded dirt road to a small parking area and restrooms at the end (see map page 104).*

Mosaic Canyon is a great introduction to the Cottonwood Mountains canyons. It's accessible but lovely, with a chance to wander through polished marble, colorful mosaic

Marble Canyon

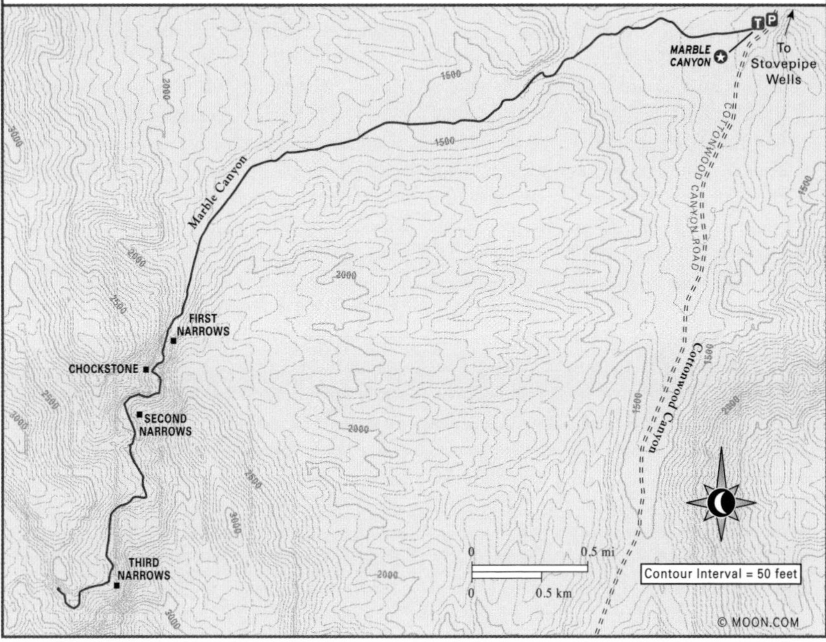

stone, and satisfying narrows. It's an easy drive to the trailhead just outside Stovepipe Wells, and the hike is short and sweet, making this one of the most popular hiking destinations in the Nevada Triangle.

The hike begins at the signed trailhead in the parking area and immediately enters a **broad wash,** which is the mouth of the canyon. The straightforward trail continues south into the canyon; ignore any side trails. The **first narrows**—pretty but shallow—begin almost immediately and wind between walls of polished marble and mosaics. These are a preview of the **second narrows,** which start behind a boulder jam at 1.1 miles (1.8 km). Bypass the boulders on the left with a moderate and tight scramble. The scenic second narrows twist through polished bedrock and rich mosaics, earning the canyon its name. The second narrows end too soon in 0.3 mile (0.5 km) at an **18-foot (5.5-m) wall.**

The hike through the first narrows can generally be made by anyone, as it follows the gravel canyon floor. It does require a few slippery rock scrambles over polished bedrock along the way.

★ Marble Canyon

Distance: *3.2 miles (5.1 km) round-trip (to end of second narrows)*
Duration: *2-4 hours*
Elevation gain: *445 feet (136 m)*
Effort: *Moderate*
Access: *High-clearance and 4WD vehicles*
Trailhead: *At the mouth of Marble Canyon, 13.4 miles (21.6 km) along Cottonwood Canyon Road. The first 8.6 miles (13.8 km) have some tricky sections but are doable with a high-clearance vehicle. A 4WD vehicle may be necessary for the remaining 4.8 miles (7.7 km), or you can hike this section* *(see map page 105).*

A rough, scenic drive into the Cottonwood Mountains pays off in the sculpted narrows and hidden petroglyphs of Marble Canyon. The petroglyphs are plentiful but faint, inspiring full attention to your surroundings. The real highlights are the canyon narrows, twisting in colorful corridors that shoot up to frame small pieces of the sky.

The drive to the canyon is half the fun, or half the battle, depending on your vehicle. Cottonwood Canyon Road is a dirt road that starts from Highway 190 in Stovepipe Wells, east of the campground entrance; look for a small airstrip. The road starts off with a bang, spitting through sand. Eventually the ground becomes more solid, but the road is washboard with some gravel near the end of this stretch.

At the 8.6-mile (13.8-km) mark, the road enters the Cottonwood Canyon wash and becomes much rougher. A 4WD vehicle is recommended past this point. If you continue driving, there are many places to turn around if needed. At 10.8 miles (17.4 km), the road splits off toward Cottonwood Canyon; stay right to continue to Marble Canyon. The road is marked with a very faint sign that is easy to miss. At 13.4 miles (21.6 km), the road ends at the canyon mouth.

The trail is immediately rewarding as it enters the sheer and colorful **narrows;** look for limestone beds with black chert nodules. This first section of the trail ends at a **chockstone** wedged between the canyon walls. Some people turn around here, but the **second narrows**—the most spectacular on this hike—lie just beyond this easily passable barrier. Bypass the chockstone with a trail on the right to head into the second narrows. They are deep, twisting, polished, and impressive. The sculpted high walls keep the passage cool and dim even in the heat of the day. The **third narrows** start in another 2.4 miles (3.9 km), after a walk through the mid-canyon. They're less impressive than the first two, but they have walls of polished black and white marble.

If you drove to the canyon mouth, a hike through the second narrows is easy and will take an hour or two; it's an easy day hike. Add another 3-4 hours of hiking if you parked before the wash.

BIKING

In the Stovepipe Wells region, smooth highways sail through iconic desert landscape, and rugged backcountry roads meander through scenic canyons. Consider cycling the bell curve of **Highway 190** through Stovepipe Wells to Furnace Creek, 25 miles (40 km) southeast. You might have to share the road with some cars, Jeeps towing campers, and RVs towing Jeeps, but there are services at either end to regroup and refresh with a cold beverage and snacks.

Salt Creek Road

Access via Hwy. 190, 4 miles (6.4 km) from the intersection with Scotty's Castle Rd.

Amid open desert, Salt Creek flows miraculously, its banks lined with pickleweed, framed by eroded mud hills, supporting a tiny pupfish population that isn't found anywhere else in the world. It makes a fine biking destination approximately 11 miles (17.7 km) east of Stovepipe Wells. Take paved Highway 190 east for approximately 7 miles (11.2 km) to the intersection with Scotty's Castle Road. Turn south. After another 4 miles (6.4 km), turn right onto the signed, graded dirt road for Salt Creek and follow it 1 mile to the parking area at the end. The full distance is 24 miles (38.6 km) and takes 2-3 hours.

Titus Canyon Road

Access via Hwy. 374, 2.7 miles (4.3 km) east of park boundary

Mountain biking Titus Canyon Road offers spectacular views through the canyon, towering rock formations, petroglyphs, a ghost town, and the impressive canyon narrows. The graded gravel road is 27 miles (43 km) one-way, starting off Highway 374 in Nevada, about 2.7 miles (4.3 km) east of the park boundary, and running west to the mouth of Titus Canyon at Scotty's Castle Road. Grades can be steep on Titus Canyon; fortunately they're usually working in your favor as they head downhill, losing elevation all the way to

1: Fall Canyon **2:** Mosaic Canyon **3:** Marble Canyon

1
2
3

the salt flats of the valley floor. There are a few cliff-huggers, and the route is the most popular backcountry driving road in the park, so you'll need to watch out for passing vehicles. Pull over if you want to stare in wonder and awe, which will be often. Allow 3-4 hours.

Titus Canyon Road was closed to cars and bicycles in 2024 due to flood damage. Check the National Park Service's Alerts page (www.nps.gov/deva/planyourvisit/conditions.htm) for current road conditions.

Cottonwood Canyon

Access via Hwy. 190 at Stovepipe Wells

The road through Cottonwood Canyon has the distinction of being the only road into the remote and lightly visited Cottonwood Mountains. It's a rugged backcountry road, sandy at the beginning and rocky in the canyon. The grade stays fairly even, and the payoff is a scenic canyon and green Cottonwood Springs. The road is 18 miles (29 km) one-way from its intersection with Highway 190 at Stovepipe Wells to the road's end at the first spring in Cottonwood Canyon. Allow 5-6 hours for a total of 36 miles (57.9 km) round-trip.

Rhyolite

Access via Beatty, NV

Gravel bike riders can make the short trip from Beatty, Nevada, to the ghost town of Rhyolite, about 6 miles (9.7 km) one-way, or 45 minutes to the east (allow 1-2 hours round trip). Close-up views of the open desert along Daylight Pass Road lead to the impressive ruins of the old ghost town. Once you arrive, your bicycle will continue to be an asset. The town of Rhyolite has graded dirt tracks crisscrossing its exposed acres leading to the cemetery, the red-light district, and the mine ruins.

CLIMBING

The area around Stovepipe Wells is a jackpot for rock climbers.

Grapevine Mountains

Fall Canyon and Red Wall Canyon are in the Grapevine Mountains, north of Titus Canyon. Both stand out for soaring canyon walls and lovely colors. While these are rewarding destinations for hikers, rock climbing will take those hikes to the next level.

The first stretch in **Fall Canyon** is accessible by hiking, but the canyon walls also offer rock-climbing opportunities. At 2.5 miles (4 km), the canyon hits its first major obstacle at an 18-foot (5.5-m) fall, a barrier for hikers and a boon for rock climbers. Polished narrows, the tightest in the canyon, lie just beyond.

In **Red Wall Canyon,** the canyon narrows start 2.8 miles (4.5 km) into the hike and 2.3 miles (3.7 km) above the canyon mouth. The narrows wind through beautiful red canyon walls and end way too soon at a 25-foot (7.6-m) wall. Climbing this obstruction gives you access to the final section of the narrows; of course, the nicest part is the most difficult to reach.

Funeral Mountains

Monarch Canyon, which is divided into upper and lower sections, is located in the northern Funeral Mountains. Highlights in **Upper Monarch Canyon** include the small but well-preserved remains of Indian Mine and Monarch Spring. **Lower Monarch Canyon** eventually leads to an unexpected waterfall, a product of Monarch Spring Creek spilling over the 180-foot (55-m) drop that divides the upper and lower canyons. The lower canyon has the best rock-climbing opportunities in the form of carved falls, found in the main side canyon about 2.2 miles (3.5 km) in.

Tucki Mountain

Mosaic Canyon, Grotto Canyon, and Stretched-Pebble Canyon are scenic neighbors, located south of Stovepipe Wells in the rock formations of Tucki Mountain. **Mosaic Canyon,** close to Stovepipe Wells, is one of the most popular and easily accessible hiking destinations in the area. Many visitors hike its lower canyon to see the polished mosaics and marble that form the undulating canyon walls. The first and second narrows offer opportunities for rock-climbing fun, while the third narrows provide access to a deep and twisting gorge.

Grotto Canyon is something of a sacred place among rock climbers—a web of narrows and falls, some in the deep shadows of Tucki Mountain, while others reach up briefly to the sunlit surface. Rock climbing is a necessity to explore this labyrinth. Grotto Canyon is east of Mosaic Canyon; access it 2.4 miles (3.9 km) east of Stovepipe Wells, across from the parking area for the Mesquite Flat Sand Dunes.

Food and Accommodations

STOVEPIPE WELLS

Stovepipe Wells has a campground, a hotel, a restaurant, a saloon, a gift shop, a convenience store, and a gas station with the cheapest gas inside the park boundaries.

Stovepipe Wells Hotel

51880 Hwy. 190; 760/786-7090; www.deathvalleyhotels.com; $144-226

All things being relative, Stovepipe Wells Hotel is centrally located. The hotel has 83 simple rooms, some renovated and a few original to Stovepipe Wells, that are substantially cheaper than those at Furnace Creek, making it a good place to set up base camp to explore the Nevada Triangle as well as to make forays into other regions of the park. Deluxe rooms include two queen beds or one king and have views of the Mesquite Flat Sand Dunes. Standard rooms have either two queens or one king. Patio rooms are original to the hotel and can accommodate one or two people (no cribs or roll-aways). All rooms have air-conditioning, TVs, minifridges, coffeemakers, and private baths with showers, and access to the swimming pool is included. Rooms do not have phones; Wi-Fi is available upon request.

The **Toll Road Restaurant** (760/786-7090; breakfast 7am-10:30am, lunch 11am-4:15pm, dinner 5pm-9pm daily year-round; $11-25) serves burgers, sandwiches, and limited featured entrées, typically pasta and steak. The **Badwater Saloon** (11:30am-10pm daily) serves the accompanying drinks. A continental breakfast and coffee are available for hotel guests.

Stovepipe Wells

The **General Store** (7am-10pm daily year-round) is really a glorified convenience store and gift shop. It sells souvenir items like specialty candy and T-shirts, plus a few basics like cold sodas, beer, ice, coffee, aspirin, and sunscreen, but don't expect to find any next-level camping supplies. On the upside, the store has the cheapest gas in the park.

Camping

Stovepipe Wells Campground

190 sites; first-come, first-served; mid-Oct.-mid-May; $14

Stovepipe Wells Campground has basic tent sites and RV sites without hookups. This is a central location for exploring a big swath of Death Valley. Beyond the prime location, the campground mostly resembles a parking lot, although the surrounding desert and Cottonwood Mountains are lovely in their austerity. The campground sits right at sea level, and the sites are completely exposed, which means it can be blazingly hot and there is no privacy. Prepare to become friends with your neighbors. Amenities include picnic tables, potable water, and flush toilets. There is access to the Stovepipe Wells Hotel pool and showers ($5 per day).

Stovepipe Wells RV Park

14 sites; year-round; $40

Within Stovepipe Wells Campground is Stovepipe Wells RV Park, with full hookup sites next to the General Store. Fees include access to the hotel's swimming pool and to Wi-Fi in the hotel lobby. Spots fill up quickly. Book online well in advance.

BACKCOUNTRY CAMPING

If you're adventurous and prepared, backcountry camping is certainly a more scenic option than the developed campground at Stovepipe Wells.

Backcountry camping is not allowed off Titus Canyon Road, Mosaic Canyon Road, Grotto Canyon Road, the first 8 miles (12.9 km) of Cottonwood Canyon Road, or on the valley floor from 2 miles (3.2 km) north of Stovepipe Wells down to Ashford Mill in the Furnace Creek region. This list limits your options since it covers most of the roads that enter the region's mountains and scenic bypasses.

Cottonwood Canyon allows camping after the first 8 miles (12.9 km). There are eight excellent established campsites nestled in the canyon against a scenic, rocky backdrop.

Beyond the Boundaries

Beatty, Nevada, is a frontier town and eastern gateway to Death Valley. It's across the state line on **Highway 374,** about 9 miles (14.5 km) east of the park boundary and a 45-minute drive northeast of Stovepipe Wells. Beatty is a good place to stop for **food, gas,** and **accommodations.**

Pahrump, Nevada, is not a travel destination, but it is the closest place to get **travel essentials** and **services** if you're in a pinch. Pahrump is 74 miles (119 km, 1 hour) southeast of Beatty via US 95 and Highway 160; it's about 100 miles (161 km, 2 hours) southeast of Stovepipe Wells. Consider it a place to stop for **gas** on the way to or from Las Vegas, but not much else.

BEATTY, NEVADA

Beatty started as a rail and supply stop when the nearby town of Rhyolite and the Bullfrog Mining District were booming in the early 1900s. Even as the gold ran out and towns in the area collapsed, Beatty remained a railroad hub until 1942, when the tracks were pulled up to contribute to the World War II effort. Since then, Beatty has shifted its focus to tourism, and still has a frontier-town feel. The town's main street is lined with a row of

Beatty, Nevada

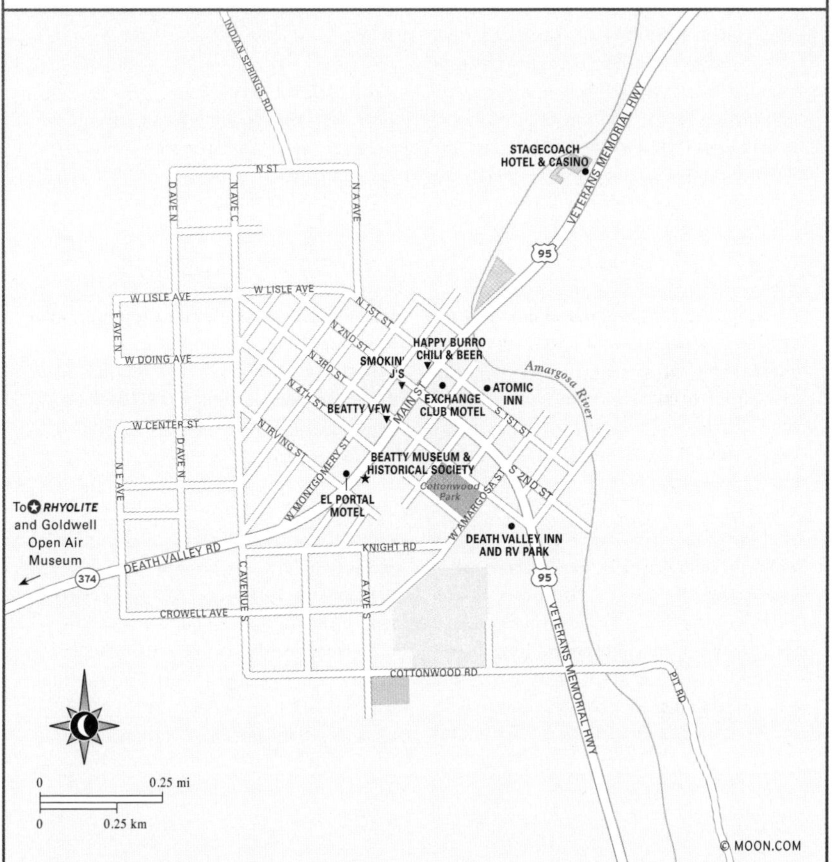

Western-facade saloons and restaurants, and you're likely to see wild burros roaming the hillsides. Beatty is a fine place to set up base camp for exploring Death Valley. It has restaurants, hotels, gas stations with cheap gas, a hardware store, a bank, and a small grocery store.

Beatty Museum and Historical Society

417 Main St.; 775/553-2303; www.beattymuseum.org; 10am-3pm daily; donation

You can learn more about Beatty's history and mining camps in the area at the Beatty Museum and Historical Society. The former church houses exhibits and artifacts highlighting the town's way of life during its railroad and mining heyday as well as research collections dedicated to the area's cultural and natural history.

Food

Happy Burro Chili & Beer

100 W. Main St.; 775/553-9099; noon-9pm Mon.-Thurs., noon-10pm Fri., 11am-10pm Sat., 11am-8pm Sun.; $6-10

The name of the Happy Burro Chili & Beer says it all. The service is friendly and the chili is delicious, made from tender pieces of steak and the perfect amount of seasoning. Plus, they bring out an arsenal of hot sauces and chili peppers to go with it. The patio can be filled with an eclectic desert mix of cowboys, old-timers, locals, bikers, European travelers, and other passers-through, recently escaped from Vegas. The limited options of chili and hot dogs (nothing vegetarian) are all cheap eats—a sign that you're outside the park boundaries. Pair that with an icy pitcher of beer and you can spend under $20.

Smokin' J's Barbecue

107 W. Main St.; 775/553-5160; noon-8pm daily; $11-28

A family-friendly joint in a town with limited options, Smokin' J's offers quality smoked brisket, pulled pork, burgers, sides, a kids' menu, and banana pudding as well as a beer selection. Order at the counter and dine inside the airy space or outside on the patio.

Beatty VFW

300 W. Main St.; 775/553-9312; 3pm-9pm daily; $9-17

When in Beatty, do what the locals do and have dinner at the VFW. The small kitchen turns out solidly executed burgers including a veggie option, French dips, fried baskets, and a shrimp scampi. Service is friendly even if you're not a local, and drinks are cheap. This is Nevada and it is a bar, so smoking is allowed, but there are a few nonsmoking tables. No one under 21 is permitted, but it offers takeout.

Accommodations

Beatty has several lodging options, from budget motels with charming signs to a casino hotel complex.

Stagecoach Hotel and Casino

900 US 95 N.; 775/553-2419; https://stagecoachhotelandcasino.com; from $98

For a whole lot of amenities, try the Stagecoach Hotel and Casino. What it lacks in charm and subtlety, it makes up for with an 80-room complex that includes a 24-hour casino, a bar, a Denny's diner, a pool, a hot tub, Wi-Fi, and satellite TV.

Exchange Club Motel

119 Main St.; 775/553-2333; https://exchangeclubbeattynv.com; from $99

The two-story property offers motel-style rooms including double queen, king, and king suites. They have done some eye-catching renovations to the exterior to entice visitors into the hotel's latest additions—a casino, speakeasy, and coffee shop are set to open in 2025.

Beatty

Atomic Inn

350 S. 1st St.; 775/553-2250; www.atomicinnbeatty.com; from $74

The Atomic Inn has converted 1980s military housing into a lightly themed budget motel that taps into the Area 51 alien mystique of the Nevada desert. The hotel's 54 rooms have fridges and free Wi-Fi.

El Portal Motel

Hwy. 374; 775/553-2912; www.elportalmotel.com; from $77

The family-run El Portal Motel offers 25 budget motel-style rooms, a seasonal pool, free Wi-Fi, and in-room fridges. The rooms are a bit dated, but the location and price make this a decent option for a stopover.

Death Valley Inn and RV Park

651 US 95 S.; 775/553-9400; https://deathvalleyinnmotel.com; from $113, RV sites $35-60

The Death Valley Inn and RV Park offers modern suite-style hotel rooms and RV accommodations with 39 pull-through sites with 50-amp hookups, restrooms, a dump station, laundry, showers, and a swimming pool.

Getting There

Beatty is right on US 95, about an hour south of Tonopah and 120 miles (193 km) northwest of Las Vegas. From Stovepipe Wells, drive 7 miles (11.3 km) east on Highway 190 to the junction with Scotty's Castle. Turn left and then right after 0.6 mile (1 km) onto Daylight Pass Road. Continue east for another 26 miles (42 km) to Beatty.

Scotty's Castle and the Eureka Valley

Somehow the words *remote* and *vast* don't quite do justice to the Eureka Valley.

These words are often used to describe Death Valley, but the Eureka Valley takes them to the next level. In this northernmost valley, the only existing modern building is the tiny pit toilet at Eureka Dunes. The trade-offs for all this remoteness are the lofty and pristine Eureka Dunes; the alien dry lake bed of "The Racetrack," where rocks move and leave tracks; the shining and desolate views of the Saline Valley from Ubehebe Peak, the highest peak in the Last Chance Range; and the copper mining camps, forgotten and few.

The one bastion of modern civilization, Scotty's Castle, exists thanks to Death Valley Scotty, an infamous swindler who convinced

Highlights

Look for ★ to find recommended sights, activities, dining, and lodging.

★ **Ubehebe Crater:** A powerful volcanic explosion created this crater, 600 feet (183 m) deep and 0.5 mile (0.8 km) across. An easy hike allows you to peer into its colorful depths (page 121).

★ **Eureka Dunes:** The Eureka Dunes are the northernmost destination in the park, so getting to them requires a special trip. Camp in the primitive campground at their base and enjoy sunset from their shining slopes (page 122).

★ **Lost Burro Mine:** There's something about the weathered camp and hand-painted sign that makes the Lost Burro Mine especially picturesque (page 124).

★ **The Racetrack:** This dry lake bed has long attracted visitors because of its strange moving rocks, which glide across its surface leaving trails (page 124).

★ **Ubehebe Peak:** This wild and rocky peak towers over the Racetrack with sweeping views of the Saline Valley (page 129).

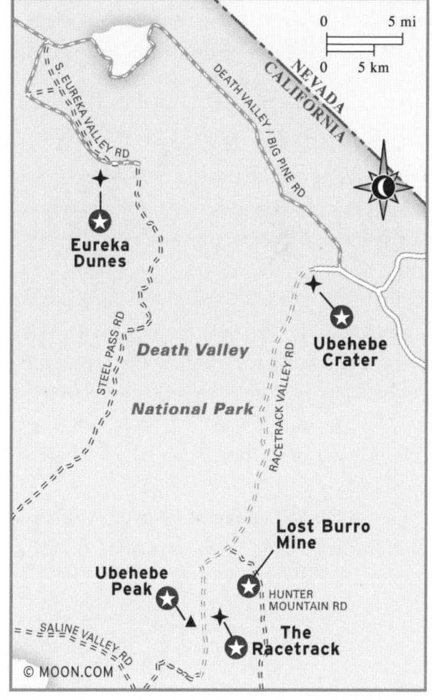

his benefactors to build this Spanish colonial-style mansion in the middle of the desert. The 1920s period-furnished castle stands high and incongruous in the rocky twists of the Grapevine Mountains. In October 2015, flash floods severely damaged its historical buildings, infrastructure, and grounds—a true display of the power water has on the Death Valley landscape. The mansion and grounds were still being restored in 2023 and are set to reopen in 2025.

The Last Chance Range divides this area, and its name alludes to the fact that it's the least accessible range in the least accessible region of the park. The sprawling and rugged Eureka Valley is studded with hidden gems. Come prepared for long drives on teeth-rattling roads and take the time to find them. Campgrounds are few and primitive, and there are no gas stations, restaurants, or lodging. The effort you spend planning to become self-sufficient will pay off with the quiet dazzle of pristine desert, gleaming sand dunes, and starry nights.

PLANNING YOUR TIME

Eureka Valley is the **least accessible** region in the park. It has one developed campground and two primitive campgrounds; there are no other accommodations, no services or food, and water is available only at Mesquite Spring Campground. Plan on roughing it and develop a strategy for exploring the area, especially if you want to spend most of your visit here. However, it is also possible to visit a destination or two in this region from one of the park hubs.

There are **three focal points** in this region: Scotty's Castle (set to reopen in 2025), Racetrack Valley, and Eureka Valley.

Scotty's Castle

Scotty's Castle was one of the most popular destinations in the park until October 2015, when flash floods severely damaged its historical buildings, infrastructure, and grounds. The 1920s mansion and grounds were still being restored in 2023, with plans to reopen in 2025. Scotty's Castle is within easy reach of both Furnace Creek and Stovepipe Wells, about an hour's drive along paved park roads.

Racetrack Valley

Despite its remoteness, **The Racetrack** is the biggest draw. Many visitors make the long and difficult drive to this eerie expanse of dry lake bed scattered with the faint trails of rocks that have skated across its surface. Access is via Racetrack Valley Road, 26 miles (42 km) of rutted, rocky washboard. Many people stay in Furnace Creek or Stovepipe Wells and turn the adventurous, 3- to 4-hour drive into a long day trip, but you could easily spend several days here. Set up camp at primitive **Homestake Dry Camp** and explore **Ubehebe Peak;** hidden mining camps like **Ubehebe Mine, Lost Burro Mine, Lippincott Mine,** and the **Goldbelt Mining District;** and even the occasional canyon.

Eureka Valley

To explore the Eureka Valley, start your trip at the **Eureka Dunes** before heading south into the park. Consider camping at the primitive **Eureka Dunes Dry Camp** so you're not rushed for time. Big Pine-Death Valley Road offers northern access to the Eureka Valley. Otherwise, it's a drive of 50 miles (81 km, 2 hours) from the town of Big Pine.

Previous: The Racetrack; Belvada Hotel; Lippincott Mine.

Scotty's Castle and the Eureka Valley

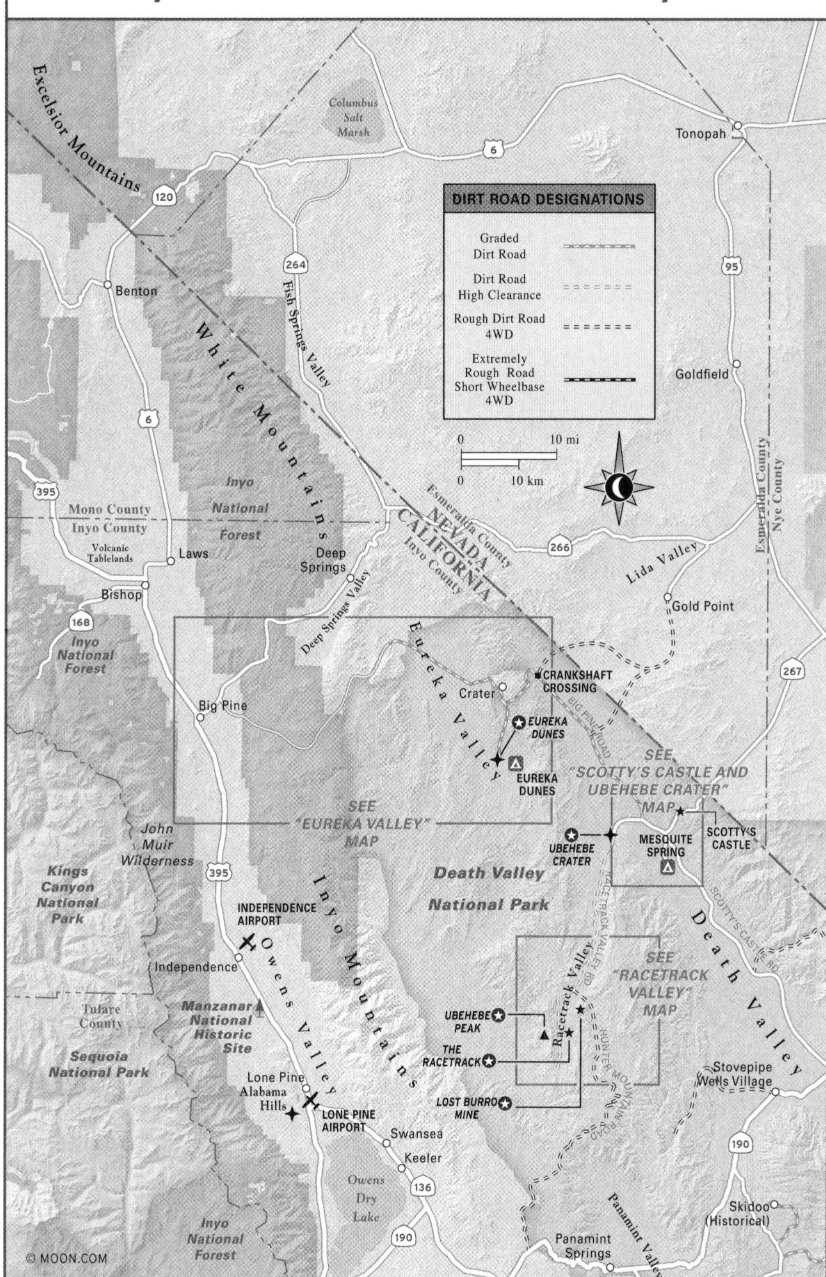

Exploring the Park

Scotty's Castle and the Eureka Valley are not places you just happen to pass through. The Eureka Valley is in the northwest region of the park, bounded by the Saline and Last Chance Ranges. To the east are the upper reaches of Death Valley itself, where it turns into a sun-baked wash running along the Nevada state line. The lower boundary of the region partly comprises the eastern flanks of the isolated Cottonwood Mountains. In a place where ruggedness and isolation are the norm, the Eureka Valley outdoes itself.

VISITOR CENTER

There is no official park hub in this region. When it reopens, **Scotty's Castle** will have a visitor center with park information and a ranger on duty during visitor center hours. The **Grapevine Ranger Station** at the junction of Scotty's Castle Road and Highway 267 is unstaffed; however, it has an automated kiosk where visitors can buy a park pass after hours. It accepts credit cards and cash. There are no park maps available at the kiosk. The closest staffed ranger station is at **Stovepipe Wells,** 42 miles (68 km) south.

PARK ENTRANCES

From the town of Big Pine on US 395, **Big Pine-Death Valley Road** travels east to loosely follow the northern boundary of the park. The road reaches the turnoff to the Eureka Dunes in about 40 miles (64 km) and the intersection with Bonnie Clare Road aka Scotty's Castle Road in 75 miles (121 km). *Note that Scotty's Castle Road (Hwy. 267) between Death Valley Road and US 95 was closed as of 2023. Check the park website for current road conditions.* Plan on more than two hours for the northern drive into Death Valley. The road is a long, graded gravel road maintained by Inyo County that can have rough washboard and washouts. After flooding it may be closed. Check road conditions. When open it offers a direct route to the remote and beautiful Eureka Dunes. If you choose to enter the park from Big Pine, be prepared, as the closest park services are 117 miles (188 km) away in Stovepipe Wells.

Due to the same flooding that damaged Scotty's Castle in 2015, Scotty's Castle Road was closed between Death Valley Road and the park boundary, where it becomes Highway 267. Road repairs are complete; however, the road will remain closed until construction in the Scotty's Castle Historic District is finished. Until the road reopens, it is not possible to access the park from Nevada via **Highway 267** and its junction with US 95, one of the main highways through Nevada. The next easiest route is from Beatty, Nevada, which is 62 miles (100 km) from Scotty's Castle. Park access is via Highway 374 and the junction of US 95. Beatty and the old mining town of Tonopah, Nevada, 94 miles (151 km) north of Beatty along US 95, can be used as a final stop for minor supplies before entering the park.

Gas and Services

Big Pine offers the closest services to the Eureka Dunes. The town has gas, accommodations, food, and basic groceries and supplies. If you are traveling a great distance, it is a good place to spend the night and regroup before entering the park. Otherwise, the closest services are at Stovepipe Wells, almost 117 miles (188 km) southeast via Big Pine-Death Valley Road and nearly four hours from Big Pine using this route. Stovepipe Wells has the cheapest gas in the park as well as a convenience store, a restaurant, and lodging.

Tonopah, Nevada, offers basic services, including accommodations, a grocery store, and gas. Although it is a small town, it is the closest service center to the Eureka Valley, 85 miles (137 km) north of Scotty's Castle. The closest services to Scotty's Castle are in **Beatty, Nevada,** 62 miles (100 km) southeast.

Driving Distances

From Big Pine to:	Distance	Duration
Grapevine Ranger Station (via Big Pine-Death Valley Rd.)	76 mi/122 km	3 hrs
Stovepipe Wells (via Hwy. 395/Hwy. 190)	117 mi/188 km	2 hrs
Furnace Creek (via Hwy. 395/Hwy. 190)	148 mi/238 km	2 hrs 45 min
Beatty, NV (via Hwy. 168/ Hwy. 266/I-95)	134 mi/216 km	2 hrs 30 min
Panamint Springs (via Hwy. 395/Hwy. 190)	92 mi/148 km	1 hr 30 min
The Racetrack (via Big Pine-Death Valley Rd./Hwy. 190)	102 mi/164 km	5 hrs
Eureka Dunes (via Big Pine-Death Valley Rd.)	50 mi/81 km	2 hrs
Gold Point, NV	90 mi/145 km	1 hr 45 min
Goldfield, NV (via Hwy. 166/Hwy. 168/US 95)	98 mi/158 km	2 hrs
Tonopah, NV (via Hwy. 166/Hwy. 168/US 95)	125 mi/201 km	2 hrs 20 min

From Grapevine Ranger Station to:	Distance	Duration
Stovepipe Wells	40 mi/64 km	45 min
Furnace Creek	51 mi/82 km	1 hr
Beatty, NV	59 mi/95 km	1 hr
Panamint Springs	71 mi/114 km	1 hr 20 min
The Racetrack	32 mi/52 km	2 hrs
Eureka Dunes	46 mi/74 km	1 hr 45 min
Gold Point, NV (via Hwy. 374/ Daylight Pass Rd./US 95)	125 mi/201 km	2 hrs
Goldfield, NV (via Hwy. 374/ Daylight Pass Rd./US 95)	125 mi/201 km	2 hrs
Tonopah, NV	152 mi/245 km	2 hrs 30 min
Big Pine (via Big Pine-Death Valley Rd.)	76 mi/122 km	3 hrs

Scotty's Castle and the Eureka Valley in One Day

- If you only have one day to spend in this region, you will have to choose: **Eureka Dunes** or **The Racetrack.** They are far-flung spots that require a full day to visit, but they are worthy of that time expenditure. They are both 2.5-3 hours one-way from Stovepipe Wells, the closest hub within the park.
- On your way to the Racetrack, make a stop at deep **Ubehebe Crater,** created by a powerful volcanic explosion.
- Once in the Racetrack Valley, several side trips add to the fun: Visit the remains of the **Lost Burro Mine** and add a hike to **Ubehebe Peak.**
- If the **Eureka Dunes** are calling your name, head north to their shimmering slopes, the northernmost destination in the park. A side trip to **Ubehebe Crater** is still on the way.
- Consider camping at the **primitive campsites** at the Racetrack or Eureka Dunes to end your day under the stars.

Sights

SCOTTY'S CASTLE

Planning Your Visit

Though **currently closed** due to the flash flooding in 2015 and a structural fire of the historical garage and visitor center in 2021, many repairs have been completed and the park plans to reopen the site to visitors. According to the NPS, Scotty's Castle is unlikely to open before late 2025. Scotty's Castle Road/Highway 267 is also closed between the Grapevine Ranger Station and US 95 to the east. You can get the latest information by calling 760/786-3200 or going online at www.nps.gov/deva.

Traditional tours of the house and grounds are on hold during renovation; however, the NPS in conjunction with the Death Valley National History Association (DVNHA) is offering **special flood recovery tours** (www.dvnha.org; most Sundays Jan.-Apr., advance reservations required; $25 plus ticketing fees). These walking tours of the grounds focus on the power of water on the Death Valley landscape as well as updates on the damage and repairs for this historical site. Each tour is limited to 10 participants, so book well in advance. Tours have a meet-up location and van shuttle to the site.

History

The history of Scotty's Castle is as unlikely as the sight of the turreted castle against the rocky hills. Walter Edward Scott, better known as **Death Valley Scotty,** was an infamous Death Valley swindler. Beginning in 1902 he convinced would-be investor after investor that he had found a rich gold deposit somewhere in Death Valley. To keep investors interested, he produced good-quality ore from other mines, but delayed actual visits to the mine with wild tales of armed gangs, ambushes, and the inferno-like environment and rough terrain of Death Valley. Ultimately his character proved to be the real investment.

What started as one of Scotty's usual swindles, this time of Chicago millionaires Albert and Bessie Johnson, turned into a lifelong friendship. Despite Albert Johnson's initial anger when he found out the claims were fraudulent, Scotty's colorful personality won him over. Scotty convinced his rich benefactors to build this Spanish colonial-style

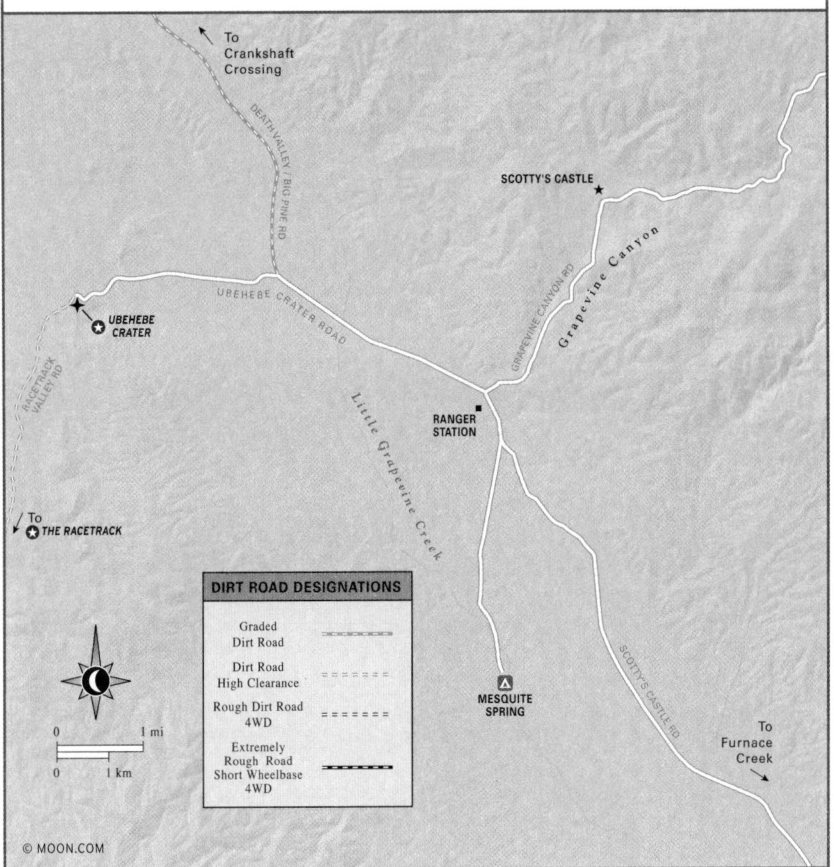

mansion, featuring stucco walls, a Spanish tile roof, and tiled walkways. Building began in 1922 and originally encompassed 1,600 acres (648 ha). When the stock market crashed in 1929, the Johnsons lost money and slowed construction on the house. Some sections, including a large swimming pool, were never fully finished.

The elaborate complex includes a main **two-story house,** an annex, and a **chiming clock tower.** The interior is fully furnished with the Johnsons' original possessions, including 1920s period furnishings, rich tapestries, mosaic tile work, arched doorways, and a spiral staircase. Underground tours reveal the inner workings of the house and thousands of tiles intended for the never completed pool.

Although Death Valley Scotty always claimed that the property was his, he lived in a humble cabin nearby. He is buried on a hill on the property, and his grave can be reached by a short hike.

EUREKA VALLEY

★ Ubehebe Crater

Access via Hwy. 190

Perhaps 300 years ago, a powerful volcanic

Eureka Valley

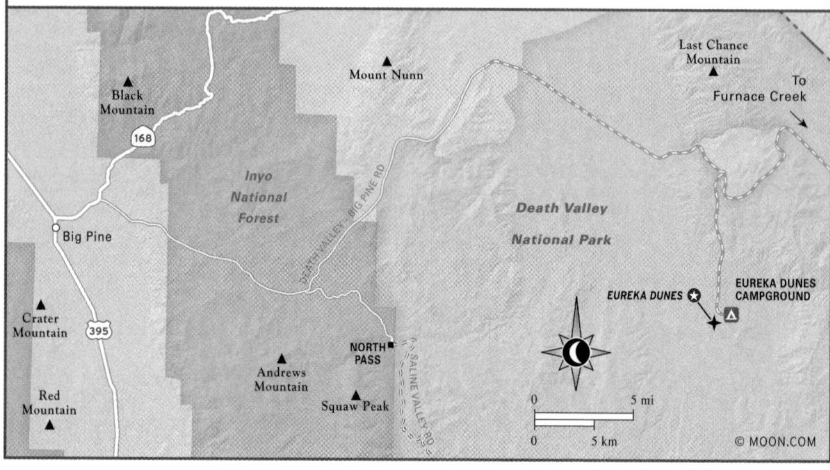

explosion created this colorful crater that measures 600 feet (183 m) deep and 0.5 mile (0.8 km) across. Ubehebe Crater is actually part of a cluster of volcanic craters that includes the **Little Hebe Crater,** a smaller and younger crater just to the west.

An easy 1.5-mile (2.4-km) round-trip **hike** around the edge of Ubehebe Crater allows you to peer down into the colorful depths of Ubehebe Crater, Little Hebe Crater, and other smaller craters. Known as maar volcanoes, the craters at Ubehebe were created through steam and gas explosions, formed when hot magma reached groundwater. Looking into their depths will give you a sense of the force of the explosion. It may be tempting to hike down to the bottom of the craters, and some people do, but it's harder to get back out.

You can see the Ubehebe Crater from the parking area, but the hike will give you better views of the cluster of craters and the striated peaks of the Last Chance Range. As you scan over the vista, especially to the north and east where you drove in, notice the cinder fields—dark layers of volcanic ash covering the landscape. The cinders came from Ubehebe Crater and will remind you again of the force of the explosion.

Directions

From Furnace Creek, head north on Highway 190 for 17 miles (27 km) to the junction with Scotty's Castle Road. Turn right and continue north for 33.4 miles (53.8 km) to the fork at the Grapevine Ranger Station. At the fork, continue left on Highway 190 for 5.4 miles (8.7 km) to the signed parking area for Ubehebe Crater. The drive takes about 80 minutes.

From Scotty's Castle, drive southwest on Scotty's Castle Road toward the intersection with Highway 190. At the intersection near the Grapevine Ranger Station, turn right onto Highway 190 and drive 5.4 miles (8.7 km) to the signed parking area for Ubehebe Crater. From Scotty's Castle, this is only a 20-minute drive.

TOP EXPERIENCE

★ Eureka Dunes

Access via Big Pine-Death Valley Rd. off of Hwy. 190

Isolated, beautiful, and pristine, the Eureka Dunes rise from the Eureka Valley floor, a gleaming mountain of sand framed by the rugged dark mountains of the Last Chance Range. The Eureka Dunes cover an area 3

Flash Floods

In October 2015, a series of unusual storms hit Death Valley in a patchwork of record-breaking rain events. Scotty's Castle got the worst of it, getting hit with over 3 inches (7.6 cm) of rain and hail in just five hours on already rain-saturated ground. Larger than any storm since **Scotty's Castle** was constructed in the 1920s, the torrent deposited debris 10 feet (3 m) high, slammed into the visitor center (historically the garage/long shed), wreaked havoc on the grounds and other historical buildings (paradoxically, this is the most water the swimming pool had ever seen at once), and wiped out Scotty's Castle Road, including over 1 mile (1.6 km) of historical concrete fence posts. The **Scotty's Castle** region is unlikely to reopen before late 2025. In summer 2022 and winter 2023, storms again hit Death Valley, shutting down the entire road network in the park, including paved and backcountry roads, and stranding visitors. The NPS, CalTrans, and local counties quickly repaired paved roads to give visitors access to Death Valley's most famous sights; however, many backcountry roads sustained sections of moderate to severe damage.

Despite Death Valley being famous for its bone-dry terrain, water has had a huge impact on the literal shape of the area. The sculpted waves of **Mosaic Canyon,** hidden slots of **Sidewinder Canyon,** and soaring **Natural Bridge** were all carved out by **flash floods.** Alluvial fans, the triangular rubble fields guarding the canyon mouths throughout Death Valley's mountain ranges, are continuously being formed by torrents of water. As flash floods sweep downcanyon, water picks up rubble, stones, plants, and artifacts as it gains momentum. If you've ever hiked or driven one of these fans, what appears as a smooth surface is jumbled and rugged, corrugated metal from mining shacks is twisted under the exposed sky, and boulders are stranded. Because of the starkness, the water that sweeps Death Valley does so with profound effect.

miles (4.8 km) wide and 1 mile (1.6 km) long; they are the tallest sand dunes in California, towering more than 680 feet (207 m) from the enclosed valley floor. At the Eureka Dunes, everything seems to be broken down to the most basic yet somehow most majestic elements.

It's hard to resist climbing the dunes—give in to this temptation. From the **Eureka Dunes Dry Camp** at the base of the dunes, a **hike** into the dunes may cover 0.5-2.5 miles (0.8-4 km), depending on how far you walk. The climb up is hard, one step forward and then a slide back. You may be climbing 300-600 feet (91-183 m), depending on which ridge you tackle. When you reach the ridgeline, you will be rewarded with more sculpted dunes and sweeping views of the valley.

In all this quiet sand and desert, it's possible that a slight rumbling sound may break the stillness. The Eureka Dunes are singing dunes, and small avalanches of sand sometimes resonate with a deep booming sound. And then there's the possibility that fighter planes from Nellis Air Force Base, to the east, may be out showing off. On one trip we were treated to an impressive air show directly in front of the dunes that had the early morning campers stopped in their tracks. The planes finally corkscrewed back over the mountains in a series of flashy moves.

In order to keep the dunes lovely for everyone, there is no sand-boarding on the dunes and no off-roading; the sand boards leave tracks that ruin the pristine views for everyone else.

Directions

The Eureka Dunes are the northernmost sight in the park, and getting to them requires a special trip—but if anything in the park deserves its own special trip, it's this. Fortunately, you can easily spend a night or two to soak in this special place. The **Eureka Dunes Dry Camp,** at the base of the dunes, has primitive camping spots with fire pits, picnic tables, and one pit toilet.

From Scotty's Castle, the dunes are

nearly 50 miles (81 km), or two hours away. Take Scotty's Castle Road southwest for 3 miles (4.8 km) to its intersection with Highway 190. Turn left onto Highway 190 and drive north for 2.8 miles (4.5 km) to the intersection with Big Pine-Death Valley Road. Turn right and continue 21.8 miles (35.1 km) to Crankshaft Crossing, marked by a sign and rusted crankshafts. Turn left to stay on Big Pine-Death Valley Road and continue 12.2 miles (19.6 km) to South Eureka Valley Road. Turn left to reach the dunes in 9.6 miles (15.4 km).

From Stovepipe Wells, the drive is 87 miles (140 km), and **from Furnace Creek,** it's 97 miles; both drives are just under three hours.

RACETRACK VALLEY

★ Lost Burro Mine

Access via Hunter Mountain Rd. off of Hwy. 190

There's something about the small weathered cabin, stone dugout, and hand-painted sign that make the Lost Burro Mine especially picturesque despite the austere setting. Tucked away in a hidden corner of the Racetrack Valley, this old gold-mining camp offers an easy stroll through a time capsule. A prospector who came across it while rounding up his burros filed the original claims for the mine in 1907. The mine chugged along in fits and starts until the 1970s, somehow managing to end up as one of the richest mines in the Ubehebe Mining District.

Today you'll see a site that's heavy on charm, but it's a humble spot that doesn't necessarily give any sign of its good track record producing gold for more than 60 years. The well-preserved **stamp mill** is easily visible on the hillside just behind the camp; its weathered timbers and metal inner workings are still standing. Strangely, no records remain to tell us if the mill was ever used. Beyond its charm, the Lost Burro Mine is interesting because it was a gold camp in a region where talc and copper were the backbone of the mining efforts.

Directions

Lost Burro Mine is accessed from **Racetrack Valley Road.** From Scotty's Castle, drive southwest on Scotty's Castle Road to its intersection with Highway 190. At the intersection near the Grapevine Ranger Station, turn right onto Highway 190 and drive 5.4 miles (8.7 km) to the signed parking area for Ubehebe Crater. Racetrack Valley Road splits off (a right turn) before the parking area and continues south into the Racetrack Valley. Follow the Racetrack Valley Road 19.4 miles (31.2 km) south to the signed Teakettle Junction. Turn left at Teakettle Junction toward Hunter Mountain, and in 3.2 miles (5.1 km) you will reach a four-way junction. The right spur ends at the Lost Burro Mine in 1.1 miles (1.8 km).

Racetrack Valley Road is a **maintained gravel road** up to the four-way junction, but the 1.1-mile (1.8-km) spur is for **4WD** vehicles. You might be able to do it with a high-clearance vehicle, but there is nowhere to turn around once you're committed. Without a 4WD vehicle, park at the four-way junction instead and walk the 1.1 miles (1.8 km) along the right spur to the camp. It's a pleasant walk and will give you views of scattered artifacts and windblown Joshua trees.

★ The Racetrack

Access via Racetrack Valley Rd. off of Hwy. 190

Maybe it's the long, white-knuckle road to the Racetrack that rattles you into a sort of delirium, but the place holds a special draw—the white expanse of dry lake bed, the dark rock formation called **The Grandstand,** the extreme stillness, and the faint tracks left by moving rocks all work together to create a surreal experience.

The dry lake bed that is the Racetrack has long attracted visitors to this extreme location because of its strangely **moving rocks,** which glide across its surface and leave trails. Until recently no one had ever seen the rocks

1: Scotty's Castle **2:** Eureka Dunes **3:** Ubehebe Crater **4:** The Racetrack

1
2
3
4

Racetrack Valley

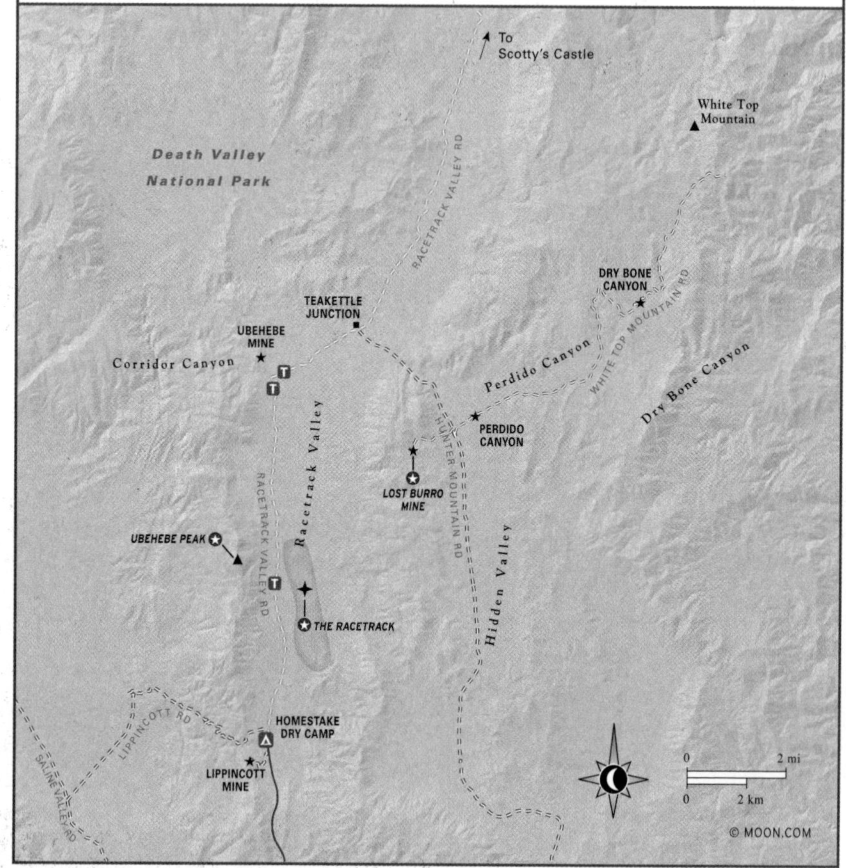

move. The evidence was the faint tracks on the expanse (known as the playa) left by the rocks themselves, which range from baseball- to boulder-size. Aliens, wind, water, and ice were popular theories. The code was cracked when researchers actually saw the rocks move. Thin ice sheets acted as sails in a light wind, enough to propel the rocks across the surface and create the mysterious tracks. But just because the mystery was solved, it doesn't make this place any less mystical.

An adventurous drive takes you to this special spot deep in the Racetrack Valley. From the start of Racetrack Valley Road, west of Ubehebe Crater, it's a long but scenic haul; take the time to pull over to appreciate the Joshua trees and soak in the desert air. You'll know you're getting close when you pass **Teakettle Junction** at 19.4 miles (31.2 km). A high-clearance vehicle is usually adequate along the length of Racetrack Valley Road, but a 4WD vehicle may be preferable or necessary at times due to flooding and washouts.

Count on a full day to visit the Racetrack. You may also be able to fit in a stop to the Ubehebe Crater and the Lost Burro Mine. If you plan to do any of the hikes in the area, get an even earlier start or camp at the primitive

Homestake Dry Camp at the southern end of the Racetrack.

Directions

Racetrack Valley Road is 26 miles (42 km) of very rough washboard road. A **high-clearance vehicle** is necessary, but you probably won't need a 4WD vehicle, depending on rains, washouts, and how recently the road has been graded. Access Racetrack Valley Road just west of Ubehebe Crater, about 20 minutes from Scotty's Castle.

At the intersection near the Grapevine Ranger Station, turn right onto Highway 190 and drive 5.4 miles (8.7 km) to the signed parking area for Ubehebe Crater. Racetrack Valley Road splits off (a right turn) before the parking area and continues south into the Racetrack Valley. Take Racetrack Valley Road 19.4 miles (31.2 km) south to the signed Teakettle Junction and continue south for another 6 miles (9.7 km) to the Racetrack.

From Furnace Creek or **Stovepipe Wells,** the drive takes more than three hours each way.

Teakettle Junction

Access via Racetrack Valley Rd. off of Hwy. 190

Adorned with an impressive array of colorful teakettles, the wooden sign that marks Teakettle Junction sits along Racetrack Valley Road 19.4 miles (31.2 km) from its beginning and marks the crossroads between **Racetrack Valley** and **Hidden Valley.** The signed junction points the way to Hunter Mountain (at the southern end of Hidden Valley), the Racetrack, and the Grapevine Ranger Station near Scotty's Castle. From here, it's only **6 miles (9.7 km) to the Racetrack.** After the long road, it's a great place for a break and a photo op.

No one really knows how the tradition started, but this famous landmark is so regularly loaded with old teakettles left by visitors that the National Park Service has to clear them out periodically.

The Grandstand

Access via Racetrack Valley Rd. off of Hwy. 190

From Teakettle Junction, Racetrack Valley Road continues south for 6 miles (9.7 km) to the first parking area, which is the turnout for The Grandstand (you can't miss it). It's hard to tear your eyes away from the dark mass of rocks rising incongruously from the center of the Racetrack's pale, smooth expanse. It's the only tall rock outcropping in the blinding flatness of the Racetrack, and it's hard to resist wanting to climb it.

To see the famous **moving rocks** in the area near the Grandstand, the best view is farther south. Continue south along Racetrack Valley Road for 2 more miles (3.2 km) and park in the small parking area at the southern end of the playa. Look carefully for the smooth, faint trails on the cracked playa surface (but avoid walking on the playa after a rain). You'll see rocks of varying size resting at the ends of these tracks.

Scenic Drives

Three main roads explore this region: Big Pine-Death Valley Road, South Eureka Valley Road, and Racetrack Valley Road. Of these, only Big Pine-Death Valley Road has paved sections, allows access to other parts of the park, and can serve as an entrance or exit route from the park, road conditions and vehicle permitting.

BIG PINE-DEATH VALLEY ROAD

Distance: *48 miles (77 km) one-way*
Duration: *2 hours*
Start: *Ubehebe Crater*
End: *Hwy. 168*
Road surface: *Gravel*
Vehicle: *High-clearance recommended*

When Highway 190, the main paved road through the park, ends at Ubehebe Crater, Big Pine-Death Valley Road takes over the north-south traverse. The 48-mile (77-km) road is mostly gravel with only 4 miles (6.4 km) of pavement. High clearance is recommended due to washboard and drainage dips. It runs along the northeastern side of the park to the northern park boundary, providing access to the **Eureka Valley Road** along the way. It continues to wander west through the Inyo Mountains, connecting with the paved Highway 168, which eventually intersects with US 395 and the town of Big Pine on the western side of the park in 70 miles (113 km).

SOUTH EUREKA VALLEY ROAD

Distance: *9.6 miles (15.4 km) one-way*
Duration: *30 minutes*
Start: *Big Pine-Death Valley Road*
End: *Eureka Dunes*
Road surface: *Sand*
Vehicle: *4WD required*

The high-clearance, dirt South Eureka Valley Road is less than 10 miles (16.1 km) long. It starts from Big Pine-Death Valley Road and ends at the Eureka Dunes, with deep sand and washboard near the dunes. An extremely rugged road for 4WD vehicles, **Steel Pass Road,** continues 29 miles (47 km) all the way to **Saline Valley Road** on the west side. The harrowing climb through the narrow, sharp dry falls of Dedeckera Canyon makes it suitable only for expert 4WD drivers with the right vehicle, extra gas and water, tools, and a detailed map.

RACETRACK VALLEY ROAD

Distance: *26 miles (42 km) one-way*
Duration: *1-2 hours*
Start: *Ubehebe Crater*
End: *The Racetrack Valley*
Road surface: *Gravel and rock*
Vehicle: *High-clearance required, off-road tires recommended*

Racetrack Valley Road may be an adventure if you're not used to driving on backcountry roads, or even if you are, depending on the time of year and the condition of the road. High clearance with off-road tires is recommended due to loose gravel and sharp rocks. This road is infamous for flat tires. From the end of paved Highway 190 at Ubehebe Crater, it drops 26 rocky miles (42 km) down to the Racetrack Valley in

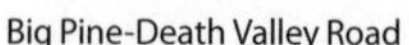
Big Pine-Death Valley Road

the eastern Cottonwood Mountains. The most popular spot is the Racetrack itself, but Racetrack Valley Road also leads to several other hikes and sites in the area. It officially ends at the **Homestake Dry Camp,** the primitive campground at the southern end of the Racetrack. From here, an incredibly rough Jeep road takes over to eventually connect with Saline Valley Road.

LIPPINCOTT MINE ROAD

Distance: *7 miles (11.3 km) one-way*
Duration: *2-3 hours*
Start: *Lippincott Mine, 1 mile (1.6 km) south of Homestake Dry Camp*
End: *Saline Valley Road*
Road surface: *Steep, rocky, not recommended*
Vehicle: *4WD required, not for casual travel*

Lippincott Mine Road has the dubious distinction of being the roughest road in Death Valley. Although it is only 7 miles (11.3 km) long, it has a reputation for being steep and narrow with cliff-edge washouts. Like Steel Pass Road from the Eureka Dunes, this road is only for expert 4WD drivers with the right vehicle, extra gas and water, tools, and a detailed map.

HUNTER MOUNTAIN ROAD

Distance: *24.5 miles (39.4 km) one-way*
Duration: *4-5 hours*
Start: *Teakettle Junction*
End: *Hwy. 190*
Road surface: *Clay, dirt, steep, and rocky in places, icy snow in winter*
Vehicle: *4WD required*

Hunter Mountain Road connects to the Racetrack Valley at Teakettle Junction. It heads south through the Hidden Valley and Goldbelt Mining District (scant remains) for 24.5 miles (39.4 km), roughly paralleling Racetrack Valley Road, until it intersects with the southern end of the Saline Valley Road at the South Pass. From the South Pass, it is an additional 15.5 miles (24.9 km, 1 hour) to reach pavement at Highway 190, 13.5 miles (21.7 km) west of Panamint Springs. It is a 4WD road with rough patches and steep grades; snow and ice may make it impassable in winter.

Recreation

HIKING

★ Ubehebe Peak

Distance: *3.8-6 miles (6.1-9.7 km) round-trip*
Duration: *2-5 hours*
Elevation gain: *2,000 feet (610 m)*
Effort: *Difficult*
Access: *High-clearance vehicle*
Trailhead: *The Racetrack via Racetrack Valley Road. Begin the trail from the Grandstand turnout, the first parking area you come to at the Racetrack. You will see the rock-lined trail heading up the mountain from the parking lot* *(see map page 131).*

This wild and rocky peak is the highest summit towering over the Racetrack in the Last Chance Range. It's a difficult climb, but you'll have sweeping views of the Racetrack the whole way up.

This hike looks intimidating from the trailhead—and it is. It's steep nearly the whole way. Unlike many Death Valley hikes, however, there is actually a trail, built by miners as a mule trail to haul out copper ore. The trail's wide start might momentarily lull you into thinking you can breeze through the hike, but a glance up at the summit will bring you to your senses. The elevation gain—nearly 2,000 feet (610 m) from the trailhead to the summit—starts quickly and never relents.

From the trailhead, **switchbacks** climb the eastern face of the mountain to the **divide** in 1.9 miles (3.1 km). At the mountain divide, the hike really pays off with views of the Saline Valley on one side and the Racetrack Valley on the other. From here you can continue up to the summit or call it a day and head back down for a 3.8-mile (6.1-km)

Scotty's Castle Hikes

Ubehebe Mine

Trail	Effort	Distance	Duration
Ubehebe Mine	Easy	0.7 mi/1.1 km one-way	1 hr
Lippincott Mine	Easy	1.1 mi/1.8 km one-way	1 hr
Corridor Canyon	Moderate	2.9-3.8 mi/4.7-6.1 km one-way	4-5 hrs
★ **Ubehebe Peak**	Difficult	3.8-6 mi/6.1-9.7 km rt	2-5 hrs

round-trip hike in about two hours. The good news is that even if you only make it to the divide, you'll still have great views and bragging rights.

At the divide there is a **junction.** To continue to the summit, take the **left trail** to stay on the main trail; it is more worn and obvious than a fainter trail that veers to the right, which leads down to copper mines and the Saline Valley. Past the divide, the trail gets even steeper and cuts through sheer mountain walls. After traversing a **lower summit,** you reach the **saddle,** the end of the trail, in 0.6 mile (1 km). From here, you must navigate a rocky ridge for 0.3 mile (0.5 km) to the windswept **summit** of Ubehebe Peak to the south. If you just make it to the lower summit, don't feel too bad—the views from here are spectacular as well.

Ubehebe Mine

Distance: *0.7 mile (1.1 km) one-way*
Duration: *1 hour*
Elevation gain: *Negligible*
Effort: *Easy*
Access: *High-clearance vehicle*
Trailhead: *On Racetrack Valley Road, drive 19.4 miles (31.2 km) south to the signed Teakettle Junction. Continue south on Racetrack Valley Road past Teakettle Junction for 2.2 miles (3.5 km). The road to Ubehebe Mine is a spur on the right (west) side of the road. Depending on how tough your vehicle is, you might be able to drive to the camp, but the best idea is to park* *(see map page 132).*

Ubehebe Peak

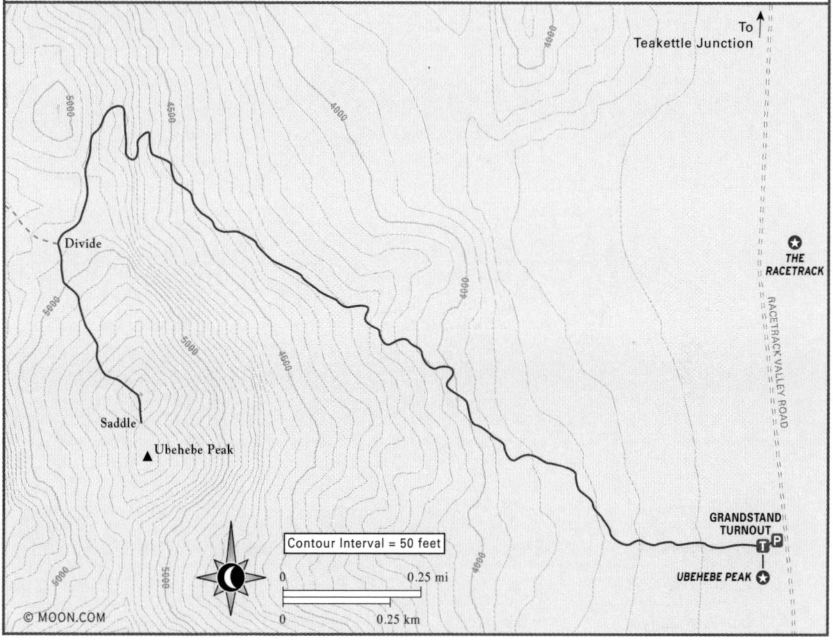

Like many Death Valley mining camps, Ubehebe Mine tells a story of isolation and perseverance. History and weather have made the camp picturesque, but the daily grind was probably not quite so charming. Ubehebe Mine started as a copper mine, but lead quickly became the focus. The mine chugged along from 1906 to 1968, until its tunnels were stripped clean. Blink and you'll miss the turnoff to this far-flung lead mining camp in the Last Chance Mountains.

From **Racetrack Valley Road,** walk 0.7 mile (1.1 km) west following the worn-out **old spur mining road.** At the **camp,** you'll find a well-preserved headframe, the remains of one cabin, and other mining artifacts, including an old cook stove, metal storage drums, and railroad tracks to nowhere. It's a beautiful, quiet spot and an easy walk.

Visiting the old mine makes a great side trip on your way out to the Racetrack. The long drive will give you a sense of the massive effort it took to get materials, vehicles, and people out here, even though they might have had it comparatively easy; Racetrack Valley Road was newly completed when the mine was starting up and conveniently passed within 1 mile (1.6 km).

Corridor Canyon

Distance: *2.9-3.8 miles (4.7-6.1 km) one-way*
Duration: *4-5 hours*
Elevation gain: *880-1,050 feet (268-320 m)*
Effort: *Moderate*
Access: *High-clearance vehicle*
Trailhead: *Take Racetrack Valley Road 19.4 miles (31.2 km) south to the signed Teakettle Junction. Continue south past Teakettle Junction for 2.2 miles (3.5 km). The 0.7-mile (1.1-km) spur to the Ubehebe Mine is on the right. It's an old rutted road, and it may be better to park and walk from here. The trail starts in the wash to the west of Ubehebe Mine (see map page 132).*

You can visit an old mining camp as well as get in a lovely canyon hike and some good

Corridor Canyon

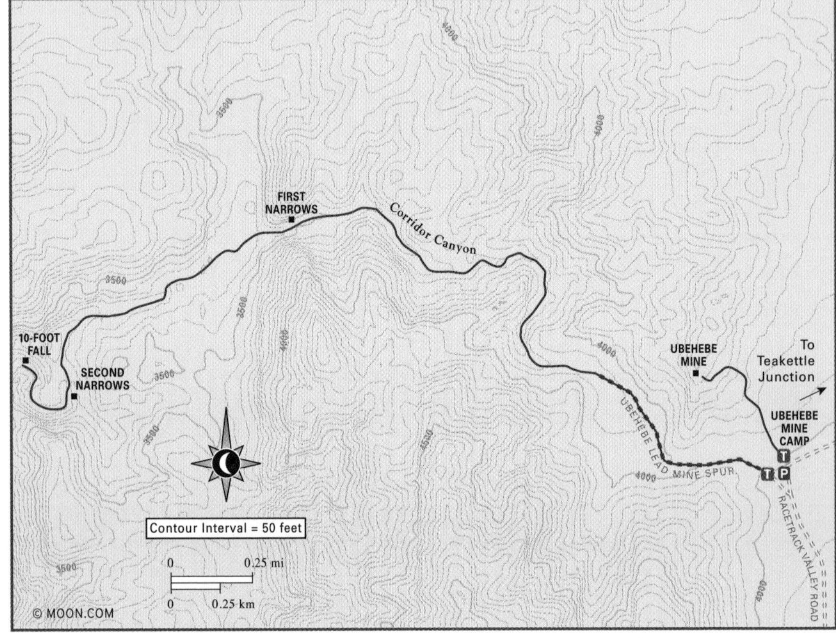

climbing with a visit to **Corridor Canyon,** which starts from the Ubehebe Mine Camp. Corridor Canyon has polished falls, narrows, a slot canyon, and the strangely special corridor with its soaring smooth walls. Hiking up-canyon toward Round Valley gives you short narrows and falls.

Corridor Canyon is part of a network of canyons. This quiet hike passes through two sets of narrows, a slot canyon, and walls of fossils before entering its namesake corridor, sliced straight and smooth for the better part of 1 mile (1.6 km). Corridor Canyon is a local name that you won't find on maps, but you can find your way to it by starting at the Ubehebe Mine.

From **Ubehebe Mine Camp,** continue west into the wash and past the camp; you will reach the smooth, gray walls of the **first narrows** in 1.5 miles (2.4 km). After only 0.2 mile (0.3 km), the narrows open to a wash in the wide main canyon. This broad landscape continues for about 1 mile (1.6 km). Make sure to orient yourself where you've walked out of the narrows; don't mistakenly follow the broad wash trending north instead of re-entering the first narrows to the east on your return.

At 2.9 miles (4.7 km), the **second set of narrows** begins. Shortly after, these are interrupted by a polished **10-foot (3-m) limestone fall.** There are handholds to climb it, but it may stop some hikers. You can turn around here for a 5.8-mile (9.3-km) round-trip hike from the Ubehebe Mine Camp, or 7.2 miles (11.6 km) round-trip from Racetrack Valley Road.

Beyond the fall, the **second narrows** continue, leading to a deep **slot canyon** in 0.2 mile (0.3 km). Just beyond the slot, **Corridor Canyon** intersects at a right angle—the highlight of this hike. You can explore in either direction, but the long, straight corridor runs to the left (south); not only is it impressive, but also there are fewer falls and impediments along this stretch. The lower corridor runs for about 0.7 mile (1.1 km), ending where the canyon makes a nearly 180-degree turn. Turning right leads to a network of canyons that end at Saline Valley Road in 9 miles (14.5 km), but navigation requires preparation, a topo map, and excellent backcountry skills. To make the return hike from the lower end of the corridor, retrace your steps 0.7 mile (1.1 km) to the slot canyon and follow your original path east to the Ubehebe Mine Camp in 3.1 miles (5 km).

Lippincott Mine

Distance: *1.1 miles (1.8 km) one-way*
Duration: *1 hour*
Elevation gain: *90 feet (27 m)*
Effort: *Easy*
Access: *High-clearance vehicle*
Trailhead: *Take Racetrack Valley Road 19.4 miles (31.2 km) south to Teakettle Junction. Continue south on Racetrack Valley Road for another 8 miles (12.9 km) to the southern end of the Racetrack playa. Continue another 2 miles (3.2 km) south beyond the playa for a total of 29.4 miles (47.3 km) from Highway 190. A small campground sign and a few graded spaces mark Homestake Dry Camp.*

Despite its extreme remoteness and lack of good access to water, the Lippincott Mine was the most active mine in the Racetrack area, producing lead, silver, and zinc in its nearly 50-year run. Evidence of this history is scattered all around the site. Old foundations, equipment, and beautifully weathered timbers are set against gorgeous views of the Racetrack Valley.

From **Homestake Dry Camp,** walk south for 0.4 mile (0.6 km) along **Racetrack Valley Road;** look for the mine's yellow water truck visible in the distance. Cabin foundations, old cook stoves, and other evidence of mine life lie scattered along the trail. The road **forks** at the water truck. The main road, **Lippincott Mine Road,** heads west up a ridge, arriving at the Lippincott Mine and great views of the Saline Valley in another 0.7 mile (1.1 km).

The Lippincott Mine Road has the dubious distinction of being one of the scariest roads in Death Valley. A road map of Death Valley shows a black-and-red color scheme, meaning you're likely to get stuck or break your vehicle. Fortunately, you don't actually have to drive this road to see the Lippincott Mine.

BIKING

You have to be a real go-getter, rewarded by a serious physical challenge, to cycle in this region. Road biking is tough due to the lack of paved roads, and the glass-smooth highways that slice through the park's other regions are mostly absent. That said, there are a few options.

Racetrack Valley Road

Access via Ubehebe Crater

Joshua trees and the hills of the Cottonwood and Last Chance Mountains make for a shifting and scenic backdrop along the fairly flat Racetrack Valley Road. It's also incredibly long: 26 miles (42 km) one-way (2-3 hours) from where it leaves the pavement at Ubehebe Crater all the way to the Racetrack—an ambitious goal for this ride. Even if you don't make it the whole way, Racetrack Valley Road is still scenic and rewarding. Depending on the time of year or day of the week, you may have the place to yourself, or you may watch a steady stream of Jeeps parade past you on their way to the Racetrack. There is no shoulder on this rocky road, but you'll be able to see and hear cars coming easily in time to pull off to the side.

Hidden Valley Road

Access via Teakettle Junction

At Teakettle Junction, turn left (southeast) to head south into Hidden Valley. Hidden Valley Road is quiet, scenic, and mostly flat, with little traffic. The road runs through several historical mining areas to the base of Hunter Mountain. (A side trip to the Lost Burro Mine is accessible via a 1.1-mile (1.8 km) right spur, 3.2 miles (5.1 km) south of Teakettle Junction.) At 13 miles (20.9 km) one-way (1-2 hours), the route ends at the **Goldbelt Spring Mining District,** which lies north of Hunter Mountain. The Goldbelt Camp has some cabin remains and an old truck. Beyond the camp, the road becomes rougher (for 4WD vehicles) and climbs steeply over Hunter Mountain.

Big Pine-Death Valley Road

Access via Mesquite Spring Campground

Big Pine-Death Valley Road runs 25 miles (40 km) one-way (2-3 hours) from the Mesquite Spring Campground area north toward Crankshaft Crossing and will give you the classic sweeping expanses of upper Death Valley. From the intersection of Mesquite Spring Campground with Highway 190, the road is paved for 2.8 miles (4.5 km) before continuing as a graded dirt road for 21.8 miles (35.1 km) north to Crankshaft Crossing. Crankshaft Crossing, named for an old crankshaft that was left as a landmark, is just a jog in the road as it heads up toward the junction with Eureka Dunes Road, but it's as good a destination as any. This area is exposed and lies at a low elevation, so set a good endpoint or turn around when you feel like it.

CLIMBING

The Cottonwood Mountains offer some fine climbing, with long, secluded canyons and good narrows. Dry Bone Canyon, Bighorn Gorge, and Perdido Canyon offer passages laced with fossils and polished falls. All are located in the White Top Mountain area of the Cottonwood Mountains at elevations over 6,000 feet (1,829 m), which means that the temperatures are cooler than at any of the valley floors.

Cottonwood Mountains

Just past the mouth of **Perdido Canyon,** dark canyon walls line a wash sprinkled with Joshua trees, providing good opportunities for climbing. Beyond this, fossil hunting is the best game here.

The leaning walls and Joshua trees of **Dry Bone Canyon** eventually lead to three sets of narrows with some polished falls for climbing. There is a formidable slot canyon after the first narrows that you will have to work your way into via a bypass and climb down from a ridge if you want to enter its depths. There are also petroglyphs in Dry Bone Canyon, a reward for carefully picking your way through this remote spot.

Bighorn Gorge has colorful high walls, polished narrows, and falls and chockstones. The falls dividing the canyon's three sets of narrows provide climbing opportunities. There are also side canyons to explore. If you're lucky, you'll see the canyon's namesake animal.

Directions

All three canyons can be accessed via Racetrack Valley Road. From Highway 190 at Ubehebe Crater, take Racetrack Valley Road 19.4 miles (31.2 km) to Teakettle Junction. At Teakettle Junction, turn left toward Hunter Mountain. Drive 3.2 miles (5.1 km) and turn left at White Top Mountain Road, just past Lost Burro Gap.

For **Perdido Canyon,** drive an additional 0.8 mile (1.3 km) and park. Perdido Canyon is 0.5 mile (0.8 km) north of the road behind the low hills at the end of the alluvial fan. For **Dry Bone Canyon,** drive 7.4 miles (11.9 km) to the wash of Dry Bone Canyon and park. For **Bighorn Gorge,** drive 10 miles (16.1 km) to a fork in the road and a divide overlooking Bighorn Gorge. Take the right spur and park at the turnout on the right. Bighorn Gorge is a wide, forested opening to the north. Beyond the wash of Dry Bone Canyon, the road gets considerably worse. When visiting Bighorn Gorge, it is also possible to park at the Dry Bone Canyon wash and hike 2.7 miles (4.3 km) to the mouth of Bighorn Gorge.

As with many sites in the vicinity of the Racetrack, getting here is half the battle. Be sure to budget at least **1.5 hours for the drive** from Ubehebe Crater. It's also a good idea to camp near the canyon mouth the night before to get an early start.

Food and Accommodations

There are **no services** in the Eureka Valley region—no hotels, restaurants, or gas. The park hubs of Stovepipe Wells and Furnace Creek are a 1- to 3-hour drive south, and the closest services are in Big Pine, about 50 miles (81 km, 2 hours) west. Bring your own food and water, make sure you have enough gas, and be prepared to camp.

CAMPING

Mesquite Spring

30 sites; first-come, first-served; year-round; $14

Mesquite Spring is the only developed campground in the region. It's a pretty campground, dotted with mesquite bushes and set along low hills less than 5 miles (8 km) west from Scotty's Castle. At an elevation of 1,800 feet (549 m), the temperature is bearable most of the year, except summer. Sites are exposed, but they're spaced far enough apart that you get some privacy. Though reservations aren't accepted, it's likely you'll get a spot May-October. Since this is one of the few campgrounds open year-round, the campground can fill on summer holiday weekends including Memorial Day, Fourth of July, and Labor Day. Stop to reserve a spot first thing in the morning; pay via an automated kiosk, which takes credit cards and cash, and put your receipt on the site marker. Amenities include picnic tables, fire pits, and access to flush toilets and water; there are no RV hookups, but there is a dump station.

Directions

The turnoff to Mesquite Spring is 0.6 mile (1 km) south of the intersection of Scotty's Castle Road and Highway 190; from the turnoff, continue 1.9 miles (3.1 km) south to the campground.

Eureka Dunes Campground

First-come, first-served; camping not recommended in summer; free

Eureka Dunes Campground is a small, primitively maintained campground located at an elevation of 2,880 feet (878 m) at the base of the dunes. It is only accessible to high-clearance vehicles. A stay here puts you within easy distance of the remote Eureka Dunes. Sites have fire pits and sturdy cement picnic tables; there is neither water nor electrical hookups, but there is a pit toilet. The area is open year-round, but camping in summer is not recommended due to high temperatures.

Directions

To get here from the intersection of Scotty's Castle Road and Highway 190, head north for 2.8 miles (4.5 km) and continue on Big Pine-Death Valley Road for 21.8 miles (35.1 km). At Crankshaft Crossing, marked by a sign and rusted crankshafts, turn left (southwest) to stay on Big Pine-Death Valley Road. The turnoff to Eureka Dry Camp is 12.2 miles (19.6 km) farther. Turn left onto the South Eureka Valley Road and drive 9.6 miles (15.4 km) to the campground at the base of the dunes. Big Pine-Death Valley Road and Eureka Dunes Road are graded dirt roads most suitable for high-clearance vehicles.

Homestake Dry Camp

First-come, first-served; free

In Racetrack Valley, your best bet is Homestake Dry Camp, an extremely remote, primitively maintained campground at 3,785 feet (1,154 m) elevation. Four camp spaces have been graded so that you can comfortably park and pitch a tent. There are no amenities, no toilet facilities, and no fires are permitted. Bring your own water. Despite the lack of amenities, the campground serves as a good base to explore the surrounding area—Ubehebe Peak, the Racetrack, Lippincott Mine, Ubehebe Lead Mine, and Corridor Canyon. The campground is only accessible by high-clearance vehicles with all-terrain tires.

Directions

To reach Homestake Dry Camp, access the Racetrack Valley Road from where it leaves paved Highway 190 and drive 19.4 miles (31.2 km) south to Teakettle Junction. Continue south on the Racetrack Valley Road for 8 miles (12.9 km) to the southern end of the Racetrack playa. Continue 2 miles (3.2 km) south beyond the playa, a total of 29.4 miles (47.3 km) from Highway 190, to a small campground sign and the graded camping spaces that mark Homestake Campground.

Backcountry Camping

Only a few roads traverse this region, so it's important to know where backcountry car camping is allowed. Camping is allowed along Racetrack Valley Road after the first mile, but there is no camping between Teakettle Junction and Homestake Dry Camp.

Camping is allowed along Hidden Valley Road away from mining sites. Turning left at Teakettle Junction and heading south along Hidden Valley Road toward **Hunter Mountain,** the road is passable in a high-clearance vehicle for 13 miles (20.9 km) to the area around Goldbelt Spring, at the base of Hunter Mountain. Beyond Goldbelt Spring, the road becomes 4WD-only as it climbs Hunter Mountain.

If you plan to rock-climb or explore the canyons in the Cottonwood Mountains, camp in the vicinity of **White Top Mountain.** White Top Mountain Road is off Hidden Valley Road; take the left turn at the junction 3.2 miles (5.1 km) south of Teakettle Junction. The road begins as passable for high-clearance vehicles, then requires a 4WD vehicle after about 5 miles (8 km). There is no camping allowed at Ubehebe Mine or Lost Burro Mine.

Historic Central Nevada

US 95

Heading beyond the boundaries into Nevada, it's easy to lose yourself on the open highway, following highway signs that lure you farther and farther north to **Goldfield,** then **Tonopah,** time capsules of the American West. From **Gold Point,** it is 15 miles (24 km) east to US 95 at the Lida Junction (Hwy. 266 and US 95), then another 15 miles (24 km) north to Goldfield (plan 30 minutes for the drive).

Gold Point

66 miles (106 km) north of Beatty, NV; free, donations appreciated

The ghost town of Gold Point, Nevada, was a mining camp in the 1860s, but it didn't become a town until 1908. The town had the usual story of boom and bust, although it was never completely abandoned. In the early 1980s, two friends began buying up the mostly abandoned property and stabilizing the cabins and town buildings. Today, the result is a Wild West gem—gritty, isolated, and authentic, open to travelers with a fascination for these kinds of tucked-away pieces of history. You can visit the town as well as stay in one of the historical houses or miner's cabins (reservations goldpointghosttown@gmail.com or 775/482-4635; reserve 7-14 days in advance, 2-night minimum stay; $150-200).

Owner Herb Robbins and his business partner, Walt Kremin, are usually on the premises, willing to open the saloon and share a beer and stories. You can wander the town to your heart's content and take pictures, but please keep in mind that this is private property with several year-round residents, so be respectful. A word to the wise: The good folks of Gold Point, Nevada, value their fierce independence and have made every effort to establish an autonomous community—avoid talking politics.

Getting There

From **Beatty, Nevada,** it is 66 miles (106 km) north (1 hour) to Gold Point via Highways 95 and 266. From Highway 266, the paved Highway 774 heads south to Gold Point in 8 miles (12.9 km).

From the **Grapevine Ranger Station** within the park, head south on Scotty's Castle Road toward Stovepipe Wells and drive 33 miles (53 km) to the junction with Daylight Pass Road (Hwy. 374). Turn left on Daylight Pass Road to head northeast toward Beatty. Drive 26 miles (42 km) to the junction with US 95. Turn left onto US 95 and drive north for 52 miles (84 km). At the signed Lida Junction, turn left onto Highway 266 and continue 7.2 miles (11.6 km). Turn left onto paved Highway 774, signed with a historical marker for Gold Point, and continue 8 miles (12.9 km). The drive from Grapevine Junction will take about two hours. Note that Scotty's Castle Road (Hwy. 267) is closed between Grapevine Junction and US 95 to the east.

Goldfield

66 miles (106 km) north of Beatty, NV on US 95, 1 hour

It's hard to know what to expect from the town of Goldfield, Nevada. Various reports contradict each other, reporting it to be a ghost town, dead and boarded up, a haunted relic, or an active place with quaint businesses. I can't say that Goldfield is alive and well, but it's not entirely dead either. More than 200 people call the town home, and it has plenty to recommend it, including early-1900s architecture, well-preserved buildings from the gold-mining era, a main street with trading posts and shops open for business, and one of the oldest continuously operating saloons in the state. Goldfield had its boom between 1905 and 1910, and for a brief time it was the largest city in Nevada.

Goldfield has a saloon (which doubles as a motel), one restaurant, and basic **supplies,** but no gas. The closest **gas** is in Tonopah, 27 miles (43 km) north, a drive of about 30 minutes.

Goldfield Hotel

69-79 Columbia Ave.

Evidence of the boom remains, especially the reputedly haunted Goldfield Hotel. The hotel is impressive in its brick grandeur, proud and sadly abandoned. Many people have made

the ghost town of Gold Point

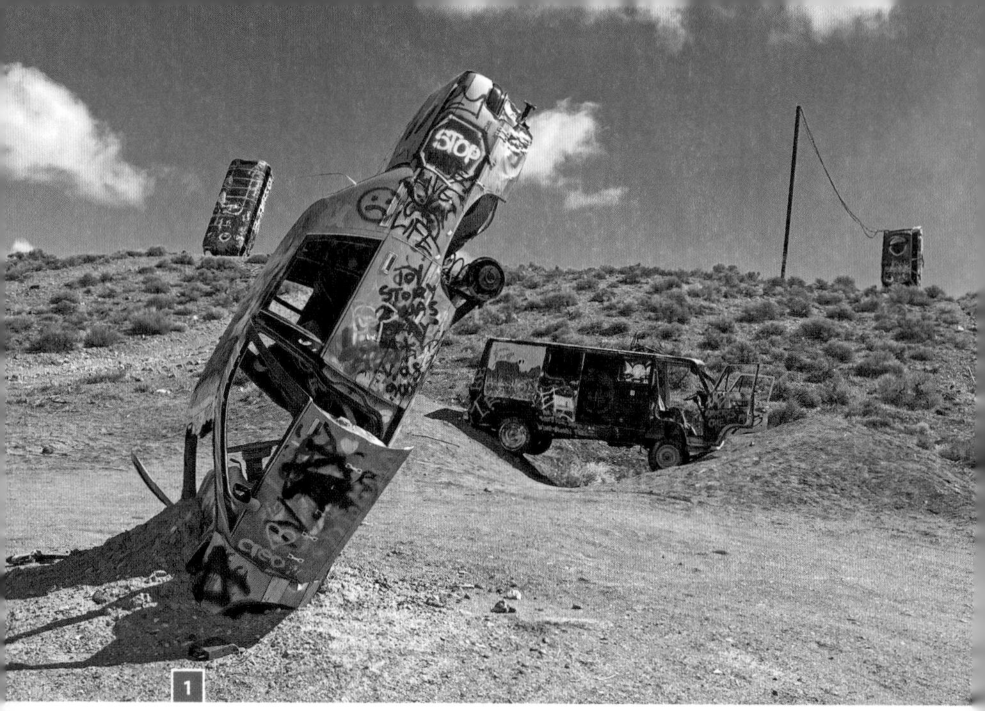

1

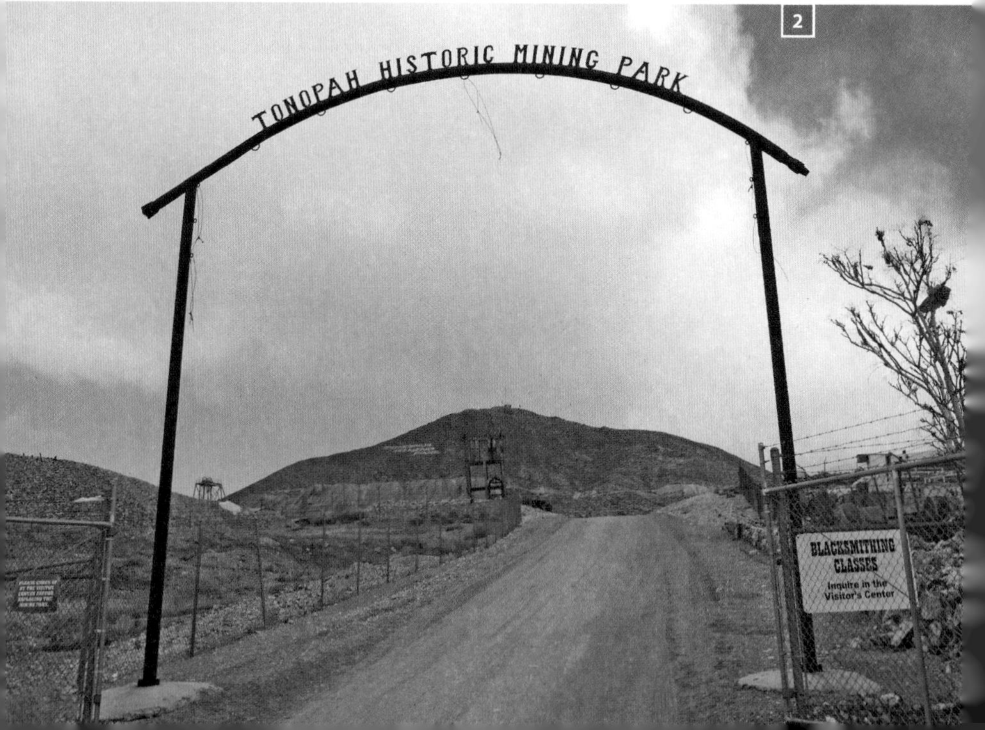

2

TONOPAH HISTORIC MINING PARK
BLACKSMITHING CLASSES
Inquire in the Visitor's Center

plans to restore the hotel over the years, but somehow it's never worked out.

International Car Forest of the Last Church

775/485-3560; free

One mile (1.6 km) southeast from downtown Goldfield, the International Car Forest of the Last Church roots us in this century with over 40 scrap cars studded, Stonehenge-style, into the earth and covered with graffiti. The creation of Nevada artists Mark Rippie and Chad Sorg, the site is free to wander.

Santa Fe Saloon

925 N. 5th Ave.; 775/485-3431; 2pm-10pm daily

The Santa Fe Saloon is a great place to quench your thirst and meet the locals. The rail yard of the Bullfrog and Goldfield Railroad is across from the bar, an interesting place to explore.

Dinky Diner

323 Crook Ave.; 775/485-3231; 8am-6pm Mon.-Sat., 8am-2pm Sun.; $7-17

Goldfield has one working restaurant—the Dinky Diner. The tiny diner turns out home-cooked American comfort food like biscuits and gravy and omelets for breakfast, adding burgers and sandwiches for lunch.

Tonopah

93 miles (150 km) north of Beatty, NV; www.tonopahnevada.com

The small town of Tonopah, Nevada, 27 miles (43 km) north of Goldfield on US 95, is an interesting mix of old and new. In Nevada, known as the Silver State, Tonopah was queen of the silver camps. The Western town has a historical downtown, two luxuriously renovated historical hotels, a brewery, and a mining park.

Tonopah Historic Mining Park

110 Burro Ave.; 775/482-9274; http://tonopahhistoricminingpark.com; 9am-5pm daily; $5 adults, $3 for seniors, children 8-17, and Nevadans, free for veterans, military, and children 7 and under

The Tonopah Historic Mining Park features a walking tour of mining tunnels, mine buildings, and artifacts. Guided off-road vehicle tours are available by advance reservation.

Mizpah Hotel

100 N. Main St.; 775/482-3030; www.themizpahhotel.com; from $159

The reportedly haunted Mizpah Hotel was built in 1907. It eventually fell into decline but was given an impressive makeover in 2011. The hotel is decorated in period furnishings, deep reds, and carved wood. A fully stocked and staffed **bar** (4:30pm-9pm daily) runs along a wall of leaded glass windows with marble tables and plush seating in addition to the bar. The **Pittman Café** (6am-10am Mon.-Fri., 6am-11am Sat.-Sun.) provides breakfast daily. The **Jack Dempsey Room,** a small full-service restaurant with period-elegant decor, is open for dinner nightly (5pm-9pm). The Mizpah is by far the best game in town for dinner and refreshments, filled with locals and travelers alike.

★ Belvada Hotel

101 S. Main St.; 775/277-3950; www.belvadahotel.com; from $159

The owners of the Mizpah Hotel bought a historical building across the street and turned it into the luxury boutique Belvada Hotel. Originally built in 1906 as the Nevada State Bank and Trust Building, it boasted posh tenants until the Great Depression when it was turned into the Belvada Apartments and eventually abandoned. A major renovation in 2020 turned it into a beautifully restored landmark with 40 thoughtfully decorated rooms. A coffee shop on the lobby floor serves Lavazza coffee drinks and pastries (6am-11am daily).

1: International Car Forest of the Last Church
2: Tonopah Historic Mining Park

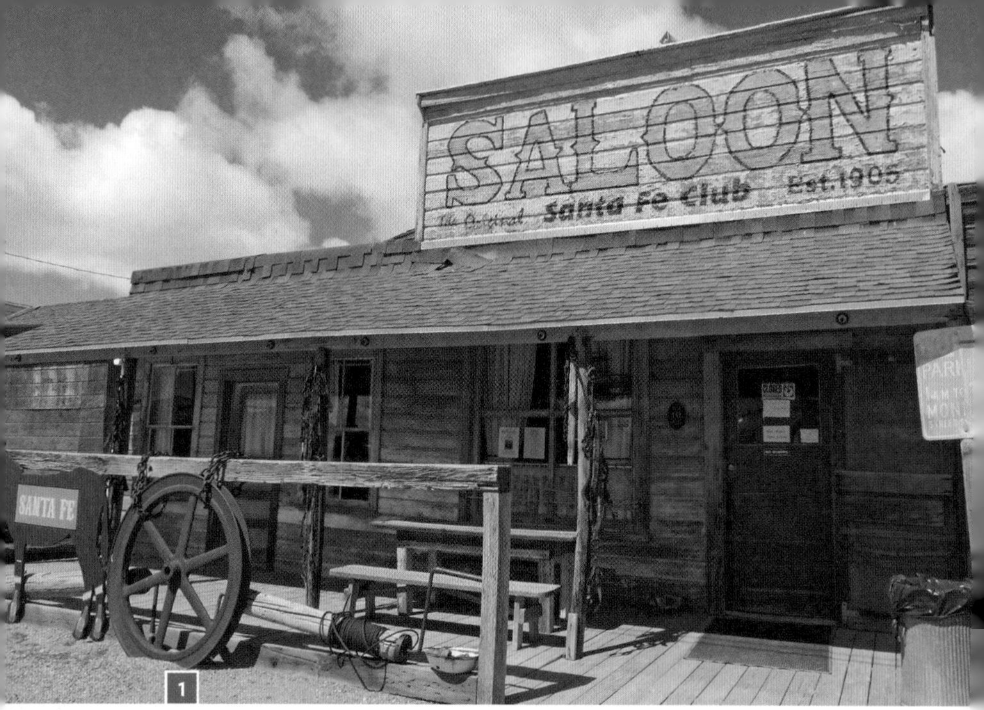

1

2

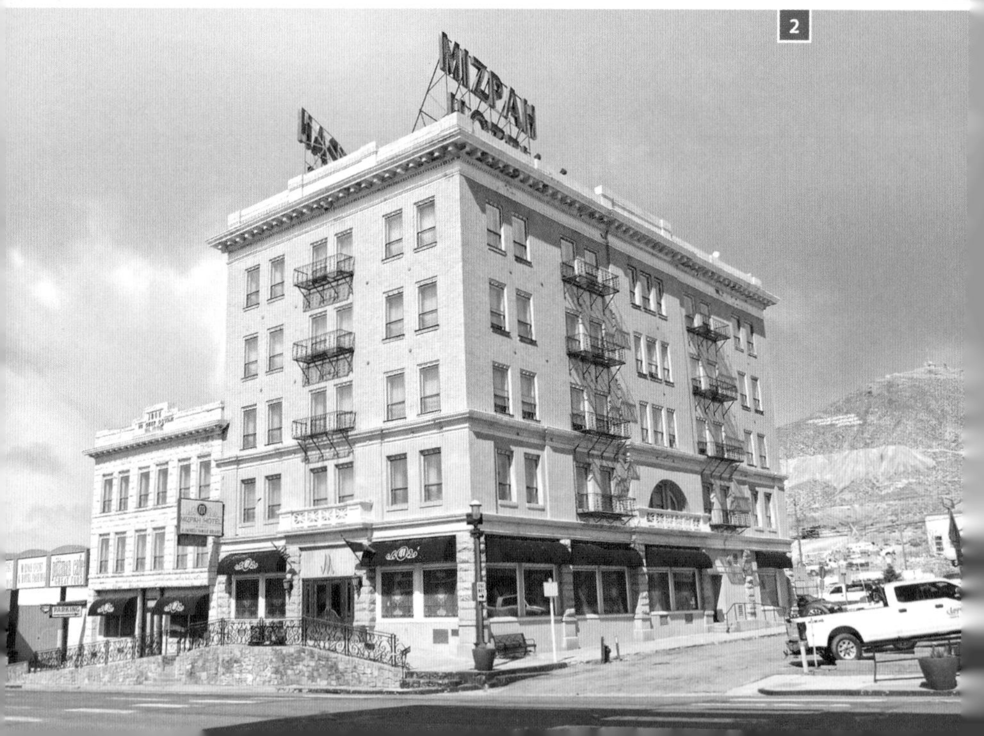

Tonopah Brewing Company

315 S. Main St.; 775/482-2000; https://tonopahbrewing.com; 11am-10pm daily; $10-18

Well-executed brews and barbecue anchor this brewpub situated in a spare, industrial space. Heaping mounds of slow-cooked pork and brisket top sandwiches and plates accompanied by classic sides like mac and cheese. Other items from the fryer and a dessert list ensure you won't leave hungry.

Getting There

It is possible to reach the towns of Gold Point, Goldfield, and Tonopah from Beatty, Nevada. From Beatty, Goldfield is 66 miles (106 km) north along US 95. Tonopah is another 27 miles (43 km) north. The turnoff to Gold Point is 52 miles (84 km) north of the center of Beatty.

When the Scotty's Castle Road is open, it is possible to reach the towns of Gold Point, Goldfield, and Tonopah, Nevada, from Scotty's Castle via Highway 267 to US 95, 26 miles (42 km) east. From the junction with US 95, turn north to reach Goldfield in 30 miles (48 km) and Tonopah in 58 miles (93 km). The turnoff to Gold Point is 16 miles (26 km) north of the junction of US 95 and Highway 267.

1: the Santa Fe Saloon in Goldfield, one of the oldest continuously operating saloons in Nevada
2: the historic Mizpah Hotel

Panamint Springs and the Saline Valley

Part of the joy of visiting Death Valley is feeling like you've come to the ends of the earth—or even that you've landed on another planet entirely—as you gaze over the cracked and alien landscape.

In the western Panamint Mountains, the relatively high number of creeks and springs, historical sites, and network of old roads that just won't die create a different kind of planet—one more akin to *Indiana Jones and the Temple of Doom* than *Star Wars*.

Old cabins and ghost camps are scattered through the wrinkled folds of the Panamints; some are forgotten, rotting into trickling springs, while others remain well visited by those still caught by the camps' mystique. Tales of silver spread through the mountains and caused

Highlights

Look for ★ to find recommended sights, activities, dining, and lodging.

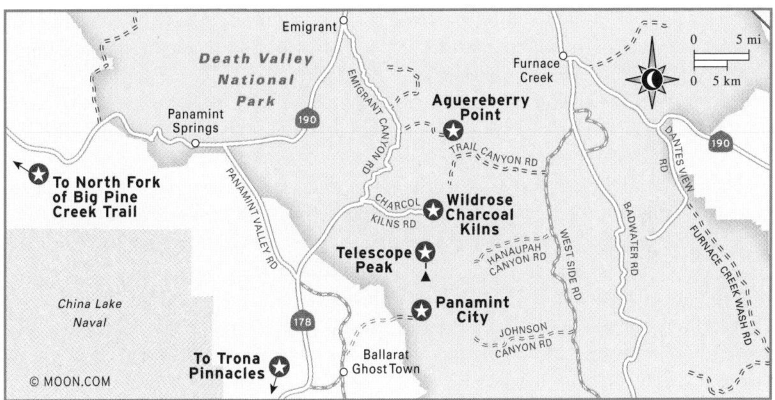

★ **Wildrose Charcoal Kilns:** Once used to make charcoal for the mining efforts in the area, these kilns now stand as works of hand-engineered beauty (page 149).

★ **Aguereberry Point:** A hermit miner built the road to Aguereberry Point. His legacy is most certainly the spectacular views of the valley that he gave us (page 151).

★ **Panamint City:** The hike to this silver-boom ghost town follows the scenic but strenuous Surprise Canyon. Crawl over waterfalls, trudge through creek beds, and scramble over rocks—all the while wondering how a road was ever built here (page 167).

★ **Telescope Peak:** The 14-mile (22.5-km) hike to reach this highest peak in the park is well worth every switchback, affording sweeping views of Death Valley to the east and Panamint Valley to the west (page 169).

★ **North Fork of Big Pine Creek Trail:** All of the hiking in the John Muir Wilderness is spectacular, but this trail near Big Pine is particularly special, with over five glacial lakes (page 186).

★ **Trona Pinnacles:** Limestone tufa formations rise from an ancient lake bed to create a place that is haunting and powerful (page 204).

towns like Panamint City to swell and burst. Today, some time and effort can take you to these hulks of history to marvel at the sheer determination that got people and equipment up to these remote and rugged locations. The western Panamint canyons are wet by comparison to the rest of Death Valley, and it's not unheard of for a flood to wipe out everything in its path, scouring a canyon down to the bare rock, marooning trucks and equipment. Of course, there's the marvel of seeing water in the desert, plummeting down a canyon to form waterfalls and pools or gurgling along the surface, all making for a wet and wild hiking experience.

Joshua tree forests, a salt lake, and one washboard road make the Saline Valley a time capsule of tourism—Death Valley before Death Valley was a destination. In the Saline Valley, you give up your civilized right to a cell phone for a quiet and beautifully varied landscape. Driving Saline Valley Road will take you past rarely visited sand dunes and give you access to quiet ghost camps and scenic canyons.

Death Valley is known for its contrasts, and the Panamint Springs area is no exception. The drop from Telescope Peak, the highest mountain in the park, down to the valley floor is a dizzying 11,049 feet (3,368 m), higher than the South Rim of the Grand Canyon. Enter Surprise Canyon from the blazing-hot ghost town of Ballarat only to have to fight your way through dense greenery, scrambling over waterfalls and past sculpted white canyon narrows. Winter brings snow and ice at the higher elevations; summer brings scorching sun. All year long brings the possibility of wind that has no scruples about scooping up your camping equipment to sacrifice to the desert gods. This western side of Death Valley will grab you with the stinging silence of the Saline Valley and rope you in with the untamed canyons of the Panamint Mountains. People come back year after year and season after season—it's different every time.

PLANNING YOUR TIME

This wild and diverse region is a favorite of the 4WD crowd as well as desert history buffs—4WD trails and historical sites dominate the landscape. But developing a plan of attack is key. The jutting elevation, long and lonely roads, twisting canyons, and adventurous hikes guarantee that you won't be able to do everything in one driving tour. Pick your sights, pick your drives, pick your hikes, and explore this region with a full tank of gas and everything else you need to survive, including water.

Concentrate your exploration on **three areas:** the Emigrant and Wildrose Canyon area, the western Panamint canyons, and the Saline Valley. Beyond the park boundaries, the John Muir Wilderness offers camping, hiking, fishing, and spectacular alpine scenery.

Emigrant and Wildrose Canyon Area

The Emigrant Canyon and Wildrose Canyon area is the **most accessible** in this region. Setting up a nice base camp at the **Wildrose Campground** allows easy access to notable hikes as well as fragments of mining history around the Harrisburg Flats region. Plan **three days:** one day to hike Telescope Peak, one to hike Wildrose Peak and visit the charcoal kilns, and one day to see everything else.

The high mountain elevations in this region mean that it might be possible to extend the Death Valley season and escape the summer heat. Telescope Peak, the highest point in the park, has snow most of the year, and most of the campgrounds in nearby Wildrose Canyon are only open **late spring-fall,** the opposite of the schedule in the rest of the park. The upper-elevation hikes are best during early summer.

Previous: Wildrose Charcoal Kilns; a creek in the Eastern Sierra along the John Muir Trail; Trona Pinnacles.

Panamint Springs and the Saline Valley

To Bishop
Big Pine
Inyo National Forest
SEE "BIG PINE" MAP
NORTH FORK OF BIG PINE CREEK TRAIL
395
SEE "THE SALINE VALLEY" MAP
Eureka Dunes
DEATH VALLEY / BIG PINE RD
267
Death Valley National Park
Ubehebe Crater
WAUCOBA SALINE ROAD
Kings Canyon National Park
INDEPENDENCE AIRPORT
Independence
Palm Spring
Nye County
NEVADA
CALIFORNIA
Inyo County
Dry Bone Canyon
The Racetrack
SALINE VALLEY ROAD
Alabama Hills Regional Recreation Area
Lone Pine
Mexican Spring
Marble Canyon
190
Stovepipe Wells Village
SEE "JOHN MUIR WILDERNESS" MAP
GRAPEVINE CANYON
136
Sequoia National Park
Owens Lake
NORTH PASS
Inyo National Forest
Panamint Springs
PANAMINT VALLEY RD
AGUEREBERRY POINT
Olancha
SEE "EMIGRANT AND WILDROSE CANYONS" MAP
WILDROSE CHARCOAL KILNS
TELESCOPE PEAK
PANAMINT CITY
Inyo County
Tulare County
FS 22S05
Ballarat Ghost Town
China Lake Naval Weapons Center
Sequoia National Forest
178
Anvil Spring
NINE MILE CANYON RD
SIERRA WAY 431
Trona
Inyo County
Kern County
TRONA AIRPORT
Inyo County
San Bernardino County
Onyx
Indian Wells
Inyokern
MATURANGO MUSEUM
Ridgecrest
TRONA PINNACLES
14
Inyo County
San Bernardino County
0 10 mi
0 10 km
Red Rock Canyon
REDROCK RANDSBURG RD

DIRT ROAD DESIGNATIONS
Graded Dirt Road
Dirt Road High Clearance
Rough Dirt Road 4WD
Extremely Rough Road Short Wheelbase 4WD

Western Panamint Canyons

Ballarat, on the eastern edge of the Panamint Valley against the western Panamint Mountains, is a good jumping-off point for exploring the Panamint canyons with a **4WD vehicle** or **backpacking.** All canyon roads require a 4WD vehicle, but it is still possible to explore some wonderful canyon hikes with a regular SUV. Even a passenger car can access a few special places.

Saline Valley

All areas of the Panamint Springs region are remote, but the Saline Valley might win a competition for which gets the fewest visitors. **Saline Valley Road** traverses the region, beginning in the north near the town of Big Pine and intersecting with Highway 190 farther south, west of Panamint Springs. To drive Saline Valley Road takes the better part of a day without stops, no matter where you're coming from. You will probably need a **high-clearance vehicle,** but a 4WD vehicle is usually not necessary, except when rain and snow have created hazardous driving conditions.

Plan at least **three days** to explore this area, and consider camping at primitive Warm Springs camp, with a central location in the Saline Valley. The best times to visit are **spring** and **fall.** Summer sees blazing temperatures; in winter, rain and snow can render Saline Valley Road impassable.

John Muir Wilderness

The John Muir Wilderness is adjacent to Death Valley National Park, along the western side. Paved US 395 traverses the region north south and is a jumping off point for both the wilderness and Death Valley.

The John Muir Wilderness is a major destination for camping, hiking, and fishing in summer. In winter there are opportunities for skiing and snowboarding. Fall brings spectacular leaf displays. Roads may close in winter and spring due to snow, and services can be limited. Spend **one day** to sightsee along US 395 and do a hike or visit a lake. Many visitors stay for a week or more, camping in the many developed campgrounds and hiking and fishing in summer or staying in a cabin or ski resort for recreation in winter.

From the John Muir Wilderness region, the best way to access Death Valley National Park is through Panamint Springs, the park's western entry point. From the towns along US 395, the drive takes between 45 minutes and 1 hour 45 minutes along paved roads that are open year-round.

Exploring the Park

The Panamint Springs region is a vast and geographically diverse area located on the western side of the park. At its upper end, the isolated Saline Valley lies tucked between the Inyo and Cottonwood Mountains, traversed only by the rough Saline Valley Road.

The lower section of this region is dominated by the western Panamint Mountains, the term referring to the western slope of these rugged mountains. The Panamint Mountains form the western edge of the park boundary and essentially create a barrier between the Panamint Valley to the west and Death Valley to the east. The barrier is highly effective and dictates the way you visit the park.

Choose a side: Will it be the western or eastern canyons? The eastern canyons feed into Death Valley itself. The Death Valley National Park boundary is somewhere in the middle of the Panamint Mountains. Only one road goes all the way through to the other side—Goler Canyon via Mengel Pass—but this is not a viable route for casual sightseeing.

VISITOR CENTER

There are **no visitor centers** or entrance stations in this region of the park. The only

Driving Distances

From Panamint Springs to:	Distance	Duration
Stovepipe Wells	30 mi/48 km	30 min
Furnace Creek	55 mi/89 km	1 hr
The Racetrack	100 mi/161 km	3 hrs 30 minutes
Eureka Dunes	120 mi/193 km	3 hrs 30 minutes
Olancha	45 mi/72 km	45 min
Lone Pine	50 mi/81 km	1 hr
Independence	65 mi/105 km	1 hr 15 min
Big Pine	93 mi/150 km	1 hr 30 min
Bishop	107 mi/172 km	2 hrs
Ridgecrest	70 mi/113 km (via Trona-Wildrose Rd.) or 100 mi/161 km (via US 395)	1 hr 30 min
Trona	48 mi/77 km (via Trona-Wildrose Rd.)	1 hr

services are in Panamint Springs, the main hub and the only place that offers food and lodging. Otherwise you're camping. It is possible to use Panamint Springs Resort as a base camp for day trips, but longer drives and hikes might cut it close to get back by dinnertime.

PARK ENTRANCES

Highway 190 is the main route into the park from the west side. The paved road bisects the region, entering the park at the Panamint Springs Resort. From here, it is a drive of 30 miles (48 km) east to Stovepipe Wells, the closest official park entrance station, and 56 miles (90 km) east to Furnace Creek, the main park hub.

Three roads feed into the park from **US 395.** From the west, **Highway 190** splits from US 395 at Olancha. From Olancha, it is 45 miles (72 km) east to Panamint Springs. From the north and west, **Highway 136** leaves US 395 south of Lone Pine (24 mi/39 km north of Olancha) to head east, intersecting with Highway 190 in 18 miles (29 km). Highway 190 then continues 30 miles (48 km) east to Panamint Springs. The total distance from Lone Pine to Panamint Springs is about 50 miles (81 km).

From the south, **Highway 178** splits east from US 395 at Inyokern. Highway 178 then heads 34 miles (55 km) east through Ridgecrest before swinging north through the mining town of Trona, where it becomes **Trona-Wildrose Road.** Just south of the park boundary, Trona-Wildrose Road splits. Panamint Valley Road leads 14 miles (22.5 km) north to Highway 190, just east of Panamint Springs, while Wildrose Canyon Road heads directly west to the Wildrose Canyon and Emigrant Canyon areas.

Trona-Wildrose Road is subject to washouts, especially the section south from the Panamint Valley Road split with Ballarat Road, 22 miles (35 km) north of Trona. Check road conditions ahead of time. If the road is closed, use the paved Nadeau Street, 18 miles (29 km) north of Trona and 3.8 miles (6.1 km)

Panamint Springs and the Saline Valley in One Day

- Your first destination will be the **Wildrose Charcoal Kilns,** beautifully hand-engineered monuments to mining once used to make charcoal.
- The 4.5-mile (7.2-km) (9 mi/14.5 km round-trip) trail to **Wildrose Peak** begins just behind the kilns, switchbacking up through juniper and conifer forest with views of the canyons below.
- After this effort, your final stops will be some easy car sightseeing. From here, drive north to **Aguereberry Point Road.** You will pass the remains of **Aguereberry Camp,** once home to miner Pete Aguereberry, on your way to Aguereberry Point. At 1,000 feet (305 m) higher than popular Dante's View, it offers sweeping views across Death Valley.
- If you're not up for the 4- to 5-hour trek to Wildrose Peak, opt for the short walk to **Darwin Falls,** near Panamint Springs Resort.
- If you have time, add on a drive through **Lee Flat,** the largest Joshua tree forest in the park, before dinner at **Panamint Springs Resort.**

south of Ballarat. From Trona, turn left onto Nadeau Street to continue heading north for 8.1 miles (13 km). Turn right onto graded and unpaved Slate Range Road. Slate Range Road intersects with Panamint Valley Road in 4.9 miles (7.9 km). Follow Panamint Valley Road north to Highway 190, then drop back down into the Wildrose Canyon area via Emigrant Canyon Road.

Gas and Services

Big Pine is located on US 395, about 43 miles (69 km) north of Lone Pine. The town provides the northernmost access to the park via either the North Pass of Saline Valley Road or Big Pine-Death Valley Road. Big Pine offers gas, lodging, food, and outdoor supplies. It also provides a refueling stop for people heading into or out of the Sierra Nevada to the west or Death Valley to the east.

Lone Pine, south on US 395, is a busy little town filled with hikers, climbers, and travelers on their way to northern lakes and ski resorts. Services include motels, restaurants, groceries, outdoor supplies, and gas. If you have had a long drive to the area and want to make a fresh entrance to Death Valley the next day, this is an excellent place to stop, regroup, and venture on.

If you blink, you'll miss **Olancha**—and you'll also miss your last chance to fill up on gas before turning east off US 395 toward Panamint Springs, 45 miles (72 km) away. Stopping here, just south of Lone Pine, can save you the sticker shock of Panamint Springs.

In the Indian Wells Valley, **Inyokern, Ridgecrest,** and **Trona** offer southern access to the park; all have gas stations and convenience stores. Trona is the last stop for gas before the park, but gas stations may not be open after business hours. Play it safe and fill up in Ridgecrest, a good-size town with grocery stores, hotels, and most of the common chain stores. If you forgot something or need supplies, you can probably find it here. For a charming place to stay near the park boundary, Lone Pine is a better bet.

Sights

EMIGRANT AND WILDROSE CANYON AREAS

★ Wildrose Charcoal Kilns

Emigrant Canyon Rd.; free

Once used to make charcoal for the mining efforts in the area, the Wildrose Charcoal Kilns now stand as works of hand-engineered beauty. The kilns are made of cut limestone, quarried locally and cemented with gravel, lime, and sand. They stand approximately 25 feet (7.6 m) tall, their walls curving gracefully inward to form a beehive shape. The Modock Consolidated Mining Company built them in 1877 to fuel the smelters of lead-silver mines in the Argus range to the west. The structures were designed to reflect as much interior heat as possible, but who knew that sound waves have similar properties? Open arched doorways lead to the interior of the kilns; stomp around on the floors of each one to capture the hollow echoes. Each kiln stands as a mini cathedral, the echoes swelling to the industry that once rang out across the canyon.

If you hike along the **Wildrose Peak Trail,** which starts at the first charcoal kiln, you'll see tree stumps along the mostly forested trail. The trees were cut down and fed to the kilns to support the mining operations that were king here. This is an easy trip from Wildrose Campground or on your way to hike Wildrose Peak or Telescope Peak.

Directions

From Panamint Springs, drive 16 miles (26 km) east on Highway 190 to Emigrant Canyon Road. Turn right onto Emigrant Canyon Road and drive 21 miles (34 km) south to the road's end. The kilns are 7 miles (11.3 km) past Wildrose Campground. The road is paved most of the way; the last 2 miles (3.2 km) of gravel are slightly rough but should be suitable for most cars.

Aguereberry Camp

Aguereberry Point Rd.; free

Pete Aguereberry came to Death Valley in 1905 in search of gold and found it, working what would become the **Eureka Mine** until his death in 1945. The hill where Pete

Aguereberry Camp

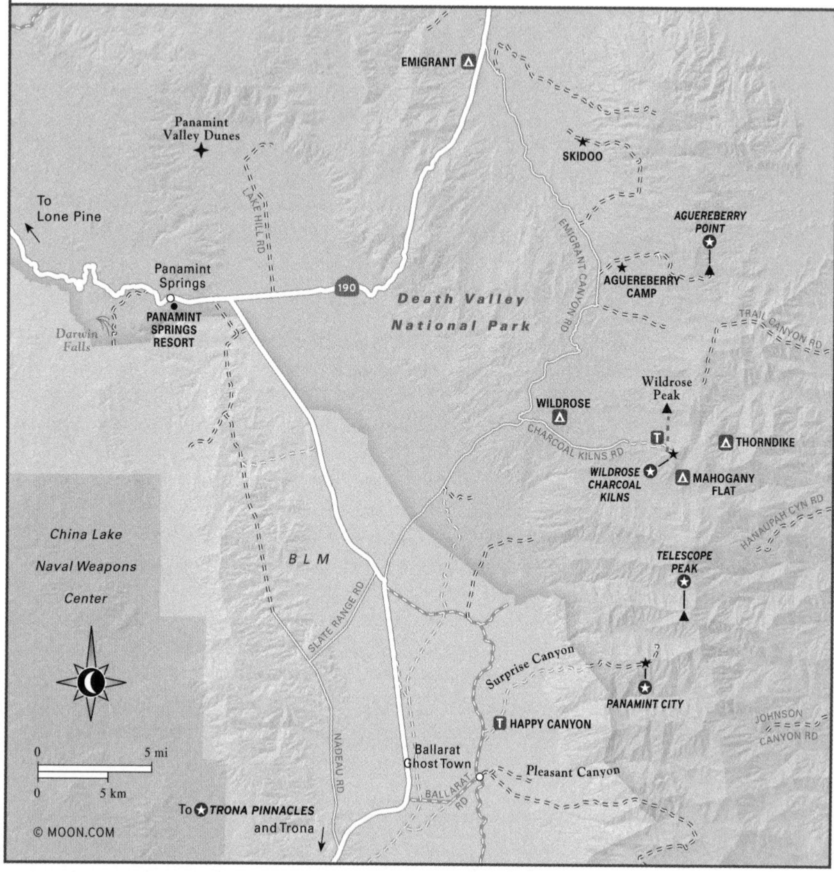

Agueereberry originally filed claims with fellow prospector Shorty Borden attracted a temporary mining camp called Harrisburg. In 1907 Pete had control of the Eureka Mine, and the few hundred people that had set up their tents in the hopes of cashing in eventually left. He nearly singlehandedly built and worked the Eureka Mine for 40 years, carving out a permanent life in the fleeting world of mining.

Today you can explore the **original camp,** visible from Aguereberry Point Road. One of the three **cabins** was Pete Aguereberry's, built in 1907 and still partially furnished. Remains of the Eureka Mine can be explored just over the hill to the south behind the camp. Wander around to find the mine site, look for flat places where the tent city stood, and keep your eye out for tin cans and other camp artifacts.

Directions

From Panamint Springs, drive 16 miles (26 km) east on Highway 190 to Emigrant Canyon Road. Turn right onto Emigrant Canyon Road and drive 10.3 miles (16.6 km) south. Turn left (east) onto Aguereberry Point Road and continue 1 mile (1.6 km) to Aguereberry

Camp. The road leading directly to the camp is closed, but it is a short walk to the site. Alternately, a second turnoff leads to the Eureka Mine. Both the camp and mine are in close proximity and easy to explore on foot together.

★ Aguereberry Point

Aguereberry Point Rd.; free

Pete Aguereberry, a miner who took his place in Death Valley history through sheer perseverance, built the road to Aguereberry Point to show friends his favorite view. His legacy is most certainly the spectacular views he gave us of Death Valley—across the valley floor southeast to Badwater Basin, the Black Mountains, and the green oasis of Furnace Creek.

Directions

From Panamint Springs, drive 16 miles (26 km) east on Highway 190 to Emigrant Canyon Road. Turn right onto Emigrant Canyon Road and drive 10.3 miles (16.6 km) south. Turn left (east) onto Aguereberry Point Road and continue a little over 6 miles (9.7 km), past Aguereberry Camp, to the road's end. The road requires a **high-clearance vehicle,** especially on the last hill (0.5 mi/0.8 km) until the point where spectacular views await.

Skidoo

7 miles (11.3 km) off Emigrant Canyon Rd.

As far as mining towns go, the town of Skidoo lived to a ripe old age, producing gold from 1906 until 1917. Now only mining tunnels and scattered artifacts indicate the region's boom. A rare and well-preserved **stamp mill** is located beyond the townsite. Views of Death Valley are spectacular.

Directions

From Highway 190, drive 9.4 miles (15.1 km) south to Emigrant Canyon Road and turn left onto the modestly marked, dirt Skidoo Road. The long and slowly winding road is graded and passable by most cars, but a **high-clearance vehicle** is recommended. You'll reach the townsite of Skidoo in approximately 7 miles (11.3 km).

The stamp mill is about 2 miles (3.2 km) past the townsite. To reach the stamp mill, continue past the townsite, staying left at the first fork. The road splits again, and any of the paths offer a view of the stamp mill, although the left fork leads most directly to it. The last mile (1.6 km) of road is rough, climbing up the hillside with rocky patches, with only a small parking area. If you are driving a passenger vehicle, park and walk the last mile.

WESTERN PANAMINTS

The western Panamints are formidable and sheer, with a rich mining history and enough springs and creeks to keep your hiking exciting and fresh.

Ballarat

23 miles (37 km) from Panamint Springs

Ballarat had its heyday between 1897 and 1905 as a resupply and entertainment center serving the nearby gold and silver mines. At its height, it claimed all the institutions of civilization, including a post office, a school, general stores, a jail, and more than its share of saloons. The only thing lacking was a church, an oversight that has not gone unnoticed by people who pay attention to this kind of history.

Although the post office closed in 1917, Ballarat continues to be a nerve center of sorts for this remote area and is a must-stop for news about road, camping, and hiking conditions. As in other canyons in the area, storms and water levels can quickly change the road to Surprise Canyon and the trail itself since the trail follows the stream-carved canyon walls.

The town has a **trading post** that serves as a welcome center, gift shop, and museum. While the store does not have regular hours, there is usually a caretaker on-site. The only supplies available are icy cold drinks and a few maps.

The caretakers have changed over the years, but they are typically very knowledgeable

1
Aguereberry Point
Elev. 6433 ft.
2
BALLARAT
TRADING POST
THE OUT POST–WELCOME
STORE
OPEN

about the area past and present as well as road and hiking conditions. They can offer helpful tips and will likely be in tune with any major Death Valley news before the National Park Service can get the word out. While here, consider making a small donation toward maintaining this historical space.

The semi-ghost town is also worth a stop in its own right. Newer trailers are mixed in among the original adobe structures and wood cabins. The original **jail** has been slightly restored and is open to visitors. You're free to wander around the town, but the buildings behind the store are off-limits. The **cemetery** is just west of town, surrounded by a wrought-iron fence.

Charles Manson's final hideout, the **Barker Ranch,** is in the vicinity. A truck reputedly owned by the Manson family now sits in front of the general store with other vehicles, quietly rusting against the mountain backdrop.

While there are no services in Ballarat, camping is allowed with permission from the caretaker.

Directions

From Panamint Springs, take Panamint Valley Road south for 14 miles (22.5 km); continue right for 9 miles (14.5 km) as it turns into Trona-Wildrose Road. A historical marker will direct you to the turnoff for the town via Ballarat Road.

You can also reach Ballarat from the north via Indian Ranch Road, 0.4 mile (0.6 km) south of Panamint Valley Road. Less than 12 miles (19.3 km) on this graded dirt road will take you to the town. All routes are dusty but fairly level, and you should be able to make the trip in any type of vehicle.

THE SALINE VALLEY

In some ways, the Saline Valley is a smaller, more rugged, and more isolated Death Valley. The formidable Inyo Mountains jut toward the sky on the west side, and the Panamint Mountains form a barrier to the east. If you make it all the way out here, you likely have some specific destination in mind. Saline Valley Road is a highly scenic drive through beautiful desert. Two passes give rise to some dizzying views as well as access to the pristine Saline Valley Dunes, the spiky acres of Joshua trees at Lee Flat, the historic Salt Tramway, and rugged, rewarding canyons with some mining ruins.

Saline Valley Road is the only road with access to the remote Saline Valley. The rough road ranges from graded dirt to high clearance and parallels the western boundary of the park for about 80 miles (129 km), from Highway 190 in the south to Big Pine Road in the north. From end to end, the drive takes 6-7 hours. *This drive is not to be undertaken lightly.* Heavy rain can cause flooding and washouts; be sure to check the Inyo County website (www.inyocounty.us) for current road status. See page 159 for information on how to safely travel this road.

There are **no services** in the Saline Valley.

Lee Flat Joshua Tree Forest

23 miles (37 km) northwest of Panamint Springs

Lee Flat is home to the most impressive Joshua tree forest in the park, covering more than 4,000 acres (1,619 ha) of valley and hillsides. The trees thrive here both in height and sheer quantity, dominating the landscape with their jaunty, spiky presence.

Lee Flat is a high-desert valley, and a drive through the graded roads will skew your idea of what a desert should look like. Mounded green hills keep you snaking along at an elevation of more than 5,000 feet (1,524 m). The cool air snaps, a relief from the desert floor. In spring, wildflowers pop out at every turn. Pull off the road to wander through this place, which feels bright, spacious, timeless, and secret all at once.

Directions

From the **South Pass** near Panamint Springs, set aside 3-4 hours for the leisurely, scenic drive to Lee Flat. The best access to Lee Flat is via Saline Valley Road. From Panamint Springs, head west on Highway 190 for 14.7

1: Aguereberry Point **2:** Ballarat Trading Post

The Saline Valley

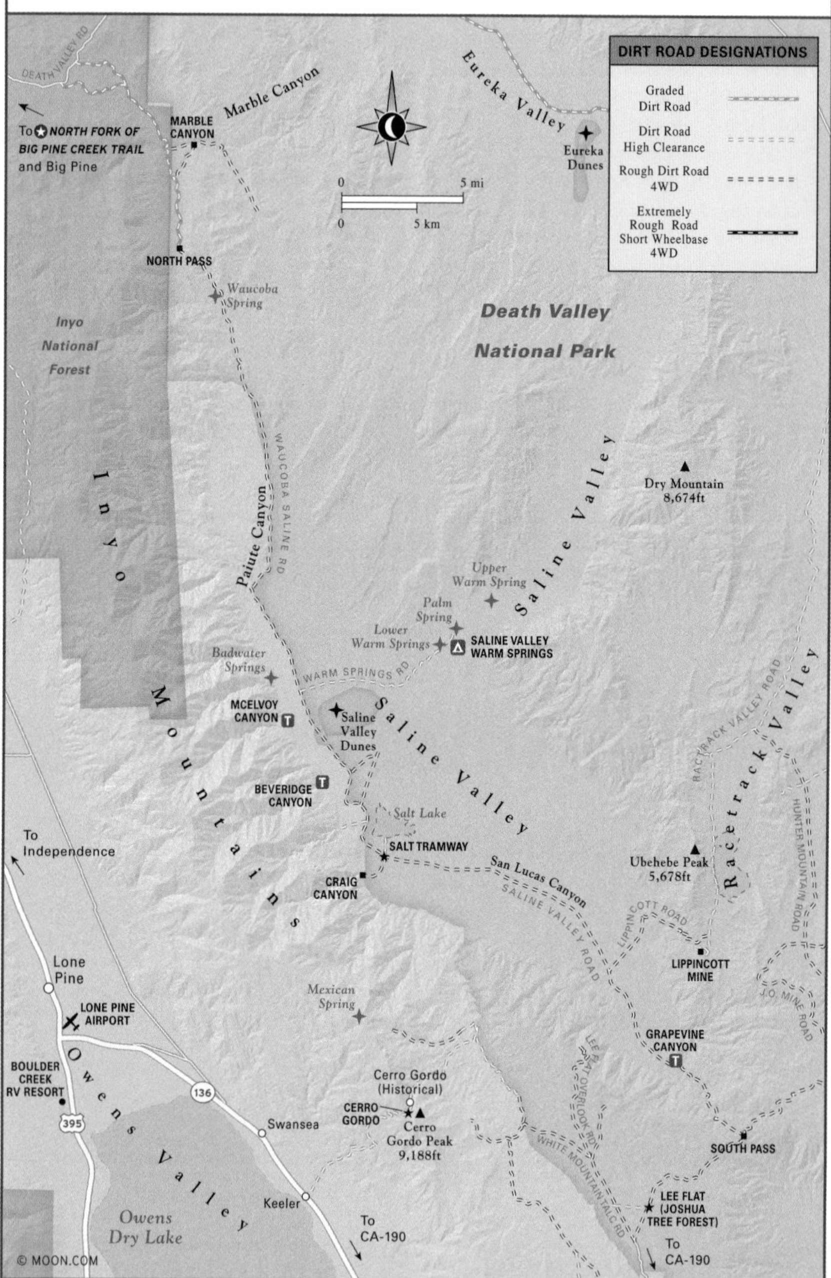

miles (23.7 km), turn right and follow Saline Valley Road north for 8.2 miles (13.2 km) to a fork. The left fork leads to Lee Flat Road; the right fork continues along Saline Valley Road. Turn left onto Lee Flat Road to venture deeper into the thick of this special place.

Salt Tramway

35 miles (56 km) north of Hwy. 190

Death Valley saw many grand mining dreams go head-to-head with the incredibly rugged landscape. The venture for halite, humble table salt, rivaled the biggest. White Smith was an attorney who came to work for the local borax mines as a teamster. It was his vision of the halite deposits at the appropriately named Salt Lake that became responsible for the operation.

To mine the salt, an aerial tramway was built in 1912-1913. The tramway consisted of a series of massive wooden towers that climbed 7,700 feet (2,347 m) over 13.5 miles (21.7 km). The salt was mined through a system that required flooding the playa and then letting the water evaporate. The revealed salt deposits were then loaded into buggies and transported by wooden cart to the tramway terminal. The tramway carried the salt, bucket by bucket, over the rugged terrain to Owens Valley on the other side of the Inyo Mountains. More than 30,000 tons of salt were transported in its 12 years of operation. Although the mine had some periods of idleness, it closed for good in 1933 at the height of the Great Depression.

In 1974 the Salt Tramway was placed on the National Register of Historic Places. You can see part of the tramway as you head north through the South Pass on Saline Valley Road in the area of Salt Lake. Some of the tramway towers are visible south of the road, where they cling to the side of the sheer Inyo Mountains. While they may look tiny, dwarfed by the mountains, the towers' true size is apparent on the valley floor. North of the road, the massive, solidly built timbers extend along an access road toward Salt Lake.

Lower Tramway

To walk out to the lower tramway, take the short maintenance road that passes three tramway towers to end at Salt Lake. **Salt Lake** is a salt-crusted expanse, sometimes covered with a shallow layer of water after a rain. From Saline Valley Road, the first tram tower is less than 0.5 mile (0.8 km) away. The road passes two other towers and ends at the lake's edge. Wooden stakes mark the shallow ponds used for salt evaporation.

Upper Tramway

An extremely rugged and strenuous **trail** (used to build and maintain the Salt Tramway) leads to the upper tramway towers. Looking at the tiny towers clinging to the side of the Inyo Mountains, try to imagine how this feat of engineering was achieved in the harsh terrain, remote location, and unforgiving weather. An insane level of persistence and vision, mind-boggling to contemplate, made this a reality.

The trail travels more than 5 miles (8 km) past the first **10 control towers.** However, a walk just to the base of the Inyo Mountains along Salt Tramway Road leads past several towers to end at the biggest tower on the valley floor in less than 2 miles (3.2 km). Where the maintenance road intersects with Saline Valley Road, take the very faint south fork toward the Inyo Mountains for less than 0.5 mile (0.8 km) to its end. The trail starts as the continuation of the maintenance road along the valley floor; in less than 2 miles (3.2 km), it meets the base of the Inyo Mountains. From this point, the trail becomes extremely strenuous—switchbacks up the mountain are very precarious with sheer drop-offs. This section of the trail requires research and preparation.

Directions

The tramway crosses Saline Valley Road about 35 miles (56 km) north of Highway 190 (via the **South Pass**). From the south, the tramway is about 5 miles (8 km) south of the Saline Valley Dunes. As the towers come into view, look for the unsigned road that leads directly to them, connecting them along the valley floor.

Saline Valley Dunes

Saline Valley Rd.

The first time I came out to the sand dunes, I was so busy using them as a landmark to get to Saline Valley Warm Springs that it didn't occur to me to admire them on their own. These sand dunes in the Saline Valley are isolated and pristine, set strikingly against the stark Inyo Mountains. By all means—stop your car, get out, and explore the dunes.

The Saline Valley Dunes are wide and shifting, covering only about 2.2 square miles (5.7 sq km); the highest dunes are about 20 feet (6.1 m) tall. They might not look impressive from the road, but it's easy to become immersed in this undulating sea of sand. As the sand ripples toward the mountains, creating a smooth place to walk, yours might be the only human tracks. When ready, follow your tracks back to your car.

Directions

The sand dunes are less than 1 mile (1.6 km) from **Saline Valley Road** and are easily visible from the road. A short access spur, about 1.5 miles (2.4 km) south of Warm Springs Road, heads east toward the foot of the dunes in less than 0.5 mile (0.8 km). The spur is very faint, not much more than a 4WD track; if you can't find it, park and walk the short stretch from Saline Valley Road.

Saline Valley Warm Springs

From North Pass: 29.1 miles (46.8 km) to Saline Valley Warm Springs Rd. turnoff, 7.5 miles (12.1 km) to Lower Warm Springs; from South Pass: 30.6 miles (49.2 km) to Saline Valley Warm Springs Rd. turnoff, 7.5 miles (12.1 km) to Lower Warm Springs

The Saline Valley Warm Springs have been cultivated for decades by people seeking to make an idyllic place to camp and relax in this isolated location. In the 1960s and 1970s, this was a hippie hot spot. The National Park Service took over management of the land in 1994, with a compromise that allows a caretaker and visitors to maintain and regulate the area. The tradition of being free and naked in the great outdoors has continued, and many people treat the springs as clothing-optional.

Although this is an extremely remote spot, many people make the trek to the springs; it can get very busy, especially on long weekends in spring and fall. For your own enjoyment, and to experience the peaceful surroundings, avoid these times if possible. The springs can be accessed via either the **North or South Pass,** depending on your vehicle, current road conditions, and your point of origin.

There are three sets of warm springs. Allow a minimum of **three days** to visit: one day to drive in, one day to soak and relax, and one day to return. Most people stay for several days or weeks, getting into the peaceful groove of soaking and relaxing. The Saline Valley Warm Springs have a year-round caretaker, and over the years many improvements have been made: warm **outdoor showers, restrooms** (pit toilets), and impeccably maintained springs and grounds.

Be prepared for blazing sun in the summer, cold temperatures in the winter, and the possibility of stinging sandstorms year-round (consider bringing goggles). The wind out here is no joke, and it will grab a tent or other belongings in a moment. On one trip, I woke to find my entire camp alcove shelter had blown away without a trace. If you find it in some distant canyon in the Saline Valley, you're welcome to it.

Lower Warm Springs

Campsite: free

The Lower Warm Springs are lush and serene, with a shaded rock pool and a cultivated green lawn where people gather, picnic, and relax—this is where most of the action is. There are fewer than 10 free **campsites** tucked away in the mesquite trees nearest the main springs. When those are full, other campsites spill

---

1: Joshua trees at Lee Flat **2:** The historic Salt Tramway carried salt from the valley floor across the Inyo Mountains. **3:** the remains of a mining camp in Marble Canyon **4:** Saline Valley Warm Springs camp

1
2
3
4
7YUJ016

out into the exposed desert or toward Palm Spring.

Palm Spring

Palm Spring, 0.7 mile (1.1 km) east on Warm Springs Road, is a little quieter. By contrast, it is austere and exposed to the blinding glare of the desert. It's a surreal experience to be sitting chest-deep in the natural mineral waters, at eye level with the expanse of desert but protected from its cold, heat, and stinging sand. Some people camp here or between Lower Warm Springs and Palm Spring. **Camping** is open desert camping with car camping and walk-in camping zones; campsites are not defined.

Upper Warm Springs

The Upper Warm Springs are 2.4 miles (3.9 km) northeast on Warm Springs Road, which gets progressively rockier. A **high-clearance vehicle,** and possibly a 4WD vehicle, is necessary. It's also a nice hike from Lower Warm Springs or Palm Spring. The upper spring is a deep-blue pool, in the most natural state of the three, and is surrounded by a fence to fend off **wild burros,** which roam freely in the area. Camping is prohibited within 100 feet (30 m) of source springs.

Marble Canyon

20 miles (32 km) from Big Pine

Marble Canyon is a scenic **ghost camp** located in the Inyo Mountains on Saline Valley Road via the North Pass. Marble Canyon was first mined around 1882, but the most intensive efforts occurred in the 1930s and continued until the 1960s. Today, the remains of the large gold placer mine include cabins and mining headframes scattered around the canyon floor.

Saline Valley Road goes directly through the site. Getting out of the car to explore will reveal several **cabins** of varying ages, along with **mine works.** The oldest cabins with stone foundations are located in the wash of Marble Canyon along a primitive spur, the unmarked Jackass Flats Road.

Directions

Marble Canyon is best reached via the **North Pass.** From Big Pine, drive east on Highway 168 for about 2 miles (3.2 km). Turn right onto Big Pine-Death Valley Road and continue east for about 12 miles (19.3 km). Turn right onto Saline Valley Road to head south. Marble Canyon lies at the bottom of a series of switchbacks, more than 6 miles (9.7 km) from Big Pine-Death Valley Road. The road veers east into Marble Canyon and then curves in a sharp right to follow Opal Canyon to the south; Marble Canyon begins at the curve.

From the curve in Saline Valley Road, Jackass Flats Road continues east into the wash of Marble Canyon for about 1.5 miles (2.4 km), then turns right (south) into Opal Canyon. To explore Marble Canyon, either walk this road or drive and park near the turn. The road is rough; a **high-clearance vehicle,** possibly a 4WD vehicle, is necessary.

The drive can also be done as a day trip from Saline Valley Warm Springs; it's about 1.5-2 hours each way. From the junction of Warm Springs Road and Saline Valley Road, head north for about 26 miles (42 km) to Marble Canyon.

Scenic Drives

The western Panamints border the Panamint Valley, starting on Bureau of Land Management land and stretching east into Death Valley National Park. The **4WD routes** here are rugged with shifting conditions, and they require technical skill and equipment. Only one road goes through clear to the other side—the Goler Canyon road via Mengel Pass—but to call Mengel Pass a road is a stretch. It's a cliff-hugger and a nail-biter. Do not attempt it unless you have experience and the right equipment. Other canyon drives in the area only flirt with the mountain passes before they head back down to the Panamint Valley. Roads in Jail Canyon and Pleasant Canyon, for example, nose their way toward Death Valley but end without going all the way through. To the north, the Saline Valley Road traverses the remote Saline Valley, nearly 80 miles (129 km) pavement to pavement.

Saline Valley Road

Distance: *80 miles (129 km) one-way*
Duration: *6-7 hours*
Start: *Hwy. 190*
End: *Big Pine Rd.*
Road surface: *Gravel with rocks, washboard, and sand in segments*
Vehicle: *High-clearance required, 4WD recommended*

Saline Valley Road's condition has improved over the years, but it remains long, nearly 80 miles (129 km) pavement to pavement from Highway 190 in the south to Big Pine Road in the north. Despite its remoteness, many people drive this road in all forms of vehicle—from apocalyptic 4WD desert beasts with military tires to adorable little VW buses with matching curtains. When the road is dry in optimal conditions, it is passable by any manner of vehicle, but the going is not smooth. Rocks, washboard, sand in places, and the sheer length of the road make it an endurance test; getting a flat or two is a distinct possibility. On the bright side, alpine forests, abundant Joshua trees, stellar views, remote sand dunes, bird's-eye views of the Saline Valley, and access to powerfully beautiful canyons make it worth the haul.

As a rule, a **high-clearance vehicle** and

Saline Valley Road

all-terrain tires are necessary, but the road and weather conditions may necessitate a 4WD vehicle with additional clearance.

During good weather in fall and spring, the road conditions are generally good, with **graded gravel** allowing for moderate speeds of 25-35 mph (40-56 km/h). Winter can bring snow, ice, and road closures; carry chains. Any inclement weather can turn the road treacherous with deep mud, sand, and washouts. Inyo County maintains the road and closes it during these times, so always check road conditions before driving and obey any road closures. Summer brings intense heat and keeps most visitors away, and can also precipitate road closures.

Even in optimal conditions, *this drive is not to be undertaken lightly.* If you plan to drive this road, **bring extra food, water,** and **tools,** and be prepared for anything. Even on a good day, it is possible that the washboard road could cause mechanical failure or a flat tire. And a flat tire here could mean being stranded for days. If you get into a true emergency, Saline Valley Warm Springs has a year-round caretaker generally available with a radio and the ability to contact the outside world. During spring and holiday weekends, there may be traffic to the hot springs, but the rest of the year, don't count on rescue from other vehicles passing by.

From end to end, the drive takes 6-7 hours, depending on your vehicle and the road conditions. There are two points of entry to the Saline Valley Road. Depending on where you enter the Saline Valley, the road is referred to as driving through the North or South Pass.

North Pass

The north entrance, or North Pass, is a mountain pass that reaches 7,300 feet (2,225 m) elevation; it can be snowy in winter. The closest services are at the town of **Big Pine,** a few miles west of where Saline Valley Road emerges onto the pavement at **Big Pine-Death Valley Road.**

South Pass

The South Pass is another mountain pass that reaches just under 6,000 feet (1,829 m) elevation; it can also be snowy in winter. The closest services to the south are at **Panamint Springs,** 13 miles (20.9 km) east of where Saline Valley Road emerges onto **Highway 190.** Most people use the South Pass to access sites along the road, especially the remote Saline Valley Warm Springs.

Panamint Valley and Indian Ranch Road

Distance: *14.7 miles (23.7 km) one-way*
Duration: *1 hour*
Start: *Panamint Valley Rd., Trona-Wildrose Rd., and Lower Wildrose Canyon Rd. junction*
End: *Trona-Wildrose Rd. junction*
Road surface: *Dirt*
Vehicle: *High-clearance recommended*

Indian Ranch Road is a graded, dirt road that travels along the base of the Panamint Mountains, paralleling the Trona-Wildrose Road. It gives access to 4WD roads and hikes into Panamint Mountain canyons notable for their springs, cabins, historical sites, and mining sites. Although the road is outside the park boundary, it provides the only access to several canyons within Death Valley National Park. Beyond being an access road, Indian Ranch Road is a pleasant detour and has a few sites that are worth a stop, including Ballarat and Warm Sulphur Springs. From the north, the road begins at a signed junction 14.2 miles (22.9 km) south of Panamint Springs where Panamint Valley, Trona-Wildrose, and Lower Wildrose Canyon roads meet. The road reconnects to pavement 14.7 miles (23.7 km) south where it intersects the Trona-Wildrose Road. Indian Ranch Road is maintained by Inyo County and is typically an easy drive for any vehicle; however, inclement weather can cause areas of rough washboard or mud. The condition of the canyon roads and canyon access can also change drastically with storms or inclement weather.

Warm Sulphur Springs

6.3 miles (10.1 km) south of Trona-Wildrose Rd.

Vegetation-dense marshland and a series of small, permanent ponds mark the spring at the base of the Panamint Mountains. Cattails and grasses soak in the spring water, and groves of screwbean mesquite contrast with the salt-saturated ground. The area is located 6.3 miles (10.1 km) south of the Trona-Wildrose Road (or 5.6 mi/9 km north of Ballarat) and marked by a wooden BLM sign.

Surprise Canyon

5.3 miles (8.5 km) south of Indian Ranch Rd. junction

Sculpted rock, a lively creek, and lush vegetation form a striking combination in the narrows of Surprise Canyon. A 4.1-mile (6.6 km) high-clearance road climbs a steep alluvial fan, entering the canyon at 2.3 miles (3.7 km) to end at **Chris Wicht Camp,** named for the superintendent of the Campbird Mine in the mid-1920s, also a saloonkeeper and one-time mayor of Ballarat. The camp was in use on and off from the 1870s and now serves as the trailhead for Surprise Canyon.

The canyon's highlight is the dazzling white, sculpted walls of the **narrows** 0.8 mile (1.3 km) into the hike. The trail follows the creek, which sometimes stretches to the canyon walls, making the creek and hiking trail one and the same at times. Over the course of the 0.5-mile (0.8-km) narrows, the stream is graced with polished slickrock, cascades, and low waterfalls with willows and rush lining the banks.

Beyond the narrows, the canyon opens up, and an old mining road follows the valley to the ghost town of Panamint City at 5.5 miles (8.9 km).

The canyon road starts from Indian Ranch Road 5.3 miles (8.5 km) south of the Indian Ranch junction or 2 miles (3.2 km) north of the general store in Ballarat.

Happy Canyon

6.1 miles (9.8 km) south of Indian Ranch Rd. junction

A road used to go through Happy Canyon to small gold and silver mines as well as a camp and mill. Now it goes only a short distance in, and the rest of the canyon is overgrown by spring vegetation and is part of the Surprise Canyon Wilderness. Its upper canyon, accessed only by extreme bushwhacking, lies within the Death Valley National Park boundary.

From its intersection with Indian Ranch Road, Happy Canyon Road travels 2.1 miles (3.4 km) to just inside the canyon, drops into a wash, and ends 0.3 mile (0.5 km) later at the wilderness boundary. A creek runs through the canyon, connecting a series of densely vegetated springs. The creek begins in the wash beyond the end of the road, and canyon narrows can be found in 0.4 mile (0.6 km).

Happy Canyon Road begins 6.1 miles (9.8 km) south of the Indian Ranch junction or 1.1 miles (1.8 km) north of the general store in Ballarat.

Pleasant Canyon

Ballarat, 11.7 miles (18.8 km) south of the Indian Ranch Rd. junction

The rugged road that winds through Pleasant Canyon leads to forested mountains, backcountry cabins, and historical gold-mining camps of the western Panamint Mountains. A **4WD vehicle is mandatory** for this drive.

Heading east into the Panamint Mountains, a high shelf road hugs the canyon wall with several steep, narrow sections. An alternate route has its own perils. The canyon springs are one of the highlights of the lower canyon. If you choose the alternate route you will be driving directly in the creek, tunneling through greenery. **Clair Camp,** located 6 miles (9.7 km) inside the canyon, has the most extensive ruins in the canyon, with stone dugouts, cabins, relics of daily life, and a mill for processing ore. It is doable as a full-day hike. The **Ratcliff Mine,** adjacent to Clair Camp, has the remains of two tramways that serviced its lower tunnels as well as striking views of the Panamint Valley below.

The road to the World Beater Mine branches off to the right 1 mile (1.6 km) past Clair Camp. The **World Beater Mine**'s highlights include a rustic cabin and the ruins of a stone stamp mill.

Beyond the mines in **Upper Pleasant Canyon,** you'll come to a spring feeding into a tub. Burros love this spot, so all water should be purified, even if it comes from the pipe. Just beyond, a side road on the left leads to the **Porter Mine** and **Stone Corral** in upper Happy Canyon just inside the Death Valley National Park boundary. The stone ruins were once the property of Panamint Tom. He is the brother of Hungry Bill, a Shoshone who famously cultivated gardens and orchards in Johnson Canyon and sold the fresh fruit and vegetables to miners over the mountain in the silver boomtown of Panamint City. Panamint Tom was famous in his own right for his horse raids as far as Los Angeles.

On maps, it may appear doable to drive a return loop through South Park Canyon. However, South Park Canyon is closed to full-size vehicles. The road through this canyon has many dangerous sections, including Chicken Rock, a high, steep, canted bit of road that slopes directly toward the precipitous mountainside. Rollovers on this section of road are well documented and not uncommon. The Bridge is a dangerously washed-out section of road patched with a bridge made of telephone poles. If you are intrigued by South Park Canyon, consider hiking it instead.

Pleasant Canyon Road begins 50 yards (46 m) south of the general store in Ballarat, heading northeast from the signed junction.

Ballarat

11.7 miles (18.8 km) south of the Indian Ranch Rd. junction

Original adobe structures and wood cabins are mixed in with newer trailers at this semi-ghost town set on the shimmering salt flats of the Panamint Valley floor, dwarfed against the dramatic backdrop of the Panamint Mountains. Ballarat had its heyday between 1897 and 1905 as a resupply and entertainment center serving the nearby gold and silver mines. The town has a **trading post** that serves as a welcome center, gift shop, and museum.

While there are no services in Ballarat, camping is allowed with permission from the caretaker.

Recreation

HIKING

Darwin Falls

Distance: *2 miles (3.2 km) round-trip*
Duration: *1.5 hours*
Elevation gain: *220 feet (67 m)*
Effort: *Easy*
Access: *Passenger vehicle*
Trailhead: *From Panamint Springs, drive 1 mile (1.6 km) west on Highway 190. Turn left onto a graded dirt road and continue to the parking area just past the fork at 2.5 miles (4 km). The right fork leads to the falls (see map page 164).*

The marvel of Darwin Falls is that they exist at all. The hike to the first falls is an easy and quick detour from Panamint Springs. A short **1-mile (1.6-km) walk** along a canyon creek leads you to a sight to behold: actual water streaming over slanted bedrock. This is where most people stop. About 1.5 hours should get you to the falls and back in time for a nice lunch on the Panamint Springs Resort patio.

The hike is not pristine wilderness, however; a pipeline follows the well-used trail. The area is also an active wash, and signs of flooding, churned dirt, and rocks are everywhere. Three more waterfalls lie beyond the first falls, but they require climbing and very careful navigation. *Do not attempt this casually.* Any hiking around waterfalls can be extremely dangerous.

Panamint Valley Dunes

Distance: *7 miles (11.3 km) round-trip*
Duration: *4-5 hours*

Panamint Region Hikes

Trail	Effort	Distance	Duration
Darwin Falls	Easy	2 mi/3.2 km rt	1 hr 30 minutes
McElvoy Canyon	Moderate	1.6 mi/2.6 km rt	2 hrs
Surprise Canyon	Moderate	1.6-2.6 mi/2.6-4.2 km rt	4 hrs
Grapevine Canyon	Moderate	2.6 mi/4.2 km rt	2 hrs
Panamint Valley Dunes	Moderate	7 mi/11.3 km rt	4-5 hrs
Wildrose Peak	Moderate	9 mi/14.5 km rt	4-6 hrs
Beveridge Canyon	Moderate to strenuous	1 mi/1.6 km rt	1 hr
★ **Panamint City**	Strenuous	11 mi/17.7 km rt	10-12 hrs
★ **Telescope Peak**	Strenuous	14 mi/22.5 km rt	7-9 hrs

Elevation gain: *750 feet (229 m)*
Effort: *Moderate*
Access: *Passenger vehicle*
Trailhead: *From Panamint Springs, drive east for 4.5 miles (7.2 km) to Big Four Mine Road (labeled "Lake Hill" on maps). Turn left and drive the graded road for 5.8 miles (9.3 km), to the first sharp right turn, and park.*

These star-shaped dunes are in the northern reaches of Panamint Valley, accessible only by a **long desert walk across sand.** Dunes have a magnetic pull that draws us close, something that tells us those mountains of sand will be even more fascinating close up. For the Panamint Valley Dunes, we can only hope that this pull lasts the 3.5 miles (5.6 km) of hiking over the flat, exposed sand that's required to reach them.

Grapevine Canyon

Distance: *2.6 miles (4.2 km) round-trip*
Duration: *2 hours*
Elevation gain: *466 feet (142 m)*
Effort: *Moderate*
Access: *High-clearance*
Trailhead: *Spur road off of Saline Valley Road (see map page 165).*

The soaring canyon walls, eerie boulder piles, and dense greenery enclosing a perennial stream recommend this short hike in the Saline Valley. Relative to other hikes in this area, it is easy to find, easy to follow, and instantly rewarding.

From the spur road and open area, hike east-northeast up a low rise for 0.2 mile (0.3 km) before dropping down into Grapevine Canyon. There are several burro and/or human trails to follow. At the canyon edge, the foot trail becomes more distinct. It winds down a rocky bluff to the floor of the wash below. Take note of where you came down for the return. Hiking from the small turnout, walk down to the canyon wash via a short slope below the road.

Continue walking upcanyon, following the sandy wash. The gorge deepens, strewn with boulders and framed by soaring granite bluffs. At 1.3 miles (2.1 km), you will come to a large spring enveloped by dense willows trussed with grapevine. The contrasts here are striking: the green of the spring against

Darwin Falls

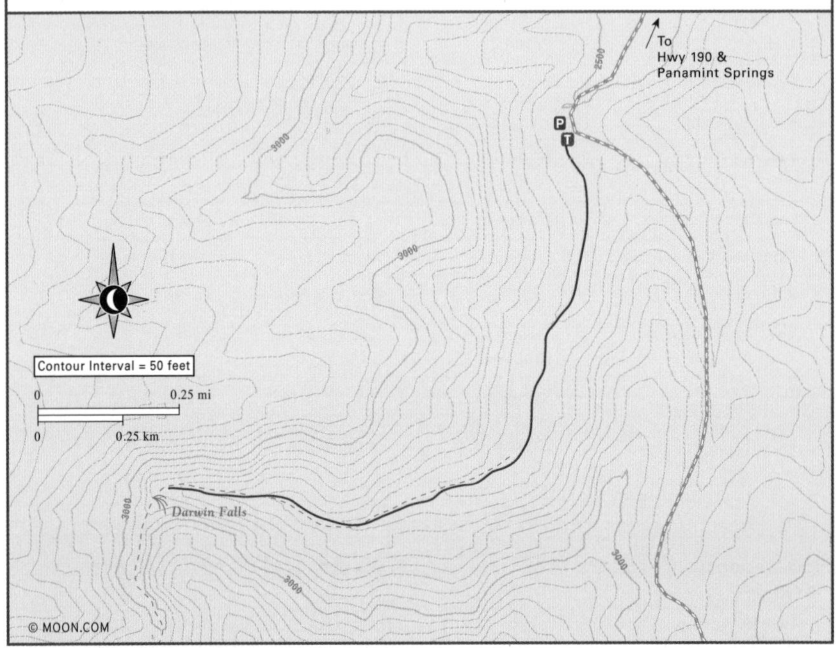

the gold of the cliffs, fringed and wild against stark and impassive. When I was here last, the spring was guarded by a territorial wild burro. In most years, a tiny stream flows downcanyon past the looming granite cliffs. Even if it is not flowing, this is a special place worth the short trek.

From Panamint Springs, drive 13 miles (20.9 km) west on Highway 190 to Saline Valley Road. Turn right and drive 19 miles (31 km) north on Saline Valley Road to a spur road on the right. The 0.2-mile (0.3-km) spur road leads to a level open area at the foot of a hill of granitic boulders. This spur road is 4.7 miles (7.6 km) north of South Pass (highest point on the southern end of the Saline Valley Road, marked by a viewpoint and intersection with Hunter Canyon Road). At 4.5 miles (7.2 km), Saline Valley Road crosses Grapevine Canyon wash, takes a sharp left, and climbs out of the wash. Grapevine Canyon will be on your right, trending north. Alternatively, you can park at a small turnout on the right overlooking the canyon. This turnout is just before the spur road (4.6 mi/7.4 km north of South Pass). It takes about 1.5 hours to get to the trailhead from Panamint Springs. Coming from the north and Saline Valley, the spur road is 5.2 miles (8.4 km) south of Lippincott Road.

McElvoy Canyon

Distance: *1.6 miles (2.6 km) round-trip*

Duration: *2 hours*

Elevation gain: *530 feet (162 m)*

Effort: *Moderate*

Access: *High-clearance/4WD*

Trailhead: *From Panamint Springs, drive 13 miles (20.9 km) west on Highway 190 to Saline Valley Road. Turn right and drive 34.5 miles (55.5 km) north on Saline Valley Road. A faint, unmaintained road leads west toward the Inyo Mountains and the deep cut of McElvoy Canyon. The road is 7.6 miles (12.2 km) north of the Salt Tramway Junction (1 mi/1.6 km south of Warm Springs*

Grapevine Canyon

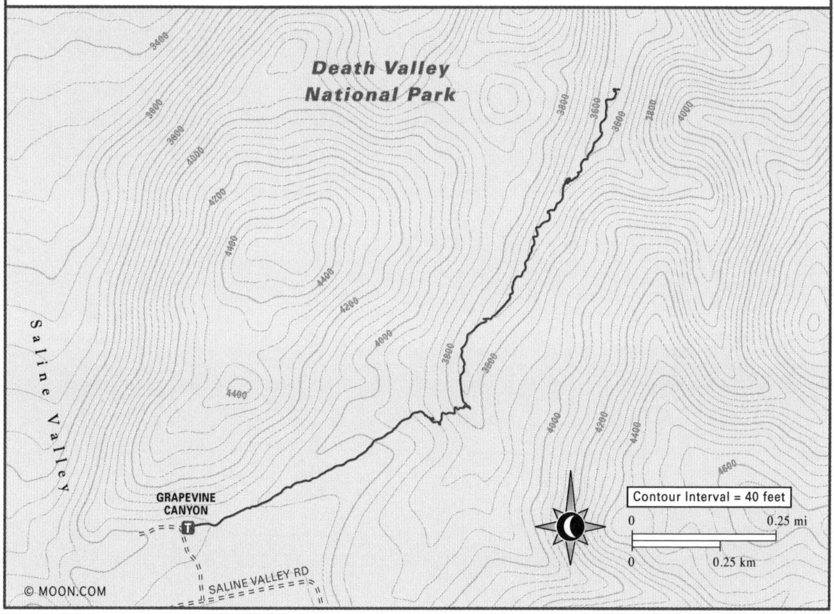

Rd.) and is hard to follow, requiring a high-clearance vehicle and a 4WD vehicle in places. The road continues up a rough alluvial fan just south of McElvoy Canyon to end in 1 mile (1.6 km).

A deep canyon, a waterfall, and a bubbling creek create a cool world far removed from the surrounding desert of the Saline Valley. You have to make the journey into McElvoy Canyon on faith, since there is no sign of this lively creek and waterfall until you're on top of it.

From the end of the road to McElvoy Canyon, walk northwest a few hundred yards toward the canyon entrance until you reach the edge of a **deep wash.** Follow the bank for a short distance toward the mountains until you find a break that lets you walk down into the wash. An **unmarked trail** will be visible leading down into the wash and continuing toward the canyon mouth.

Soon the magic begins, and you'll be walking along a **bubbling creek.** Following the creek will take you to the canyon mouth in about 0.5 mile (0.8 km) from the edge of the wash. In another 0.3 mile (0.5 km) you will reach a **grotto waterfall,** cool with hanging ferns. There is a second waterfall 0.5 mile (0.8 km) beyond the first, but it involves a moderate rock-climb over a dry slant to the right of the creek to get you beyond the grotto.

Beveridge Canyon

Distance: *1 mile (1.6 km) round-trip*
Duration: *1 hour*
Elevation gain: *385 feet (117 m)*
Effort: *Moderate to strenuous*
Access: *High-clearance/4WD*
Trailhead: *Lower Beveridge Canyon is accessed from Saline Valley Road. A faint, primitive road starts less than 32 miles (52 km) north of Highway 190 via the Saline Valley Road's South Pass (4 mi/6.4 km south of Warm Springs Rd.) to climb a fan toward the canyon mouth. Follow the road as far as you can, then park and walk* *(see map page 166).*

Beveridge Canyon shares a name and canyon with Beveridge, a fabled ghost town deep in

Beveridge Canyon

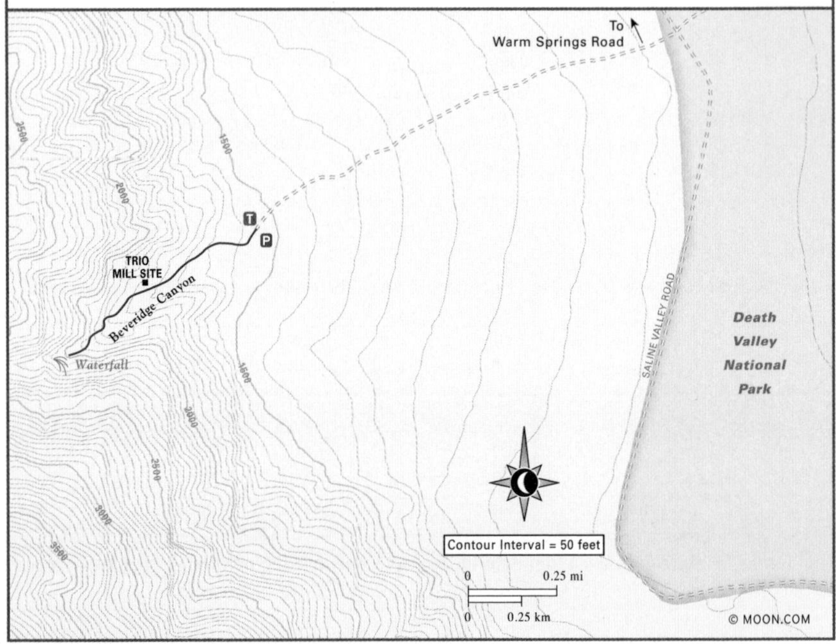

the Inyo Mountains, reputed to be the remotest ghost town in the Mojave Desert. The only way to reach the ghost town of Beveridge is via the upper canyon in the Inyo Mountains Wilderness. The lower canyon has its own intense beauty and draw, if you can get through even a piece of it.

Depending on where you park, you will reach the abandoned **Trio Mill Site** and camp in about 0.3 mile (0.5 km), walking west along the road toward the canyon mouth. The camp is littered with antique equipment, a truck graveyard, and a decaying cabin whose yard is dotted with metal junk sculptures and other deteriorating buildings (this is private property).

The camp is on the edge of a very rocky, boulder-filled wash that leads to the canyon mouth and the first **waterfall** in about 0.2 mile (0.3 km). Sculpted narrows, waterfalls, and intense greenery fill the canyon. Hiking beyond the first waterfall is extremely strenuous and requires rock-climbing skills; however, it is possible to hike to the first waterfall without any special moves. Beveridge Canyon is generally water-filled but may dry up at the lower elevations during extremely dry years.

TOP EXPERIENCE

Surprise Canyon

Distance: *1.6-2.6 miles (2.6-4.2 km) round-trip*
Duration: *4 hours*
Elevation gain: *665 feet (203 m)*
Effort: *Moderate*
Access: *High-clearance recommended*
Trailhead: *From Ballarat, drive 2 miles (3.2 km) north along Indian Ranch Road to the signed turnoff for Surprise Canyon. At the junction, turn right (west) and drive 4 miles (6.4 km) up the road to the historic Chris Wicht Camp; park in the small parking area. The road is rocky and steep, but it is maintained by Inyo County and typically does not require 4WD* (*see map page 168*).

Chris Wicht Camp is named for the superintendent of the Campbird Mine in the mid-1920s. The camp was in use on and off from the 1870s and now serves as the trailhead for Surprise Canyon. At the far (east) end of the parking area, an unsigned but well-established **trail** follows a creek east into the canyon.

The reason for the canyon's name becomes abundantly clear as you encounter the lush greenery and narrows of this lovely place. Surprise Canyon serves as the main hiking thoroughfare to the picturesque ghost town of Panamint City, but it's also worth exploring on its own.

Be prepared for an **erratic trail.** It follows the canyon and is difficult to lose, but it crisscrosses the creek to avoid the need to bushwhack through the deep vegetation at the canyon floor. At times the trail and the creek are one and the same. If you just give in to the fact that you're going to get wet, this can be part of the adventure.

Aim for the **narrows,** a highlight of the canyon with their smooth marble walls and mossy waterfalls. The narrows begin 0.8 mile (1.3 km) into the hike and last for about 0.5 mile (0.8 km). You'll need to do some rock scrambling to get through here. The hike up through the narrows will only take a few hours, but if it's hot, you might want to allow time for resting by the creek, soaking your feet in the cool pools, and picnicking next to the splashing water. This is a good place to visit in **late spring,** and you might be satisfied to splash through the canyon, enjoying the contrast of the water with the hot desert air and the slight relief from the elevation.

Beyond the narrows, the trail follows the canyon to the ghost town of Panamint City at 5.5 miles (8.9 km).

★ Panamint City

Distance: *11 miles (17.7 km) round-trip*
Duration: *10-12 hours*
Elevation gain: *3,660 feet (1,116 m)*
Effort: *Strenuous*
Access: *High-clearance recommended*
Trailhead: *From Ballarat, drive 2 miles (3.2 km) north along Indian Ranch Road to the signed turnoff for Surprise Canyon. At the junction, turn right (west) and drive 4 miles (6.4 km) up the road to historic Chris Wicht Camp; park in the small parking area. The road is rocky and steep, but it is maintained by Inyo County and typically does not require 4WD (see map page 168).*

This is a long, strenuous hike but worth every rocky step. The destination, the silver-boom ghost town of Panamint City, is scenic, well preserved, and forested with junipers and pinyons. There are cabins, a mill, and artifacts for days. The relatively high elevation of the area (5,000-8,000 ft/1,524-2,438 m) means that the canyon and surrounding mines can be cold and snowy in winter, while summer can be broiling. The best time to hike is in **spring.**

Don't be fooled by the 5 miles (8 km) to the ghost town. The hike is long and demanding. It zigzags up the scenic but strenuous **Surprise Canyon,** a destination in its own right. There is a beaten path most of the way, but the problem is that there isn't just one path. Spur paths dead-end, and you will definitely do some bushwhacking. Just when you've given up all hope of ever reaching Panamint City, when you've become convinced that you've wandered up a side canyon and lost the trail completely, pause, have a snack, regroup, and trudge on. Panamint City is just around the next corner, or the next. Watch out for rattlesnakes, and don't give up. You'll be fine as long as you're following the canyon. All roads lead to Panamint City.

From **Chris Wicht Camp,** follow the unsigned but well-worn trail east into the canyon. The trail follows Surprise Canyon for the first 1.3 miles (2.1 km). The **narrows** begin at 0.8 mile (1.3 km), and they require some rock scrambling to get through. The trail crosses the creek several times; plan on getting wet. Past the narrows, look for steel poles as the trail bypasses the canyon high on the south side to avoid the creek. What was once a road is now not much more than a scree-filled trail suitable for goats. A road used to go through Surprise Canyon all the way to Panamint City. Even after the road washed out, it was

Surprise Canyon and Panamint City

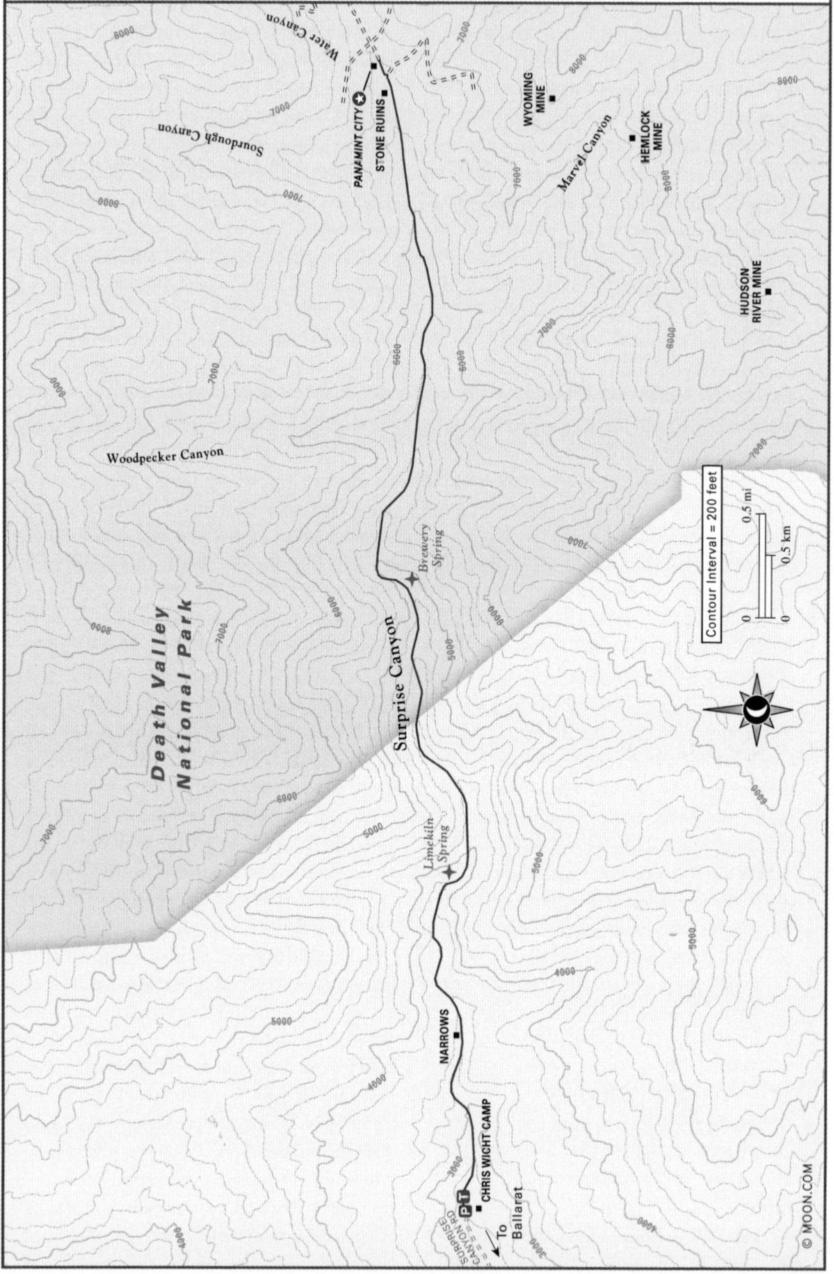

Water Canyon
PANAMINT CITY
STONE RUINS
Sourdough Canyon
WYOMING MINE
HEMLOCK MINE
Marvel Canyon
HUDSON RIVER MINE
Woodpecker Canyon
Brewery Spring
Surprise Canyon
Death Valley National Park
Limekiln Spring
NARROWS
CHRIS WICHT CAMP
SURPRISE CANYON RD
To Ballarat
Contour Interval = 200 feet
0.5 mi
0.5 km

a favorite pastime of the 4WD set to climb their way up to the townsite, winching up the waterfalls and taking all day to get there. The canyon is a great example of the desert reclaiming the land, and it's hard to imagine that a road ever went through here.

After the canyon narrows, you'll pass two springs. **Limekiln Spring,** at 1.8 miles (2.9 km), is signaled by a huge wall of hops, which some people call grapevine; according to the caretaker at Ballarat, they are actually hops. The next spring, 3.1 miles (5 km) in, is called **Brewery Spring.** The trail through Brewery Spring leads directly through the creek under a tunnel of trees and vines. This is the last water before Panamint City, more than 2 miles (3.2 km) away.

Past Brewery Spring, the canyon jogs to the east, and you're on the home stretch. The final mile (1.6 km) is grueling, but with its two tracks, you can tell that this was actually a road at some point. It would take a military-grade vehicle to actually clear the rocky terrain today. You'll know you're almost there when you see the iconic brick smokestack of the mill. Suddenly **stone ruins** begin to spring up by the trail. This was Main Street, and from here, you make your grand entrance into town.

Panamint City was founded in the early 1870s and saw mining efforts until the 1980s, when a series of floods wiped out the road leading to the town. The town had a tough and lawless reputation, so much so that Wells Fargo refused to open a bank here. To solve the problem of not having a bank, 450-pound (204-kg) silver ingots were cast and transported, unguarded, to Los Angeles. There were no reported thefts after this.

The plumbing of the old townsite still works, and you might be able to count on tap water from some of the old pumps. Although the trail is blessed with an abundance of water, all water should be treated, even from the pumps at Panamint City. The **Wyoming Mine** and road are visible high up on the mountain. **Sourdough Canyon,** on the left just before you reach the brick smelter, has a mill and camp worth exploring on an easy stroll. **Water Canyon** continues north of town and veers to the left. The old Thompson camp in Water Canyon has a few cabins, just past where the road crosses the creek. If you push on, you'll see the remains of a 1957 Chevy and, in this green space that borders the creek, the remains of an old water tank. It is overgrown, but there's just enough space to squeeze in and soak your feet in the cold water.

Backpacking

This is a long and strenuous hike; as a day hike, it is exhausting and doesn't give you time to explore the area. Panamint City is best done as a backpacking trip with one day to hike in, a day to explore and relax, and a day to hike out. Once you've reached the ghost town, set up camp and explore at your leisure.

If you can't make it all the way to Panamint City in one day, signs of **campsites** appear just past Brewery Spring. This is the last water before Panamint City, and if you continue through, you'll be splashing along the trail as you head through a tunnel of vines and trees. This area seems like too much of a snake magnet for my taste, but it's not the worst idea to camp just beyond the spring and make the last leg of the trip without your heavy pack. About 1 mile (1.6 km) past Brewery Spring, where the canyon jogs to the north and then east again, there's a great campsite in the crook of the canyon, elevated from the trail with a wind wall, flat spaces for tents, and lots of nice rocks for sitting.

TOP EXPERIENCE

★ Telescope Peak

Distance: *14 miles (22.5 km) round-trip*
Duration: *7-9 hours*
Elevation gain: *2,929 feet (893 m)*
Effort: *Strenuous*
Access: *High-clearance; 4WD may be necessary*
Trailhead: *Mahogany Flat Campground, at the end of Wildrose Canyon Road* *(see map page 170).*

The highest peak in Death Valley, Telescope

Telescope Peak

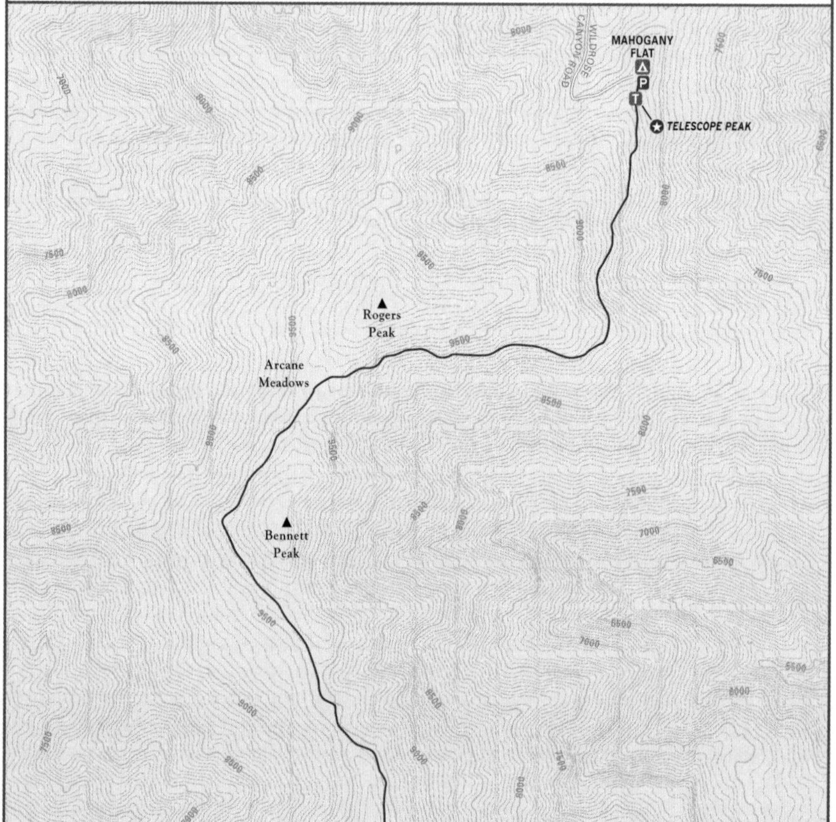
MAHOGANY FLAT
WILDROSE CANYON ROAD
TELESCOPE PEAK
Rogers Peak
Arcane Meadows
Bennett Peak
Telescope Peak
Contour Interval = 50 feet
0
0.5 mi
0
0.5 km
© MOON.COM

Peak is snow-covered most of the year. It juts vertically from the valley floor to tower 11,049 feet (3,368 m) above Badwater Basin, the lowest point in Death Valley. The 14-mile (22.5-km) hike to reach the peak is worth every switchback and is one of the few maintained trails in the park. This hike gives and gives, with sweeping views of Death Valley to the east, Panamint Valley to the west, and sometimes both at once. It's a great place to cap off extensive travel in Death Valley. If you've been wandering down in the canyons and valley floors, this is your chance to have a personal travel retrospective.

The straightforward trail starts out in a forest of pinyon, juniper, and mahogany, then swings around **Rogers Peak,** slowly gaining elevation until you reach open, windswept **Arcane Meadows** at 2.4 miles (3.9 km). From here, the Panamint Valley and the Argus Range come into view. You'll see the trail snaking along the ridge toward Telescope Peak, slowly getting closer and in sight the whole hike. The next 2 miles (3.2 km) along the ridge are fairly level. To the west are sweeping views toward Tuber and Jail Canyons; to the east, you'll see the three forks of Hanaupah Canyon.

About 4 miles (6.4 km) in, the hike starts to climb again—the last mile (1.6 km) is steep switchbacks. The landscape gets increasingly windswept, barren, and rocky as the elevation reaches dizzying heights. Ancient and gnarled bristlecone pines dot the trail above the tree line. It's not just the amazing views that will take your breath away—the lack of oxygen at this elevation may make the long set of switchbacks to the summit slow going. Soak it all in from the top as you look from the salt flats of Death Valley to the distant Sierra Nevada range.

Late spring, **May or June,** is the best time to do this hike. Most of the rest of the year sees the trail covered in snow and ice. In summer a haze can settle in over the valleys and lessen the views.

Wildrose Peak

Distance: *9 miles (14.5 km) round-trip*
Duration: *4-6 hours*
Elevation gain: *2,164 feet (660 m)*
Effort: *Moderate*
Access: *Passenger vehicle*
Trailhead: *Wildrose Charcoal Kilns (see map page 172).*

This pretty, well-maintained trail lures you on with juniper trees, conifer forests, sparkling ancient schist, and glimpses of the canyons below. Stretches of welcome shade for hiking and the relatively high elevation make this a good choice for **late spring** or **early summer.**

The clearly marked trail begins at the **westernmost charcoal kiln.** The trail starts out fairly level, but this is small comfort because sooner rather than later you'll have to start climbing. The trail is intermittently steep up to the **saddle,** at 2.1 miles (3.4 km), where you have sweeping views of Death Valley. If you are not set on reaching the summit, this is a rewarding place to stop and turn around.

After climbing again, the trail reaches a **second saddle,** with more views, at 3.1 miles (5 km). From here, Wildrose Peak is 1.1 miles (1.8 km) farther via a **steep trail;** it feels like you're climbing straight up the side of the mountain, and then comes a series of increasingly steep and tight switchbacks. The views become more and more impressive as you look down into Death Valley Canyon, Trail Canyon, and Death Valley itself. The scenery becomes as rarified as the air, and you'll begin passing gnarled and ancient bristlecone pines.

Beware a **false summit** 0.2 mile (0.3 km) before the actual summit. Just as you're about to start celebrating your ascent, you'll see the trail continues along a ridge to the actual summit. Fortunately, this is an easy, level stroll. You're rewarded for your pain and suffering with panoramic views from the windswept **summit.** The tiny road you see in the distance to the northeast is Aguereberry Point Road.

Wildrose Peak

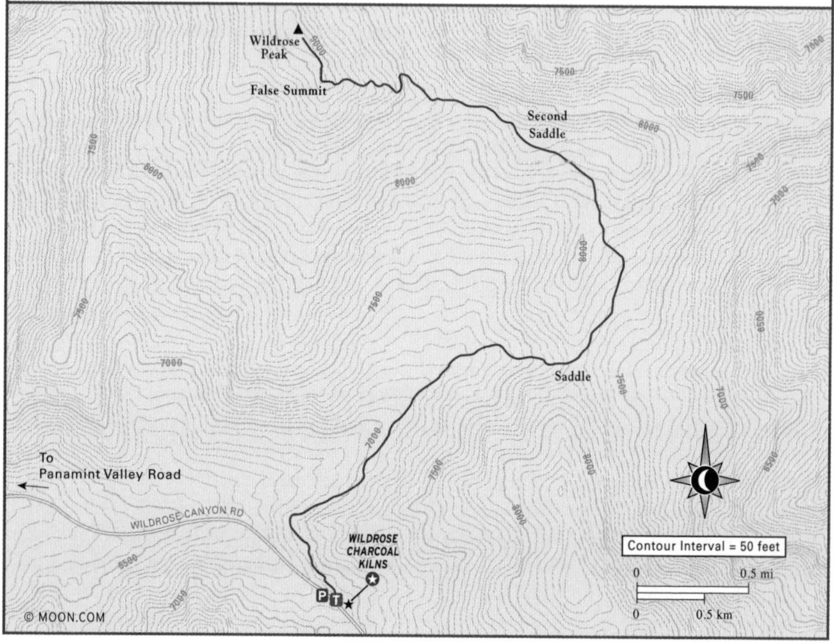

BIKING

This region is way too rugged and the distances too great to be suitable for most bike rides. However, the few paved roads that crisscross the western side of the park are tempting—a road cyclist's dream of freedom with miles of pavement set against the sparseness of the rolling hills and carved drama of the mountains. Roads are wide and swooping, and you'll feel like a raven soaring over the desert floor. A few rugged routes offer remote vistas with historical significance.

Highway 190

Access from Panamint Springs

Highway 190, past Panamint Springs, winds dramatically into the park. It is 31 miles (50 km) (one-way) east to Stovepipe Wells and 45 miles (72 km) (one-way) west to Olancha and US 395. Set your own destination, since there's nothing much on either side of Panamint Springs. You'll be rewarded by views, more views, and smooth road.

Trona-Wildrose Road

Access from Trona

Biking the road from Trona offers similar hardship and reward. From the mining town of Trona, Trona-Wildrose Road climbs the length of Panamint Valley, more than 50 miles (81 km) (one-way) north to Panamint Springs Resort, which will surely seem like heaven on earth after that journey. The road stretches out seemingly endlessly. Though there is minimal traffic, be wary of the lack of shoulder; even the scariest RV towing a Jeep, however, will most likely have room to pass you safely.

Skidoo Road

Access via Emigrant Canyon Rd., 9.4 miles (15.1 km) south of Hwy. 190

Skidoo Road begins 9.4 miles (15.1 km) south

of Highway 190 on Emigrant Canyon Road. Modestly marked, it is a graded dirt road that leads to the townsite of Skidoo (no structures) in approximately 7 miles (11.3 km). The ride affords wide-open desert views and leads to the now-leveled site that bustled in gold production from 1906 to 1917, unheard-of longevity in this climate of boom and bust. Continue another 2 miles (3.2 km) for the real reward: a visit to the well-preserved stamp mill and stunning views across the salt pan of Death Valley.

Aguereberry Point Road

Access via Emigrant Canyon Rd., 10.3 miles (16.6 km) south of Hwy. 190

The scenic climb to Aguereberry Point begins 10.3 miles (16.6 km) south of Highway 190 off Emigrant Canyon Road. For 6 miles (9.7 km) the road, the dream of subsistence miner Pete Aguereberry, traverses steep grades. Aguereberry built the road to show friends his favorite view. It ends at a point giving wide views of Badwater Basin, the Black Mountains, and the green oasis of Furnace Creek. One possible starting point is Emigrant Campground to the north. Over the 18 miles (29 km) from Emigrant Campground (2,100 ft/649 m) to Aguereberry Point (6,433 ft/1,961 m), the elevation gain is intense. Be prepared for an uphill haul with a huge payoff.

CLIMBING

The Panamint Springs region is a wet and wild world of possibility for rock climbing. Many canyons in the region were sculpted by water, creating carved falls and undulating canyon walls, features that may look like a buzz-kill to hikers but signal that the fun is just about to begin for rock climbers. Much of the water that formed the canyons is still present, creating refreshing challenges for those who attempt to hike and climb here. Breaking out your climbing skills and equipment can give you access to the upper reaches of canyons that don't give up their secrets so easily.

Darwin Falls offers a short stroll to a humble waterfall, impressive mostly due to its bone-dry location in the Panamint Valley. However, just beyond the lower waterfall lie three more waterfalls, increasingly tall and slender streams of water dropping into the stone-lined pools below.

Inyo Mountains Wilderness

Beveridge Canyon, McElvoy Canyon, and Craig Canyon are a power trio in the Inyo Mountains Wilderness, clustered near the Salt Tramway and Warm Springs Road. A trip here brings you to deep gorges and tumbling waterfalls, enticing you to push through to the next round. These three climbs require technical skills, climbing experience, and, in some cases, equipment.

The deep narrows at the mouth of **McElvoy Canyon** have a hiking trail that leads first to one waterfall and then another. Beyond the second waterfall, a technical climb bypasses that waterfall and leads to narrows and a third waterfall.

A creek and waterfalls dominate **Beveridge Canyon,** making it both spectacularly beautiful and impossibly rugged at the same time. Climb past the first two waterfalls to reach the wet narrows, high and sweeping polished white marble. Beyond this, three waterfalls lead through the narrows, taking you deeper into the creek and waterfalls only to effectively end at the final waterfall, 60 feet (18.3 m) high and topped with a chockstone.

Craig Canyon, by comparison, is refreshingly dry. The goal here is to get to the colorful and winding narrows 2 miles (3.2 km) into the deep canyon, an adventure-filled day that requires getting past nine falls and many boulder jams.

Food and Accommodations

PANAMINT SPRINGS

Panamint Springs Resort

40440 Hwy. 190; 775/482-7680; www.panamintsprings.com; 7am-9:30pm daily year-round, $226-326, general store 8am-8pm daily

Panamint Springs Resort offers the only accommodations, food, supplies, and gas within the park boundaries on the west side of the park. The rustic resort opened in 1937, when the first toll road across the Panamint Valley was built from Stovepipe Wells. Today, it's a welcome and unexpected sight as you cross into Death Valley, rising out of the desert floor and beckoning with a deep veranda and fan palms.

The resort has affordable motel rooms, cabins, a cottage, tent cabins, RV spaces, and tent sites. Rooms are very basic and do not offer televisions, refrigerators, or coffeemakers. Panamint Springs is a pet-friendly resort; however, pets must be declared before check-in.

There are no phones in any rooms, and cell phones will not work here. Panamint Springs has limited phone connectivity reserved for hotel staff; however, it does offer complimentary satellite internet access. Bandwidth is limited and reserved for sending brief messages (no streaming). There is a general store with basic supplies, gas, and an ATM.

Panamint Springs Resort Restaurant

40440 Hwy. 190; 775/482-7680; noon-8:30pm Mon.-Thurs., noon-9pm Fri., 7am-9pm Sat., 7am-8:30pm Sun. year-round

The Panamint Springs Resort restaurant serves appetizers, salads, burgers, chicken tenders, and fish-and-chips. Weekend breakfast is standard American fare including scrambled eggs and French toast. On weekdays breakfast items are available at the general store. The **bar** serves wine and a wide selection of American craft brews and imports. The downside of having all this great stuff in the middle of nowhere is that it can get very busy. Rooms can get fully booked months ahead of time, especially for holiday weekends. Tour buses have been known to pull up and swamp the dining area. Of course, this gives you a chance to sip a cold craft beer on the porch while you wait, but don't be surprised that you're not the only one who knows about this not-so-hidden gem.

CAMPING

Panamint Springs Resort Campground

40440 Hwy. 190; 775/482-7680; www.panamintsprings.com; 8am-8pm daily year-round; $15 tent sites, $65-85 tent cabins, $30-60 RV sites

The Panamint Springs Resort Campground has a total of 76 accommodations, including **tent cabins** (1-5 people), **RV sites** (30- and 50-amp hookups), **tent sites** (1 tent, 1 vehicle), and one group site. All sites have fire pits; most have picnic tables. Amenities include potable water and flush toilets. Best of all, the campground has hot showers (free with a site, fee for non-guests), a rarity in Death Valley campgrounds (Furnace Creek, the crowded hub on the other side of the park, is the only other campground with showers). The campsites can fill quickly, so make reservations well ahead of time. Panamint Springs is a pet-friendly resort; however, pets must be declared before check-in. There is a surcharge of $5 per reservation for pets in RV and tent sites. Electric vehicle charging is also available ($20 charge).

Emigrant Campground

10 sites; first-come, first-served; year-round; free

Emigrant Campground is a tiny tent-only

1: views of the Panamint Range from Panamint Springs Resort Campground **2:** Panamint Springs Resort Campground **3:** Panamint Springs tent cabins **4:** restaurant at Panamint Springs Resort

1
2
3
4
RESTAURAN
BURGERS-SALA

campground at the junction of Highway 190 and Emigrant Canyon Road. It's a pretty spot that more closely resembles a day-use area. Sites are small, close together, and exposed to the open desert. It's too small to serve as a base camp for several days, but it will do in a pinch. At 2,100 feet (640 m) elevation and with no shade, it can be uncomfortably hot in summer, although cooler than the valley floor (but almost any place is cooler than the valley floor). Amenities include picnic tables, drinking water, and restrooms with flush toilets. No fires are allowed.

Directions

Emigrant is directly off paved Highway 190, approximately 21 miles (34 km) east of Panamint Springs, so it's easy to access and centrally located.

Wildrose Campground

23 sites; first-come, first-served; year-round; free

Wildrose Campground is tucked away at the lower end of Wildrose Canyon, surrounded by mesquite and low hills. At 4,100 feet (1,250 m) elevation, the camp sits at a good midlevel point to avoid the scorching temperatures of the valley floor in summer and the snow of the higher elevations. Unlike the seasonal campgrounds at the higher elevations of the canyon, Wildrose is open year-round and rarely fills up. Its level sites don't offer privacy or shade, but it's a peaceful campground in a quiet and lovely section of the park. It's a great place to set up a base camp for exploring the Emigrant Canyon and Wildrose Canyon areas, with easy access to Skidoo, the Wildrose Charcoal Kilns, Wildrose Peak, and Telescope Peak. Amenities include picnic tables, fire pits, potable water, and pit toilets; the campground is also accessible to small trailers.

Directions

To get here from the north, take Emigrant Canyon Road south toward Wildrose Canyon from Highway 190 for approximately 21 miles (34 km), to the end of Emigrant Canyon Road. From the south, Trona-Wildrose Road veers past it approximately 46 miles (74 km) north of Trona. Trona-Wildrose Road is prone to washouts. Pay attention to park alerts, and check for road closures before planning your route.

Thorndike Campground

6 sites; first-come, first-served; Mar.-Nov.; free

Rocky and remote Thorndike Campground is perched between the canyon walls high up in Wildrose Canyon. This campground lies between Wildrose Campground, downcanyon, and Mahogany Flat, at the top of the canyon, which means it can get overlooked. Since it's lightly visited, you should have no problem getting a spot; you might even have it all to yourself. The combination of steep canyon walls, a perch off the winding canyon road, and winds whipping downcanyon through gnarled juniper trees gives this place a wild and forgotten feel. The sheerness of the canyon walls cuts in on the daylight hours, so when the sun dips, it can get chilly. Bring firewood, as the nights can get surprisingly cold, even in summer. However, this can be a welcome relief when it's too hot at lower elevations.

Almost all campsites are shaded—a rarity in Death Valley. Amenities include picnic tables, fire pits, and pit toilets; there is no drinking water available (the closest drinking water is at Wildrose Campground, about 8 mi/12.9 km downcanyon). If you want to hike both Telescope Peak and Wildrose Peak, this is a great home base.

At 7,400 feet (2,256 m) elevation, snow can make access impossible for vehicles November-March.

Directions

To get here from the north, take Emigrant Canyon Road south toward Wildrose Canyon from Highway 190 for approximately 21 miles (34 km), to the end of Emigrant Canyon Road at Wildrose Campground. At Wildrose Campground, take Wildrose Canyon Road another 9 miles (14.5 km) up the canyon. The pavement ends at 7 miles (11.3 km), at the

Wildrose Charcoal Kilns. The gravel road is steep and rocky from here. A **high-clearance vehicle** is necessary; a 4WD vehicle is preferable when navigating snow, ice, or washouts. The road is not accessible to trailers. From the south, drive Trona-Wildrose Road 46 miles (74 km) north of Trona to the Wildrose Campground, and then drive an additional 9 miles (14.5 km) up Wildrose Canyon Road. Keep in mind that Trona-Wildrose Road is prone to washouts. If the road is closed, you might have to bypass it.

Mahogany Flat Campground

10 sites; first-come, first-served; Mar.-Nov.; free

Perched at the top of Wildrose Canyon, Mahogany Flat Campground offers cool temperatures, sweeping views, and access to Telescope Peak, the highest mountain peak in the park. At 8,200 feet (2,499 m) elevation, expect cool nights, which can be a lifesaver in the summer. Many people use this campground as a jumping-off point to hike Telescope Peak, since the trailhead starts just outside the campground. It gets some traffic because of the popularity of Telescope Peak, but you are still likely to find a spot.

Amenities include picnic tables, fire pits, and pit toilets; there is no drinking water available (the closest water is at Wildrose Campground, about 9 mi/14.5 km downcanyon). Snow may make the campground inaccessible November-March.

Directions

To get here from the north, take Emigrant Canyon Road south toward Wildrose Canyon from Highway 190 for approximately 21 miles (34 km), to the end of Emigrant Canyon Road at Wildrose Campground. At Wildrose Campground, take Wildrose Canyon Road another 11 miles (17.7 km) up the canyon to the end of the road at the campground. The road gets slightly steeper and rockier past Thorndike Campground. A **high-clearance vehicle** is necessary; a 4WD vehicle is better when navigating snow, ice, or washouts. From the south, drive Trona-Wildrose Road 46 miles (74 km) north of Trona to Wildrose Campground, and then drive an additional 11 miles (17.7 km) up Wildrose Canyon Road until it ends at the campground.

Backcountry Camping

Depending on where you go, backcountry camping could be your only option—or your best option.

In the Emigrant Canyon and Wildrose Canyon areas, developed campgrounds are the best bet; the most tempting backcountry choices here are off-limits. Backcountry camping is not allowed off Skidoo Road, Wildrose Canyon Road, or Aguereberry Point Road. These are all considered day-use-only roads and are some of the few roads in the area.

Western Panamint Canyons

When exploring the western Panamint canyons, backcountry camping is the only choice, unless you commute from Panamint Springs or Wildrose Canyon for day explorations only. Of course, this limits your fun. The western canyons, including **Surprise Canyon** and **Pleasant Canyon,** are popular backpacking and 4WD trails. Many of these canyons begin on Bureau of Land Management (BLM) land and cross into the jurisdiction of Death Valley National Park. When camping on BLM land, or for any backcountry camping, camp in a site that has already been disturbed (sometimes called a dispersed site or dispersed camping). To locate dispersed sites, look for pullouts or spurs off the road that are hard-packed and devoid of vegetation. These are not labeled as campsites, but if you know what to look for, you can have an enjoyable backcountry experience.

If you want to set up a main base camp or give yourself a fresh start for backpacking or exploring the 4WD trails in the canyons, the ghost town of **Ballarat** is a good place to start. There are no supplies, but you will be strategically located to get your fill of old mining camps, rocky creeks, and sculpted canyon walls.

Saline Valley

Saline Valley Warm Springs has primitive camping spots. These sites are used primarily by people visiting the springs. There are well-maintained pit toilets and outdoor shower stations with water piped from the hot springs. There are no fees for camping, and drinking water is not available. From Saline Valley Road, the primitive 6.8-mile (10.9-km) road to the camp can be sandy and hard to follow.

John Muir Wilderness

The John Muir Wilderness (www.fs.usda.gov) is not an aside—it's a destination, with jewel-like turquoise glacial lakes, craggy snow-covered peaks, glaciers, and meadows. Extending for nearly 100 miles (161 km) along the crest of the eastern Sierra Nevada range, this dazzling wilderness area has miles of trails for day hikes and backpacking trips. The iconic John Muir and Pacific Crest Trails cut through this area; Mount Whitney, the highest peak in the contiguous United States at 14,505 feet (4,421 m), marks the southern end of the John Muir Trail. This wilderness area lies to the west of Death Valley National Park, with 85 miles (137 km) between Mount Whitney and Badwater Basin, the highest and lowest points in the contiguous United States Many visitors combine a trip to the John Muir Wilderness and Death Valley. From Panamint Springs, the western exit from Death Valley, it is a one-hour drive to Lone Pine at the foot of Mount Whitney and the Sierra Nevada. The drive highlights the dramatic intersection of desert and mountain and gives access to alpine adventures.

The John Muir Wilderness is also a huge angler destination. Many of the lakes are stocked with trout, and creeks rush through all the major canyons and drainages. Most campgrounds in the area are established along creeks, so you don't even need to leave camp to find a good fishing spot.

The area is best visited **late spring-early fall** due to the high elevation and possibility of snow and ice. Many campgrounds are closed in winter, and roads may be closed due to snow.

Orientation

Road access to the John Muir Wilderness is along US 395. This rural highway divides mountain from desert terrain, providing access to the eastern Sierra Nevada on the western side and Death Valley on the eastern side. Some of the same gateway towns along US 395 that provide access to Death Valley are also jumping-off points for the John Muir Wilderness. From north to south, these small, scenic towns are **Bishop, Big Pine, Independence,** and **Lone Pine.**

FROM BISHOP/ HIGHWAY 168

Of the US 395 towns, Bishop provides the most extensive paved-road access into the John Muir Wilderness. From the town center, Line Street turns into Highway 168, heading west toward the mountains into scenic Bishop Canyon. Bishop Creek is the splashing through-line of the region, carving out the north, middle, and south forks of Bishop Canyon. North Lake Road and South Lake Road branch off Highway 168, giving access to the north and south forks of Bishop Canyon, while Highway 168 gives access to the middle fork. The three roads in the region roughly parallel the creek, and all campgrounds are creek-adjacent. Together the North Fork, Middle Fork, and South Fork of Bishop Creek make up the Eastern Sierra's largest watershed and a region sprinkled liberally with alpine lakes, many accessed by an extensive

John Muir Wilderness

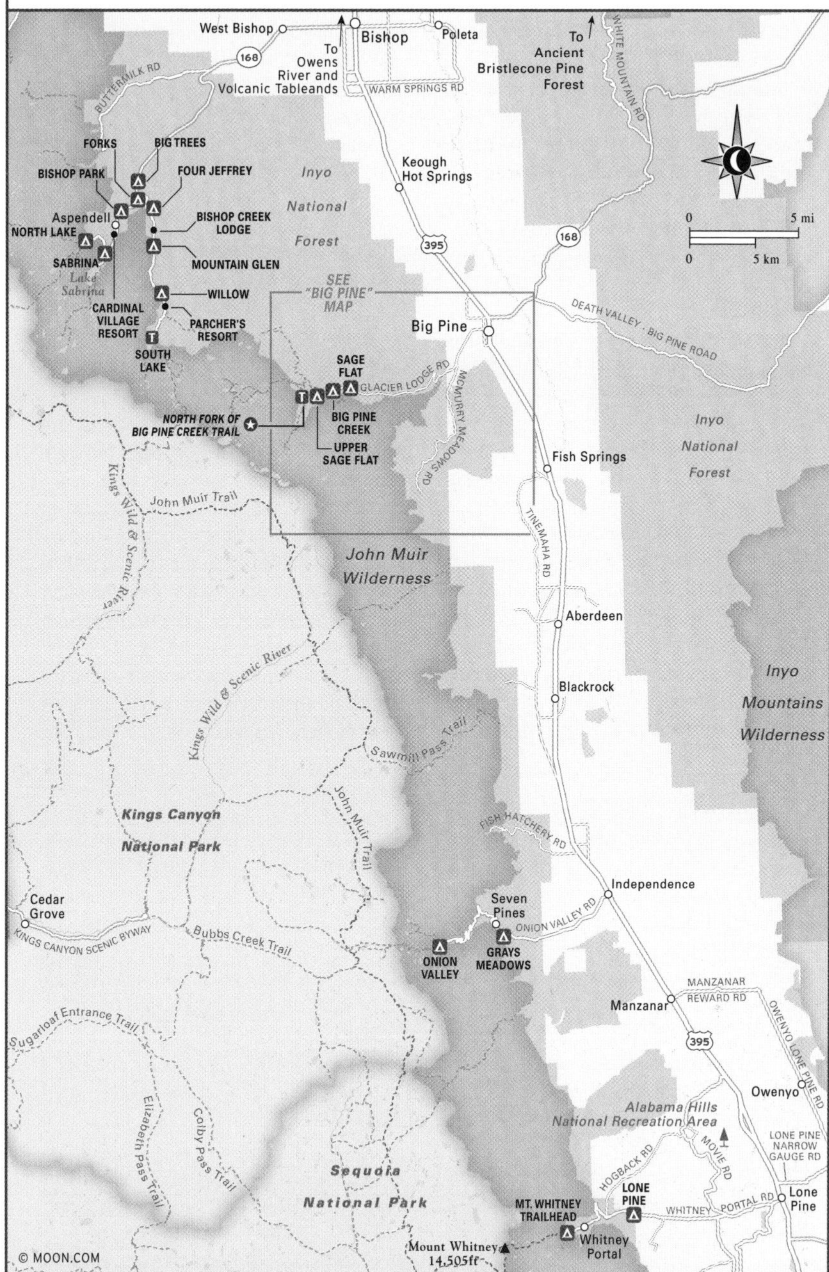

high-country trail network. The North Fork and South Fork have trail systems that continue over the Sierra Crest, eventually leading to Kings Canyon National Park on the western side of the mountains.

Pick up wilderness permits and find out trail, campground, road, weather, and backcountry conditions at **White Mountain Public Lands Information Center** (798 N. Main St.; 760/873-2500; www.fs.usda.gov; 8am-noon and 1pm-4:30pm Tues.-Sat. May-Oct., call for winter season virtual service).

Directions

To reach the North Fork, head west on Highway 168, signed South Lake and Lake Sabrina, from Bishop for 18 miles (29 km). A right turn on North Lake Road leads to the North Fork of Bishop Creek. Tiny **North Lake** is popular for fishing, the North Lake Campground, and hiking trails.

To reach the Middle Fork of Bishop Creek, head west on Highway 168 from Bishop for 15 miles (24 km) to the signed junction with South Lake. Continue on the main (right) fork for another 4 miles (6.4 km) to end at **Lake Sabrina,** a popular fishing and boating destination.

To reach the South Fork of Bishop Creek, head west on Highway 168 from Bishop for 15 miles (24 km) to the signed junction with South Lake. Take the left fork (South Lake Road) for an additional 7 miles (11.3 km) to end at **South Lake,** a scenic, 170-acre (69-ha) alpine gem nestled at 9,768 feet (2,977 m), where many trailheads converge.

Highway 168 and South Lake Road pass by numerous developed campgrounds, rustic lodging, and a vast network of hiking trails.

Boating and Fishing

The John Muir Wilderness near Bishop is an especially popular spot for anglers. The high-country lakes around the Eastern Sierra are stocked with brook, golden (native to California), rainbow, cutthroat, and even brown trout. There are myriad backcountry fishing spots here, some accessible by paved roads and others only by hiking. If you really want to get serious about it, the Department of Fish and Game has an *Eastern Sierra Backcountry Fishing Guide* (www.fs.usda.gov) showing detailed maps to backcountry lakes and streams with a key to the type of fish in each.

The season runs **May-October** due to the potential for high snow and road closures the rest of the year. Anyone 16 years or older must

the Sierra Nevada rising above the desert boulders of the Alabama Hills

have a valid California long- or short-term sport fishing license. They are available online (www.ca.gov) or at many sporting goods stores.

Lake Sabrina, South Lake, Intake 2, North Lake, and the three forks of Bishop Creek (North, Middle, and South) are the most obvious choices, and are all reachable by car. That said, all campgrounds are creek-adjacent, making fishing an option that pops up everywhere.

Lake Sabrina

Lake Sabrina (elevation 9,128 ft/2,782 m) was created in 1907 by damming the Middle Fork of Bishop Creek. Despite the concrete dam, the lake is a scenic destination. Day-use visitors fish off the dam as well as from the shoreline. **Lake Sabrina Boat Landing** (760/873-7425; www.lakesabrinaboatlanding.com) is open Memorial Day weekend-September, offering boat and pontoon rentals and a small store with bait, tackle, ice, drinks, and snacks. A café serves breakfast and lunch, wine, beer, pie, and ice cream on a deck overlooking the lake (pie and coffee 8am-5pm daily; kitchen and beer counter 8am-3pm Fri.-Sun.).

South Lake

In addition to being a destination for scenery gazing, South Lake offers boating and fishing; the lake is populated with wild and stocked trout for conventional and fly fishing. South Lake has a boat landing managed by **Parcher's Resort** (760/873-4177; www.parchersresort.net; Memorial Day weekend-mid-Oct.; 7am-6pm summer, 8am-6pm fall). The store rents kayaks and pontoon boats in the summer season, depending on the water level (since it is a reservoir, water levels can vary). Call for boat availability. The store also offers fishing, camping, and vacation basics including tackle, beer and soda, ice, staple grocery items, firewood, charcoal, sundries, and gifts. The shores of South Lake are wild, rocky, and steep. The best lake access is from the boat landing.

Intake 2

Located 16 miles (26 km) southwest of Bishop on Highway 168 and 0.5 mile (0.8 km) south of Intake 2 Campground, Intake 2 is the lowest-elevation lake in Bishop Creek Canyon and is easy to fish. It is heavily stocked with rainbow trout and popular for shore fishing and tubing. It also has wheelchair-accessible fishing. No boat rentals or services are available.

North Lake

North Lake is a pond by comparison to Lake Sabrina and South Lake; though small, it's not short on natural beauty or good fishing. It is on a narrow dirt road less than 1 mile (1.6 km) south of North Lake Campground, giving it a backcountry feel.

Mac's Sporting Goods

425 N. Main St.; 760/872-9201; www.macssportinggoods.com; 8am-5pm daily

In Bishop try Mac's Sporting Goods for friendly, knowledgeable staff and the basics to outfit your Eastern Sierra fishing trip, including rod and reels, lures, bait hooks, and artificial and live bait.

Reagan's Sporting Goods

963 N. Main St.; 760/872-3000; www.reaganssportinggoods.com; 8am-5pm Mon.-Sat., 8am-3pm Sun.

Reagan's offers a large selection of sporting goods for fishing and hunting, as well as some camping supplies.

Hiking

Due to all the great hikes and fishing spots, parking can be scarce at South Lake. The road ends at an upper parking area set aside for overnight hikers. A lot just below this is designated for day hikers. Get there early (before 9am) for good parking, or take the slacker approach and get there around noon when the first round of go-getters are returning from their hikes. Even if parking is difficult, trails thin out quickly past the trailheads due to the number of destinations.

Piute Pass

Distance: *10.7 miles (17.2 km) round-trip*
Duration: *5-7 hours*
Elevation gain: *2,300 feet (701 m)*
Effort: *Moderate*
Access: *Passenger vehicle*
Trailhead: *North Lake Campground*

The Piute Pass hike is a classic Sierra experience. It begins at the north end of the North Lake Campground and steadily gains elevation over 5 miles (8 km) (it is 10.7 mi/17.2 km round-trip to Piute Pass and back). The trail crosses several streams to pass a string of alpine lakes and ponds, including Loch Leven and Piute Lake, until it caps off at windswept Piute Pass (elevation 11,377 ft/3,468 m), overlooking glacier-carved backcountry. For some, the pass is the portal into a longer backpacking trip; you may be tempted as you look out over the landscape from this well-earned vantage point.

Lamarck Lakes

Distance: *5.2 miles (8.4 km) round-trip to Lower Lamarck Lake; 6.4 miles (10.3 km) round-trip to Upper Lamarck Lake*
Duration: *3-4 hours*
Elevation gain: *1,500 feet (457 m)*
Effort: *Difficult*
Access: *Passenger vehicle*
Trailhead: *North Lake Campground*

The Lamarck Lakes hike climbs steeply through aspen groves and lodgepole pine forest toward sweeping views and two alpine lakes. The hike gains 1,500 feet (457 m) in elevation from the trailhead (9,400 ft/2,865 m) to Upper Lamarck Lake (10,900 ft/3,322 m). Round-trip, it covers 5.2 miles (8.4 km) to Lower Lamarck Lake and 6.4 miles (10.3 km) to Upper Lamarck Lake. The Lamarck Lakes trail is an excellent day hike; it is more lightly traveled than Piute Pass since it does not continue as a thru-hike across the Sierra Nevada.

Blue Lake

Distance: *6 miles (9.7 km) round-trip*
Duration: *3-4 hours*
Elevation gain: *1,310 feet (399 m)*
Effort: *Difficult*
Access: *Passenger vehicle*
Trailhead: *Lake Sabrina parking area*

The hike to Blue Lake is the first to reach the many spectacular hiking destinations in the glacial-carved Sabrina Basin portion of the John Muir Wilderness. From the signed trailhead below the dam, the trail parallels Lake Sabrina's eastern shore before it gets steeper, crossing open granite slabs with views of the lake. Blue Lake appears after 2.8 miles (4.5 km). The best access is a stream crossing where the stream crosses the trail. Call it a day here or continue on to other excellent destinations in this network of lakes. The trailhead is below the final parking area on the east side (this will be on the right if you have parked and are walking back down the road).

Hungry Packer Lake

Distance: *12.6 miles (20.3 km) round-trip*
Duration: *6-10 hours*
Elevation gain: *2,773 feet (845 m)*
Effort: *Moderate*
Access: *Passenger vehicle*
Trailhead: *Lake Sabrina parking area*

The trek to Hungry Packer Lake provides solitude and a chance to traverse the glacial-carved Sabrina Basin, passing many other destination-worthy lakes and streams along the way. From the signed trailhead below the dam, the trail parallels Lake Sabrina's eastern shore before it gets steeper, with Blue Lake appearing after 2.8 miles (4.5 km). Make a right at the junction near Blue Lake's shore to continue on. The grades are less steep beyond Blue Lake, and there are views of Dingleberry Lake after another 1.4 miles (2.3 km). From there you will hike through granite boulder-studded meadows before reaching spectacular Hungry Packer, framed by triangular Picture Peak. The trailhead is below the final parking area on the east side (this will be on the right if you have parked and are walking back down the road).

Treasure Lakes

Distance: *6 miles (9.7 km) round-trip*

Duration: *3-4 hours*
Elevation gain: *1,360 feet (415 m)*
Effort: *Moderate*
Access: *Passenger vehicle*
Trailhead: *South Lake parking area*

A 6-mile (9.7-km) round-trip hike to Treasure Lakes takes you to a duo of alpine gems tucked into a sheer, craggy mountain fortress. The destination is a spectacular place to take in the scene from either of the lake's rocky shores and eat lunch. The journey isn't too bad either, crossing icy mountain streams past stands of wildflowers as the trail gains elevation. At 6 miles (9.7 km) round-trip, the hike is long enough to leave you proud of your accomplishment but manageable enough to leave you with the energy for an icy post-hike beverage at the Bishop Creek Lodge just down the road. The trailhead, like other trails in the area, begins at the far end of the top parking area near South Lake. You'll have sweeping views of South Lake before the trail turns into the forest to switchback up toward the lakes.

Lower Marie Louise Lake

Distance: *3.6 miles (5.8 km) round-trip*
Duration: *2-3 hours*
Elevation gain: *935 feet (285 m)*
Effort: *Moderate*
Access: *Passenger vehicle*
Trailhead: *South Lake parking area*

Short and sweet, the hike to Lower Marie Louise Lake is a 3.6-mile (5.8 km) round-trip with a pretty and secluded payoff. The hike clocks in at well under three hours, and although the first 0.5-mile (0.8-km) and last 0.6-mile (1-km) stretches are steep, the distance makes the trail very manageable, even for children. I have hiked this trail with a six-month-old strapped to my chest (she napped her way past spectacular views of South Lake, picturesque streams, wildflower meadows, and pine forest). The trail shares the trailhead with the Treasure Lakes and Bishop Pass hikes, so the first stretch has the most traffic. At 0.8 mile (1.3 km), the trail forks toward Bishop Pass (left). In another 0.6 mile (1 km), a spur trail to the left leads to Marie Louise Lakes while the main trail continues to Bishop Pass. At this point you will likely leave most other hikers behind, and may find that you have the lovely Marie Louise Lakes all to yourself. Lower Marie Louise Lake is serene and forested, chock-full of trout, and a lovely place for a picnic. To find the small upper lake, follow the shoreline left to pick up a short trail to **Upper Marie Louise Lake.**

Bishop Pass

Distance: *11.4 miles (18.3 km) round-trip*
Duration: *4-5 hours*
Elevation gain: *2,172 feet (662 m)*
Effort: *Moderate*
Access: *Passenger vehicle*
Trailhead: *South Lake parking area*

Earn spectacular mountain scenery and a string of alpine lakes along the full-day hike to Bishop Pass. Views from the trail become impressive after **Long Lake** (2.3 mi/3.7 km in), affording views of the jagged, granite fortress of the Inconsolable Range and lofty Chocolate Peak and Mount Goode. However, if you decide to call it at Long Lake and turn around, this is a fine destination for a day hike (4.6 mi/7.4 km round-trip). Bishop Pass marks the line between the Eastern and Western Sierra as well as the Inyo National Forest and Kings Canyon National Park. Hardy hikers prepared for backpacking may use this trail to continue, connecting with the John Muir Trail or the Pacific Crest Trail through remote and breathtaking alpine wilderness. Other shorter destinations that spur off the Bishop Pass trail include **Bull Lake** (4.2 mi/6.8 km round-trip) and **Chocolate Lakes** (5.3 mi/8.5 km round-trip). To reach these scenic destinations, follow the trail marker to Bull Lake from the Bishop Pass trail. The Chocolate Lakes (there are three) begin 0.5 mile (0.8 km) beyond Bull Lake.

Tyee Lakes

Distance: *7.6 miles (12.2 km) round-trip*
Duration: *4-5 hours*
Elevation gain: *2,135 feet (651 m)*
Effort: *Difficult*

Access: *Passenger vehicle*

Trailhead: *Signed trailhead on Highway 168 just before Willow Campground*

A steady uphill trail leads through aspens and lodgepole pines to a chain of four unique lakes. Tyee Lakes does not share the South Lake trailhead of many other hikes in the area, cutting out some of the crowds. The unusual name comes from a brand of salmon eggs bait, although rainbow and brown trout are the fish you will find here. The Tyee Lakes trail begins approximately 5 miles (8 km) north of the intersection of Highway 168 and the turnoff for South Lake. Look for a wooden bridge and sign for Tyee Lakes on your right. If you reach Willow Campground, you have gone too far.

Camping and Accommodations

North Lake

11 sites; June-Sept.; first-come, first-served; $27

Perched at 9,300 feet (2,835 m) elevation, North Lake Campground is a lovely campground adjacent to the North Fork of Bishop Creek. It offers 11 shaded sites scattered among tall Jeffrey and lodgepole pines, 8 with small parking spots and 3 that require a short walk in. The road to reach the campground is winding and narrow, part pavement and part gravel; trailers and RVs are not allowed. North Lake Campground is popular with thru-hikers, day hikers, and more casual campers. The turnover can be high because people use it as a jumping-off point for backpacking trips.

Lake Sabrina

www.fs.usda.gov; first-come, first-served; $30

Several US Forest Service campgrounds are directly off paved Highway 168 between Bishop and Lake Sabrina. They are all along Bishop Creek, offering scenic camping as well as fishing opportunities. Amenities include flush and/or vault toilets, fire rings, picnic tables, and drinking water. **Big Trees Campground** (7,400 ft/2,256 m; May-Oct.), approximately 9 miles (14.5 km) from Bishop, is the first campground you come to on the way up the mountain. It offers 16 campsites set among, well, big trees (large Jeffrey pines). Some sites are large enough for campers or RVs. Past Big Trees, the road gets narrower and windier; most campsites beyond this are tent-only with a few options for smaller rigs.

The romantically named **Intake 2** (8,200 ft/2,499 m; May-Oct.), approximately 16 miles (26 km) from Bishop, is named for a small fishing lake. There are 5 walk-in sites on the lakeshore and 11 car-camping sites near the creek above Intake 2. **Bishop Park Campground** (8,400 ft/2,560 m; May-Oct.), approximately 16 miles (26 km) from Bishop, is popular, with grassy lawns and sites on the banks of Bishop Creek. It maintains 21 sites, many of them walk-in tent sites. Large RVs are not recommended, but a few sites can accommodate small campers or trailers. **Sabrina Campground** (8,900 ft/2,713 m; May-Sept.) is the closest campground to Lake Sabrina, about 3 miles (4.8 km) away. Like the other campgrounds in the area, it runs along the Middle Fork of Bishop Creek; some sites are closer to the creek than others. It offers 18 campsites, some shaded and some sunny.

Cardinal Village Resort

321 Cardinal Rd., Bishop; 760/873-4789; www.cardinalvillageresort.com; $100-500

Cardinal Village Resort, open the last weekend in April-last weekend in October, is at an elevation of 8,500 feet (2,591 m) in the small community of **Aspendell.** Cardinal Village was built in the early 1900s to serve a nearby gold mine. The mine closed in the 1930s, and in 1946 Cardinal Village began serving anglers and their families. The resort now offers 13 rustic cabins, most of which were originally miners' homes, along with two newer structures, for groups ranging 1-16 people. Four cabins are available during the winter months, though the café is closed in winter. No pets are allowed. It is the closest lodging to the Lake Sabrina, North Lake, and Intake

1: Tyee Lakes **2:** Four Jeffrey Campground **3:** Sage Flat Campground **4:** historic Bishop Creek Lodge

1
2
3
4
CREEK
LODGE
MOUNTAIN-LODGE

2 fishing destinations. For hiking, it is only a few miles to trailheads for Piute Pass and Lamarck Lakes and miles of backcountry hiking and alpine lakes. The on-site **Cardinal Café** (8am-3pm daily, summer only) serves a basic American menu, including hot breakfasts, burgers, beer, and wine, with wood-fired pizza in summer. A small store stocks clothing, gifts, books, and maps.

South Lake

www.fs.usda.gov

Campgrounds in the South Lake region range from the 106-site, RV-friendly Four Jeffrey Campground to tiny Mountain Glen, with 5 sites and no piped water. The US Forest Service campgrounds are all located along South Lake Road and adjacent to the South Fork of Bishop Creek. The only campground in the area that takes reservations is Four Jeffrey Campground.

Forks Campground (7,800 ft/2,377 m; May-Oct.; $30; no reservations) offers 21 sites among tall Jeffrey pines and aspens, some creekside. Located near the junction of the South Fork and Middle Fork of Bishop Creek, this is the lowest-elevation campground along South Lake Road, making it easiest to access for campers and trailers. **Four Jeffrey Campground,** the next on the way up the mountain, is the largest campground in the Bishop area, offering 106 sites, some reservable (8,100 ft/2,469 m; 877/444-6777; www.recreation.gov; May-Oct.; $30). Don't let the large number of sites scare you away; this is a lovely campground with a high desert and low alpine feel. Some sites are scattered across sage flats dotted with pine, offering spectacular views of the surrounding granite mountains. Others are along aspen-lined Bishop Creek. The campground is good for tent camping as well as campers and RVs.

Mountain Glen (8,500 ft/2,591 m; May-Sept.; $25; no reservations; natural/unpiped water only) is a small, charming campground offering five sites tucked into an aspen grove along Bishop Creek. **Willow Camp** (9,000 ft/2,743 m; May-Sept.; $25; natural/unpiped water only) is a lovely, tiny campground offering eight walk-in sites nestled along Bishop Creek. This is the last campground before South Lake.

Two historical lodges along South Lake Road offer cabins and amenities. **Bishop Creek Lodge** (2100 S. Lake Rd., Bishop; 760/873-4484; www.bishopcreekresort.com; Apr.-Oct.) is a great stop for day hikers, visitors, and destination weekenders. The **Bishop Creek Lodge Café and Bar** (bar 8am-4pm Sun.-Thurs., 8am-8pm Fri.-Sat., kitchen 11am-8pm Fri.-Sat.) offers a simple menu with pizza, burgers, french fries, and salads as well as a full bar and local brews. Bishop Creek Lodge began in the 1920s as Schober's Lodge, and the bar and café is still operating from the original log cabin.

Parcher's Resort (760/873-4177; www.parchersresort.net; Memorial Day weekend-mid-Oct.) is a rustic mountain retreat established in 1921 by W. C. and Marie Louise Parcher for recreation. It offers cabins, RV sites, a small store, and a boat launch. It is the closest lodging to South Lake—less than 1 mile (1.6 km) south of the Bishop Pass trail, South Lake Boat Landing, and other hiking and fishing. The property offers 19 rustic cabins that can accommodate 2-6 people ($150-329) and three RV sites with hookups ($75). The South Lake Boat Landing rents fishing boats and pontoon boats for half and full days ($75-325) and tandem kayaks by the hour ($15 per hour).

FROM BIG PINE/ GLACIER LODGE AREA

Big Pine is the most popular gateway town to the John Muir Wilderness, offering some of the most spectacular hikes in the area.

Hiking

★ North Fork of Big Pine Creek

Distance: *16 miles (26 km) round-trip*
Duration: *8-10 hours*
Elevation gain: *3,440 feet (1,049 m)*
Effort: *Strenuous*
Access: *Passenger vehicle*

Trailhead: *Glacier Pack Train station*

The North Fork of Big Pine Creek is so rich with spectacular alpine lakes that no one bothered to name them all. A 16-mile (26-km) hiking loop passes First, Second, Third, Fourth, Fifth, Sixth, Seventh, and Black Lakes in a full-day hike that soars to 11,200 feet (3,414 m). Cut out 3 miles (4.8 km) and some elevation by skipping Sixth and Seventh Lakes. The lakes are linked in a chain of granite bowls, fed by the Palisade Glacier, the southernmost glacier in the United States. Because of the pristine water source, all lakes except one are a dazzling turquoise color (hint—Black Lake is not turquoise). Park at a dirt parking area across from the Glacier Pack Train and begin the hike behind the corrals. The good news is that if you are not up for the 16-mile (26-km) or even the 13-mile (20.9-km) loop, there are several other spectacular destinations within easier reach. At 2 miles (3.2 km) you will reach a waterfall. At 2.7 miles (4.3 km), the Lon Chaney cabin, completed in 1930 for the famous actor, provides a respite next to a calmly idyllic stream. You can also do an out-and-back hike to Second Lake (it's hard to choose, but this might be the most stunning) in a 9-mile (14.5-km) trek.

Camping and Accommodations

US Forest Service Campgrounds

877/444-6777; www.recreation.gov; $23-25

US Forest Service campgrounds in this area include **Sage Flat** (7,400 ft/2,256 m; 28 sites; first-come, first-served; mid-Apr.-mid-Nov.), **Upper Sage Flat** (7,600 ft/2,316 m; 21 sites; May-mid-Oct.), and **Big Pine Creek** (7,700 ft/2,347 m; 30 sites; May-mid-Oct.). All are pretty, shaded canyon campgrounds with water and toilets. The campgrounds are just off Glacier Lodge Road and are visible from the road.

Glacier Lodge

Glacier Lodge Rd., 11 miles (17.7 km) west of US 395; 760/938-2837; www.glacierlodge395.com; Apr.-Nov.; tent or RV sites $38-65, cabins $189-219

Spend the night at Glacier Lodge along Glacier Lodge Road, which heads west into mountain wilderness and US Forest Service lands. Glacier Lodge is a historical mountain retreat built in 1917. The lodge itself burned down in 1998, but it still offers rustic cabins as well as RV and tent camping.

Getting There

The North Fork of Big Pine Canyon and the John Muir Wilderness are reached by heading west from Crocker Avenue, in the center of Big Pine, and continuing 10 miles (16.1 km) west on Glacier Lodge Road. The road leads to campgrounds, Glacier Lodge, and spectacular alpine hikes.

FROM INDEPENDENCE/ ONION VALLEY ROAD

The tiny town of Independence is popular with day hikers visiting the alpine lakes of lovely Onion Valley and thru-hikers connecting with the backcountry of Kings Canyon National Park on the western side of the mountain range via Kearsarge Pass. The pass is the shortest, lowest, and one of the most well-graded trails over the Pacific Crest.

Hiking

Kearsarge Pass

Distance: *11 miles (17.7 km) round-trip*
Duration: *5-7 hours*
Elevation gain: *2,623 feet (799 m)*
Effort: *Strenuous*
Access: *Passenger vehicle*
Trailhead: *Right side of Onion Valley Road between the lower and upper hiker parking areas*

The main trail leading to Kearsarge Pass entices day hikers as well as thru-hikers looking to connect with the Pacific Crest Trail on the western side of the Sierra Nevada range. The trail begins on the right side of the road between the lower and upper hiker parking areas. To reach the parking areas, follow Onion Valley Road west for 13.7 miles (22 km). From the trailhead, it is 11 miles (17.7 km) to Kearsarge Pass and back, with 2,623 feet (799 m) of elevation gain. If this seems like too much of a commitment, **Gilbert Lake,** at 2.3 miles (3.7 km) into the Kearsarge Pass trail, makes a fine destination.

Camping and Accommodations

US Forest Service Campgrounds

877/444-6777; www.recreation.gov; $25-29

The area offers several US Forest Service campgrounds with reservable sites as well as sites available on a first-come, first-served basis. Onion Valley Campground (9,200 ft/2,804 m; June-Oct.) is a great choice if you're positioning yourself for a big hike. It offers 29 mountainside sites up to 25 feet (7.6 m) long; trailers are not recommended except for tent trailers. The campground has drinking water, vault toilets, and firewood for sale. If you are a more casual camper and hiker, consider camping at one of the lower-elevation campgrounds: Lower Grays Meadow and Upper Grays Meadow Campgrounds are both approximately 6 miles (9.7 km) west of Independence. These sites have more sunlight, more privacy, and a more laid-back vibe (at the top there is a lot more gear and hike preparation). Lower Grays Meadow and Upper Grays Meadow (6,000 ft/1,829 m elevation; May-Oct.) sit along Independence Creek in high desert landscape. Lower Grays Meadow offers 52 sites, and Upper Grays Meadow offers 35, with sites ranging from sunny, desert sagebrush and pine to shaded, walk-in creekside spots. Some sites may be available on a first-come, first-served basis. Sites include picnic tables and fire rings, with vault toilets on-site.

Getting There

From the center of Independence, Onion Valley Road climbs west into the John Muir Wilderness, passing through sagebrush and pine to a higher glacier-carved landscape. The road ends in just over 13 miles (20.9 km) at Onion Valley Campground. Two parking areas give access to the campground and trailheads.

FROM LONE PINE/ WHITNEY PORTAL ROAD

Whitney Portal (elevation 8,374 ft/2,552 m) refers to the end of Whitney Portal Road, which begins in Lone Pine and stops at the closest paved point to the summit. It attracts day hikers, thru-hikers, day-use visitors, and campers. From Lone Pine, Whitney Portal Road heads west for 12 miles (19.3 km), snaking up the flanks of Mount Whitney, providing spectacular views of the Owens Valley below, to end at the hiking and wilderness gateway. Horseshoe Meadows Road intersects Whitney Portal Road after 3 miles (4.8 km) and continues its own 19-mile (31-km) mountain route with exceptional views and hiking and camping access.

Hiking

Mount Whitney

Distance: *22 miles (35 km) round-trip*
Duration: *12-14 hours*
Elevation gain: *6,100 feet (1,859 m)*
Effort: *Strenuous*
Access: *Passenger vehicle; permit required*
Trailhead: *Whitney Portal*

From Whitney Portal, fit hikers tackle the shortest route to the Mount Whitney summit, a 22-mile (35-km) round-trip day hike. A preapproved permit is necessary and available via lottery (www.recreation.gov). Thru-hikers can access the classic **John Muir Trail** at the summit of Mount Whitney, which extends more than 200 miles (320 km) to Yosemite Valley. The trailhead for the under-appreciated Whitney Portal National Recreation Trail also begins here and covers 4 miles (6.4 km) one-way to end at the car-accessible Lone Pine Campground, nestled between the town of Lone Pine and the base of Mount Whitney. Even if you're not undertaking a massive trek, Whitney Portal is worth a visit for the sweeping views along the drive (don't look down; there are no guardrails) as well as the portal itself. At the top you'll find a day-use picnic area, small fishing pond, store and restaurant, and a waterfall to admire.

Camping and Accommodations

Lone Pine Campground

42 sites; www.recreation.gov; May-Oct.; $29

The campgrounds at the Whitney Portal largely serve as a base camp for Mount Whitney and John Muir Trail hikers. For the casual camper, the best bet is Lone Pine Campground (6,000 ft/1,829 m elevation). The 42 sites nestle among the sagebrush near Lone Pine Creek, in addition to one walk-in group site. Some sites are up to 40 feet (12.2 m) long and will fit small RVs or campers, but there are no hookups. Sites include fire pits, and there are vault toilets in the campground. Firewood is available for purchase. Some first-come, first-served sites are available.

Mount Whitney Trailhead Campground

25 sites; May-Oct.; $18 per night; no reservations

Mount Whitney Trailhead Campground offers 25 walk-in sites (8,300 ft/2,530 m) with flat tent pads and fire grates. Piped water and vault restrooms are available. The campground is geared toward Mount Whitney summit and thru-hikers, and stays are limited to one night.

Whitney Portal Campground

43 sites; www.recreation.gov; May-Oct.; $28 per night

The Whitney Portal Campground, also called the **Mount Whitney Family Campground** (8,100 ft/2,469 m), is for more casual campers and hikers. The 43-site campground is adjacent to Whitney Creek, with some reservable sites and some available on a first-come, first-served basis.

Supplies

Whitney Portal Store

760/876-0030; www.mountwhitneyportal.com; 9am-6pm daily May and Oct., 8am-8pm daily June-Sept.

The Whitney Portal Store serves up burgers, pancakes, and beer—carbs for hungry hikers. It also carries last-minute hiking supplies and souvenirs. The people-watching is great from the tiny patio as grizzled thru-hikers and day tourists comingle.

Getting There

From Lone Pine, follow Whitney Portal Road west for 12 miles (19.3 km) as it climbs over 4,500 feet (1,372 m) in elevation. The road passes the Mount Whitney campgrounds before ending at a parking area near the Whitney Portal Store.

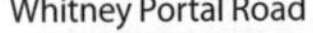

Whitney Portal Road

US 395

US 395 is a rural highway at the intersection of desert and mountain terrain, with Death Valley to the east and the steep granite mountains of the eastern Sierra Nevada to the west. It provides access to Death Valley as well as the John Muir Wilderness. Its small, scenic towns provide services and supplies and make good jumping-off points for exploration. There are also hot springs, petroglyphs, cultural sites, and an ancient pine forest in the region. From north to south, these towns are Bishop, Big Pine, Independence, and Lone Pine.

The town of **Bishop** doesn't offer direct access to Death Valley, but if you're coming from the north, this is a good place to regroup and stock up before exploring the park. It also makes an excellent base camp if you plan on spending some time in the John Muir Wilderness.

The town of **Big Pine** provides **supplies, gas,** and two access points for exploration into Death Valley. Heading east on **Highway 168,** a right turn leads to **Big Pine-Death Valley Road,** which stretches 75 miles (121 km) southeast, passing the North Pass of the Saline Valley Road and the Eureka Dunes before dropping down to meet the northern terminus of Scotty's Castle Road. It is a good refueling or jumping-off point for exploring the John Muir Wilderness.

The tiny town of **Independence** is situated 26 miles (42 km) south of Big Pine and 16 miles (26 km) north of Lone Pine and does not offer direct access to Death Valley. There is beautiful camping and hiking just west of town in the Onion Valley area of the John Muir Wilderness, but fewer services make it less popular as a base camp.

The town of **Lone Pine** provides direct access to Death Valley. From the center of town **Highway 136** drops southeast to intersect with **Highway 190** and eventually the visitor outpost of Panamint Springs in 50 miles (81 km). It makes a good jumping-off point to visit the Whitney Portal region of the John Muir Wilderness as well as Death Valley.

BISHOP

Bishop, 15 miles (24 km) north of Big Pine, is a historical mountain town with a picturesque main street set against the granite backdrop of the Sierra Nevada range. The **Mule Days** festival, held every Memorial Day weekend, celebrates the town's pioneer history. It is the largest populated town in Inyo County (just under 4,000) and an outdoor gateway to the Sierra Nevada and myriad rock-climbing sites.

The Paiute-Shoshone Indians control land in the area, and evidence of ancient Native American settlement is prevalent, especially to the east of town in the Volcanic Tablelands area, where there are several impressive petroglyph panels.

Sights

Laws Railroad Museum

395 Silver Cyn Rd.; 760/873-5950; www.lawsmuseum.org; 10am-4pm most days; $10 donation, children under 12 free

Laws Railroad Museum, on the site of the original Laws railroad station, includes the original depot, post office, and agent's house, as well as other buildings used to re-create this slice of history.

Owens Valley Paiute-Shoshone Cultural Center

2300 W. Line St.; 760/873-8844; www.bishoppaiutetribe.com/owens-valley-paiute-shoshone-cultural-center; 10am-4pm Tues.-Sat.; free

Owens Valley Paiute-Shoshone Cultural Center is a museum showcasing the art and way of life of local native groups, including cultural displays, a veterans memorial, environmental displays, artifacts, and historical archives. A gift shop offers arts and crafts by local tribal artisans.

Volcanic Tablelands

Loop begins 3.6 miles (5.8 km) north of Bishop

The Volcanic Tablelands are austere desert plains between the Sierra Nevada and the White Mountains, east of the town of Bishop. The rolling sage lands have a quiet beauty that may not be immediately recognizable. Further exploration reveals a landscape that shifts with the light, strange volcanic mounds, songbirds, and sage, all framed by the jagged, snowcapped peaks of the formidable Sierra Nevada range. The region was formed around 700,000 years ago by the erupting Long Valley Caldera to the northwest. The area is popular for rock climbers (exceptional bouldering opportunities) and solace seekers. The highlight is evidence of Native American settlement in the form of several impressive petroglyph groupings. These mystical symbols etched into rock were the work of ancestors of the present-day Paiute-Shoshone, possibly made by shamans connecting with the spirit world, by hunters for hunting magic, or as a symbolic map of the universe. The sites include Red Mountain, Chidago, and Fish Slough Petroglyphs. They are all located along Fish Slough Road.

Loop Drive

Distance: *40 miles (64 km) round-trip*

Duration: *2-3 hours*

Start: *Bishop, intersection of US 395 and Hwy. 6 on the north end of town*

End: *Bishop, intersection of US 395 and Hwy. 6 on the north end of town*

Road surface: *Dirt and gravel*

Vehicle: *High-clearance recommended*

A loop drive from Bishop along Fish Slough Road and Highway 6 takes about 40 miles (64 km) and 2-3 hours to absorb some of the Volcanic Tablelands and visit historical sites. Highway 6 is paved, and Fish Slough Road is graded gravel, normally accessible with any vehicle. The northern section of the loop begins at the intersection of Chidago Canyon and Fish Slough Road. The southern section ends at the intersection of Five Bridges Road and Fish Slough Road. In 2013, nearby Chalfant Petroglyphs were severely damaged by vandalism and theft, and information surrounding the petroglyph sites has been more guarded since then. A good map is available from www.bishopvisitor.com. Check out the Trip Planning section for a map of Backroad Tours in the Eastern Sierra (routes 13 and 14). Fish Slough refers to Owens River wetlands. In contrast with the stark volcanic landscape, Fish Slough is characterized by lush, green riparian wetland. It is home to the Owens pupfish, thought to be extinct by 1948 but rediscovered in the 1960s and still around today.

Owens River

The Owens River is most famous for its fight over water, immortalized in the movie *Chinatown*, but today the river is an idyllic waterway popular for fly fishing and floating. To access the river from Bishop, take Line Street east for 3 miles (4.8 km). Turn right onto an unmarked road just before a small bridge. This road heads south, roughly paralleling the river with several popular spots for swimming, fishing, and floating. Strangely, much of the land is managed by the Los Angeles Department of Water and Power. Dispersed camping is not allowed in most places along the river. Pay attention to signs.

Hot Springs

Keough's Hot Springs Resort

800 Keough Hot Springs Rd., Bishop; 760/872-4670; www.keoughshotsprings.com; tent and RV sites $30-35, tent cabins $160; day-use 11am-6pm Mon. and Wed.-Fri., 9am-6pm Sat.-Sun.; adults $14, children 3-12 $10, children 2 and under $5

Keough's Hot Springs Resort, 8 miles (12.9 km) south of Bishop, has RV sites, tent sites, tent cabins, a giant hot-spring-fed swimming pool (86-92°F/30-33°C depending on season), and a smaller hot pool (104°F/40°C) for day-use or overnight guests. The resort was established in 1919 and shows its age, but the pool is a welcome break if you are camping or hiking in the heat of summer. Showers are included.

Benton Hot Springs

55137 CA-120, Benton; 760/933-2287; www.bentonhotsprings.org; from $85

Benton, 40 miles (64 km) northeast of Bishop, has a long history of settlement, first by Native Americans for its hot springs, then as a traveler stop for the nearby mining towns of Bodie and Aurora as well as its own silver-mining works. Today the town has picturesque ruins and Benton Hot Springs, which offers rooms and camping. Seven inn rooms ($169) and a miner's cabin ($139) share three outdoor tubs that are always open. Breakfast in the main dining room is included. Four private houses ($219-279)—two historical—have private tubs. There are also 12 tub sites for camping or RVs (no hookups; $85-95). All sites feature a private hot tub fed by natural hot springs, a picnic table, and a fire pit. This delightfully remote location makes for a low-key destination or place to unwind mid-trip. Main activities include soaking, stargazing, and forgetting your day-to-day worries. No day use.

Outfitters and Supplies

Bishop has the survival basics for civilization as well as the backcountry, including banks, hardware stores, grocery stores, and pharmacies, as well as hiking outfitters and sporting goods stores.

Sage to Summit

312 N. Main St.; 760/872-1756; www.sagetosummit.com; 9am-9pm daily

Sage to Summit offers ultralight equipment dedicated to fast-packing, trail running, and generally covering as much mountain ground as quickly as possible. You can also shop online.

Eastside Sports

224 N. Main St.; 760/873-7520; www.eastsidesports.com; 9am-6pm daily

Eastside Sports is a well-stocked store even for the jaded gearhead: backpacking, mountaineering, climbing, camping, travel, and outdoor sports. It also rents some of its gear: backpacks, sleeping bags, tents, and pads, plus bouldering pads and other items.

Manor Market

3100 W. Line St.; 760/873-4296; 6am-8pm Sun.-Thurs., 6am-9pm Fri.-Sat.

Skip the packing at home and get it all at the Manor Market. This homey store stocks local produce, gourmet foods and staples, and a well-curated wine and beer selection. The attached hardware store has everything else.

Food and Drink

Astorga's Mexican Restaurant

2206 N. Sierra Hwy.; 760/872-3849; www.astorgasmexicanrestaurant.com; 11am-8:30pm daily; $8-24

Astorga's Mexican Restaurant is a family-friendly Mexican joint serving up all the things you want after a day of hiking in a homey space with a patio. Burritos, combination plates, fajitas, and tamales are served alongside margaritas, beer, and wine.

★ Eric Schat's Bakery

763 N. Main St.; 760/873-7156; http://schatsbakery.com; bakery 6am-6pm daily, Fri. until 7pm; sandwiches 8:30am-3:30pm Mon.-Thurs., 8:30am-4pm Fri.-Sat., 8:30am-5pm Sun.

Have a plan before you go into Eric Schat's Bakery or you'll end up with everything: Pastries, donuts, coffee cakes, coffee, cookies, freshly made sandwiches, picnic items, and towering racks of bread (including authentic Basque-style sheepherder bread) are available at this popular institution established in 1938.

★ Back Alley Bowl and Grill

649 N. Main St.; 760/873-5777; www.thebackalleybowlandgrill.com; 11am-9pm daily; lunch $9-16, dinner $19-28

A locals' favorite and the worst-kept secret in town, this combination restaurant and bowling alley offers a full-service restaurant and bar. The lunch menu features burgers,

1: petroglyphs northwest of Death Valley **2:** Benton Hot Springs

1

2

BENTON HOT SPRINGS
EST · 1852
See BENTON
WORLD FAMOUS HOT SPRINGS
MI. BACK ON HWY. 120

sandwiches, salads, soups, and appetizers of the fried variety, while dinner steps it up with steaks and seafood entrées.

Yamatani

635 N. Main St.; 760/872-4801; 4:30pm-9pm Tues.-Sat.; $7-22

Yamatani brings some of the coast to the mountain with sushi, teriyaki, tempura, sake, and more. The restaurant offers a sushi bar as well as full-service dining in a lightly decorated dining room with wooden tables and Japanese screens.

Whiskey Creek Restaurant

524 N. Main St.; 760/873-7777; www.whiskeycrk.com; 11am-8:30pm Tues.-Sat.; lunch $11-18, dinner $16-39

Whiskey Creek Restaurant serves up high-end comfort food, steaks, pasta, and seafood in a wood and brass bar and, when the weather is good, on an outdoor patio.

Looney Bean

399 N. Main St.; 760/873-3311; www.looneybeanbishop.com; 6am-4pm daily

Looney Bean offers specialty organic coffee, baked goods, all-day breakfast, lunch bowls, and vegan and gluten-free offerings in a space filled with local art and gifts. Vegan options include a vegan breakfast burrito and vegan lunch bowl. Wi-Fi is available.

Owens Valley Distilling Co.

237 E. South St., Unit E; 442/228-5041; www.owensvalleydistillingcompany.com; noon-8pm Thurs.-Sat., 4pm-8pm Sun.; $7-13

Owens Valley Distilling Co. offers a premium cocktail menu featuring its spirits in a stylish industrial space. A small, curated food menu is available to balance the cocktails, including a Chicago-style hot dog, Italian beef sandwich, and a few bar snacks. There are also rotating guest food vendors starting at 5:30pm some days. Bottle sales are available.

Accommodations

Bishop offers the most lodging of the US 395 mountain towns nearest to Death Valley. Accommodations include one luxury hotel, chain hotels, and motor court motels. Book lodging ahead of time, because it is sold out during Mule Days in late May and in early October for the Lone Pine Film Festival. The town can book quickly during other festivals or events, too.

If you're a vintage sign geek, the motor court motels of Bishop will entice you. None are destination lodging: They have charming exteriors and basic budget interiors, but they meet your basic lodging needs, have social media-worthy signs, and are walking distance to Bishop's shops, restaurants, and bars. Rates vary widely depending on season and availability; they can balloon on busy weekends in summer or when there is a special event in the area.

★ Bishop Creekside Inn

725 N. Main St.; 760/872-3044; www.bishopcreeksideinn.com; from $180

By far the best hotel in Bishop, Bishop Creekside Inn offers clean, stylish, well-appointed rooms that feel luxurious if a little corporate. A natural creek runs through the property (hence the name), with some of the rooms overlooking. The seasonal swimming pool makes for an excellent place to unwind after a morning of hiking or a day of dusty travel. A complimentary breakfast buffet is better than most, with fresh-baked biscuits as well as scrambled eggs, sausage, and other hot items. For all this, the rates are reasonable.

Bishop Village Motel

286 W. Elm St.; 760/872-8155 or 888/668-5546; www.bishopvillagemotel.com; $119-164

Bishop Village Motel offers a heated seasonal pool, family suites, and suites with kitchens. Rooms are basic budget motel rooms, but its location a few blocks off the main drag makes it both quiet and convenient.

Eastside Guesthouse & Bivy

777 North Main St.; 760/784-7077; https://eastsideguesthouse.com; $134-224

Eastside Guesthouse is set back on a grassy

lawn with ponds and patios. The model is a cross between a hostel and a small boutique hotel with lodging ranging from private family suites to bunkhouses.

Brown's Town Campground RV

219 Wye Rd.; 760/873-8522; www.brownscampgrounds.com

Brown's Town Campground RV, 1 mile (1.6 km) south of Bishop, offers 150 grassy sites for tents and RVs (with hookups). Amenities include hot showers, restrooms, laundry, a café, and a general store.

Getting There

Bishop is on US 395, approximately 3.5 hours south of Reno, Nevada, and 4 hours north of Los Angeles. There is no direct route to Death Valley from Bishop; however, if you are coming from the north or west, this is an excellent stop to regroup, stock up, and spend the night for an early start time to make your final drive into Death Valley.

BIG PINE

Big Pine (elevation 3,989 ft/1,216 m) provides the northernmost and remotest access to the park via either the **North Pass of Saline Valley Road** or **Big Pine-Death Valley Road.** The town offers gas, lodging, food, and outdoor supplies. It also provides a refueling stop for people heading into or out of the Sierra Nevada to the west or Death Valley to the east.

Food

Copper Top BBQ

442 N. Main St.; http://coppertopbbq.com; 11am-8pm Wed.-Sun.; $7-25

The Copper Top BBQ has good takeout portions of barbecue tri-tip, pork, and chicken smoked on-site as well as outdoor tables for families and picnics. Hearty meals include a choice of meat as well as rolls and a side, while sandwiches are a meal of their own. Kids items, classic sides, sweets, and craft beers round out the stick-to-your-ribs menu.

Brewed Awakening

120 S. Main St.; https://brewedawakening395.square.site; 5am-1:30pm Mon.-Sat.; $4-10

A homey coffee shop on Main Street serves iced, hot, and blended coffees, flavored lattes, and a tea assortment alongside coffee shop fare. The breakfast menu includes a scrambled egg and sausage platter and bagels, while lunch adds a Polish hot dog and grilled paninis.

Rossi's Place

142 S. Main St.; 760/938-2308; 5pm-8pm Fri.-Sat.; $8-20

Rossi's Place is a small café with pizza, sandwiches, and salads as well as beer, wine, and cocktails. It is a favorite local spot with a rustic Western feel.

Accommodations

Big Pine Motel

370 S. Main St.; 760/938-2282; from $99

Big Pine Motel has curb appeal with its vintage motor court-style rooms and grassy lawn. Rooms are basic budget motel rooms suitable for an overnight before heading through the mountains.

Starlight Motel

511 S. Main St.; 760/938-2011; $119-139

Starlight Motel offers clean, basic rooms in a shaded setting with a deck and outside seating. It is a decent option for a hiking base camp or proximity to the Ancient Bristlecone Pine Forest.

Supplies

Carroll's Market

136 S. Main St.; 760/938-2718; 9am-8pm daily

Carroll's Market has groceries, produce, and wine as well as fishing and camping supplies for your mountain adventure.

Hi-Country Market & Hardware

101 N. Main St.; 760/938-2067; www.bristleconemotel.com; 6am-11pm daily

Hi-Country Market & Hardware is a one-stop shop for gas, firewood, water, ice, last-minute

Big Pine

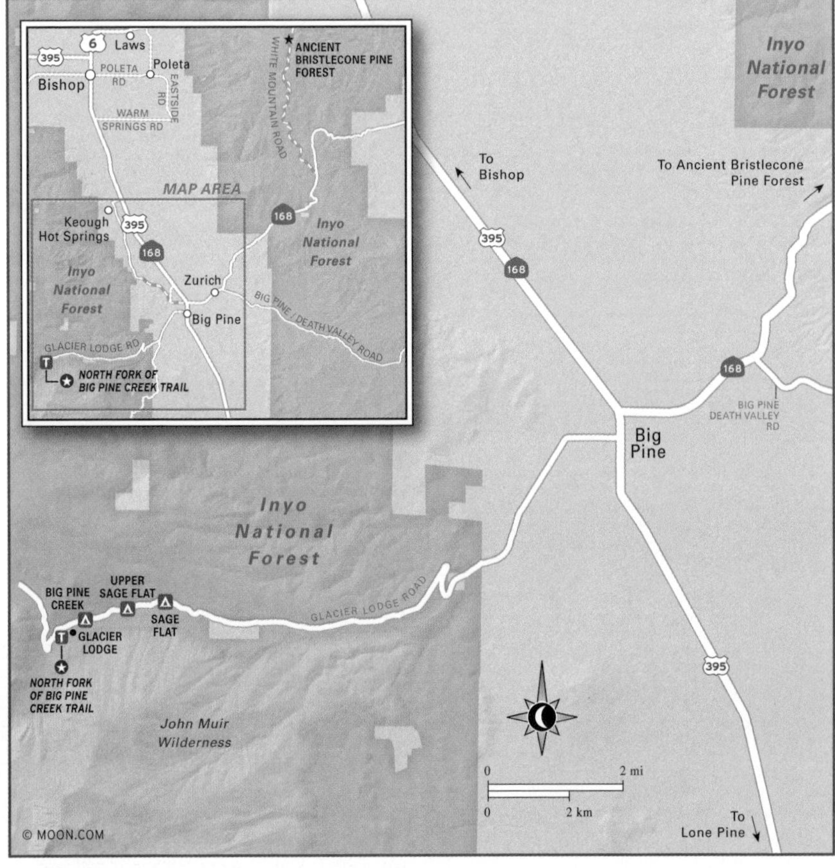

groceries, prepared foods, and camping and fishing supplies. It also has an extensive hardware section.

Getting There

Big Pine is located on US 395, about 43 miles (69 km) north of Lone Pine and 15 miles (24 km) south of Bishop.

INDEPENDENCE

Originally founded in 1862 as a US Army camp during a period of white settlement and violence, Independence became an official town in 1866. Today it boasts a historical inn, the Eastern California Museum, a bona fide French restaurant, a few motels, a gas station, and a historical main street including the Inyo County Courthouse where Charles Manson was arraigned in 1969 on charges of arson and possession of stolen vehicles near Death Valley. It's a tiny if charming blip on the map, usually overshadowed by the larger town of Lone Pine 15 miles (24 km) to the south. There is beautiful camping and hiking just west of town in the Onion Valley area, but fewer services make it less popular as a base camp.

Sights

Eastern California Museum

155 N. Grant St.; 760/878-0258; www.inyocounty.us/residents/things-to-do/eastern-california-museum; 10am-5pm Sun.-Tues. and Thurs.-Sat.; donation

Maintaining the cultural and natural history of Inyo County, the small Eastern California Museum houses thousands of photographs and artifacts representing life from Death Valley to Mono Lake. It was founded in 1928 to archive a quickly vanishing way of life in the Eastern Sierra, with original categories including Indian anthropology, botany, geology, mineralogy, and history.

Food and Accommodations

★ Still Life Café

135 S. Edwards St.; 760/878-2555; call ahead, usually open for dinner Wed.-Sun.; $18-29

You might have to blink twice to make sure this unexpected French colonial bistro truly exists in this speck of a western town. Still Life Café is presided over by Malika Adjaoud in the kitchen and daughter Kanza pouring the wine. If you are rushing to get to or back from somewhere, stop in Bishop or Lone Pine instead. If you have time to relax, the impeccably cooked food is worth the wait. Salmon burgers, spaghetti Bolognese, or braised lamb shank may be on the specials list. Hours are capricious. If it happens to be open when you are driving by, stop in—or call ahead to make sure it is open.

Ray's Den

405 N. Edwards St.; 760/878-8030; https://raysden.com; $125-155

Ray's Den offers clean, basic lodging for families, hikers, and anglers. Its location in Independence along US 395 makes it a good stopover on the way to Death Valley. The stop offers more than convenience, set against the glorious backdrop of the Sierra Nevada range.

Mt. Williamson Motel

515 S. Edwards St.; 760/878-2121; www.mtwilliamsonmotel.com; $145-155

Mt. Williamson Motel makes for a good base camp for hikes into the Onion Valley and John Muir Wilderness. The motel offers basic budget rooms as well as eight rustic cabins with refrigerators, microwaves, and Wi-Fi. The motel caters to backpackers and thru-hikers, offering services that include lodging, receiving and holding resupply packages, breakfast, laundry, and transport to and from the Onion Valley Campground.

Getting There

Independence lies directly on US 395, 65 miles (105 km) northwest of Panamint Springs. To get there, take Highway 190 west for 30 miles (48 km). Continue straight on Highway 136 for 17 miles (27 km) until reaching US 395. Turn north and drive 17 miles (27 km) to the town of Independence. It is 15 miles (24 km) north of Lone Pine.

MANZANAR NATIONAL HISTORIC SITE

US 395, Independence; 760/878-2194 ext. 3310; www.nps.gov/manz; visitor center 9am-4:30pm daily, auto-tour road and grounds sunrise-sunset daily; free

With the granite wall of the Sierra Nevada looming to the west and blazing desert to the east, it's easy to understand how this remote site was chosen as a war detainment camp. Harder to fathom is the political climate that led to over 110,000 Japanese American men, women, and children being detained in 1942 during the political paranoia of World War II. Also difficult to imagine: the reality of daily life in this often inhospitable place. A walking or driving tour of the grounds of Manzanar National Historic Site reveals the meager living conditions as well as the gardens, orchards, and extensiveness of the complex. A tour of the visitor center tells the story of some of the thousands of detainees.

MOUNT WHITNEY FISH HATCHERY

1 Golden Trout Circle; 760-876-4128 or 760-878-2970; https://mtwhitneyfishhatchery.net; 10am-3:30pm Fri.-Sun.

This unlikely attraction features parklike

Ancient Bristlecone Pine Forest

The **Ancient Bristlecone Pine Forest** (760/873-2500; www.fs.usda.gov; 6am-10pm daily summer only, visitor center 10am-4pm Thurs.-Sun.; $3 per person, max $6 per vehicle, children under 18 free), in the White Mountains east of Big Pine, has some of the oldest trees in the world, including the Methuselah Tree, dated at more than 4,800 years old.

White Mountain Road winds into the mountains and provides breathtaking views of the Sierra Nevada range and Owens Valley. Stop in at the **Schulman Grove Visitor Center** (760/873-2400; June-Oct.), then have a look at the **Schulman Grove,** accessible from the visitor center parking lot.

The **Patriarch Grove** lies 12 miles (19.3 km) north of the Schulman Grove on a graded dirt road and is home to the world's largest bristlecone pine. There are picnic tables, restrooms, and interpretive trails at this quiet grove.

Allow at least **three hours** for a round-trip visit from Big Pine to see the Schulman Grove. Add an additional 2-3 hours to visit both groves. The campgrounds along the Glacier Lodge Road are a good overnight option.

bristlecone pine

HIKING

Three interpretive hiking trails (1-5 mi/1.6-8 km) traverse the Schulman Grove, offering close-up views of bristlecone pines, historical mining cabins, and the Methuselah Tree. Two interpretive loop hikes explore the Patriarch Grove, one offering close-up views of the trees and another overlooking the basin below. It's a surreal experience to wander through the ancient trees and think about the changes the world has seen as they stood quietly growing into their gnarled shapes above a landscape that was once covered by glaciers.

GETTING THERE

From Big Pine, follow Highway 168 east for 13 miles (20.9 km) to White Mountain Road. Turn left (north) and drive 10 miles (16.1 km) to the Schulman Grove Visitor Center. For road closures and conditions, contact the Inyo National Forest Ranger Station (760/873-2400). Plan **one hour** for the drive from Big Pine. Plan an additional hour from Big Pine to reach the Patriarch Grove.

grounds, early 20th-century architecture, and educational exhibits. A commanding building on the site was built in 1917, constructed of local rock. A pond surrounded by native vegetation is no longer used for hatching fish, but it does make a fine spot for a stroll. Bring a picnic for lunch under the mature trees or take a break from the road while soaking in some shade and history.

LONE PINE

This charming Old West town serves as the portal to Mount Whitney, the highest peak in the contiguous United States at 14,505 feet (4,421 m). Buildings with Western facades line the town's Main Street, with snow-covered Mount Whitney an impressive backdrop. Lone Pine is a tourist town, fully equipped with hotels and motels, restaurants, a grocery, and outdoors outfitter stores. There are bars, cafés, and shops for browsing.

Museum of Western Film History

701 S. Main St.; 760/876-9909; www.museumofwesternfilmhistory.org; 9am-4pm Sun., 9am-5pm Mon.-Sat., closed major holidays; $5

The Museum of Western Film History showcases the history of movies filmed in the nearby Alabama Hills. The museum has an interpretive handout guide to the area, or you can just wander through and enjoy the formations.

Food and Drink

Several restaurants along the main street serve a range of fare, including steaks, pizza, Chinese, and Mexican food.

Frosty Chalet

500 N. Main St.; 11am-8pm Wed.-Mon. May-Oct.; $5-9, cash only

Frosty Chalet is an old-school ice cream and burger shack with classic soft serve, milkshakes, and griddle burgers. This is a great stop with kids.

Bonanza

104 N. Main St.; 760/876-4768; 11am-8pm daily; $14-19

Bonanza is a classic diner with red booths and a lunch counter. It serves up hot plates of Mexican food of the rice, beans, and melted cheese variety along with cold beer.

Seasons Restaurant

206 S. Main St.; 760/876-8927; 5pm-9pm Tues.-Sat., hours may vary; reservations recommended; $16-40

The closest thing to fine dining in town, Seasons serves fish, seafood, pasta, and steaks as well as a few regionally influenced specialties including medallions of elk and rainbow trout. The well-executed steaks, full bar, and pleasant space make this a favorite of tourists passing through.

Merry Go Round

212 S. Main St.; 760/876-4115; 11am-2pm Wed.-Fri., 4:30pm-8:30pm daily; $18-28

The Merry Go Round offers Chinese fare in a converted carousel with a cozy patio. The Chinese menu includes well-executed classics like Kung Pao chicken and sweet and sour shrimp.

★ Alabama Hills Café & Bakery

111 W. Post St.; 760/876-4675; www.alabamahillscafe.com; 5am-3pm Mon.-Tues. and Thurs.-Sun.; $8-19

For breakfast, the Alabama Hills Café is a winner. This unassuming, tucked-away spot serves freshly baked bread and heaping plates of breakfast and lunch to fortify locals, hikers, and other visitors.

Jake's Saloon

119 N. Main St.; 760/876-5765; noon-2am daily

At Jake's Saloon locals hold down the barstools in this divey watering hole. Hikers, tourists, bikers, film crews, and others on their way to Death Valley or Tahoe shuffle through as well. Pool tables and shuffleboard provide the entertainment. For such a Western town, it's currently Lone Pine's only saloon. The tempting-looking Double L Saloon down the street has closed.

Accommodations

Summer is the busy season in Lone Pine, and hotels can fill ahead of time. Summer and holiday rates, both substantially more expensive, may also apply. The Lone Pine Film Festival is held every year in October. The town and all surrounding lodging from Olancha to Bishop can book solid. If you are visiting the area during this time, book early.

★ Dow Villa Hotel

310 S. Main St.; 760/876-5521; www.dowvillamotel.com; $77-189

Built in 1923, the historical Dow Villa Hotel is a refurbished period hotel with a seasonal pool and a year-round hot tub. Stay in the original hotel or the motor-court rooms, which were added later.

Trails Motel

633 S. Main St.; 760/876-5555; from $110

Lone Pine also has several basic budget motor-court-style motels, including the Trails Motel. The motel is a good option for the price, offering clean rooms with minifridges and microwaves as well as a seasonal swimming pool.

Boulder Creek RV Resort

2550 US 395; 760/876-4243; www.boulder creekrvresort.com; tent $50, RV $80, cabin $195

RV accommodations, tent sites, and cabins can be found at the Boulder Creek RV Resort. The property also features a swimming pool and hot tub, a playground, laundry and shower facilities, and a market.

Outfitters and Supplies

Elevation

150 S. Main St., Lone Pine; 760/876-4560; www.sierraelevation.com; 9am-7pm Sun.-Thurs., 9am-8:30pm Fri.-Sat.

Well-stocked climbing and mountaineering shop Elevation outfits climbers and hikers and dispenses serious knowledge in the form of a great outdoors guide selection. Elevation also offers some rentals: crampons, snowshoes, backpacks, and bear canisters.

Gardner's True Value

104 S. Main St.; 760/876-4208; 8am-6pm Mon.-Sat.

Gardner's True Value is a chock-full hardware store that also offers camping basics and fishing licenses.

Lone Pine Market

119 S. Main St.; 760/876-4378; 8am-9pm Sun.-Wed., 8am-10pm Thurs.-Sat.

Lone Pine Market is a small-town grocery store with the basics. The produce section can be a little tired, but it's fine for stocking up on last-minute essentials.

Gifts

Lone Pine Rocks and Gifts

235 S. Main St.; 760/876-1010; www.lonepinerocksandgifts.com; 9am-6pm daily

Modeled on a classic western trading post, Lone Pine Rocks and Gifts has been a Lone Pine institution since the 1960s. It caters to rockhounds as well as casual tourists, stocking gems and minerals from nearby Owens Valley and around the world. The shop also stocks Indigenous pottery and sundries.

Information

At the literal crossroads to Death Valley and the Eastern Sierra, the **Eastern Sierra Visitor Center** (US 395 and Hwy. 136, Lone Pine; 760/876-6200; 8am-4:30pm daily), 2 miles (3.2 km) south of Lone Pine, is chock-full of hiking, backcountry, history, and field guides for visiting the lake-laced Sierra Nevada or heat-cracked Death Valley.

Getting There

Lone Pine lies directly on US 395, 50 miles (81 km) west of Panamint Springs. To get there, take Highway 190 west for 30 miles (48 km). Continue straight on Highway 136 for 17 miles (27 km) until reaching US 395. Turn north and drive 2 miles (3.2 km) to the town of Lone Pine.

Alabama Hills

Lone Pine is right on the edge of the Alabama Hills, the scenic, rocky Sierra Nevada foothills near Mount Whitney. It was named for mining prospectors sympathetic to the Confederate cause during the Civil War. The outstanding scenery attracted filmmakers beginning in the 1920s, and westerns, sci-fi movies, and other films have been shot here, making it a landscape that looks iconic and familiar to visitors. The area now known as **Movie Flats** is where most of the movies were filmed. Take a short hike through the Alabama Hills; the popular **Mobius Arch** is an easy 20-minute loop.

Getting There

To get to the Alabama Hills from US 395 in Lone Pine, turn west onto Whitney Portal Road and drive 2.7 miles (4.3 km) to Movie Road. Turn right onto Movie Road and follow the many dirt roads through the area.

1: Mount Whitney Fish Hatchery **2:** Manzanar National Historic Site **3:** Cerro Gordo ghost town **4:** Red Rock Canyon State Park

1
2
慰霊塔
3
4

A self-guided **tour map** is available online (https://inyocountyvisitor.com).

THE OWENS VALLEY

The Owens Valley stretches along the base of the Panamint Mountains that guard the western edge of Death Valley. The landscape here straddles the zone between desert and mountain. The tiny town of Olancha at the southern end of the Owens Valley offers few services, but it does provide a direct route into Death Valley. As you drive along Highway 190 en route between Olancha and Death Valley, you might see big, blue **Owens Lake** on your GPS map. But make no mistake; this has not been a viable lake for more than 100 years, since the California Aqueduct was built. The Owens Valley follows the path of the Owens River, bordered by the Sierra Nevada range to the west and the Inyo Mountains to the east. It extends approximately 80 miles (129 km) between the US 395 towns of Olancha and Bishop.

Olancha

The tiny village of Olancha offers gas and one lodging option. It lies 30 miles (48 km) west of the western park boundary and offers direct access via Highway 190. It is 45 miles (72 km) west of Panamint Springs.

Olancha RV Park and Motel

1075 US 395, Olancha; 760/764-0023; www.bishopmotels.net; RV sites $59, tipi $99, motel $129-139

The Olancha RV Park and Motel offers tipis, motel rooms (some with kitchenettes), and RV spots with hookups as well as a café and seasonal swimming pool. The on-site café serves breakfast, burgers, and salads with veggie options.

Cerro Gordo

760/876-5030; 9am-5pm daily

The well-preserved remains of the Cerro Gordo ghost town stand high in the Inyo Mountains, monument to its life as a silver town located a steep 8 miles (12.9 km) from the alkali floor of the hot and windswept Owens Valley below. Cerro Gordo was a thriving silver producer with mines in operation 1865-1938. Pablo Flores originally discovered the rich silver veins of Cerro Gordo, Spanish for "Fat Hill." The things that it had going for it (besides rich silver veins) were water and wood. Smelters were erected in Cerro Gordo and on Owens Lake. By 1869, the property was the largest producer of silver and lead in California, delivering so much silver bullion to Los Angeles, 275 miles (445 km) away, that the squalid little town (LA, that is) relied on Cerro Gordo as a lifeline. Today, the property is privately owned and maintained by people passionate about its history.

Getting There

From the town of Olancha on US 395, take Highway 190 east for 14.6 miles. Turn left (north) onto Highway 136. Drive 4.6 miles north to the town of Keeler. Turn right on Cerro Gordo Road (signed). The road ends at the ghost town in 7.7 miles (12.4 km). Cerro Gordo Road climbs steeply, gaining nearly 1 mile (1.6 km) in elevation from Keeler (elevation 3,600 ft/1,097 m) to Cerro Gordo (elevation 8,500 ft/2,591 m). Very steep grades make high-clearance/4WD (a vehicle with some power) desirable; however, the road is graded and maintained and may be passable with any vehicle. In bad weather, the road could be impassable, even with 4WD.

INDIAN WELLS VALLEY

Ghost towns, some more living than others, and high concentrations of Native American rock art make this area worth digging into. Located on the southwestern edge of Death Valley, the Indian Wells Valley is roughly bounded by **Highway 14** to the west, **Trona Road** to the east, and **Highway 178** to the north. The major access point is the intersection of **US 395** and Highway 178 in Inyokern. You'll travel through the Indian Wells Valley if you're coming from the south, but it's worth a detour from any direction.

To the south, the intersections of Highway

14, US 395, and Highway 178 form the Indian Wells Valley. **Ridgecrest** is your best bet for gas, supplies, and services. From here, Highway 178 heads north into the park.

East of Ridgecrest lies the **Searles Valley** and the long, dusty drive to the Trona Pinnacles.

Inyokern

Indian Wells Brewing Company

2565 Hwy. 14, Inyokern; 760/377-5989; www.mojavered.com; brewery 10am-5pm daily, grill 10am-4pm weekends

At the Indian Wells Lodge and Brewing Company, kids will love the rows of novelty sodas—bacon soda, anyone?—and adults can enjoy the craft beers. The brewing company is positioned over an artesian spring and uses its water source wisely, brewing flavorful beers like the Mojave Red and Death Valley Pale Ale. There's a green lawn along with picnic tables where you can sample a beer, have lunch, or give the kids a chance to run around. On weekends, the brewery opens Uncle Virgil's Backyard, a small lunch counter, and serves up burgers, fries, and hot dogs.

Getting There

Inyokern is 70 miles (113 km) south of Lone Pine, about a one-hour drive along US 395. In Inyokern, Highway 14 leads southwest to Red Rock Canyon State Park, while Highway 178 cuts east to Ridgecrest, Trona, and the Trona-Wildrose Road, a southern gateway to the Panamints. US 395 continues south to the almost ghost town of Randsburg in 24 miles (39 km).

Ridgecrest

Maturango Museum

100 E. Las Flores Ave., Ridgecrest; 760/375-6900; www.maturango.org; 10am-5pm Mon.-Sat., noon-4pm Sun.; $5 adults, $3 seniors, military free

The Maturango Museum offers tours to one of the biggest and best-preserved groupings of Native American rock art in the country. The Coso Rock Art District, a National Historic Landmark, hosts a dizzying array of rock art. It's a shallow, rocky canyon with just the right kind of rocks for the wind to have varnished them with a dark smoky glaze over thousands of years. These rocks, covered with "desert varnish," are a prime canvas for petroglyphs, created by chipping into the rock.

Once you get over the initial awe of seeing so much ancient rock art all in one place, you can try to figure out what it all means. There's no definitive guide to the meanings, and many petroglyph symbols will probably remain great unsolved desert mysteries. What you will see are lots of bighorn sheep, hunting scenes, and elaborate pictures of shamans, rain, and other abstract symbols. These could have been part of shamanistic quests, religious ceremonies, or historical documentation. This is an amazing place, but it also happens to be within the boundaries of the Naval Air Weapons Station China Lake. It might seem counterintuitive, but this location has probably preserved the site; it's a sad fact that many well-known rock-art sites get vandalized.

The Maturango Museum holds **tours** most weekends in March-June, and these sell out. Check the website in late winter and early spring, and reserve a tour as soon as the schedule is posted. The tour is loosely guided by volunteers who have clearance to be on the base, but you'll be able to wander around and soak it in at your own pace.

Getting There

The Maturango Museum is off Highway 178 in Ridgecrest. From the junction of US 395 and Highway 178 in Inyokern, follow Highway 178 east for 9.5 miles (15.3 km).

Red Rock Canyon State Park

Hwy. 14, Cantil; 661/946-6092; www.parks.ca.gov; $6

Red Rock Canyon State Park is a little slice of Utah in the California desert. The red rock formations create a scenic drive through the area and a lovely place to hike. It's one of those unusual places that is easy to access but is as lovely as if you had hiked far from the highway. It's also a good place to set up a base camp to explore the Indian Wells region west of Death Valley.

Ricardo Campground

Ricardo Campground Rd.; 50 sites; first-come, first-served; year-round; $25

Ricardo Campground features primitive campsites and miles of hiking trails through beautiful rock formations and cliffs. Sites are easily reached off the paved campground road and are spaced wide apart, tucked up against the red canyon cliffs. The campground has potable water, pit toilets, fire rings, and picnic tables.

Getting There

Red Rock Canyon State Park is near the intersection of Highway 14 and US 395 in the Mojave Desert. From Randsburg, head west on Redrock Randsburg Road for 20 miles (32 km) to the intersection with Highway 14. Turn right (north) on Highway 14 and drive 5 miles (8 km) to the park entrance.

THE SEARLES VALLEY

The Searles Valley is situated between the Slate and Argus Ranges, south of Panamint Valley and east of Ridgecrest and US 395. Take Highway 178 east from the Kern River Valley and watch the landscape shift from California golden homestead to pioneer death trap. It has the draw of otherworldly rock formations and long stretches of austere desert. Coming from the rolling foothills of the Sierra Nevada, the land turns harsh and alien, beautiful in its own way.

The mining town of **Trona** is worse for the wear after two earthquakes hit in 2019, but it has a fascinating history as a company town, evident by the historical buildings mixed in with the new.

★ Trona Pinnacles

20 miles (32 km) east of Ridgecrest; www.blm.gov; free

The Trona Pinnacles are haunting and powerful. You can see them from the highway on the long, dusty drive out, a draw to keep going. The pinnacles were formed through a geologic anomaly in which calcium-rich groundwater met ancient alkaline lake water over thousands of years to form tufa formations. What you see now is a ghost lake with alien spires. If you look hard, you can see where the water line used to be on the distant mountain range. It's the only hint of water you'll find out here. There is a small parking area with restrooms. From there, wander on several unmaintained trails through the formations.

Getting There

The Trona Pinnacles are on BLM land about 20 miles (32 km) east of Ridgecrest and south of the historical and active mining town of Trona. Access the signed dirt road that leads to the pinnacles from Highway 178 about 7.7 miles (12.4 km) east of the intersection of Highway 178 and Trona-Red Mountain Road. The 5-mile-long (8-km) dirt road from Highway 178 to the Trona Pinnacles is usually accessible to regular passenger vehicles, but the road may be closed during the winter months after a heavy rain.

Background

The Landscape

GEOGRAPHY

Death Valley is located in the northern Mojave Desert on the eastern side of California's Sierra Nevada range. The Mojave (also spelled Mohave, the term used by the Mohave Tribal Nation) is a high desert area occupying a large swath of southeastern California and parts of southern Nevada, southwestern Utah, and northwestern Arizona. Death Valley National Park lies in the northeast section of the greater Mojave, mostly in California, with a small section, called the Nevada Triangle, in Nevada. Death Valley sits within the Great

Basin, a hydrographic distinction that means all drainage of waterways is internal; no rivers lead to the sea.

During the series of ice ages from 1.8 million to 10,000 years ago, Death Valley was colder, with a climate more like British Columbia—glaciers and snowpacks in the Sierra Nevada drained into vast lakes and shallow drainage pools. When the climate shifted, it became hotter and more arid; the pools dried, leaving behind fossil lakes full of silt, clay, and minerals. Clear evidence of these plant-free playas can be seen in places like **The Racetrack, Badwater Basin,** and the **Trona Pinnacles.**

The evaporated lakes resulted in concentrated mineral beds that set the stage for mining activity. This area is known for its richness of mineral wealth, and it has a long and notorious mining history. Death Valley was settled by European Americans in the mid-19th century for its gold and silver despite harsh unknown territory and limited water sources. Mining operations eventually expanded to include borax, talc, gypsum, salt, and other minerals mined from these ancient mineral beds.

The "basin and range" topography is characterized by extremes in elevation: steep mountain ranges trending in the same direction, interspersed with deep valleys. The deepest of these is Death Valley, for which the park is named. During times of flood, water becomes a raging force as it hurtles through water-cut canyons and spills sediment at the canyon mouths in alluvial fan formations. These triangle-shaped spillages are prominent when driving through Death Valley and are often the first obstacle to cross by car or on foot if you're trying to visit one of the valley's many fascinating canyons.

Wind, combined with other geologic processes, creates desert features such as sand dunes, desert varnish, and desert pavement. Desert varnish and desert pavement are unique to arid environments and are often found around alluvial fans. **Desert varnish** is a reddish-brown coating of clay manganese and iron oxides found on rocks. The varnish darkens over time and can be used to date rock formations. Native Americans used desert varnish as a canvas for petroglyphs, chipping it away to reveal the lighter-colored rock underneath. **Desert pavement** is a sturdy, compact rock surface of pebbles and broken rocks. One theory suggests that these rocks are left behind when the wind sweeps away smaller particles, while another attributes the distinct ground covering to the shrinking and swelling of clay soil, which pushes pebbles to the surface.

GEOLOGY

Throughout Death Valley, the earth's history is exposed in striking formations and tortured geologic features. A formation is a geologist's grouping of the stratified rock that forms the landscape, as determined by age and duration. Formations can also be associated with geographic and climatic conditions. Death Valley has a complex set of at least **23 formations.** The oldest rocks in Death Valley are found in the steep Black Mountains above Badwater Basin and are approximately 1.7 billion years old. Many of the rocks are ancient, but the stark topography, with its sheer rises and drops, is relatively recent.

Ancient Seas

In the Paleozoic era (570 million years ago), the northern Mojave was a tidal area filled with shallow seas stretched along the coastline. Marine deposits built up over a span of millions of years. Some of these deposits are still visible, like the 700-million-year-old Noonday Dolomite in **Mosaic Canyon.** This quiet accumulation of sedimentary deposits in shallow waters drew to a close about 250 million years ago, and a much more cataclysmic era began, marked by colliding tectonic plates and magma plumes.

Previous: the Ibex Dunes.

Death Valley Dunes

First-time visitors to Death Valley may be surprised that the park is not a vast sea of sand. Sand dunes cover less than 1 percent of Death Valley National Park, but they are striking features, sometimes visible from long distances. Wind is a crucial factor in creating sand dunes, driving loose particles from dry riverbeds or lake beds, dry washes, and canyons until they reach a barrier such as the sheer mountains ringing the valley. The trapped sand piles up, migrating and shifting as the wind continuously sculpts these sand-scapes.

Dunes are categorized by shape, which tells you something about the way they were formed and their migration patterns. **Star dunes** are the highest, with ridges rising to a peak. The **crescent-shaped dunes** are more common, shaped by winds that blow constantly in the same direction. Prevailing winds that blow at an angle shape the **linear dunes,** characterized by their long, straight, or sometimes undulating lines.

These graceful, clean expanses compel us to climb them. Look carefully for signs of more complex life—delicate insect and animal tracks, and plants that grow from reserves of water hidden within dune systems. The following sand dune tour highlights each system's unique setting and features.

- The **Mesquite Flat Sand Dunes** (page 92) are visible from long distances along the valley floor near Stovepipe Wells, and are easily accessed from a parking area off Highway 190. This extensive dune system covers many acres and includes star, linear, and crescent shapes.

- The **Ibex Dunes** (page 73), tucked away in the southeast corner of the park, offer isolation and easy hiking from the unmaintained dirt road that leads to the dunes. Hiking up the graceful sand ridges of the Ibex Dunes affords good views of the Saddle Peak Hills and a hidden talc mine. It's a great stop to pair with a visit to the lovely Saratoga Spring, just a few miles away along the same road.

- The **Panamint Valley Dunes** (page 162) are swept up against the dark Cottonwood Mountains in the far upper reaches of the Panamint Valley. Although you can see them gleaming in the distance from Highway 190, the closest road stops more than 3 miles (4.8 km) short, making them some of the remotest dunes in the park. The cross-country hike to reach them will all but guarantee you have these impressive dunes to yourself.

- If you find yourself in the Saline Valley, stop your car, get out, and walk less than a mile (1.6 km) to reach the long, low **Saline Valley Dunes** (page 156). They're easy to pass by, but it's well worth stopping to get a closer look. Up close, they become low waves of sculpted sand hills, each rise giving way to another until you're immersed in the dunes. Follow your own footsteps to get back to your car.

- If sand dunes can be regal, the **Eureka Dunes** (page 122) earn that adjective. They are the tallest and most extensive dune system in the park, with the tallest of the dunes reaching nearly 700 feet (213 m). The Eureka Dunes are also "singing dunes" or "booming dunes," one of only about 40 worldwide. From time to time they emit a low booming sound like a distant airplane, caused by the motion of moving sand grains. It's a long drive to the Eureka Valley in the northernmost reaches of the park, but well worth it. Camp in the primitive campsites at the foot of these dunes and make a destination of it.

Volcanism

The Mesozoic era (245-65 million years ago) marked a period of radical shifts in the landscape. As the Pacific plate became subducted under the North American plate, friction generated massive heat, melting rock and forming magma. The newly formed magma rose to the surface in a chain of volcanoes. The ocean was gradually pushed 200 miles (320 km) west during the upheaval, leaving the northern Mojave Desert high, if not yet dry.

Deep magma plumes intruded the earth's

crust and cooled, forming crystallized formations known as plutons. Granite is one of these plutonic rocks and is exposed in outcrops throughout sections of Death Valley, including the upper **Warm Spring Canyon** in the Panamint Mountains, **Hunter Mountain** in the Cottonwoods, and Emigrant Canyon around **Skidoo.** Volcanic activity continued to shape the landscape well beyond these dramatic shifts. Scattered volcanic debris is common in the valleys, and hot springs have been tapped in the Saline and Owens Valley. At Naval Air Weapons Station China Lake, on the southwest side of the park, the navy harnessed the region's geothermal energy to create a clean power plant.

Basin and Range

Death Valley as we know it today started to gain its rough building blocks 65 million years ago in the Cenozoic era, but it didn't take the topographic shape associated with the northern Mojave—high, sheer ranges perforated by deep basins—until much later. Scenic **Titus Canyon** gives us the earliest known records of Cenozoic rock formations. The land then was probably broad and rolling with valleys, grasslands, lakes, and woodlands in a warm, wet climate. The fossil record reveals clear evidence of mammals, including rodents, tapirs, horses, and titanotheres, a bulky, horned animal that shares ancestry with the horse and rhino.

As these idyllic grasslands faded, tectonic movements formed the two main faults that define Death Valley. The **Northern Death Valley-Furnace Creek Fault Zone** follows the western side of the Amargosa Range, and the **Southern Death Valley Fault Zone** follows the western foot of the Black Mountains. These active faults form one of the longest running fault systems in California. Meltwater and precipitation filled the area with a series of shallow lakes; when these lakes evaporated, they left the mineral and salt-rich legacy that shaped the mining history of Death Valley. The crust is still dynamic. US Geological Survey studies indicate that parts of Death Valley may still be rising or falling a foot (0.3 m) every 500 years.

CLIMATE

Death Valley is one of the driest and hottest places in the western hemisphere, with scalding temperatures at the lower elevations in summer. In July 1913, Furnace Creek hit 134°F (57°C), the highest recorded atmospheric temperature on earth. The **summer** average is 115°F (46°C). Strangely, Death Valley's extreme heat is often a selling point—many visitors come specifically intent on experiencing it. There are no bodies of water or cloud cover to mitigate temperature, and the low-lying valleys trap heat. The same conditions can create bitter cold in **winter.** The same year that produced that record high also produced the record low of 15°F (-9°C). Cold is more likely at the upper elevations, hit with strong winds and cold fronts from the Pacific Ocean. A temperature of 0°F (-18°C) is not uncommon, and Telescope Peak, the highest peak in the park at 11,049 feet (3,368 m), is snow-capped for a good part of the year.

Death Valley's arid climate is partly caused by the imposing Sierra Nevada range, which towers more than 9,000 feet (2,743 m) to the west. As storms roll in from the Pacific Ocean, they hit the western side of the Sierra Nevada, wringing out most of their moisture before continuing on into the eastern desert. This rain shadow effect accounts for the 2 inches (5 cm) of annual rainfall in Death Valley, compared to as much as 60 inches (152 cm) of rain on the western side of the Sierra Nevada. Four mountain ranges lie between the Pacific and Death Valley, each squeezing out the last bits of moisture from storm clouds as they head inland.

Death Valley holds dazzling topographic extremes within its boundaries, and temperatures and precipitation vary widely depending on the season and elevation. From the sizzling salt flats of Badwater Basin, 282 feet (86 m) below sea level, to the snow-covered summit of Telescope Peak at 11,049 feet (3,368 m) is a distance of only 15 miles (24 km). These drastic changes in elevation support a range of temperatures and diverse ecology. That means if it's 100°F (38°C) at Badwater Basin, it may be 60°F (15.5°C) at the top of Telescope Peak.

The good news is that it's possible to find a comfortable environment to visit, whether in summer or winter. **Spring** and **fall** are mostly temperate and pleasant, but unexpected weather—including monsoons and dust storms—can swoop in year-round, wreaking havoc in a short time. Strong winds and sandstorms occur frequently on the valley floor, and with little warning; these can last anywhere from a few minutes to a few days. Dust storms are formed by approaching cold fronts and can tear up anything not tied down, causing whiteout conditions. Rainstorms can trigger flash floods, picking up force in mountain canyons and causing washouts on the sunbaked desert floor.

ENVIRONMENTAL ISSUES

Nonnative Species

It takes a specially adapted plant or animal to survive in Death Valley's severe climate. Most of the species that do are native, having adapted to Death Valley's specific conditions. A few nonnative species have stuck around, however, competing with native plants and animals for precious water resources.

Tamarisk

Originally from the eastern hemisphere, tamarisk trees were planted in the United States in the 1800s for ornamentation, shade, windbreaks, and erosion control. The trees were eventually planted in Death Valley by pioneers, the Civilian Conservation Corps, and even the National Park Service (NPS) in the early days. Tamarisk is resilient and looks lovely, but it's a major water suck in the northern Mojave Desert, where riparian environments are rare and fragile. You'll see tamarisk trees in areas where there is a substantial underground water supply; they crowd out native plants and animals and salinize the soil by dropping salty leaves. The bush variety, called salt cedar, has pink blooms in spring and gives riparian areas a lush look. The tree variety, athel, adorns old mining camps like the well-watered **Ibex Spring** camp and adds a picturesque quality to the old cabins. The NPS has made efforts to remove the plants from Saratoga Spring, Eagle Borax Works, Warm Spring Canyon, and other sites. Today, tamarisk abounds in riparian areas in the dry Southwest, to the detriment of the native plants.

Burros

Wild burros were introduced to Death Valley in the 1860s and used as pack animals when mining ruled the land. Originally from the Sahara in Africa, burros are strong animals acclimated to life in the arid desert. They can also tolerate as much as 30 percent water loss by body weight and replenish it in five minutes of drinking. Inevitably some burros escaped or were released when people moved on, and the wild burro population in Death Valley soared.

The NPS set a goal to remove all burros from within Death Valley National Monument's boundaries. In an enormous effort from 1983 to 1987, more than 6,000 burros were captured and put up for adoption. The NPS also built a 37-mile (60-km) fence along the eastern border to keep wild burros from straying over from Nevada. In 1987 the NPS declared their efforts over, claiming that they had removed all wild burros from all the hidden nooks and crannies of the park. However, seven years later, in 1994, the national monument became a national park that included an additional million acres and inherited a whole new crop of burros. The **Saline Valley,** in particular, is home to several of the curious animals. They also stray into the relatively well-watered canyons on the western side of the Panamint Mountains. At this point many visitors feel that they are as much a part of the park as indigenous species, but ultimately they throw off the biological balance by competing with other animals, specifically bighorn sheep, for precious water resources.

Air Pollution

Air pollution is not always present in Death Valley, but when it does appear, it can diminish the spectacular views for which the park is known. Some of the air pollution is generated within the park when the wind whips up loose particles and dust from dry lake beds and the open desert. The largest source, however, is industrial and auto emissions in urban centers like Los Angeles, hundreds of miles away. **Spring** and **summer** days have the worst hazy air.

Night Sky

Death Valley National Park is one of 16 parks in the United States that the **International Dark-Sky Association** (www.darksky.org) has designated an International Dark Sky Park. It is so remote that it remains free of the light pollution of major cities or smaller urban areas. Even Las Vegas, more than 110 miles (177 km) east, doesn't affect the inky, starry sky.

The spectacular night skies are one of the park's draws, and the NPS regards them as a natural treasure to be maintained. The NPS has reduced excessive outdoor lighting and has improved lighting facilities to reduce glow and glare. It maintains its commitment to protect natural darkness, and Death Valley is one of the few places in the country where it is possible to experience the awe of truly dark skies. For those of us used to cities, the sight can be spectacular.

Plants and Animals

PLANTS

The widely varying landscape of Death Valley forms biological islands to which specialized species of plants and animals have adapted. Sand dunes, desert wetlands, and high desert woodlands represent the wide array of habitat. Most wildlife can range and breed across landscapes, but plants remain in specific locations conducive to their survival. Water availability and temperature are strong influences.

Desert Lowlands

In the desert lowlands, plants must be able to adapt to heat, salt, and very little water. The lowest basins hover near or below sea level and include Death Valley, Saline Valley, and Panamint Valley. Dry lake beds, called playas, are remnants of Pleistocene-era lakes and have salt concentrations so high that they block plant growth. As salt levels lessen toward the edges, some plants are able to take root even in soils that are still relatively salty. **Pickleweed,** or picklebush, is one of most salt-tolerant species and can tolerate 6 percent salinity, twice the salinity of the ocean. A succulent shrub, pickleweed stores salt in its segmented, fleshy stems. A healthy crop of pickleweed can be found at Salt Creek, where it thrives along the muddy banks of this exposed desert stream.

Low-lying areas farther from the playa are less salt-heavy. As the salinity decreases, soil can support plants such as arrowweed or mesquite. **Mesquite** can tolerate 0.5 percent salinity. The plant has a long taproot, sometimes longer than 50 feet (15 m), and can anchor itself in sand dunes where other plants can't reach water, making it a great indicator of subsurface water; desert wells are often located near mesquite thickets. Mesquite is a wide-ranging species that played a vital role in Native American life for food, fuel, and housing.

Other plants that do not have a way to adapt to salinity or faraway water sources adapt by developing mechanisms to cope with infrequent access to water. **Desert holly** shrivels up to reduce the rate of photosynthesis and its need for moisture. The leaves turn silvery to reflect more light.

Creosote is very common across the western hemisphere. This bush can continue photosynthesis after 30 months with no rain and withstands heat, cold, drought, and flooding. It has staggering longevity: One species has individuals dated to 11,700 years old. The first creosote bushes arrived in the Amargosa Desert east of Death Valley approximately 9,000 years ago but did not reach the mountains until 5,000 years ago. Some of the creosote plants we see today may have been some of the first plants in the Mojave Desert.

The lower elevations of the northern Mojave also support about 20 species of desert **cactus.** They occur in hot lowland valleys from 1,000-9,500 feet (305-2,896 m) to mix with the junipers and pinyons. The spines and ribs deflect heat and help preserve water, and the spines also deter animals from eating them.

Transition Elevations

The midlevel elevations, 1,300-5,900 feet (396-1,798 m), receive more rain and thus support more varied plantlife. Since the Mojave Desert's boundaries are not clear-cut, **Joshua trees** are often considered an indicator plant, signaling that the biological landscape has transitioned to the Mojave. Joshua trees are large, top-heavy yuccas with a spiky upper branch system that can reach more than 30 feet (9 m) in height. They were named by Mormon settlers, who were reminded of the biblical story of Joshua reaching his arms up in prayer. Joshua trees grow in places that receive snowfall and take advantage of the small amounts of groundwater and deeper soil of these locations; they occur between lowland and higher-elevation vegetation, with the highest concentrations at 3,500-5,000 feet (1,067-1,524 m) elevation. Joshua trees don't have growth rings, so they are hard to date; instead, they are measured by their size and growth rates, which are about 3 inches (7.6 cm) per year in the first 10 years and 1.5 inches (3.8 cm) per year after. Large, cream-white flowers bloom in spring and are pollinated by the yucca moth. Good places to see Joshua trees include Lee Flat along the Saline Valley South Pass, the Racetrack Valley Road, and Joshua Flats along the Big Pine-Death Valley Road.

Wildflower season (mid-Feb.-mid-July) in the desert is a rare and elusive phenomenon; it doesn't happen every year. The perfect conditions have to be in place—well-timed rain intervals from Pacific storms between late fall and early spring, the right amount of warmth, and an easing up of the extreme drying desert winds. Wildflowers survive by sprouting only when these optimal conditions occur, then going out bright and fast, turning to seed again to lie dormant until another germination year. It's a wildly exultant time when the basins are filled with fragile, short-lived color.

The National Park Service provides a weekly spring wildflower update on the Death Valley National Park website (www.nps.gov/deva/learn/nature/wildflowers.htm), pointing visitors to the best places to see wildflowers and describing their bloom status. Wildflower season runs mid-February-mid-July and begins at the lower elevations, creeping up to the higher elevations as the season wears on. Mid-February-mid-April, wildflowers can be seen in the foothills and alluvial fans of the lower elevations such as those along the Badwater Road. Early April-early May, wildflowers may be found in the canyons and higher valleys like the Racetrack Valley. May-mid-July, wildflowers pepper the higher mountain peaks and woodlands such as those of Wildrose and Telescope Peaks.

Desert Woodlands

Pinyon-juniper woodland marks the desert high-elevation tree line at around 6,000 feet (1,829 m). **Pinyons** and Utah **junipers** usually grow together in scrub forest on gravel or bedrock. This forest signals a change in water availability and elevation since it needs 9 or 10 inches (23 or 25 cm) of annual precipitation, a significant amount of water in the desert. Pinyon trees with mature pinecones have rich, nutritious seeds—pine nuts, which were among the important food sources for Indigenous people in the northern Mojave.

Wildrose Canyon and Wildrose Peak are good locations to see these woodlands.

Limber pine and **bristlecone pine** forests rise above the pinyon-juniper belt in the Inyo, Panamint, and part of the Grapevine Mountains. A good place to see this forest is Mahogany Flat, elevation 8,100 feet (2,469 m), in the Panamint Mountains. A trail from here leads to Telescope Peak, the highest point in Death Valley National Park. Limber pines appear at about 9,000 feet (2,743 m). Bristlecone pines appear at about 10,000 feet (3,048 m). It is the oldest living tree on earth, and some individuals are thousands of years old. The oldest ring count approaches 5,000 years. Limber and bristlecone pines are gnarled and stark. Although they grow in cold, arid elevations not usually conducive to plantlife, these conditions may also help them. There are few fungi or insects, and forest fires sparked by lightning are uncommon since there is little ground cover.

ANIMALS

Death Valley's landscape often looks barren, but there is a surprising amount of wildlife diversity. Approximately 380 species of birds have been documented along with 51 species of mammals and 41 species of reptiles and amphibians. Riparian environments, sand dunes, coniferous areas, and desert woodlands each have their own habitat. There are even six fish species in Death Valley. Five of these are not found anywhere else. The best places to see fish are freshwater marshes: Saratoga Spring, where you can find the Saratoga Spring pupfish, and Salt Creek, with the Salt Creek pupfish.

All animals in the northern Mojave have adapted to the harsh climate and have developed ways of avoiding the worst extremes and ways to conserve precious resources. Most cold-blooded animals, such as snakes, lizards, tortoises, and reptiles, hibernate in winter. In summer, some animals do the opposite, in a process called estivation. Metabolism lowers, and the animal—for example, the Mojave ground squirrel—lives on stored body fat from midsummer until fall or winter. During midday some animals, like snakes and coyotes, retreat to shade or dens. Lowland animals are mostly nocturnal and hunt at night or at dawn. The beefy and distinctive chuckwalla lizard stores extra water in the fatty tissues of its tail. Other animals get all or nearly all their water from plants.

Mammals

Bighorn sheep are often associated with the northern Mojave, but it is uncommon to see these elusive animals, although their droppings are abundant in canyons such as Ashford Canyon. They are well adapted to steep, rocky mountain passages and can survive in sparsely vegetated areas as long as they have access to water every few days. Bighorn sheep were common in the mid-19th century, but hunting and disease from domestic sheep drastically cut their numbers. The rise of feral burros introduced competition for vegetation and water. Burro reduction programs initiated by the NPS and Bureau of Land Management (BLM) were geared toward protecting habitat for bighorn sheep.

The top-rung carnivore in the desert, the **mountain lion** or puma lives at upper elevations, preying on bighorn sheep and deer. The smaller cousins of these predators, **bobcats,** live at lower elevations and prey on smaller mammals and birds.

Birds

Some birds, like roadrunners, are here year-round, but for most others, Death Valley is a migratory stop from November through March. Birds congregate near water, like the Saline Valley freshwater marsh. Other birds migrate within the region. Ravens survive year-round in the hottest parts of Death Valley; they are intelligent and adaptable.

Desert Tortoise

An emblematic Mojave Desert animal, the desert tortoise lives 60 to 100 years. It hibernates in winter and estivates in summer, living in a 3- to 10-foot (0.9- to 3-m) burrow underground, and forays out in fall and spring. It can store a quart of water. Desert tortoises have become increasingly rare, although as recently as the 1950s they were one of the most commonly seen native animals in the Mojave. They have faced threats from habitat destruction and competition for food. Land development, livestock grazing, and off-highway-vehicle recreation destroy burrows; cars and recreational vehicles may crush tortoises. They were put on the federal threatened species list in 1990. You might be able to see a tortoise behind the Shoshone Inn in Shoshone Village or at the Jawbone Canyon rest area off US 395.

Salt Creek Pupfish

A few animal species have become stranded in biological islands in the rare desert wetlands. During the late Pleistocene, Mojave pupfish filled the lakes and streams. They survived as the water shrank, becoming isolated from the network of water. Now each riparian environment has its own specialized pupfish, with the entire population of the species confined to one pool or creek.

Bats and Arthropods

Arthropods include insects, spiders, and scorpions. **Scorpions** look like a crustacean or a strange sea creature, evoking the region's watery history. **Bats** are predators of arthropods. All over the world, including the California deserts, bats have lost roosting and foraging areas. The thousands of abandoned mines in the Death Valley area make good roosting locations and substitute for lost habitat. Open mine shafts can be dangerous, but wildlife biologists encourage property owners, including the federal government, to close off shafts with grated metal bars instead of filling them entirely with dirt.

History

INDIGENOUS HISTORY

During the end of the last glacial age, there were marshes and savannas in the desert lowlands, making them conducive to human settlement. Archaeological evidence from a number of sites confirms human habitation in the northern Mojave Desert for at least 11,000 years. There is evidence of camps near the shores of Lake Manly in Death Valley. As the lakes dried up and it became hotter and more inhospitable in the low-lying valleys, year-round human occupation dwindled. There is scarce evidence of human settlement between 4,500 and 7,500 years ago, a particularly arid period in natural history. From 4,500 years ago, the climate became more temperate, and hunter-gatherer cultures evolved in the region. They developed a way of life that allowed them to survive in this severe landscape.

When European Americans came on the scene in the 1800s, there were four cultural groups that had perfected a life in the difficult terrain in and around Death Valley: the **Kawaiisu** people to the south, the **Southern Paiute,** the **Owens Valley Paiute,** and the **Western Shoshone** in Death Valley itself. The Shoshone were part of a larger Shoshone Nation that extended from western Wyoming to eastern Oregon, eastern California, and central Nevada. The groups moved seasonally between the desert floor and mountain camps, seeking favorable climate and seasonal plants. Winters were spent hunting and harvesting wild grasses and mesquite beans in the low desert valleys. In summer they moved to the cooler mountain elevations, where pinyon pine nuts were the staple. The group of Shoshone people at Furnace Creek in the heart of Death Valley called themselves Timbisha. Although the Spaniards had established coastal missions in California beginning in 1769, the European invasion of North America didn't begin to affect the groups living in the harsh interior, east of the

Preserving Historical and Cultural Sites

INDIGENOUS SITES

Death Valley has been home to Indigenous people for thousands of years. Signs of their ancient culture, with its powerful connections to the land, are scattered across Death Valley, often blending in with the landscape. Stone alignments, rock walls, and rock art can be found in the **Greenwater Valley** area. Native American village sites are in the remote canyons of the **Saline Valley.** The secluded and rugged **Cottonwood Mountains** hide petroglyphs in deep mountain canyons.

Sadly, there is a code of silence that surrounds most of these sites due to the threat of **vandalism.** The only Indigenous rock art site readily disclosed in Death Valley is in the popular but rugged Titus Canyon at Klare Spring; as a result, this impressive panel of petroglyphs has been badly vandalized.

MINING SITES

Pioneer settlement and mining moved in and stole Indigenous territory, leaving historical traces throughout the lonely canyons and hills of Death Valley. Visit the **Ibex Spring mining camp,** a remote and scenic ghost camp in one of the lightly visited areas of the park. As you walk toward the camp, you might be struck by the isolation, the incongruousness of the palm trees against the barren rocky hills, the jagged cabins alone with the sun and wind. As you get closer, you may be struck by something else: a water tank riddled with bullet holes, or sheetrock cabin walls that looked like they've been punched in. It's still a fascinating spot, but the years of vandalism have taken their toll.

PRESERVING SITES FOR THE FUTURE

Death Valley is so vast that it's easy to go a day without seeing another soul. Because of its scale, many places in the park are lightly patrolled, and we as visitors are tasked with taking care of this monumental natural and cultural resource. Adding graffiti to an ancient petroglyph or thoughtlessly and illegally shooting up a mining camp may seem extreme, but these acts are common. Even less egregious behaviors, such as removing a rusted can from a ghost camp, for example, take a toll and chip away at historical sites. Along with the natural beauty of Death Valley, its historical and cultural sites tell the story of Death Valley and contribute to its fascination. Indigenous sites are still sacred to the Timbisha Shoshone people, who continue to have strong ties to the land. Do not disturb these sites in any way. Leave them for others to discover and enjoy.

Sierra Nevada range, until the early 19th century. With mining and eventually tourism, an all-too familiar story of Native American displacement occurred with the Timbisha Shoshone people, who had called Death Valley home for thousands of years.

PIONEERS

After Lewis and Clark finished their exploratory journey through the West in 1806, fur trappers set up camp in the Rocky Mountains, beaver populations were soon exhausted, and traders began exploring farther west into the Great Basin region. A small group of traders led by Spaniard **Antonio Armijo** struck out to find a reliable route from New Mexico to California. Armijo traveled west from the present location of Las Vegas and followed the elusive desert river, the Amargosa, to the west and south. The Amargosa River flows mostly underground and disappears for good at the southern end of the Death Valley sink. Armijo left the trail there, but he was the first European American to visit the desert basin that would become Death Valley. His trail became the Spanish Trail, used as a trading route and the original route for migrant pioneers coming to the area in the 1840s.

In the 1840s the famous Death Valley 49ers were seeking a way to the Sierra Nevada, where gold camps and wild speculation were beginning to boom. Tens of thousands of people flocked to the West, seeking their fortunes along the few established routes. The north-south route along the base of the Sierra Nevada range, the present-day US 395, had been defined, but the area to the east was still unexplored. A group of 400-500 migrants in 110 wagons left from Salt Lake City under the guidance of Jefferson Hunt. The plan was to follow the Spanish Trail. Partway into the trip, 20-year-old **Captain Orson Smith** convinced some of the members of the wagon train to leave the Spanish Trail and follow him on a shortcut to the goldfields. After only 25 miles (40 km) into this so-called shortcut, the group encountered a deep canyon. Many of the party realized their mistake, cut their losses, and turned around to rejoin the initial group and successfully take the Spanish Trail to the Sierra Nevada. A smaller group of 27 wagons and 100 people somehow made it past this canyon and continued west across the desert, where they encountered the bleak, salty wildness of the Death Valley sink in December 1849.

This was unprecedented territory for nonnative people, and they were faced with the extreme basin and range topography, with its sheer mountains and desolate lowlands. The groups continued to fracture into smaller and smaller units, feeling their way west through various rugged routes to the base of the Sierra Nevada. The **Pinney party** comprised 11 men traveling on foot. They ran low on food, and two men split off, eventually making their way to Owens Lake to be nursed back to health by the Paiute people. In 1862 the skeletons of nine men were found near the Death Valley Dunes, and were presumed to be the rest of the Pinney party.

Possibly the most famous contingent of wanderers was the **Bennett-Arcane group,** comprising seven wagons and about 30 men, women, and children. After entering the salt flats, they turned south instead of following the Jayhawkers to the north. Exhausted and discouraged by the sheer Panamint Mountains, they eventually set up camp, most likely at today's Bennett's Well, off the West Side Road. Two men, William Lewis Manly and John Rogers, went for help, returning 26 days later to rescue the remaining group. In the interim another smaller group led by **Harry Wade** found their way southwest. Somehow only one member of the Bennett-Arcane group had died while awaiting rescue. As they walked over the southern Panamints with their lives, having long since abandoned and burned their wagons, one of the party supposedly turned and said, "Goodbye, death valley," naming North America's deepest basin.

COMPETING LAND-USE VISIONS

Death Valley and its surrounding mountain ranges were signed into national monument status in 1933. More than 60 years later, in 1994, the monument was declared a national park, more than doubling the size of the protected lands. At 3.4 million acres (1.4 million ha)—over 5,000 square miles (12,950 sq km)—it is the biggest national park in the contiguous United States. The vastness and wide-open spaces of the northern Mojave Desert might make it seem like there's plenty of land to go around, but competing interests have often dictated the way the land is used. Miners, ranchers, off-road-vehicle recreation enthusiasts, the military, Native American groups, and conservationists have clashed in and around the northern Mojave Desert.

The Military

Military bases flank the park boundaries on two sides. **Naval Air Weapons Station China Lake** lies to the southwest, and **Fort Irwin National Training Center** to the northeast. Chosen for the vastness and seeming emptiness of the region, these military bases take up large swatches of the northern Mojave. Both were home to Native American groups for at least 15,000 years. When the

China Lake facility's boundaries were established in 1943, it included one of the largest known concentrations of petroglyphs in the western hemisphere. The **Coso Rock Art District** in the Coso Range Canyons covers a 99-square-mile (256-sq-km) area with more than 50,000 documented petroglyphs. While the site no longer has easy public access, the navy has a policy of stewardship toward cultural and natural sites located within the boundaries of the facility and allows for military-approved guided public tours of the rock art. Unlike the few well-known rock art sites in Death Valley, there is virtually no contemporary graffiti—being located inside a military base has arguably protected them.

Also within the boundaries of the China Lake facility are the **Coso Hot Springs,** on the National Register of Historic Places. The springs were used by Native Americans dating back to the Coso people and later the Northern Paiute and Timbisha as a cultural and healing ritual site. Local Native American groups still have access to the springs for ceremonial purposes. In the 1920s a hot springs resort was built at Coso Hot Springs, and the ruins of this resort still stand.

At times, visitors to Death Valley are reminded of the proximity of military operations. Especially in the Saline Valley, tucked against the western Inyo Mountains or the Eureka Dunes, high up in the northern Last Chance Range, it is possible for military planes to swoop in literally out of the blue to buzz the surreal mountainscapes with maneuvers. Although both military centers have sought to expand their acreage into the surrounding desert, they operate under relatively clear mandates from Congress. Much of the current debate over land use is about areas outside their borders.

Mining

Death Valley's rich mineral resources were known from the time of the famous 1849 rush for gold, but most of the attention was focused on the western Sierra Nevada and the Comstock Lode in Nevada. The area around Death Valley didn't have its first mining heyday until the early 1870s, when the silver-mining town of **Cerro Gordo** in the Inyo Mountains grew into a sizable silver-mining camp and drew attention to the area.

Panamint City sprouted up next, drawing hundreds of eager investors and miners to the silver veins in the Panamint Mountains. By 1874 Panamint City had swelled to a rowdy town of 2,000 people with a reputation for lawlessness and violence. By 1875 the boom was over. Small mining camps spread through the Panamints and other mountain ranges around Death Valley, appearing and being abandoned as the veins played out and people moved, along with their possessions and sometimes even buildings, to newer sites. The eastern side of Death Valley gained much attention after 1900 when towns like **Chloride City** and **Rhyolite** gained momentum. Rhyolite was the largest town in the Death Valley area, with a population of 5,000-10,000 during its heyday, 1905-1911. The teens and 1920s saw interest in lead and copper mining, and mining efforts crept into remote places like the Racetrack Valley.

When Death Valley became a national monument in 1933, mining was briefly suspended, but Congress created a loophole to allow the continuation of mining claims. In the 1930s mining claims were at their highest as the Depression brought people seeking alternative ways to eke out a living. These were small-time pocket miners, working small deposits of minerals that would support a few families. Gold fever had given way to more practical dreams. **Talc** and **borax** fever, for instance, though not nearly as romantic-sounding, had taken hold, and mining companies worked the land, maximizing technology to pull out even low-grade ore.

In 1971, when the third borax rush took off, attitudes toward the land had changed. In the 1800s people had swarmed the land for what they could eke out of it, but more than 100 years later most people saw that same land as something in need of protection. Mining practices had changed: Old mining practices had been relatively unobtrusive, and miners hand-dug pockets of ore, leaving the overall landscape intact. Newer methods included open-pit and strip mining, which vastly degraded the landscape and changed its shape. Individuals seeking their fortunes had given way to mining corporations seeking wealth in highly visible locations within a national monument. Congress sought to get the number of mining claims within the monument's boundaries under control when it passed the **Mining Act of 1976.** Before the Mining Act, there were more than 4,000 claims in Death Valley; by the time Death Valley officially became a national park in 1994, there were fewer than 150. The last one, Billie Mine, a borax mine located along the Dante's View Road, closed in 2005.

Tourism

The economy of Death Valley began to transition from mining to tourism in the 1920s, and in 1933 Congress approved Death Valley as a **national monument.** The first toll road designed for visitors was completed in 1926. It followed the contours of present-day Highway 190 from Towne Pass on the west side to Stovepipe Wells. The tourist village of Stovepipe Wells, briefly called Bungalow City, was completed in 1926.

The national monument designation protected the land, but Congress conveniently left a loophole for mining. Mining and tourism are inextricably intertwined in Death Valley history in many ways. The Pacific Coast Borax Company actually built some of the first lodging for visitors, completing the elegant Furnace Creek Inn (now the Inn at Death Valley) in 1927 and investing money in the tourism potential of the land as mining claims played out.

Mining and tourism both began to boom in the middle of the 20th century, coexisting within the national monument. With mining claims somewhat regulated with the passage of the Mining Act of 1976, the park turned to other issues of conservation and public debate. Also in 1976, Congress attempted to create a plan that would encompass a wide range of land-use interests by establishing the **California Desert Conservation Area** on land managed by the BLM outside the park's boundaries.

The debate continued to rage until there was a sweeping attempt to shift priorities, in the form of the **California Desert Protection Act of 1986.** The legislation languished until 1994, when it was finally signed into existence. It added an additional million acres to the national monument to create the new and better-protected Death Valley National Park. It also added land and protected status to the newly created Joshua Tree National Park and the Mojave National Preserve. The act also acknowledged the claims of Native American groups, ordering a study to find reservation land for the Timbisha Shoshone people.

The Timbisha Shoshone People

Beginning with the arrival of the first European American migrants in the mid-1850s, the Timbisha Shoshone people were displaced from their land and way of life as mining camps and towns sprang up and took control of water and other natural resources. They gradually acculturated, doing manual labor for road building, mining, ranching, and construction.

When Death Valley became a national monument in 1933, the focus for the land shifted toward conservation and tourism. Mining was also allowed, and mining claims continued to grow well into the 1970s. The Timbisha Shoshone, who were tied to the land through their lifestyle, religion, and history, were the only interest group completely left out of land management.

Following the national monument designation, the NPS built the Timbisha a 60-acre (24-ha) adobe village next to Furnace Creek, but they were forbidden to continue using the land for their subsistence lifestyle. Their first political triumph came on the heels of the Mining Act of 1976, which marked a shift in attitudes toward the land. In 1983 the Timbisha Shoshone gained formal federal recognition. When Death Valley became a national park in 1994, the act required a study to find them reservation land within their native region. In 2000 the **Timbisha Land Act** set aside 300 acres (121 ha) of homeland for the Timbisha Shoshone, along with provisions granting them access to national park lands for religious activities.

Wilderness

The wide-open spaces of the desert function as a canvas for the dreams and beliefs of the many people who visit and call it home. The vastness of Death Valley inspires a certain feeling of independence and solitude, and it is easy to embrace a feeling of open possibility, as opposed to the feeling that you are visiting an attraction. This might account for the competing visions about the way the land is used and protected.

During the 20th century, two increasingly divergent political viewpoints became clear. One contingent wanted to continue to eke out a living from the land with mining, ranching, and other economic activity. Others held the idea that the scenic, geological, ecological, and historical resources of the northern Mojave Desert need to be protected. These two points of view are not always mutually exclusive, but they represent two vastly different political perspectives and continue to create political tension at Death Valley and the surrounding areas.

Within the park, debates continue over "wilderness" designations, which have closed some 4WD roads. A wilderness designation adds protection from land development, although roads still intersect it. Most of the park—93 percent—is designated wilderness. Debates also continue over how historical sites like cabins should be maintained and who should be responsible. A visit to a place like the Ibex Spring camp makes it clear what the NPS is trying to prevent. Sheetrock walls are punched out, an old water tank is riddled with bullet holes, and weathered timbers have been pulled from cabins and used as fuel for bonfires.

Debates beyond the park's boundaries have become fiercer on land managed by the BLM in both California and Nevada, and mining and ranching battles on BLM land have received media coverage. In Death Valley National Park and beyond its boundaries, the northern Mojave Desert continues to inspire a fierce sense of independence, passion, and inspiration.

Essentials

Getting There

Death Valley National Park is at the southeastern side of central California, bordering Nevada on the east. A small portion of the park, the Nevada Triangle, is in Nevada. The closest major cities are Las Vegas, 140 miles (225 km) southeast, and Los Angeles, 300 miles (485 km) southwest. Most of the park is easily accessible year-round, although some higher-elevation locales may close due to snow during winter. Highway 190 is the major route that bisects the park; it is open year-round. It passes through the two main park hubs, Stovepipe Wells and Furnace Creek.

SUGGESTED ROUTES

West

US 395 is the main route traversing the eastern side of California between the Sierra Nevada range and the Nevada border. Routes to Death Valley via US 395 work best for travelers coming from the north or west. From US 395 there are two routes into the Death Valley region.

Highway 190 runs east from the tiny town of Olancha, with a gas and café stop.

Highway 136 runs east from Lone Pine, a bigger town with hotels, restaurants, gas, and other services. Highway 136 joins Highway 190, which crosses into the park boundary at the Panamint Springs Resort, with its motel, restaurant, general store, gas, and campground. The resort has park information and can be used for exploring areas on the western side of Death Valley. The closest park hub is Stovepipe Wells, 30 miles (48 km) east.

Southwest

Highway 14 cuts across the Mojave Desert from the Los Angeles area to join **Highway 178** in the town of Ridgecrest before heading northeast into the park. Ridgecrest is a moderate-size town on the edge of the Naval Air Weapons Station China Lake. It has the most services, including hotels, restaurants, groceries, and outdoors stores. It's a good place to fill up on gas and grab any supplies you've forgotten.

Highway 178 enters the park and joins **Highway 190** just east of the Panamint Springs Resort, about 1.5 hours from Ridgecrest. The closest park hub is Stovepipe Wells, another 30 miles (48 km, 30 minutes) northeast. Between Ridgecrest and Highway 190 where it enters the park, Highway 178 is prone to washouts; check road conditions before taking this route.

East

If you are using **Las Vegas** as your travel hub or entering Death Valley from the east, there are several eastern routes. Depending which route you take, travel time is 2-3.5 hours from Las Vegas.

US 95 is a main route in Nevada that parallels both the state boundary and Death Valley. There are two points to enter Death Valley from US 95. The first route leaves US 95 south on **Highway 373** at Amargosa Valley and then runs west, via a right turn at Death Valley Junction, onto **Highway 190** into the park. Amargosa Valley has a gas station and a convenience store, but there's no gas at Death Valley Junction.

North on US 95 is the gateway town of Beatty, Nevada. From here, **Highway 374** leads south into the park. Beatty has lodging, restaurants, and gas and makes a good driving stop; it is also a good base camp for exploring the park.

The shortest route leaves from **I-15 South** to follow **Highway 160** through Pahrump, Nevada. A left turn on Bell Vista Road takes you to Death Valley Junction, California, where **Highway 190** continues into the park.

Southeast

I-15 begins in San Diego and runs north, passing about an hour east of Los Angeles. It is the main road between Southern California and Las Vegas. From Baker, which is a good gas and convenience-store stop, **Highway 127** runs north, intersecting with **Highway 190,** the main park route. This is the fastest route into the park from the Los Angeles area.

FROM LAS VEGAS

Las Vegas is the closest major city to Death Valley, less than three hours away. It has a major airport with flights from most US cities and offers car, RV, and 4WD vehicle rentals as well as equipment and supplies to prepare for your trip.

Previous: Ash Meadows National Wildlife Refuge.

Car

I-15 intersects with US 95 north of McCarran International Airport. To reach **Death Valley Junction** (2.5 hours, 140 mi/225 km) from Las Vegas, take US 95 north for 88 miles (142 km) to Amargosa Valley, Nevada. Turn left (south) onto Highway 373 and drive 24 miles (39 km) southwest. Highway 373 becomes Highway 127 when it crosses into California. At the tiny outpost of Death Valley Junction, turn right (west) onto Highway 190 and continue west for 30 miles (48 km) to the park hub at Furnace Creek.

From Las Vegas via **Beatty, Nevada** (2.5 hours, 160 mi/260 km), take US 95 north for 116 miles (187 km). Turn left (south) onto Highway 374 and drive 19 miles (31 km) southwest to Beatty Cutoff Road at the Hells Gate junction. Turn left onto Beatty Cutoff Road, and drive 10 miles (16.1 km) south to Highway 190. Turn left onto Highway 190, and drive 11 miles (17.7 km) south to Furnace Creek.

From Las Vegas via **Pahrump, Nevada** (2 hours, 120 mi/193 km), take I-15 south. Exit on Nevada Highway 160 West. Drive 60 miles (97 km) to Pahrump, Nevada. Turn left on Bell Vista Road and drive 30 miles (48 km) to Death Valley Junction, California. Turn right on Highway 127 then left on Highway 190 after approximately 300 feet (91 m). Drive 30 miles (48 km) to Furnace Creek Visitor Center.

Air

Harry Reid International Airport (LAS; 5757 Wayne Newton Blvd.; 702/261-5211; www.harryreidairport.com) is a major international airport positioned to serve Nevada and parts of Arizona and California. It's located near I-15 and US 95 in Las Vegas. More than 30 commercial carriers land here, including Aeroméxico, Alaska Airlines, American, Delta, JetBlue, Southwest, and United.

Ground transportation is outside Terminal 1's baggage claim area and on Terminal 3's Level Zero. If you're staying overnight in Las Vegas, group shuttles from the airport are available to many of the major hotel-resorts. **Taxis** are available from the airport and the Rent-A-Car Center. Some taxis do not take credit cards. Rideshare drop-off is available at the Terminal 1 and Terminal 3 departure curbs. Rideshare pickup is located in designated areas in the parking garage. Walk-up limo services are also available.

Car Rental

Car rentals are located at the **Rent-A-Car Center** (7135 Gilespie St.; 24 hours daily), 3 miles (4.8 km) from the airport. Courtesy shuttles from the airport take you to the rental car center. The center is close to I-15 and I-215 as well as the Las Vegas Strip.

Tours

Chartered day tours to Death Valley are available from Las Vegas. These tours often leave from popular hotels along the Las Vegas Strip and take visitors to some of the park's highlights. Companies like **Incredible Adventures** (800/777-8464; www.incadventures.com) offer SUV, van, and private tours.

RV Rental

Many RV rental agencies have offices in Las Vegas, including **Cruise America** (800/671-8042; www.cruiseamerica.com) and **El Monte RV** (888/337-2214; www.elmonterv.com). Direct rental RV shares are also offered through companies like **Outdoorsy** (www.outdoorsy.com) or **RVshare** (www.rvshare.com).

Smaller vehicles suit the Death Valley terrain better than big RVs, and they allow for more versatility in travel. Camper vans out of Las Vegas are available through companies that include **Native Campervans** (877/550-5335; https://nativecampervans.com), **Escape Campervans** (877/270-8267 or 310/672-9909; www.escapecampervans.com), and **Indie Campers** (23865 Hawthorne Blvd., Torrance; 855/661-3485; https://indiecampers.com).

Equipment Rental

REI (710 S. Rampart Blvd.; 702/951-4488; www.rei.com), centrally located in Las Vegas's Boca Park, rents car camping and hiking gear, climbing gear, and mountain bikes. **Basecamp** (2595 Chandler Ave.; 702/357-9513; www.basecampoutdoorgear.com) rents backpacking, camping, and camp kitchen gear from a warehouse less than a mile (1.6 km) from Harry Reid International Airport.

Accommodations and Food

There are many major hotel chains and accommodations convenient to the airport and highways. For that Vegas experience, the Las Vegas Strip is lined with casino resort hotels. The city is also a dining destination; many resort hotels have multiple restaurants to suit a variety of different tastes and price points, some with celebrity chefs to draw in crowds beyond the hotel guests.

To steer clear of the clamor of the Strip, head toward the west side of town to **Red Rock Casino Resort & Spa** (11011 W. Charleston Blvd.; 702/797-7777; www.redrockresort.com), which is close to Red Rock Canyon National Conservation Area.

FROM LOS ANGELES

Approximately 300 miles (485 km) south of Death Valley, Los Angeles has a major international airport with regular flights from US and international cities. LA has all the civilization you could possibly need to prepare for your trip, including car, RV, and equipment rentals.

Car

The drive from Los Angeles to Death Valley takes about four hours, depending on your destination within the park. You can plan your route via the western park entrance at Panamint Springs or the eastern entrance and Furnace Creek.

Western Entrance

Head north out of Los Angeles on US 101 to Highway 170 and onto I-5. From I-5, take Highway 14, the Antelope Valley Freeway, north toward Palmdale and Lancaster. Drive 120 miles (193 km) north to Indian Wells, where Highway 14 joins US 395. Continue north on US 395 for 42 miles (68 km) to the town of Olancha. Turn right (east) onto Highway 190 and continue 45 miles (72 km) to **Panamint Springs.** Stovepipe Wells lies 29 miles (47 km) east of Panamint Springs; Furnace Creek is 53 miles (85 km) east of Panamint Springs.

Eastern Entrance

Head east out of Los Angeles on I-10, the San Bernardino Freeway. After approximately 10 miles (16.1 km), around West Covina, follow signs for I-605 north. Follow I-605 north for approximately 5 miles (8 km), then take the exit onto I-210 east, the Foothill Freeway. Continue east on I-210 for 27 miles (43 km), then follow signs for I-15 north toward Barstow. Stay on I-15 north for 130 miles (209 km) until its intersection with Highway 127 at the town of Baker. Take the Highway 127/Kelbaker Road exit toward Death Valley and drive north on Highway 127 for 87 miles (140 km) to Death Valley Junction. Turn left (west) onto Highway 190 and drive another 30 miles (48 km) west to **Furnace Creek.**

Air

Los Angeles International Airport (LAX; 1 World Way; 855/463-5252; www.flylax.com) is a major international airport and hub about 16 miles (26 km) southwest of downtown Los Angeles. It is one of the busiest airports in the world. The main airport serves the Los Angeles area with eight terminals, plus the Tom Bradley International Terminal (Terminal B).

Airport shuttles, hotel shuttles, and private parking shuttles can all be accessed at the upper Departures level identified by red curbside pylons. Ride app services, transportation network services, and taxis are located at the LAX-it lot next to Terminal 1. A **FlyAway Bus** service (no reservations; 24

hours daily) offers the best public transportation from LAX to downtown (Union Station) and the San Fernando Valley (Van Nuys). Free shuttles to public transportation hubs are also available from the Lower/Arrivals level. For the **Lot South/LAX City Bus Center,** pickup is from the Lower/Arrivals level at the pink LAX shuttle sign in front of each terminal. Several public bus lines connect at the center. Metro users should wait at the pink LAX shuttle sign and board the **Metro C Line (Green Line)** shuttle.

Car Rental

Approximately 20 car-rental companies operate at Los Angeles International Airport; all vehicle rental companies are located off-site. Companies offer courtesy shuttles that pick up customers at the Lower/Arrivals level of all terminals outside baggage claim under the purple Rental Car Shuttles sign.

RV Rental

A few RV rental agencies have offices in Los Angeles, including **Cruise America** (800/671-8042; www.cruiseamerica.com). Direct rental RV shares are also available through companies like **Outdoorsy** (www.outdoorsy.com) or **RVshare** (www.rvshare.com). Camper van rentals are available through **Escape Campervans** (4858 W. Century Blvd., Inglewood; US 877/270-8267 or international 310/672-9909; www.escapecampervans.com), **Lost Campers** (8820 Aviation Blvd., Inglewood; 415/386-2693 or 888/567-8826; www.lostcampersusa.com), and **Indie Campers** (23865 Hawthorne Blvd., Torrance; 855/661-3485; https://indiecampers.com).

Equipment Rental

There are several REI locations around the Los Angeles area. The **REI Arcadia** (214 N. Santa Anita Ave., Arcadia; 626/447-1062; www.rei.com) is east of Los Angeles, directly off I-210, and rents camping and hiking gear as well as climbing gear.

FROM PALM SPRINGS

Some visitors fly direct into Palm Springs, then head north along this remote and circuitous route to enter the park at its eastern access.

From Palm Springs, take Highway 111 west for 10 miles (16.1 km) to merge onto I-10. Follow I-10 west for 40 miles (64 km) until the junction with I-215. Take I-215 north for 15 miles (24 km) and continue north as the freeway joins with I-15. In about 60 miles (97 km), I-15 crosses I-40 in Barstow. Keep left to stay on I-15 and continue another 62 miles (100 km) north to Baker (a good place to fill your tank before heading into the park). At Baker, turn north onto Highway 127. You'll pass Tecopa in about 50 miles (81 km), or one hour; Shoshone lies 8 miles (12.9 km) farther. In another 27 miles (43 km), you'll reach Death Valley Junction; take Highway 190 west for 30 miles (48 km) to the park hub at **Furnace Creek.**

It's also possible to take US 395 north from I-15 near Victorville and enter the park from the south, via Ridgecrest and the Trona Road, or from the west via Olancha and Highway 190.

The total drive time will be about **4.5-5 hours** to cover the 300 miles (485 km) from Palm Springs. In winter, chains may be required on the stretch of I-15 between the Angeles and San Bernardino National Forests.

Getting Around

DRIVING

Death Valley's vast distances and lack of a park transportation system mean that you will likely spend a lot of time driving. Although heat-related issues are one of Death Valley's dangers, car accidents are the number one source of injury.

Roads

Death Valley has more than 1,000 miles (1,610 km) of paved and dirt roads. When planning a trip, make sure you know what type of road you'll be traveling. **Graded dirt roads** are regularly maintained and usually passable in an ordinary passenger vehicle. **Dirt roads** are rougher but generally only require a high-clearance vehicle, like a small SUV. **Rough dirt roads** usually require a 4WD vehicle. On extremely rough dirt roads, a short-wheelbase 4WD vehicle and driving expertise are required. These roads are no joke—slanted bedrock, boulders, and sheer drop-offs can make for a harrowing drive even for experienced drivers. *Do not attempt extremely rough dirt roads without expertise and the proper vehicle.*

These extreme situations aside, people have different comfort levels and are willing to push their cars to different performance levels. Use common sense to judge the situation, and be aware that backcountry roads can quickly become difficult and narrow with little possibility of turning around.

Roads can also change status. For example, a windstorm can cause sandy conditions and make a generally high-clearance-only road a 4WD road. Water can have a similar effect. The Harry Wade Exit Route generally only requires a high-clearance vehicle but can become a 4WD road when the Amargosa River flows across it at certain times of the year, creating muddy conditions. In winter, be prepared for snow and ice at higher elevations. In summer, avoid remote roads at low elevation because of the possibility of mechanical failure.

Road conditions can change quickly in Death Valley due to floods, wind, snow, and other factors. In the event of a **flash flood,** even paved roads can be wiped out. Avoid canyon roads during rainy weather due to the possibility of flash floods. To keep updated on Death Valley's current road conditions, visit the **Death Valley Alerts & Conditions** page on the park website (www.nps.gov/deva/planyourvisit/conditions.htm).

Gas

Plan your fuel stops in advance and maintain a full tank before traveling long distances. Fuel is only available within the park at **Furnace Creek, Stovepipe Wells,** and **Panamint Springs.** There is no fuel available at Scotty's Castle. If you're planning a backcountry drive, make sure you have more than enough gas to get you there and back.

Outside the park the closest fuel stops are at **Beatty, Nevada,** on the east side; **Shoshone** to the southeast; and **Olancha, Lone Pine,** and **Big Pine** to the west. Many small communities around the park's boundaries do not have gas. Because of Death Valley's remoteness and its status as a tourism destination, gas prices are significantly cheaper outside the park. It's a good idea to fill up before entering Death Valley. Inside the park, Stovepipe Wells has the cheapest gas.

Maps and GPS

The National Park Service (NPS) strongly advises against navigating with a GPS receiver in Death Valley, and for good reason. Those who rely exclusively on GPS navigation can end up in life-threatening situations. When venturing beyond the paved park roads, use these tips to get safely around the park.

Park Maps

Always carry a basic park map and use it to get a general sense of the lay of the land. Park maps are included with every Death Valley Visitor Guide and are available for free at the **Furnace Creek Visitor Center** and **Stovepipe Wells Ranger Station.** This map is accurate enough to get you around the paved park roads and major graded dirt roads. Panamint Springs is a privately owned resort, but they usually have free copies of the visitor guide in the general store. You can also download one (www.nps.gov/deva/parknews/newspaper.htm) from the park website. Interactive maps are available via a new National Park Service app (go.nps.gov/app) that has up-to-date information about all 423 national parks in one app.

Unlike other national parks, Death Valley does not have entrance stations along its main roads. Begin your trip at one of the park hubs to pay your entrance fee, grab a map, and take advantage of the visitor center or other services.

Death Valley Backcountry Roads

For venturing into the backcountry, pick up a *Death Valley Backcountry & Wilderness Access* map at one of the visitor centers or ranger stations. This map has slightly more detail than the basic park map, but its best feature is a list of backcountry roads with road descriptions, including the type of vehicle needed and the distances involved.

For more detailed planning and backcountry visits, I recommend Tom Harrison Maps' *Death Valley National Park,* which includes mileages, road conditions (paved, dirt, 4WD), and elevation. The NPS also recommends the National Geographic *Death Valley National Park* Trails Illustrated map. Both maps are available at visitor centers and ranger stations in the park where the Death Valley Natural History Association has kiosks.

RV TRAVEL

Having an RV can provide a great base camp in Death Valley's often windy, exposed landscape. But with the steep basin and range topography, you'll also need to plan your entrance route carefully.

The easiest RV route into the park is via **Highway 190** from the east via Death Valley Junction and Highway 127. It is also possible to enter via Beatty and Highway 374 (Daylight Pass Rd.). At the split on Daylight Pass Road, the Beatty Cutoff is suitable for RVs but descends through some sharp, narrow curves. Highway 374 (Mud Canyon Rd.) also has some curves.

From the west, the mountain passes along Highway 190 toward Panamint Springs are steep and narrow. Through Towne Pass, there are grades of 7 to 9 percent; extra-long RVs are not recommended on this stretch. To enter from the west, follow **Highway 178** north from Ridgecrest to enter the park via the paved Trona Wildrose Road (subject to closure, so check road conditions) and Panamint Valley Road.

Once inside the park, the main roads—**Highway 190** and **Badwater Road** (Hwy. 178)—are paved and easily drivable. However, other popular roads are not suitable for RVs or trailers: Titus Canyon Road, Skidoo Road, Upper Wildrose Canyon Road, Aguereberry Point Road, and Racetrack Valley Road. Some roads do not allow RVs and trailers over 25 feet (40 km) in length: Artist's Drive, Dante's View Road, Emigrant Canyon Road, and Lower Wildrose Canyon Road.

RV sites are available at Furnace Creek, Texas Spring, Sunset, Mesquite Spring, Stovepipe Wells, and Panamint Springs Campgrounds, although only Furnace Creek, Stovepipe Wells, and Panamint Springs have full hookups. Beatty, Nevada, has RV accommodations and can be a good base camp. Shoshone, at the junction of Highways 127 and 178, also has RV accommodations.

TOURS

4WD Tours and Rentals

Over 1,000 miles (1,610 km) of dirt and paved roads unravel across the park to the springs, dunes, mountains, canyons, and historical sites

Death Valley Road Guide

ROAD	TYPE	ACCESS
Aguereberry Point Road	graded dirt road	high-clearance
Ashford Canyon Road	dirt road, rough dirt road	high-clearance first 2 miles (3.2 km); 4WD last mile (1.6 km)
Badwater Basin Road	paved	passenger vehicle
Beatty Cutoff	paved	passenger vehicle
Big Pine-Death Valley Road	graded dirt road	high-clearance
Chloride Cliff Road	dirt road to rough dirt road	high-clearance to Chloride City spur; 4WD thereafter
Cottonwood Canyon Road	rough dirt road	high-clearance first 8 miles (12.9 km); 4WD thereafter
Daylight Pass Road (Hwy. 374)	paved	passenger vehicle
Darwin Falls Road	graded dirt road	passenger vehicle to trailhead; 4WD thereafter
Echo Canyon Road	rough dirt road	high-clearance first 3 miles (4.8 km); 4WD thereafter
Greenwater Valley Road	graded dirt road	high-clearance
Ibex Spring Road	dirt road	high-clearance
Hanaupah Canyon Road	rough dirt road	high-clearance first 5 miles (8 km); 4WD thereafter
Hunter Mountain Road	dirt road	high-clearance through Hidden Valley to Hunter Mountain; 4WD thereafter
Harry Wade Road (Harry Wade Exit Route)	rough dirt road	high-clearance, but may require 4WD
Ibex Dunes Road (spur from Saratoga Spring Road)	dirt road	high-clearance to dunes; 4WD thereafter

strewn across the immense landscape. Guided 4WD tours are available through **Farabee's Jeep Rentals** (101 CA-190, Furnace Creek; 760/786-9872; https://farabeejeeps.com; Sept.-May; $165-345 per person) to take you past some of the park's highlights as well as to more remote locations. Tours are also offered to some of Death Valley's classic sights like The Racetrack and Titus Canyon, and custom tours are available for two or more people. Tours range 3-8 hours.

Farabee's also rents 4WD vehicles, specializing in fully equipped Jeeps outfitted with sturdy off-road tires and 2-in-1 suspension lift to get you over boulders, washouts, and places that would otherwise seem crazy to attempt. A

ROAD	TYPE	ACCESS
Johnson Canyon Road	rough dirt road	high-clearance first 6 miles (9.7 km); 4WD thereafter
Lippincott Mine Road	rough dirt road	expert 4WD only
Lower Titus Canyon Road (to parking area and hiking access)	graded dirt road	passenger vehicle
Phinney Canyon/ Strozzi Ranch Road	rough dirt road	high-clearance first 12 miles (19.3 km) to Strozzi/Phinney Junction; 4WD thereafter
Racetrack Valley Road	dirt road	high-clearance, but may require 4WD
Saline Valley Road	dirt road	high-clearance, but may require 4WD
Saratoga Spring Road	dirt road	high-clearance
Scotty's Castle Road	paved	passenger vehicle
Skidoo Road	dirt road	high-clearance
South Eureka Road	graded dirt road	high-clearance preferable
Steel Pass Road	rough dirt road	expert 4WD only
Titus Canyon Road	dirt road	high-clearance, but may require 4WD
Trona Wildrose Road	mostly paved	passenger vehicle; may be impassable after rain
Warm Springs Road (Saline Valley)	dirt road	high-clearance; may be impassable after rain
Warm Spring Canyon Road	graded dirt road to rough dirt road	high-clearance first 10 miles (16.1 km) to Warm Springs Camp; 4WD into Butte Valley; expert 4WD only over Mengel Pass
West Side Road	graded gravel road	high-clearance

Spot GPS tracking device is provided should you run into trouble.

Four-wheel-drive or SUV rentals are also available through numerous major car-rental companies, but many of these are not intended for off-highway use; many car-rental agencies write into their policies that cars must be kept on paved roads.

Horse Trail Tours

Except for walking or riding a burro loaded down with gold-prospecting equipment, riding a horse may be the most historically correct way to experience Death Valley. The Ranch at Death Valley offers guided trail rides through its **Furnace Creek Stables** (760/614-1018; www.oasisatdeathvalley.com;

Beware of GPS

Whether you are using a paper map, a GPS receiver, or a combination, at some point in exploring beyond the main paved roads, you may find that you're heading toward a dubious-looking road. Part of the reason that GPS navigation is so dangerous within Death Valley is that it does not always know the current state of the roads. The Death Valley region has been crisscrossed with roads throughout its time as a mining mecca. Many of these roads have fallen into disuse, and some have been actively closed by the NPS. However, they continue to exist in the map data that is used by GPS systems.

In addition, due to the extreme basin and range topography of Death Valley, very few roads traverse some of the steep mountain ranges in the park. Those that do are often rugged 4WD-only trails. GPS receivers are designed to calculate the shortest route from one place to another, which could send you on a difficult or dangerous path if you're trying to drive as the crow flies.

The NPS is actively working with GPS mapping companies like TomTom, Google, and Navteq to fix the navigation situation. For your safety, if you are heading toward a road that does not look passable, do not assume it will eventually work out. Do not proceed if the road does not look like something that is suitable for your car. Roads can quickly become impassable, with no place to turn around.

Oct.-May; $90-145 per person). One-hour guided horseback tours take you across the valley floor, and two-hour rides make a foray into the foothills of the Funeral Mountains with views of the valley.

Recreation

HIKING

There are few developed and maintained hiking trails in Death Valley. Many trails follow old mining roads, canyons, or other natural features. A few popular trails in the Furnace Creek and Stovepipe Wells area are well marked and easy to follow. Other trails require more research and preparation.

For long day hikes, certain wilderness areas, or multiday backpacking trips, bring along the appropriate topo map in paper or electronic form. The company Gaia GPS offers an offline topo map app, available for tablets. Maps for Death Valley National Park are available. These electronic maps must be downloaded before your trip, as they will not be available in the park, where there is no Wi-Fi or cellular data access.

When hiking, wear light-colored clothing, sunscreen, sunglasses, and a hat with a wide brim. Layer your clothing to be prepared for changes in elevation. Carry plenty of water, and do not hike at low elevations during summer. Tell someone where you are going and when you expect to return. When hiking in remote locations, I leave a note in the window of my car listing my destination, date, and time.

BIKING

It's easy to be impressed by Death Valley's vastness, and it's possible to leave thinking that's the main selling point. With the right timing, a bike tour can be the perfect way to see some of the park's finer points. Bicycles are allowed on all park roads that are open to public vehicular traffic and on designated bike routes. Bikes are not allowed on closed roads (even if hiking is allowed), service roads, off-road, in wilderness areas, or on any trail. Riding single file is the rule.

The wide-open spaces and relatively light

traffic make Death Valley a great place for road biking; however, biking requires a high level of planning, particularly for water. Water is not readily accessible, even along the main park highways; plan to carry extra water and to treat any backcountry springwater before drinking it. The Furnace Creek Visitor Center offers drinking water for refillable water bottles.

Summer in Death Valley is too hot for most activities, and physical exertion, especially at the lower elevations, can be dangerous. If you avoid the heat of the summer months, cycling can be ideal, with clear dry air, few cars, and routes to fit all abilities. Plan cycling routes for early morning or under the desert night sky. Avoid biking in canyons if there is a storm approaching. The NPS recommends sunglasses, proper clothing, and extra food and water for a safe trip.

Bicycle rentals are available in Furnace Creek at **Desert Outfitters** (760/786-2345; www.oasisatdeathvalley.com; 9am-5pm daily). The shop offers e-bikes and road bikes in a range of men's and women's sizes for half-day and full-day rentals. When Desert Outfitters is closed, bike rentals are available through the general store.

BACKCOUNTRY CAMPING

Death Valley has more than 3 million acres (1.2 million ha) of wilderness and more than one million visitors per year, giving everyone plenty of space to stretch out. With a little planning, it's possible to snag a gorgeous scenic camping spot with as much privacy as you could want, all for the price of admission to the park.

The desert is fragile, but by adhering to some basic rules you can leave the least impact, preserving it for others. Backcountry camping is permitted **at least 2 miles (3.2 km) from paved roads;** try to camp in places that have previously been used for camping. Hard-packed or gravel ground is the most resistant to impact. Avoid walking in water, trampling vegetation, and walking on delicate soil surfaces. Camping is prohibited along several of the park's major dirt roads. Check out the park's website (www.nps.gov/deva) for a complete list of prohibited camping areas and guidelines.

RANGER PROGRAMS

Ranger programs are offered daily in winter and spring (Dec.-Mar.), including ranger-guided canyon walks and ranger talks. The schedule varies and is available online (www.nps.gov/deva) and in the visitor center. Regular programs include Harmony Borax Works ranger talks, night-sky viewing, and adventure hikes. Winter **Paleontology Tours** are daylong guided hikes to fragile paleontological sites that are normally closed to the public; these tours are available on a limited basis by reservation only up to two weeks in advance (877/444-6777; www.recreation.gov). Other guided walks and demonstrations are offered on such diverse subjects as Badwater Basin and stone tool-making. Since the closure of Scotty's Castle due to flood in 2015, the NPS and Death Valley National History Association have added special flood recovery tours, which are walking tours of the Scotty's Castle grounds for an up-close look at the power of water to shape the Death Valley landscape (www.dvnha.org; $25; registration required).

Travel Tips

There is **no cell phone reception** in Death Valley National Park, with the exception of Furnace Creek and Stovepipe Wells. Depending on your provider, you may also luck into a tiny window of cell service at unpredictable moments. Do not rely on your cell phone for communication.

Cell service is unpredictable to nonexistent in many areas around the park. On the western side of the park, there is cell service in the town of Lone Pine and along US 395. On the eastern side of the park, there is cell service in the town of Beatty and along US 95. Many individual businesses provide wireless internet for guests.

INTERNATIONAL TRAVELERS

The closest gateway city for international travelers to fly into is **Las Vegas.** The drive from Las Vegas to Death Valley takes 2-3 hours along paved highway roads that are open year-round. Along the way, you will cross the state line from Nevada to California, but there are no stops, checkpoints, or special concerns along this route. The states of California and Nevada recognize a valid driver's license issued by a foreign jurisdiction (country, state, territory). An international driver's license is not necessary.

Visas and Passports

Visitors from most other countries must have a valid passport and a visa to enter the United States. You may qualify for the Visa Waiver Program. To check, apply online with the **Electronic System for Travel Authorization** (http://esta.cbp.dhs.gov/esta); make sure you have a return plane ticket to your country of origin dated fewer than 90 days from your date of entry. Holders of Canadian passports do not need visas or visa waivers. To learn more about visa and passport requirements, visit http://travel.state.gov.

In most countries, the local US embassy or consulate should be able to provide a **tourist visa.** The average fee for a visa is US$185. While a visa may be processed as quickly as 24 hours on request, plan at least a couple of weeks, as there can be unexpected delays, particularly during the busy summer season (June-Aug.).

Los Angeles is home to **consulates** from many countries around the globe. If you should lose your passport or find yourself in some other trouble while visiting California, contact your country's offices for assistance. To find a consulate or embassy, check online (www.state.gov) for a list of all foreign countries represented in the United States. A representative will be able to direct you to the nearest consulate.

Customs

Before entering the United States from another country by air, you'll be required to fill out a customs form. Check with the US embassy in your country or the **US Customs and Border Protection** (www.cbp.gov) for an updated list of items you must declare. Prescription medications should be in their original containers and transported along with the doctor's prescription or written statement from your physician that they are necessary while traveling. Inform TSA officers of any medically necessary liquids and/or medications as well as accessories such as freezer bags or syringes. For information about current regulations on domestic flights, visit the **Transportation Security Administration website** (www.tsa.gov).

If you are driving into California along I-5 or another major highway, prepare to stop at **Agricultural Inspection Stations** a few miles inside the state line. You don't need to present a passport or a driver's license; instead, you must be prepared to present any fruits and vegetables you have in the vehicle.

In an effort to prevent known pests from entering the state and endangering crops, travelers are asked to identify all the produce they're carrying in from other states or from Mexico. If you are carrying produce, it may be confiscated on the spot.

Money

California and Nevada businesses use the **US dollar** ($). Most businesses also accept the major credit cards Visa, MasterCard, Discover, and American Express. ATM and debit cards work at many stores and restaurants, and ATMs are available at banks and in some local businesses like convenience or grocery stores. Within Death Valley, ATMs are limited. Currency exchange offices are available at any international airport.

Visiting the National Parks

Death Valley National Park draws many international travelers year-round who often add in trips to other nearby national parks or wilderness areas, including **Yosemite, Sequoia and Kings Canyon, John Muir Wilderness,** and **Joshua Tree.** While these national parks appear relatively close on a map, they span a wide range of climates, distances, and geography. If you're planning a trip to multiple destinations, your itinerary should consider the following factors for safe and efficient travel.

Seasonal Access

All national parks are open year-round, but depending on the time of year, certain areas and roads may have limited access—or no access—as well as limited services. The season for parks in the **Sierra Nevada** (Yosemite, Sequoia and Kings Canyon, John Muir Wilderness) generally runs **April-October.** The most popular time to visit is summer. During winter, heavy snows often close mountain roads for months at a time.

Desert parks (Death Valley, Joshua Tree) operate on a reverse schedule—their season runs **October-April.** During summer, the heat at low elevations makes activities such as hiking dangerous and may prompt road closures. Winter is generally a good time to visit Death Valley and other desert areas, although snow can cause road closures even in desert mountains.

Road Conditions

When planning your visit, be aware that maps may not show road conditions. For example, most roads that run east-west across the rugged Sierra Nevada range **do not provide through-access in winter**—including **Highway 120,** the main route through Yosemite National Park.

Also consider the type of road when planning a route. On a map, many backcountry or unpaved roads may look like they provide a shortcut, but rough road conditions may make the trip longer than it appears—or make it dangerous, depending on the state of the road. Stay on paved park roads. If you do plan to travel in the backcountry, make sure you are properly prepared.

ACCESS FOR TRAVELERS WITH DISABILITIES

Death Valley may be known for its ruggedness, but it is still possible to experience many of the park's natural wonders and historical sites without going into rough backcountry or traveling on a trail that does not meet ADA standards.

An **Access Pass** (www.nps.gov) is available for free to US citizens or permanent residents with permanent disabilities. Passes can be obtained at a visitor center or ranger station in Death Valley. The pass is part of the National Parks and Federal Recreational Lands Pass Series and can be used to cover entrance fees at 2,000 other locations, including national forests and national wildlife refuges.

All museums, visitor centers, and contact stations within the park abide by ADA-compliant guidelines and are accessible to all visitors. This includes the Furnace Creek Visitor Center, the Borax Museum at Furnace Creek, Scotty's Castle Visitor Center and

Accessible Death Valley

These recommended destinations include drives and sights easily seen from parking areas as well as two ADA-accessible trails. Roads are paved or graded dirt, and in most cases there are no formal parking spaces.

- **Ash Meadows National Wildlife Refuge** (page 77): Graded dirt roads throughout the refuge lead to wheelchair-accessible boardwalks through the Mojave's largest remaining oasis. Roads should be accessible for any vehicle, including a van with a lowered floor; however, road conditions are always subject to change.
- **Badwater Basin** (page 46): A paved road leads to a paved parking area, where a wheelchair ramp allows access to the salt flats.
- **Devil's Golf Course** (page 46): A graded dirt road leads to a small parking area with close-up views of strange salt formations.
- **Mesquite Flat Sand Dunes** (page 92): A paved road to the parking area offers close-up views of these dunes.
- **Eureka Dunes** (page 122): A graded dirt road leads to the foot of spectacular sand dunes.
- **Ubehebe Crater** (page 121): A paved road leads to a small parking area at the edge of a colorful volcanic crater.
- **Trona Pinnacles** (page 204): A graded dirt road leads to haunting tufa rock formations left over from an ancient lake bed.
- **Artist's Drive** (page 48): This short, scenic drive on a paved road offers beautiful views of colorful hills.

Museum, and the Stovepipe Wells Ranger Station. In addition, the grounds at Scotty's Castle are accessible to all visitors.

Most **developed campgrounds** within the park have accessible sites and accessible restrooms, including Furnace Creek and Sunset Campgrounds in the Furnace Creek area, Stovepipe Wells Campground, Emigrant Campground in the Panamint Springs area (which does not accommodate RVs or campers), and Mesquite Spring in the Scotty's Castle area. For the most scenic and pleasant accessible camping, Mesquite Spring is the best bet. Most sites are paved, widely spaced, and flat—even those not designated as ADA compliant. There are accessible restrooms with flush toilets.

Throughout the park, **accessible restrooms** with flush toilets are located at the Furnace Creek Visitor Center, Stovepipe Wells General Store, Scotty's Castle Visitor Center, and Emigrant Campground picnic area. Pit toilets, located at many sights and campgrounds throughout the park, are also accessible, including those at Badwater Basin and the Eureka Dunes.

There is only one accessible hiking trail in the park: the **Salt Creek Trail** in the Stovepipe Wells area. A small parking area leads to a boardwalk trail that covers a 1-mile (1.6-km) loop alongside Salt Creek. Outside the park boundaries, the **Ash Meadows National Wildlife Refuge** has wheelchair-accessible boardwalk trails. Although accessible trails are limited in the area, there are many sights and drives available to visitors with physical disabilities.

- **Titus Canyon Road** (page 97): This one-way, 27-mile (43-km) road may not be appropriate for a van with a lowered floor. Carefully consider this drive, check road conditions, and proceed with caution.
- **Harmony Borax Works** (page 42): A graded dirt road leads to a small parking area. The road should be accessible for any vehicle, including a van with a lowered floor; however, road conditions are always subject to change.
- **Wildrose Charcoal Kilns** (page 149): A graded dirt road leads to a parking area. The road should be accessible for any vehicle, including a van with a lowered floor; however, road conditions are always subject to change.
- **Warm Springs Camp** (page 48): A graded dirt road. Depending on road conditions, this drive may not be appropriate for a van with a lowered floor. Carefully consider this drive, check road conditions, and proceed with caution.
- **Goldfield** (page 137): A paved road leads to the small Nevada mining town. There are dirt roads throughout the town.
- **Rhyolite** (page 94): A graded dirt road should be accessible for any vehicle, including a van with a lowered floor; however, road conditions are always subject to change.
- **Salt Creek** (page 94): A graded dirt road leads to a parking area; a wheelchair-accessible boardwalk traverses a 1-mile (1.6-km) loop along the banks of Salt Creek. The road should be accessible for any vehicle, including a van with a lowered floor; however, road conditions are always subject to change.

PEOPLE OF COLOR

Much of the local economy in the Death Valley region is based on tourism, and its small gateway towns welcome diverse visitors from all over the world. The largest percentage of visitors to national parks, however, continue to be white. National Park Service data from the most recent 10-year study confirms that only 23 percent of park visitors were people of color. Death Valley's gateway towns are small, rural communities with primarily white populations. On the western side of the park, for example, census data show the tiny town of Lone Pine to have a population that is 65.6 percent white. On the eastern side of the park, the small community of Beatty is 90.9 percent white.

Consider visiting the following websites for more information:

- The National Park Foundation's Outdoor Exploration program actively encourages diversity in public lands, partnering with organizations to teach valuable skills and make the outdoors more inviting for BIPOC and other historically excluded communities. The site features stories and programs designed to encourage enduring connections to the parks (www.nationalparks.org/area-of-work/outdoor-exploration).
- Latino Outdoors is a hub of learning resources designed to support and connect the Latino outdoors community. Website tutorials feature practical information for hiking and backpacking. The Las Vegas chapter brings people together to explore the wonders of the Mojave Desert through outings and educational partnerships (https://latinooutdoors.org).

LGBTQ+ TRAVELERS

Death Valley National Park sees over one million visitors per year filtering through the park's main service hubs and a handful of gateway towns surrounding the park boundaries. Much of the local economy is based on tourism, and the small, rural towns are used to welcoming travelers. The closest city with an actively gay scene is Las Vegas, 2-3 hours from Death Valley and a great travel hub for visiting the park. The city is famous for being an adult playground with an openness that extends to the LGBTQ+ community. The main cluster of LGBTQ+ nightclubs and businesses is colloquially called The Fruit Loop, referring to a section of Naples Street near the University of Nevada, although there are businesses outside the district that cater to a LGBTQ+ clientele.

Consider visiting the following websites for more information:

- Gaze at the National Parks podcast (https://gazeatthenationalparks.com)
- Vegas.com (www.vegas.com/lgbt-travel)
- Queer in the World (https://queerintheworld.com/moving-to-lgbt-las-vegas)

TRAVELING WITH CHILDREN

Death Valley can be a fun place for kids. The Mesquite Flat and Eureka Dunes give them a place to run or dig in the sand. Mosaic Canyon, Golden Canyon, and Natural Bridge offer the chance to do some canyon exploring. Salt Creek is full of tiny fish. Stovepipe Wells and the Ranch at Death Valley both have family-friendly lodgings with swimming pools to give everyone a break in the midday heat. When sightseeing, pack extra snacks and make sure children are properly hydrated and slathered with sunscreen. Kids will appreciate the Wild West experience in ghost towns and mining areas, but be sure to keep a very careful eye on children—there are exposed mining shafts in the park, old mining equipment and structures can have sharp or rusty edges, and rusty cans and broken glass can be found at historical sites.

The **Junior Ranger Program** is designed for children ages 5-13 and offers a structured way for kids to learn about the park and enjoy a sense of stewardship. Pick up a copy of the Junior Ranger booklet at any visitor center, then have the kids complete age-appropriate activities, do a park project, and attend a ranger program.

TRAVELING WITH PETS

If possible, leave your pets at home when visiting Death Valley. Pets are allowed in the park, but they are not allowed on any trails or more than 100 feet (30 m) from a road or picnic area. Pets are allowed in campgrounds, but again are not allowed to stray more than 100 feet (30 m). There is a limit of four pets per site in campgrounds. Pets cannot be left unattended at any time, especially in a vehicle. High temperatures can be extreme and could quickly harm a pet locked in a car, even with the windows cracked. Dogs must be on a leash no longer than 6 feet (1.8 m) at all times. Wild coyotes in the park could be potentially dangerous to pets that are off-leash.

SENIOR TRAVELERS

US citizens or permanent residents ages 62 and older can purchase an **America the Beautiful Senior Pass** (lifetime \$80, annual \$20) at any visitor center or ranger station in Death Valley or online at www.nps.gov. The pass is part of the National Parks and Federal Recreational Lands Pass Series and can be used to cover entrance fees at 2,000 locations, including national parks and national wildlife refuges. It also provides discounts on some facility amenities, useful at campgrounds. If you already have a Golden Age or Golden Access Pass, both are good for entry into the park.

Desert Survival Tips

Death Valley's vast spaces, remote roads, and weather extremes can create potentially risky situations, but traveling is not any more dangerous than in other national parks if you are prepared for the unique environment. Know what weather to expect and where you're going, and be prepared for the unexpected.

TELL SOMEONE WHERE YOU ARE GOING

Whether you're hiking, driving, or a combination, make sure you tell someone where you are going and when to expect your return. Death Valley covers a huge area, and in the event that you are stranded, the search effort can be pinpointed. For hiking, obtain a voluntary backcountry permit from the ranger station. For backcountry camping, permits are voluntary or mandatory depending on the location.

BRING SUPPLIES

Temperatures can fluctuate 40 degrees between day and night. Bring a sleeping bag or emergency blanket even if you do not plan to be out overnight. Pack appropriate clothing for a range of temperatures, and be prepared for cold temperatures at night. Always bring extra water and extra nonperishable food that does not have to be cooked. GPS navigation is notoriously unreliable in the park. Be prepared with a paper map or an electronic offline map and a charger. Cell phones do not work in the park. Be prepared to survive until help arrives if you are stranded.

VEHICLE BREAKDOWNS

Sharp rocks, long bumpy roads, and heat can cause your vehicle to break down. Always drive with a full-size spare tire. A fix-a-flat tire kit may also be helpful. Getting two flat tires is not an unheard-of situation on Death Valley's back roads. If you are stranded, stay with your car until help arrives. It is much easier to spot a big metal car that flashes in the sunlight than a person walking. Also, it is dangerous to overexert yourself in the heat of Death Valley, so hiking out to safety is not generally the best option. Be prepared with extra supplies including food, water, and warm clothes.

WINDSTORMS

The wind can be a relentless companion in Death Valley, especially in spring, with nights generally windier than days. Wind can be a minor irritant or it can seriously impact your visit and create potentially dangerous situations. At times, wind can descend in the form of a windstorm preceded by a cold front. There may be very little warning, and a dark cloud may be the only indication that a windstorm is approaching. Always stake tents and secure other camp belongings such as camp chairs. Windstorms can create whiteout conditions with serious visibility limitations. If you are driving, use headlights and be prepared to pull over if visibility becomes limited to the degree that driving is dangerous.

Health and Safety

HEAT

Heat is the biggest health threat in Death Valley. The hottest conditions occur at the lower elevations during summer. Furnace Creek and the valley floor south toward Badwater Basin log the highest temperatures in the park and can be dangerously hot **May-October.** Many visitors choose to visit Death Valley in summer, and it is possible to do so safely if you take some precautions. *Avoid hiking or other outdoors exertion at low elevations during summer.* In summer, confine hiking to high elevations or go out early in the morning or late in the evening; stick to paved roads for touring at low elevations. When hiking or exploring outdoors, wear a wide-brimmed hat, sunglasses, and proper sun protection. Lightweight, light-colored breathable clothing can offer better protection than sunscreen—wear both.

Contrary to popular belief, Death Valley is not hot everywhere all the time. Its arid desert climate, however, does create extremes in temperature. Many upper mountain elevations are prone to ice and snow in winter. Telescope Peak, the highest point in the park, is snowcapped most of the year. Hike at higher elevations in summer and lower elevations in winter.

DEHYDRATION

It's crucial to drink plenty of water, especially during physical activity. Signs of heat exhaustion include **dizziness, nausea,** and **headaches.** If these occur, get into the shade and drink plenty of water or sports drinks.

Drink at least 1 gallon (4 liters) per day, or more depending on your level of physical activity. Always carry extra water—at least 5 gallons (19 liters) extra if you are traveling in the backcountry. If you run out of water, all water in the park is potable. Water is available at visitor centers, ranger stations, and museums and at most campgrounds, including Furnace Creek, Sunset, and Texas Spring in the Furnace Creek area; Stovepipe Wells; Mesquite Spring in the Scotty's Castle area; and Emigrant and Wildrose Campgrounds in the Panamint Springs area.

HANTAVIRUS

Hantavirus, or hantavirus pulmonary syndrome, is an uncommon but potentially life-threatening respiratory illness that is transmitted to humans by rodents. Humans encounter the virus by inhaling air contaminated with rodent urine, droppings, and saliva. In Death Valley, many old structures such as cabins and mining tunnels carry the threat of hantavirus. The threat is especially prevalent in enclosed spaces. Symptoms may develop between one and eight weeks after exposure and include fatigue, fever, and muscle aches. Early treatment increases the likelihood of complete recovery. Be *very* careful when exploring old structures. Look for nests and droppings, try not to kick up dust, and limit or avoid time in spaces that could be contaminated.

WILDLIFE

Death Valley has its share of venomous animals, though they are rarely life-threatening to humans. The desert **tarantula** and giant desert hairy **scorpion** produce toxins sufficient to immobilize a small animal. To a human, their bite may be comparable to a bee sting.

The **Mojave rattlesnake** (also called Mojave green) is known to be one of the most venomous and deadly of North American species. These snakes tend to hunt at night in rocky areas and open vegetation, like Joshua tree flats or creosote scrub. The **sidewinder** and **Panamint rattlesnake** are also venomous. The sidewinder likes sandy hills and dunes; you may see its distinctive J-shaped trail in the sand. It loops along so that only two points of its body have to touch the hot sand. The Panamint rattlesnake prefers rocky slopes and mountain areas. Fortunately, rattlesnakes announce their presence by rattling their tails. If you hear a rattle, stop moving and slowly back away from the sound. The best way to avoid getting bitten by any animal is to give it space—and never put your hands and feet where you cannot see. For a rattlesnake bite, seek immediate treatment at the nearest hospital or emergency room.

Resources

Suggested Reading

Death Valley's history, strange geography, and potential for solitude and adventure have inspired enthusiasts, scholars, and travelers to chisel out hundreds of books about this region. This list offers a few suggestions to help navigate a trip to Death Valley or better understand this unusual place.

INTRODUCTORY GUIDES

Naylor, Roger. *Hottest Place on Earth.* Tucson: Rio Nuevo Publishers, 2013. A conversational blend of history, photography, and fun facts, this guide introduces the potential visitor to Death Valley's main attractions, ghost towns, roads, and hikes.

Page, David T. *Yosemite & the Southern Sierra Nevada: Includes Mammoth Lakes, Sequoia, Kings Canyon & Death Valley.* 3rd ed. Woodstock, VT: The Countryman Press, 2017. This guide takes on history, hiking, points of interest, lodging, food, and towns in helpful snippets spanning the Eastern Sierra and into Death Valley.

Tweed, William C., and Lauren Davis. *Death Valley and the Northern Mojave: A Visitor's Guide.* Los Olivos, CA: Cachuma Press, 2003. An introduction to Death Valley and the northern Mojave including geology, climate, plants and animals, Native American history, mining history, and the advent of tourism. Colorful photography and region-specific information will entice the first-time visitor or anyone interested in the area.

HIKING AND EXPLORATION

Bryan, T. Scott, and Betty Tucker-Bryan. *The Explorer's Guide to Death Valley National Park.* 4th ed. Boulder, CO: University Press of Colorado, 2022. This classic travel guide includes geological, human, and natural history. It's best known for detailed descriptions of roads to scenic and historical destinations, and is extremely useful for touring Death Valley's backcountry routes.

Cunningham, Bill, and Polly Cunningham. *Hiking Death Valley National Park.* 2nd ed. Guilford, CT: FalconGuides, 2017. A lightweight guide to 57 day and overnight hikes in the park.

Digonnet, Michel. *Hiking Death Valley: A Guide to Its Natural Wonders and Mining Past.* 2nd ed. Palo Alto, CA: Michel Digonnet, 2016. The most comprehensive hiking guide to Death Valley to date, this book is indispensable for exploring the region. Detailed trail directions and topo maps are included.

Digonnet, Michel. *Hiking Western Death Valley National Park: Panamint, Saline, and Eureka Valleys.* Palo Alto, CA: Michel Digonnet, 2009. A comprehensive hiking guide focused on western Death Valley's geologic and cultural history, with detailed trail directions and maps. A must-have.

Fredericksen, Devon, and Reed Harvey. *50 Classic Day Hikes of the Eastern Sierra.* Bishop, CA: K. Daniels & Associates, 2012. A well-curated and user-friendly guide to spectacular hikes in the Eastern Sierra region, this book details trails to alpine lakes, boulder-strewn passes, and historical mining sites. The high print quality and numerous color photos are a bonus.

Giacomazzi, Sharon. *Exploring Eastern Sierra Canyons: Bishop to Lone Pine.* Mendocino, CA: Bored Feet Press, 2009. This thorough hiking guide is packed with enough detailed information and enthusiasm to get you out on the trail. Information about rustic resorts, camping, history, and pack stations adds to its value as a resource.

Mitchell, Roger. *Death Valley SUV Trails.* Oakhurst, CA: Track & Trail Publications, 2006. This guide to 40 four-wheeling excursions contains detailed driving directions, historical notes, and difficulty ratings for each drive.

HISTORY

Crum, S. J. *The Road on Which We Came: A History of the Western Shoshone.* Salt Lake City: University of Utah Press, 1994. Most histories of Death Valley focus on its mining history. This book, written by an enrolled tribe member, offers a comprehensive Native American history of the Great Basin Shoshone.

Green, Linda W., and John A. Latschar. *Historic Resource Study: A History of Mining in Death Valley National Monument.* Denver: National Park Service, 1981. A historical resource study conducted by the National Park Service to assess the cultural value of mining sites in Death Valley in relation to land conservation goals. Contains interesting history of mining sites in and around the Death Valley region.

Jones, Robert C. *Death Valley Ghost Towns: As They Appear Today.* 3rd ed. Kennesaw, GA: Robert C. Jones, 2013. This practical guide contains a brief history, directions, photos, a description of remains, and a rating system for all sites to help visitors to decide whether or not to make the trek.

Lingenfelter, R. E. *Death Valley and the Amargosa: A Land of Illusion.* Berkeley, CA: University of California Press, 1986. The classic history of Death Valley, spanning a century from the 1830s, when the first Europeans opened a trail through the area, to 1933, when Death Valley became a national monument. Focuses on Death Valley's mining history and also discusses Native American history and Death Valley's journey from mining to tourism.

Lingenfelter, R. E. *Death Valley Lore: Classic Tales of Fantasy, Adventure, and Mystery.* Reno: University of Nevada Press, 1988. Historical collection of accounts of Death Valley gleaned from the popular media of the late 19th and early 20th centuries, when adventurers, prospectors, and explorers flocked to the land.

Palazzo, Robert P. *Ghost Towns of Death Valley.* Charleston, SC: Arcadia Publishing, 2014. Brief histories and historical photographs of Death Valley ghost towns, including buildings and local characters.

Rothman, Hal K., and Char Miller. *Death Valley National Park: A History.* Reno: University of Nevada Press, 2013. An environmental and human history of Death Valley National Park. Details the region's path to preservation and debates over land use in the northern Mojave Desert from the perspective of Native American groups, miners, ranchers, the military, tourists, wilderness advocates, and the National Park Service.

MAPS

National Geographic Trails Illustrated. *Death Valley National Park*. Evergreen, CO: National Geographic Maps, 2022. A detailed 1:165,000 topographic map with trail and backcountry road information. It has UTM grids for use with GPS units.

Tom Harrison Maps. *Death Valley National Park*. San Rafael, CA: Tom Harrison Maps, 2020. Shaded relief 1:253,440 topographic map with contour lines and vegetation. The only detailed map that includes mileage between road junctions, it is extremely useful for general navigation and backcountry travel.

NATURE AND GEOGRAPHY

Grayson, Donald. *The Great Basin: A Natural Prehistory*. Oakland, CA: University of California Press, 2011. A detailed environmental and human history of the Great Basin geographic watershed region that encompasses Death Valley. The book takes a multidisciplinary approach through history, geology, and archaeology to look at the rich and diverse ecosystems in the Great Basin.

Mackay, Pam. *Mojave Desert Wildflowers*. 2nd ed. Guilford, CT: FalconGuides, 2013. A detailed guide to wildflowers of the Mojave Desert region. Contains background on geography, climate, topography, geology, and environmental issues. Colorful photographs and plant descriptions are useful in identifying hundreds of plants.

Sharp, Robert P., and Allen F. Glazner. *Geology Underfoot in Death Valley and Owens Valley*. Missoula, MT: Mountain Press Publishing, 1997. This guide is designed to come to the rescue of the curious desert visitor or amateur geologist staring at an impressive pile of rocks, wondering how on earth it was formed. Written in guide format, the book details the geologic history of Death Valley and Owens Valley to the east.

Stewart, Jon Mark. *Mojave Desert Wildflowers*. Albuquerque: Jon Stewart Photography, 1998. Simple and elegant, this guide gets straight to the point with full-page color photographs and corresponding information that makes identifying wildflowers easy and straightforward.

Internet Resources

DEATH VALLEY

Death Valley National History Association
www.dvnha.org

The Death Valley National History Association has retail outlets for Death Valley-related books and gifts in the park's visitor centers. It also offers its excellent selection through the website's online store. The site includes information on the association's programs and events, too.

Death Valley National Park
www.nps.gov/deva

The park's official website is a great place to start planning a trip to Death Valley. It has information on where to stay (campgrounds, hotels, links to reservations) and what to visit. Visitor guides, backcountry road guides, and other information can be downloaded from the website. It also has helpful advice on weather, road conditions, and other tips for travelers to the desert.

Recreation.gov
www.recreation.gov
In Death Valley National Park, only Furnace Creek Campground accepts reservations; make them at this website.

BEYOND THE BOUNDARIES

Alabama Hills
www.blm.gov
The Alabama Hills span over 30,000 acres (12,140 ha) of public land and are known for their beautiful scenery as well as their film history. They have been the setting for many Westerns and other movies, beginning in the 1920s. The Bureau of Land Management website provides a description of the area, directions, and a downloadable *Movie Road* touring brochure.

Ancient Bristlecone Pine Forest
www.fs.usda.gov
The US Forest Service website provides crucial information on park hours, seasons, and directions as well as a phone number to check road conditions. It gives an overview of the pine groves and hikes in the area.

Ash Meadows National Wildlife Refuge
www.fws.gov/refuge/ash_meadows
The refuge's website offers tips to help plan your visit, including weather and visitor center hours as well as information about the desert oasis habitat.

Beatty
www.beattynv.info
This "gateway to Death Valley" town's website devotes several pages to visitor information, including dining and lodging in Beatty. It also links to sites for nearby attractions like the ghost town of Rhyolite.

Eastern Sierra
www.bishopvisitor.com
This website offers detailed information about attractions and exploring the outdoors as well as recommendations to dine and stay. Backcountry maps and routes for exploring the region are especially helpful.

John Muir Wilderness/Inyo National Forest
www.fs.usda.gov
This US Forest Service-maintained site has detailed information about camping, hikes, attractions, and permits.

Lone Pine
www.lonepinechamber.org
The Lone Pine website provides a good catalog of restaurants and hotels in town with contact information and links to individual business websites.

Red Rock Canyon State Park
www.parks.ca.gov
The state park's website offers basic planning information including park hours and regulations, facilities, and campground information.

Shoshone
www.shoshonevillage.com
A charming gateway town on the southeastern edge of Death Valley, Shoshone has basic visitor services. The town's website includes descriptions and contact information for all local businesses. It also includes helpful links to nearby wilderness destinations, attractions, and land-use organizations.

Index

E

F

G

H

I

JKL

M

NOP

R

S

T

UV

WZ

List of Maps

Front Map

Welcome to Death Valley National Park

Furnace Creek and the Amargosa Range

Stovepipe Wells and the Nevada Triangle

Scotty's Castle and the Eureka Valley

Panamint Springs and the Saline Valley

Photo Credits

All photos © Jenna Blough except: page 1 © Mykola Lukash|Dreamstime.com; page 5 © (top) Galyna Andrushko | Dreamstime.com; (left middle) Lloyd Tanner; (right middle) Paul Lemke | Dreamstime.com; (bottom left) Roman Slavik | Dreamstime.com; (bottom right) Glenn Nagel | Dreamstime.com; page 6 © Rinus Baak | Dreamstime.com; page 8 © William Perry | Dreamstime.com; page 10 © Maygutyak | stock.adobe.com; page 11 © Nuvisage | Dreamstime.com; page 12 © Scott Temme Xanterra Travel Collection; page 14 © (top) Dreamstime | Kelly Vandellen; page 15 © Beisea | Dreamstime.com; page 19 © Scott Temme | Xanterra Travel Collection; page 23 © Xanterra Travel Collection; page 24 © (top) Helena Bilkova|Dreamstime.com; page 25 © Abigail Marie A | stock.adobe.com; page 29 © (bottom) Scott Temme| Xanterra Travel Collection; page 30 © Jimekstrand | Dreamstime.com; page 31 © Pixy2000 | Dreamstime.com; page 32 © NPS / Kurt Moses; page 33 © Tobkatrina | Dreamstime.com; page 34 © Luckyphotographer | Dreamstime.com; page 43 © (left middle) Marcie Blough; (right middle) Bukki88 | Dreamstime.com; (bottom) Scott Temme | Xanterra Travel Collection; page 49 © Dshumny | Dreamstime.com; page 52 © Scott Temme | Xanterra Travel Collection; page 61 © (top) Laurens Hoddenbagh| Dreamstime.com; page 68 © (top) Scott Temme | Xanterra Travel Collection; (left middle) Scott Temme | Xanterra Travel Collection; (right middle) Scott Temme | Xanterra Travel Collection; (bottom) Scott Temme | Xanterra Travel Collection; page 70 © ScenincMedia | Dreamstime.com; page 87 © Galyna Andrushko | Dreamstime.com; page 93 © (top) Scott Temme | Xanterra Travel Collection; (right middle)Wisconsinart | Dreamstime.com; page 107 © (bottom) Paul Lemke| Dreamstime.com; page 125 © (top) Aruns911 | Dreamstime.com; (right middle) Scott Temme | Xanterra Travel Collection; (bottom) Mazuciukas | Dreamstime.com; page 143 © (top left) Mkopka | Dreamstime.com; (top right) Joy | Unsplash.com; page 157 © (top) Marcie Blough; (left middle) Marcie Blough; (bottom) Marcie Blough; page 159 © Marcie Blough; page 175 © (left middle) Marcie Blough; page 180 © Dean Pennala | Dreamstime.com; page 198 © Andreistanescu | Dreamstime.com; page 201 © (left middle)Woodkern | Dreamstime.com

MAP SYMBOLS

Divided Highway
Primary Road
Secondary Road
Unpaved Road
Feature Trail
Trail
Pedestrian Walkway
Railroad

Dirt Road Designations

Graded Dirt Road
Dirt Road High Clearance
Rough Dirt Road 4WD
Extremely Rough Road Short Wheelbase 4WD

City/Town
Highlight
Site
Accommodation
Restaurant/Bar
Other Location
Information Center
Parking Area

Trailhead
Camping
Park
Unique Featur
Unique Featur Hydro
Mountain
Golf Course
Regional Airpc
Place of Worshi

CONVERSION TABLES

°C = (°F - 32) / 1.8
°F = (°C x 1.8) + 32
1 inch = 2.54 centimeters (cm)
1 foot = 0.304 meters (m)
1 yard = 0.914 meters
1 mile = 1.6093 kilometers (km)
1 km = 0.6214 miles
1 fathom = 1.8288 m
1 chain = 20.1168 m
1 furlong = 201.168 m
1 acre = 0.4047 hectares
1 sq km = 100 hectares
1 sq mile = 2.59 square km
1 ounce = 28.35 grams
1 pound = 0.4536 kilograms
1 short ton = 0.90718 metric ton
1 short ton = 2,000 pounds
1 long ton = 1.016 metric tons
1 long ton = 2,240 pounds
1 metric ton = 1,000 kilograms
1 quart = 0.94635 liters
1 US gallon = 3.7854 liters
1 Imperial gallon = 4.5459 liters
1 nautical mile = 1.852 km

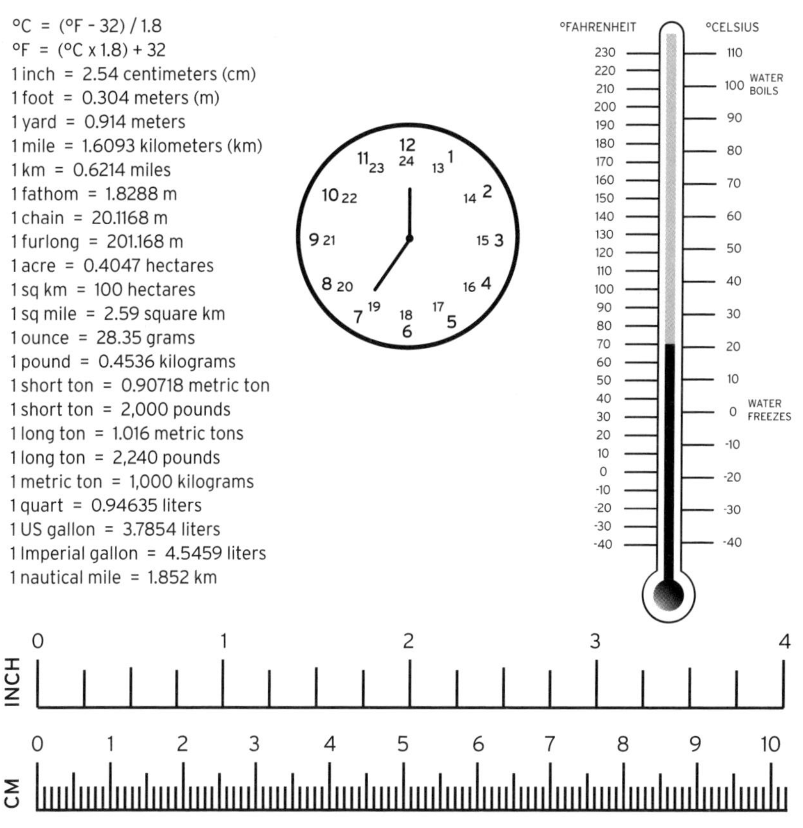

MOON DEATH VALLEY NATIONAL PARK
Avalon Travel
Hachette Book Group
1700 Fourth Street
Berkeley, CA 94710, USA
www.moon.com

Editor: Devon Lee
Managing Editor: Courtney Packard
Copy Editor: Ann Seifert
Graphics and Production Coordinator: Suzanne Albertson
Cover Design: Toni Tajima
Interior Design: Avalon Travel
Map Editor: Kat Bennett
Cartographers: Albert Angulo, Abby Whelan and John Culp
Proofreader: Deana Shields
Indexer: Rachel Lyon

ISBN-13: 9798886470406

Printing History
1st Edition — 2015
4th Edition — June 2024
5 4 3 2 1

Front cover photo: Death Valley sand dunes
© Freebilly | Dreamstime.com
Back cover photo: Manson family's truck
© Jenna Blough

Printed in China by APS